ROME AND CANTERBURY
THROUGH FOUR CENTURIES

D0912427

Cover photographs (left to right from top)

William Wake, Archbishop of Canterbury
Cardinal Consalvi by Sir Thomas Lawrence, 1819
Charles Butler, Secretary of the Catholic Committee
Henry Grattan, MP for Dublin, by F. Wheatley, 1782
Cardinal Wiseman, Archbishop of Westminster
John Rouse Bloxham, chalk study by William Holman Hunt 1888-90
Ambrose Phillipps de Lisle by Adrian Stokes, 1879
Fr Victor De Buck, S.J.
Odo Russell at time of First Vatican Council
E.B. Pusey by George Richmond, 1890
Charles Lindley Wood, 2nd Viscount Halifax, in 1881
Abbé Fernand Portal
Cardinal Mercier, Archbishop of Malines
Dr John Moorman, Bishop of Ripon
Archbishop Geoffrey Fisher
Pope Paul VI with Dr Michael Ramsey, Archbishop of Canterbury
   in Rome, March 1966
Dr Robert Runcie, Archbishop of Canterbury
Pope John Paul II

ROME AND CANTERBURY
THROUGH FOUR CENTURIES

A study of the relations between
the Church of Rome and the Anglican Churches
1530–1981

by
BERNARD and
MARGARET PAWLEY

MOWBRAY
LONDON & OXFORD

Copyright © 1974, 1981 Bernard and Margaret Pawley

First published in hardback 1974
This updated and revised paperback edition
(without photographs)
first published 1981
by A. R. Mowbray & Co. Ltd.
Saint Thomas House, Becket Street,
Oxford, OX1 1SJ

ISBN 0 264 66415 9

British Library Cataloguing in Publication Data

Pawley, Bernard
    Rome and Canterbury through four centuries. –
    Updated and rev.ed.
    1. Catholic Church – Relations – Church
    of England   2. Church of England
    – Relations – Catholic Church
    I. Title   II. Pawley, Margaret
    282   BX5129

    ISBN 0–264–66415–9

Set in Monotype Baskerville 11/12pt by Cotswold Typesetting Ltd, Gloucester and
Printed in Great Britain by The Thetford Press

CONTENTS

ACKNOWLEDGEMENTS

It is possible to produce a book of this kind only through the help of one's friends. To the Rt Revd Arthur Vogel, Bishop of West Missouri, the Revds A. J. M. Saint, Samuel Cutt, and the late Robert Gladwell, and to Prudence Hannay, considerable thanks are due for their interest, suggestions and information. Miss W. R. Clarke has typed a difficult manuscript in a characteristically indomitable manner. We thank James Herbertson, among others, for reading the proofs.

The authors express their gratitude to the Archivists and Librarians of the following institutions for their help and courtesy: the Vatican, Propaganda Fide, Anglican Centre in Rome, Bodleian, Cambridge University Library, British Museum, Public Record Office, Dr Williams' Library, Library of Sion House, Canterbury Cathedral Library and the City of Ely public library; also to the Revd Fr J. Jurich, S.J., the Revd Canon J. Dessain, the Squire de Lisle, Mrs R. Collier, Mrs. A. J. M. Saint and the President and Fellows of Magdalen College, Oxford, for the loan of unpublished papers.

For permission to quote from *William Wake* (2 vols. CUP, 1957) we are indebted to the Cambridge University Press.

INTRODUCTION

With the promulgation on 21st November 1964 of the Vatican decree on Ecumenism the history of the Christian Church entered a new era. The movement for the recovery of unity on a wide front which had had its first large-scale embodiment at the Edinburgh Conference of 1910, took on a new dimension. The great Church of Rome, two-thirds of Christendom as she then was, held aloof, officially, from the first half century of the ecumenical movement. But from 1964 she was totally and irrevocably committed to the recovery of the union of Christendom. The Churches of the Anglican Communion were in the vanguard of those who encouraged this change of heart, and the last chapters of this work record some of the unofficial attempts which were made, in faith, to bridge the gap which was the legacy of previous centuries.

The publishers, in calling for this book, rightly supposed that there was a widespread search for information which would make a background to these important events. Accordingly the authors have provided a study of the long period of darkness which led up to this new dawn. It is not of course exhaustive, or even systematic, but fragmentary. That is to say it is a study of certain personalities—visionaries, heroes one would like to call them—who kept the candles of hope burning through the dark night, often under difficult and even dangerous circumstances and against heavy discouragement.

During the course of writing, the two authors have been heavily involved in practical assignments, many of them directly connected with the newly established relationships themselves. This factor, coupled with the sheer weight of material that has come to light, has contributed to the incompleteness of the book. It is hoped that many of the remarkable episodes will encourage scholars to make fuller studies of the personalities involved; as Dr. Norman Sykes did so notably in the case of Archbishop Wake. More references than would otherwise have been justified have therefore been included in the text. But whereas time and space have dictated that certain omissions had to be made, other characters do not find their place within these pages for more deliberate reasons. Although many of the early ecumenists earned for themselves reputations of disloyalty, more extreme dissidents on either side have not been included, since their aims appear more personal than ecclesial. For example, neither the correspondence of Fr. Hyacinthe (Charles Loyson) with Archbishop Tait, nor the activities of some of the Anglican Papalists appear here.

It was the original intention that this study should begin at about the year 1850 with the establishment of the Roman Catholic Hierarchy in England. As research progressed it became clear that, contrary to what had previously been supposed, there had been much communication between members of the two Churches at earlier dates: later history would be unintelligible without going back to the beginning. The first three hundred years of division are therefore dealt with fairly rapidly in four chapters, and they lead into a description of the long-drawn-out debate on the restitution of political and civil rights to Roman Catholics, which marks the end of the old penal order and the start of more modern thinking. The book at that point goes into greater detail.

In telling this story the authors have, of course, been writing as Anglicans. They have attempted to be as objective as is humanly possible; to tell the truth about the past and also to be eirenic. If they have offended in either particular they ask to be forgiven.

Canterbury, 1974   *Bernard Pawley*
                                                      Margaret Pawley

PREFACE TO SECOND EDITION

The original material of this book has been abridged for this paperback edition. It has been brought up to date (1981); and we have taken the opportunity thus offered of making corrections. We are grateful to all who have told us of errors and have made suggestions.

Canterbury 1981

B.C.P.
M.G.P.

restoration of the true portrait leads us to emphasise two principles which have been lost sight of in the course of time. The first is that it was the Renaissance which had the major influence in shaping the changes which took place in the English Church; and the second that the breach with Rome was mainly forged in the reign of Elizabeth rather than by the dynastic troubles of the last 'catholic' king, Henry VIII.

The ecclesiastical developments of the present day are also taking place in the context of what is in effect a second Renaissance. Old habits of thought and customs are being put rigidly under review and minds are being stimulated by new triumphs of discovery. The comparison between the voyages to the new worlds of the fifteenth and sixteenth centuries and the astronauts of the twentieth is obvious: an expanding universe of new knowledge and of whole new categories of thought is the background to both epochs. New forms of art and literature, new conceptions in science and philosophy, appear in both ages. These two pairs of association are not coincidences but just two instances of man's spirit and his habits developing along parallel lines. And in both cases it can be shown that the 'cultural revolution', as the phrase now is, is the principal cause of the ecclesiastical reform. The results appear to be opposite to one another, those of the first Renaissance leading to ruptures, those of the second to the resumption of friendly relations. That is due, of course, to the differing nature of the ecclesiastical situations to be dealt with. But the general principle remains the same: a new generation of mankind, under the stimulus and exhilaration of new-found knowledge, finds its ecclesiastical apparatus out of date and sets out to find new wineskins which will be able to contain the new wine. To this general background all the main features of the Reformation, theological, ecclesiastical or political, are really incidental.

The first Renaissance was perhaps too wide a cultural experience for the world, as it then was, to contain. That may yet prove to be true of the second. But when it is remembered that Tyndale, Erasmus, Caxton, Magellan, Raphael, Machiavelli, Lorenzo de Medici, Pius II Piccolomini (Aeneas Silvius) and Alexander VI (Borgia) were all in their respective ways products of the same movement of the human spirit, its dimensions seem to defy calculation. It is not surprising that it broke up the unity of Europe and rent the Church asunder. One of the strange features of this epoch was that too great an anxiety on the part of the Church to embrace the aesthetic and moral standards of the reappearing classical culture contributed most signally to its own disruption. The new culture itself became polarised by regions; and very broadly speaking the aesthetic and moral influences of it stayed south of the Alps while philosophy, theology and politics came north to engulf the Teuton races.

New thinking and new ways of expressing religious truth led to urgent demands for ecclesiastical reform. The mediaeval church was believed to be failing both in head and members, and to be impotent in operation. The new approach to theology in the Scriptures showed up defects in the current interpretations of the catholic faith. What the Second Vatican Council set out to do in the twentieth century some of the provinces of the Church took it into their heads to do locally in the sixteenth. Princes used the situation for their own purposes, or were obliged to take hold of it to prevent religious warfare and to establish good order where it had broken down. Generally speaking, in England, as will be shown, there was no basic desire to divide the Church, or to depart from the catholic faith, but only to restore it to its primitive shape and to rid it of abuses.

Thomas Goodrich, Bishop of Ely,[1] for example, had been a colleague of Erasmus at Cambridge. Quite independently of the theological reformation on the continent, and more in the spirit of the Renaissance, he ordered, in 1539, the destruction of all monuments and ornaments in his cathedral which failed to correspond with a realistic picture of the Christian faith. Thus he destroyed all the statues and glass which depicted legendary tales about the Blessed Virgin Mary and the Shrine of St. Etheldreda, which was the centre of a totally unreal cult, as he held it to be, of the saints and which tended to obscure the general shape of the Christian scheme of salvation. In all this Bishop Goodrich could be said to typify the tendencies of his

[1] 1534–1554.

time. New critical attitudes, themselves the products of new categories of thinking, had led to dissatisfaction with certain of the outward expressions of religion. The cultus of the saints, as practised in the shrines of Christendom, had taken on the dimensions of a major abuse. The reform of the abuse opened up questionings about the doctrine which underlay it and of the authority which gave sanction to it. The solution, if it was to be effective, of this kind of problem, clearly lay in the calling of a General Council. But as the Papacy was too weak to take this step until it was too late to be effective, the provinces of the north took on their own reformation.

If the first cause of the breach was the failure of the Papacy to deal with the consequences of the Renaissance of thought by calling a Council, the second was the temporal claims of the Bishops of Rome. From the time of the bull 'Unam Sanctam' of 1302 the general claim of the Papacy was to have ultimate rights over all temporal sovereigns. The working out of this claim in practice had, as is widely known, a long history of friction and bitterness in England, as in most countries of northern Europe. Henry VIII was only one of a long line of English sovereigns who had had tiresome quarrels with the Pope over civil and spiritual jurisdiction. But even in the sixteenth century the relationship was still unsettled, the temporal claims of the Papacy and the pretensions and exemptions of the clergy still stood ready to trigger off any ammunition which might have a tendency to explode. Of the abuses and crimes of the reign of Henry VIII more than enough has been written. Henry's dispute with Rome concerned jurisdiction: even had the annulment question gone favourably for him, the jurisdictional struggle with the Papacy would have continued. Other European princes had found the papal yoke too restricting. When in 1529 Henry dismissed Wolsey he spoke of following their example. He was advocating national churches and pressing his reforms further than was expedient. Although he shifted his ground, his need for an heir was ultimately regarded as a political matter in which the safety of the realm was at stake. Henry clearly expected to be granted an annulment of his marriage to Queen Catherine, as in the case of former kings of England and of France, and members of his own family, where political issues were held to be involved.[1] But the papacy itself was now unable to act independently of political pressures.[2] To do the Pope justice, Henry's continuous provocations, which might have led to an early and total rupture of relations, were tolerated at length and contact was maintained. By 1533 the cause for annulment had lasted six years. The Pope solemnly refused Henry's petition, condemned his separation and marriage to Anne Boleyn and ordered him to take Catherine back under penalty of excommunication; though this excommunication was never promulgated. In the same year Bishops Gardiner[3] and Bonner[4] were sent by Henry to Marseilles[5] with an appeal to the Pope to call a General Council, and in effect to serve notice on the Pope that Henry appealed from him to a Council. Gardiner, arriving at Marseilles before the Pope (an interview having been arranged there by Francis I of France), had to await his arrival. The Pope visited the Embassy, but without appreciable effect, for at the end of that year he decided that the appeals were 'frivolous, forbidden and unlawful'. It was not until 1534, when Clement VII was succeeded by Paul III (Farnese), that the Papacy showed signs of concern for what was going on in the north of Europe. Even then the failure to listen to the voices of the reformers and to call a Council to deal with them, was a major cause of the subsequent breakdown. But Paul III was at least interested in trying to retain the loyalty of the English sovereign, who in his early years had supported Pope Julius II against the action of Louis XII of France. Louis had summoned an irregular Council at Pisa, with the object of deposing the Pope. When Paul III at last showed signs of

[1] Notably King John; King Louis XII of France; Henry's two sisters, Mary Tudor and Margaret, widow of James IV of Scotland. The Emperor Maximilian and Charles VIII of France also had an annulment apiece (*The Early Tudors 1485–1558*, J. D. Mackie, OUP, 1952, pp. 187, 284, 326n.).

[2] Queen Catherine was aunt to the Emperor Charles V who held the Pope a virtual prisoner.

[3] Stephen Gardiner, 1490–1555. Bishop of Winchester 1531. Deprived 1551.

[4] Edmund Bonner, 1550–1569. Last Bishop of London in communion with the Papacy. Died in the Marshalsea under Elizabeth.

[5] For details of these negotiations: *Stephen Gardiner and the Tudor Reaction*, J. A. Muller, SPCK, 1926.

wanting to call a Council, the English King, fearing that a Council might not go entirely in his favour, came out against it. In 1534, the year of the assertion of the Royal Supremacy, the marriage to Catherine was pronounced valid. But even this did not close the door to negotiations or complete any rupture of relations. In June 1535, for example, Gregory Casale, a go-between for Henry, was able to report that the 'case' might be heard more favourably than on previous occasions.

Soon after this news of the executions of Thomas More and John Fisher reached Rome and the possibilities of success were considerably lessened; but Henry supposed he might still gain a bloodless victory. He resisted the suggestions of the German princes at Schmalkeld that he should make an alliance with them.

The Pilgrimage of Grace, in the following year, showed that there was considerable support in Britain for the view that certain reforms might be effected without a permanent break. In 1537 Reginald Pole was commissioned as special papal legate to attempt a solution of the English problem, but the proposal was abortive.

In 1538 the Pope prepared once more to promulgate the bull of excommunication which had been drawn up three years previously, but never acted upon, deposing Henry and absolving his subjects from their obedience (as 'Regnans in Excelsis' would do some 30 years later). But even then the bull was not made effective, and the whole affair continued in a state of suspense. In 1540 Henry sent an embassy (Gardiner again, and Sir Henry Knyvet[1]) to the Emperor at Ratisbon, hoping thus to get himself an ally and if possible to prevent a permanent breach. It is difficult to disentangle the thread of the meetings at Ratisbon, or their preliminaries or consequences, but it seems reasonably clear that Henry's general instructions to Gardiner were if possible to use the Emperor as a means of reconciliation between himself and the Pope, his intention being that the Pope should reconsider the divorce and allow certain degrees of independence to the English Church in return for Henry's continued support against the protestant princes. Of this whole episode Gardiner was able to say, later, in a sermon in 1554, that:

[1] Muller, *Stephen Gardiner and the Tudor Reaction*, p. 96.

When the tumult was in the north, in the time of King Henry VIII, I am sure that the King was determined to have given over the supremacy again to the Pope, but the hour was not yet then come, and therefore it went not forward, lest some would have said that he did it for fear. After this, Master Knyvet and I were sent ambassadors unto the Emperor to desire him that he would be a mean between the Pope's Holiness and the King, to bring the King to the obedience to the See of Rome, but the time was neither then come, for it might have been said that it had been done for a civil policy.[1]

It is important to remember, through all this episode, that Henry, and Gardiner as his Minister, though anxious to gain a degree of independence from the Pope for the Church in England were by no means intending to be used as agents of the continental protestant reformation. Gardiner at Ratisbon commended himself, for example, to the Venetian ambassador as being a defender of 'catholic' principles and opposed to the protestants. There is evidence that Gardiner gave offence to the latter: he seems to have been well received by Henry on his return.

Whatever prospects there may have been for avoiding a permanent breach had Henry lived longer, his death in 1547 and the succession of Edward VI made them, for the time at least, much more remote. The hand of the stronger king was removed, and both Church and State were at the mercy of those who guided them during the young king's minority. Thomas Cranmer's[2] promotion to the See of Canterbury had been due in part to his willingness to aid the course of Henry's matrimonial cause. But he was also a reformer in the main tradition of the Renaissance (a son primarily of the new knowledge rather than of doctrinal innovation). With Henry's restraints removed, he proceeded immediately under the young king to institute reforms. This is not a history of these events but rather a comment on their influence on and consequences for the development of the relations between the English Church and Rome. Cranmer began with modest

[1] December. Muller, *Stephen Gardiner and the Tudor Reaction*, p. 265.
[2] 1489–1556. Archbishop of Canterbury 1532.

reforms, in the 'Order of Communion' of 1548 and the new
Prayer Book of 1549. (Pope Paul VI, speaking of the reforms
effected by the second Vatican Council, said that they could
best be compared to the process of pruning a tree, cutting out
dead wood in order to give the live shoots more room to
breathe. Cranmer, four centuries before, would have claimed
the same for his.) Like the Vatican reformers of 1962, Cranmer
in 1549 was under pressure from two conflicting parties, both
contending for their interests. It is edifying to compare Cranmer's prefaces to his Prayer Books, for example, with the
decree on the Sacred Liturgy in the Second Vatican Council
and some of the provisions consequent upon it. The comparison
is remarkably close. Had the Church of England been allowed
to continue with the 1549 Prayer Book and Ordinal the
breach might never have become as wide as it did. But there
were strong forces tugging at the English reformers from the
continent of Europe, and disciples of the great protestant
classical leaders were by that time established in positions of
influence in Britain. In 1552 the second Prayer Book of Edward
VI made its appearance. It depended for its authority not on
the sanction of the Convocations but on the State, as it was a
schedule to an Act of Uniformity. The Act said that further
changes were necessary to make the book 'More earnest and
fit to stir people to the true honouring of Almightly God'.
How far the doctrinal reforms which form the background of
the book constitute profound changes and a departure from
the 'catholic faith' has of course been a matter of controversy
through the centuries, and a deep reappraisal of the nature and
essential content of that faith is still part of the current debate.
In 1552 it was held by the continuing Romanists that the
Church of England, having made a deliberate break with
some articles of the theology of the previous century, had put
itself outside the orbit of the catholic faith. The view of the
English Reformers on the other hand was that they had
rescued the catholic primitive and apostolic faith and order
from the heretical accretions which the Roman west had added,
and that they had restored it to its original shape. But the
nature and presuppositions of the 1552 book need not detain us
further, for it was changed considerably in revisions in 1559
and 1662 and only had one year's life on its own account. For

in 1553 the young king died and was succeeded by his sister Mary Tudor.

A daughter of Henry VIII and Catherine of Aragon, declared illegitimate by the surviving Archbishop of Canterbury,[1] and brought up in the meanwhile as a strong adherent of the unreformed religion, Mary was not likely to bring peace to troubled England. Determined to restore the papal obedience at any cost and fixed also with a determination to assert her own legitimate rights as a sovereign, she inaugurated one of the most unhappy reigns of England's long history, and earned the memorable title of 'Bloody Mary'.

Gardiner was the chief link between the new regime and the old; Mary made him Chancellor of the realm. It is clear that Mary's advisers counselled her to go slow in her restoration of the papal authority. But she was determined in her course and carried Parliament with her despite two major obstacles: her known intention to marry Philip II of Spain (England's chief rival on the seas); and the unwillingness of those who had benefited by the plundering and confiscation of Church lands under Henry to surrender their new gains. In fact their consent to the restoration of papal authority over the Church was deliberately delayed, and only eventually agreed to when, in 1554, Pope Julius III gave an undertaking that properties so acquired should not be forfeit. This was written into the text of Mary's Second Act of Repeal, which annulled the ecclesiastical legislation of the previous reigns and made possible the arrival of Cardinal Reginald Pole, who was to be Mary's Archbishop of Canterbury. It is illustrative of the strange ecclesiastical confusion of those days that Pole on his appointment was still in minor orders, had to be ordained priest, and was consecrated bishop the following day. He actually said his first Mass on the day after his predecessor Cranmer was burnt alive.

On 29th November 1554 Parliament restored the papal supremacy and soon afterwards reimposed the penalties for heresy. Immediately the persecutions began which were to be the main events with which Mary's tragic reign was to be associated. Cranmer was still in office when Mary came to the throne; he and his fellow bishops (and all minor clerics) were invited to forswear certain reformed beliefs and to embrace

[1] Thomas Cranmer.

the whole of the unreformed religion. A subservient Convocation of the clergy re-accepted the doctrine of Transubstantiation by a single vote. But some of the bishops who had led
the return to a primitive catholic orthodoxy and the abandon-
ment of this among other mediaeval accretions, were made of
sterner stuff. They were given opportunities, and temptations,
to recant, but they refused. In 1555 began the notorious series
of burnings beginning with Bishops Latimer[1] and Ridley[2] and
Cranmer, Archbishop of Canterbury. Within the next three
years 300 people were similarly executed; the 'fires of Smithfield' burnt their way into the long historical memories of the
English nation. Foxe's Book of Martyrs[3] became almost an
appendage to the Bible. No one then, or for a long time afterwards, believed in toleration as a principle, but these features of
Mary's reign, consequent upon the establishment of the papal
and Spanish connections, together with the development of the
Reformation on the continent of Europe, were making a
permanent solution of the Roman problem less and less
possible.

By this time the long overdue Council of the Church had
been summoned and had had fourteen sessions, mainly at
Trent, from 1545 onwards. The Council, its membership predominantly Italian, put all possibility of reconciliation out of
the question by its decisions. For not only were the main
questions of the protestant reforms not adequately considered,
but the main doctrines under question were reaffirmed in a
most vigorous style with accompanying anathemas. The main
objective of the Council, naturally, was to salvage the life and
teaching of the Church at a time when it appeared to be
threatened; then to give impulse to a movement of revival and
renewal which would help to reconvert the heretics to the true
faith and to recover the ground which had been lost. If any
changes were to be made they were to intensify, and to give a
sharper edge to, those parts of the Christian syllabus of beliefs
which the northern provinces of Europe said were in need of

[1] Hugh Latimer, 1485–1555. Cambridge Fellow. Bishop of Worcester
1535.
[2] Nicholas Ridley, 1500–1555. Bishop of Rochester 1547; London 1550
on Bonner's deprivation.
[3] *Acts and Monuments touching matters in the Church*, John Foxe, English edition,
1563.

reform. The Latin Church, already estranged from the Greek, was now to part company with much of its membership among the nations of northern Europe.

The findings of the Council are well known, and we need do no more than to summarise them here. At Session 4 (1546) came the assertion of the equal value of Scripture and Tradition as sources of divine truth, and of the sole right of the Church to interpret the Bible and the authority of the Latin text of the Vulgate. Session 5 (1546 and 1547) struck at the root of protestant beliefs about the nature of man's salvation and codified the Roman doctrine about Justification and Merit in the form in which we now have it. It was during the thirteenth Session (1551) at which there were some Protestants present, that the doctrine of Transubstantiation, the cause of so much dispute and misunderstanding, received its final form. By the time Elizabeth came to the throne (1558) the main definitions of the Council had been made and the 'damage' (from the point of view of the preservation of the unity of the Church) was already done.

At home Elizabeth inherited a country depressed by the events of the reign already described and by the loss of England's last stronghold in France. The will of many for national independence was thereby strengthened. The statesmanlike solution of the religious problem was therefore inevitably a compromise of some sort which would preserve the fundamentals of the old religion and which would retain the loyalty of as many as possible of those who felt the inspiration of the new ideas of the Renaissance.

The Elizabethan Settlement, as it is now described, consisted mainly of enactments. The first of these was the Act of Supremacy of 1559. It is important to notice of this that the framers of the legislation regarded themselves not simply as restoring the status quo of the years of Henry VIII, but as taking an independent line in important matters. The preamble of the Elizabethan Act reads:

> that where in the time of your father of worthy memory, King Henry Eighth, divers good laws and statutes were made and established, as well for the utter extinguishment and putting away of all usurped and foreign powers and author-

ities out of this your realm . . . as also for the *restoring and
uniting to the imperial government of this realm the ancient jurisdictions . . . to the same of right belonging* . . .[1]

The Act deliberately did not restore the title of 'Supreme Head'
as used by Henry VIII, which Elizabeth held to be impious,
but uses instead the form 'Supreme Governor'. Yet the Act can
be said to be careful about the location of ultimate spiritual
authority.[2]

Ecclesiastical conformity for the reign was secured by the
passing of the Act of Uniformity in the same year. Elizabeth's
intentions in this were pacific. There had been an unmistakable
hardening of both Romans and Protestants during Mary's
reign; and Elizabeth was tired, as most of her subjects were, of
the excesses of religious strife.

There is a common tendency to exaggerate the autocracy of
the Tudor monarchs, particularly of Elizabeth herself, whose
personal character gave colour to such a tendency, but it
should not be forgotten that all her legislation was passed
without restraint by a Parliament 80 per cent of whose members were independent; whose election was quite regular; it can
therefore be said to have been enacted in a constitutional
manner. Moreover, it probably represents the consensus of most
English people who, having been forcibly transferred from one
church discipline to another three times in twelve years were
glad to settle down to a moderate regime.

These two enactments, of Supremacy and of Uniformity,
still largely determine the nature of the 'Establishment' of the
Church of England. This state of affairs is not theoretically
acceptable to the Church of Rome (the ideas of the Papacy and
of a National Church being assumed to be incompatible), so
that it should be reckoned as a major cause of disunity. The
Church of Rome claims to be guardian of the spiritual rights
and independence of the whole Catholic Church. The national
churches have seen themselves as guardians of the inherent
rights of the local church and champions of the individual
Christian against the dangers of an international ecclesiastical
despotism. The more ecumenical climate of the twentieth

---

[1] *Select Statutes and other Constitutional documents illustrative of the reigns of
Elizabeth and James I* (ed. G. W. Prothero), OUP, 1913, p. 1.
[2] ibid., Section 20, p. 12, para. XX.

century makes it possible to see these two points of view as complementary and not antagonistic; and workers for unity do not expect this issue to provide a major obstacle to progress. In the four previous centuries, however, these two principles can be held to be a major cause of antagonism, though it should be noted that the issue between them was by no means born of the Reformation, as testified by the tomb of the Martyr St. Thomas Becket in Canterbury itself.

The settlement of questions of church order by these two enactments was a simple matter in comparison with the provision of a standard of doctrinal orthodoxy for the new separated province of the Church. The Act of Uniformity set up the Prayer Book as a general point of reference in matters both ritual and doctrinal. But deductions from the implied teachings of the Book of Common Prayer would certainly be very widely drawn, and it was felt that clarity on a certain number of points should at least be attempted. A new edition therefore of Edward VI's Articles was now put forward and set up as the official standard of Anglican orthodoxy. The general intention was again to preserve the catholic faith of the undivided Church, that is of the first four general councils, rather than specifically to deny such doctrines as were felt to be unwarranted accretions of later centuries, and particularly among the decrees of the Council of Trent; and then to make as clear a definition as possible, in the heat of controversy, of contemporary doctrinal issues such as lay behind predestination and transubstantiation. The Articles were never intended to be an Anglican corpus dogmaticum. In recent years a Commission under the Chairmanship of the then Bishop of Durham (Ian Ramsey) has reassessed their position among the formularies of the Church of England and has eased the demands they made upon the consciences of subscribing ministers. The Durham report, which was heavily endorsed by the four houses of Convocation and by the laity of the Church Assembly, said of them:

The Articles are not a complete body of divinity. They are agreed propositions showing what attitude the Church of England took on certain controverted points of divinity in the sixteenth century, and are therefore in this way deter-

minative of the direction taken by Anglicanism at a particularly significant stage in its history.[1]

The 39 Articles were finally promulgated in 1571, and with
the Prayer Book and Ordinal still form the documents of
Anglican divinity. As has been said, they do not form or
contain an official confessional document to compare with the
Heidelberg Catechism or the Augsburg Confession. That the
Anglican Communion has no such charter is considered by
some its strength, by others its weakness.

There is a great change now coming over the whole field
of theological opinion, both catholic and protestant, which
suggests that all churches and confessions are labouring under
an excessive weight of definitions and dogmas, and that the
future path towards reintegration of Christian union must lead
us to see that truth, especially religious truth, is dynamic
rather than static and that the present exercise must begin
from the point where essential truths are sorted out from
peripheral ones. But here we are talking the language of 1970
and Pope Paul VI, four centuries on. Of the time of the breach
suffice it to say that each side had to regard the other as being
in error. Anglicans believed the Church of Rome to have added
to the faith and pressed upon men's consciences doctrines which
were not part of the original deposit. This situation has been
aggravated by the further Roman Catholic definitions of the
last hundred years. The Church of Rome, on the other hand,
believed that the English Church, in trying to reform the
faith, had changed it into something which it was not before;
and in trying to reform the Church unilaterally it had put itself
out of communion with the rest of Christendom and so into
schism, thus invalidating its own sacraments and orders.
Through the gap thus formed have poured many bitter waters,
each side being from that time onwards officially out of touch
with the other, following policies and developing doctrines
which were less and less mutually understandable, while
customs, formulations and even theological language diverged
and reacted. The Church of Rome became more exclusively
Latin in culture. The English Church, isolated from the Latin

[1] 'Subscription and Assent to the 39 Articles', a Report of the Archbishops'
Commission on Christian Doctrine, 1968, Section 59.

Church of southern and western Europe, found it more difficult to resist the hard doctrines of the Protestant Reformation of the north: in particular, groups within Parliament and the armed forces were influenced by Calvinistic teaching. Her distinctive position gradually began to take shape. The shape in which it emerged and in which it has for the most part endured was more the result of practical experience than of basic doctrinal speculation. The Church of England, as has been said often, is not a confessional Church: she believes herself to be the result of what happened to the English portion of the catholic Church which broke off to restore and relive her basic faith and order in the light of new experiences. The misleading conception of the Via Media has implications which do not explain the facts, for it is negative. The Anglican interpretation of catholicity has been a positive deliberate attempt towards comprehensiveness; to include and to make available as much Christian truth and order as was edifying.

Precisely because the Church of England had no confessional document, her early history naturally called forth a literature of explanation and clarification under a succession of apologists, to which those who wish to understand her should turn. The first of these was Bishop Jewel[1] whose Apologia Ecclesiae Anglicanae appeared in 1562 in Latin and in 1564 in English. For Jewel both the Scriptures and the patristic writers justified the action and the doctrinal position of the English Church. He accepted the breach with Rome, but denied it to be an act of schism:

> It is true we have departed from them; and for so doing we both give thanks to Almighty God, and greatly rejoice on our own behalf. But yet for all this, from the primitive church, from the apostles, and from Christ we have not departed . . . [Indeed] we truly have renounced that church wherein we could neither have the word of God sincerely taught, nor the sacraments rightly administered, nor the name of God duly called upon. . . . To conclude, we have forsaken the church as it is now, not as it was in old time . . . . and we are come to that church, wherein they them-

[1] John Jewel, 1522–1571. Fellow of Corpus Christi College Oxford 1542. At Frankfurt during reign of Mary. Bishop of Salisbury 1560.

selves cannot deny . . . but all things be governed purely and reverently, and as much as we possibly could, very near to the order used in the old times.[1]

In Jewel we see also the rejection of the position of the Bishop of Rome and the beginnings of the ecclesiastical 'Drang nach Osten', an Anglican tendency to look to the position of the eastern patriarchs as over against the position of the see of Rome. Jewel appealed to the Council of Nicaea to show that

> the bishop of Rome hath no more jurisdiction over the Church of God than the rest of the patriarchs, either of Alexandria or Antiochia, have.[2]

Jewel's Apology was widely translated and circulated in Europe and resulted in the first of the pamphlet exchanges[3] between the two communions, which have continued until dialogue has come to close range in present times.

Another early apologist was Richard Hooker[4] whose 'Of the Laws of Ecclesiastical Polity' appeared in 1594. He saw the Church of England the victim of a reluctant, though necessary, schism within the Body of Christ—for from that, as distinct from the Church of Rome, she was by no means separated. The ties of Christian observance, particularly that of Baptism, continued the real unity of Christian fellowship, in spite of the breakdown of ecclesiastical unity.

The Church of England had thus taken the general shape in matters doctrinal which was to continue through the centuries of separation, while the Church of Rome's course was set upon the implementation of the decisions of the Council of Trent. It must be remembered by the English, and particularly the Anglican, reader, that the Church of Rome then, as now, was not concerned only with what was happening in the Church of England; she was faced also with the fissiparous and centrifugal

---

[1] *Works*, Vol. 3, p. 90, 92 Apologia Eccl. Angl., Parker Society, Cambridge 1848.

[2] *Works*, Vol. 3, p. 59, 60 Apologia Eccl. Angl.

[3] Notably from a colony of English Roman Catholic exiles living at Louvain, headed by Thomas Harding, *Elizabethan Recusant Prose 1559–1582*, A. C. Southern, London, 1950. *The English Catholics in the reign of Elizabeth*, J. H. Pollen, London, 1920.

[4] Born ?1554; died 1600. Fellow of Corpus Christi College, Oxford 1577. Master of the Temple 1585.

behaviour of the diverse confessions of the continental protestant churches. It is therefore not surprising that the Reformation was for the Church of Rome a hardening experience,
minimising the benefit which might have come to her from the
Renaissance if such as Erasmus, Colet and More had been
allowed to guide her destinies. The great new experiences and
revelations of the Counter-Reformation immediately took on a
harsh and militant form. The glorious zeal of the missionaries
was armed with a sword to convert where persuasion failed;
the apologist who faced the new churches of northern Europe
had fleets and armies at his back to reinforce his arguments
against the heretic, and even the giant mystics and ascetics
who were the ripest fruits of the period acquired a strain of
intolerance which has made them seem remote to those outside
the ethos of the Latin Church. But in so far as these things are
regarded, from the point of the development of future relations,
as unsatisfactory, it is to be observed that they were a natural
reaction to defects on the protestant side. The diversities,
divisions, exaggerations and provocations of protestantism
served then, as they have done since, to aggravate tendencies in
the Roman Church to intolerance, exclusiveness and militancy.
That both sides resorted to the civil power to support their
divine pretensions has meant that ecclesiastical divisions and
confessional differences have taken on a quality to which wars,
politics, geography, economics and diversities of culture have
given a hardness which is proving very difficult to soften.

It is unprofitable to speculate which of the many episodes
in this sad history can be said to be the point of no return,
beyond which it was impossible for official relations to continue.
It is difficult, for example, to suppose that it was any use
hoping after the closure of the last session of the Council of
Trent in 1563. But the separation was not technically complete
until the papal bull of 1570. Legislation had already been
passed in England which brought to an end the civil jurisdiction of the Pope and secured authority over 'causes ecclesiastical and civil' for the English sovereign. But in 1570
Pope Pius V published the bull 'Regnans in Excelsis'[1] to
excommunicate the Queen and to liberate Englishmen from
their obedience to her. It is not therefore surprising that in the

[1] Full text in Prothero, p. 195.

following year Elizabeth retaliated with more stringent laws against continuing Roman Catholics.

> . . . if any person . . . shall . . . say . . . that our said Sovereign Lady Queen Elizabeth during her life is not or ought not to be Queen of this realm of England or that any other person ought of right to be a king or queen of the said realms . . . or shall by writing, printing . . . or sayings . . . affirm that the Queen . . . is an heretic, schismatic, tyrant, infidel or an usurper of the crown . . . .that then all such offences shall be deemed . . . to be high treason.[1]

The die was thus indeed cast and the breach was made. The next pope, Gregory XIII, endorsed the bull and authorised an Italian expedition against Ireland, in an attempt to defeat the English sovereign through the defection of that province. It still wanted ten years before the full panoply of the Spanish Armada should come sailing up the English Channel in an attempt to restore the unity of Christendom by conquest. From then on, at least, the whole situation was lifted out of the realm of faith and ecclesiastical politics. In the mind of the common Englishman the Pope of Rome was thought of as a political and military enemy of, and as a threat to, the English nation. The lights had gone out, and it was dark indeed.

[1] 13 Eliz. Cap. 1. Prothero, p. 58.

2
THE GULF WIDENS

The long and honourable line of those who have tried to heal the breach can be traced back to those who had laboured to prevent it happening at all in the first place. None of the climacterics of history is ever as clear cut as it is made to appear in subsequent accounts, and this is certainly true of the breach between England and Rome. The hand of caution and reluctance can be seen more on the side of Rome, it is fair to say, than on the part of England. The Papacy had much to lose from the disintegration of Christendom, while England, with the other nations of northern Europe, had much to gain, of a secular kind at least, from independence.

It is not the place of this book to recount in detail the political manoeuvres and subtleties which lay behind the ecclesiastical events; but of the international scene it can be said that during the second half of the sixteenth century France was an enemy of England, being in league with Scotland and Elizabeth's rival claimant to the throne; while Spain was in the first place in favour of conciliating the English Queen and of winning England, as Philip would have said, 'back to the Church'. Against this background we can first notice the efforts of the papacy to retain Elizabeth and England within the Roman obedience and then, when that looked unlikely, to postpone as long as possible the ultimate rupture of relations. There was a change of Pope almost immediately after Elizabeth came to the throne, Pius IV succeeding Paul IV in 1559. Pius was a man of affairs rather than a theologian, and showed an altogether more pragmatic attitude to the English question than had his predecessor. The situation seems to have been represented to him as more favourable than in fact it was.[1] In the spring of 1560 Sir Francis Englefield, one of Mary's ministers, went to Rome where with Sir Edward Carne, Mary's former ambassador, a consultation was held concerning the 'English question'. As a result Pius IV appointed a commission of five cardinals, including Morone, the 'protector' of England. By them it was proposed that Vincenzo Parpaglia, abbot of San Salvatore, should be sent to the court of Elizabeth with a note from the Pope. On 4th May 1560 Cardinal Charles Borromeo, Secretary of State, wrote to the Nuncio in Spain:

> The Pope has decided to send an embassy to the Queen of England to try to bring her back to the bosom of the Church and the obedience of the Holy See, believing that the troubles in which Her Majesty finds herself at present give some hope that the attempt may succeed. His Holiness has chosen Abbot Parpaglia for this post. . . . He will be instructed to seek all the help he can from the king of France and from Madam the Governess in Holland. It now remains for you to use your offices with his Catholic Majesty. . . .[2]

The whole expedition became a drama of rival policies, as did its successors. France wanted Elizabeth excommunicated as soon as possible, while Spain was for winning her by more subtle and gentle methods. The matter was more simply decided, however, by Elizabeth's unwillingness to receive the embassy. Parpaglia accordingly returned home from Brussels.[3] The official Vatican news was conveyed to the King of Spain in the picturesque phrase that:

> The Nuncio who was to have crossed into England has found that the sea in those parts is rougher than was anticipated in view of the obstinacy of the Queen, who does not want to receive him. He has therefore been recalled.[4]

In November 1560 came the bull announcing the resumption

[1] Bishop de Quadra, Spanish Ambassador in England, spoke of possible risings of Elizabeth's remaining catholic subjects.

[2] Vat. Archives. German Nunziatura, Vol. iv, f. 13v.

[3] For details of these embassies see *England and the Catholic Church under Elizabeth*, A. O. Meyer (trans. J. R. McKee), London, 1916.

[4] September 1560. Vat. Archives. German Nunziatura, Vol. iv, f. 40d.

of the Council of Trent, and in March 1561 the Pope decided to make a second attempt to win Elizabeth back by gentle means, perhaps to come to the Council or to send representatives, or at the very least to persuade her to release her political prisoners. The chosen ambassador this time was an Abbot Martinengo.[1] The fate of his mission was similar to that of his predecessor. Philip of Spain discouraged the visit altogether. Elizabeth hesitated as to whether to receive him or not, but her mind was finally made up this time by Cecil and a majority of the Privy Council.

These attempts at reconciliation (and there were others)[2] are worthy of inclusion, to show that there was a deep reluctance to make the separation permanent. They represent the backward glances of parting friends before they took the inevitable road of divergence. For that the separation by this time (the '60s of the sixteenth century) was inevitable there can be no doubt. Both the Reformation and the Counter-Reformation were too firmly set upon their courses for there to be any possibility that England would escape their consequences; and the hard facts of political interest on all sides bore down to make the chances of reconciliation even more remote.

The English Romanist community grew weaker as the century went on—that is until the arrival of the mission priests. Their unwillingness to join in rebellious movements in England was increased by the failure of the Pope to supply them with adequate leadership. They were for the most part prepared to be patriotic,[3] but the pressure of events made this more and more difficult. The formulas of the Council of Trent put the first strain on their loyalties. They were torn by internal dissensions.[4] In spite of their frequent appeals to Rome for help the English Roman Catholics at first received

[1] *England and the Catholic Church under Elizabeth*, Meyer, pp. 41–6.
[2] Agents sent by successive popes to try to effect reconciliation include Thomas Sackville, Gurove Bertano, Antonio and Sebastian Brushetto. 'Anglo-Roman Relations 1558–1565', C. G. Bayne, *Oxford Historical and Literary Studies*, Vol. II, OUP, 1913.
[3] Some equipped ships at their expense against the Armada and encouraged their tenants in defence of their country. *Historical Memoirs of English Catholics*, Vol. I, Charles Butler, John Murray, 1822, p. 230.
[4] For the details of the methods adopted for the care of the Roman Catholic community in England see *England and the Catholic Church under Elizabeth*, Meyer.

very little. Their whole situation, however, was completely
transformed by subsequent events. The massacre of the
Huguenots in France in 1569, the bull of 1570 and eventually
the arrival of the Armada in 1588 first created and then
consolidated a new state of affairs. Political overtones swamped
all religious differences: the loyalty of the Roman Catholic
community became suspect, a situation which had been forced
on the local scene from outside. No matter what the sentiments of
English catholic citizens were, the formulas of the Council, the
terms of the bull and the guns of the Armada spoke a different
language. Trials and executions began and in the forty-four-
year reign of Queen Elizabeth 250 people died in the religious
persecutions. Those who suffered most were the mission
priests, trained overseas and sent into the country, and members of the Society of Jesus.[1] Both, no doubt sincerely, disclaimed any political connections, but they undoubtedly aimed
to stiffen the resistance of English Roman Catholics to the
Church of England. Many of them died heroic deaths; and
each execution drove a deeper wedge between the English
Church and the hopes of a permanent reconciliation with
Rome, as those in the previous reign had done.[2]

The history of the next three centuries was going to be one of
increasing estrangement between the Church of the nation and
the small Roman Catholic minority within it. Three trends
were going to confirm that separation. The first was the growing
power of the Puritans in Parliament, with all their prejudices
against the Church of Rome, both theological and political.
Secondly, on the Roman side, was a series of disastrous provocative incidents which succeeded in antagonising the
English State authorities even further and in keeping up the

[1] It has been calculated that there were 300 mission priests and 12 Jesuits
in England at the end of Elizabeth's reign: the tensions between them mainly
concerned oversight. The secular priests canvassed at Rome for a bishop and
it was not until 1623 that they received one.

[2] Much thought and prayer has been put into the understanding of
these events in the years leading up to the canonisation of the '40 Martyrs'
in October 1970. Thanks to the totally new spirit prevailing in these
relationships the controversial sting has been drawn from the history of the
period, and the common remembrance of the martyrs of religious and
political intolerance has set the seal on the progress of the Ecumenical
Movement. The understanding and conciliatory guidance of Pope Paul VI
dominated the whole proceeding.

phobia that the Roman Catholic Church was in the last analysis a danger to the national security. Thirdly, the self-conscious life of the Anglican Church feeling the need to justify itself in relation to Rome on the one hand and the extreme currents of the Protestant Reformation on the other. Trials of Roman Catholics for treason would become fewer under the new reign, except in so far as they were provoked from time to time by events which were thought to have sinister political implications. But a general state of civil disability and exclusion was maintained. It is against this background that subsequent attempts at restoration of good relationships were made.

The death of Elizabeth and the accession of James I (formerly James VI of Scotland) brought with it a change of dynasty from Tudor to Stuart which might have been expected to bode well for church relationships. James had had dealings with the Pope and with foreign Roman Catholics (and indeed with English ones) while still on the throne of Scotland, asking their help to secure the throne of England. Under the direction of the Duc de Guise he had written as early as 1584 to the Pope (Gregory XIII) in this cause,[1] and as late as 1622 we find him addressing a letter to Gregory XV in the interests of European peace:

> Your Holiness will perhaps marvel, that we differing from you in point of Religion should now first salute you with our letters. Howbeit, such is the trouble of our mind for these calamitous discords and bloodsheds which for these late years by past have so miserably rent the Christian works, and so great is our care and daily solicitude to stop the course of these growing evils betimes so much as in us lies, as we could no longer abstain considering that we all worship the same most blessed Trinity, nor hope for salvation by any other means then [sic] by the blood and merits of our Lord and Saviour Christ Jesus . . . that you would be pleased . . . to put your hand to so pious a work and so worthy of a Christian Prince.
>
> . . . That which remains for us further to say concerning

---

[1] 19th February 1584. Span. Cal. iii 518.

this matter, this Gentleman, our subject, George Gage,[1] will deliver unto you more at large. Praying your Holiness that you will give him in all things full credence and belief.[2]

In 1599 a letter went from James in Scotland to Clement VIII.[3] When, after James's success in obtaining the crown of England, the letter came to light and its contents became known, James largely disclaimed it, for by then (1608) he had begun to learn that secret trafficking with the Pope was not regarded with favour by his subjects. The Pope's reply to this letter[4] was not enthusiastic. He was clearly hoping for James's conversion (in the absence of which he was making efforts to secure a catholic successor to Elizabeth). While still in Scotland James's queen (Anne of Denmark), herself a Roman Catholic convert, began to take part in the negotiations and wrote a number of letters to the Pope, to which she received replies.[5]

James undoubtedly also made attempts to gain the support of Roman Catholic subjects for his succession to the throne. In a letter to the Earl of Northumberland, a leading Roman Catholic noble, he said:

> As for catholics I will neither persecute any that will be quiet and give but an outward obedience to the law, neither will I spare to advance any of them that will by good service worthily deserve it.[6]

When James came to the English throne in 1603 it could be

---

[1] A Roman Catholic court messenger, one of a number of agents who went between James and Rome; another was Padre Alessandro d'Ales (who came to London at least four times); from Scotland there were numerous agents: Sir James Lindsay (who also continued to operate from England): Sir Walter Lindsay ('Secret Diplomacy of James VI', J. D. Mackie, *Scottish Historical Review*, Vol. XXI, 1923–1924, pp. 267–82).

[2] Cabala, p. 412, E.1663 30th September 1622.

[3] *James VI of Scotland and the Throne of England*, H. G. Stafford, D. Appleton Century Co., New York and London, 1940, pp. 235–6; also *English Historical Review*, 'James VI and Rome', Vol. XX, 1905, pp. 124–5.

[4] Public Record Office Rom. Trans. Bdl. 86a. Clement to James, 13th April 1600.

[5] *James VI and the Throne of England*, Stafford, pp. 238–9 and *Clement VIII und Jakob I*, A. O. Meyer. Rom. 1904 for transcripts (in German) of the letters in the Vatican Archives.

[6] Quoted by D. Harris Willson, *King James VI and I*, Jonathan Cape, 1956, p. 148–9.

said that the prospect for at least a modus vivendi between the Church of England and the Roman Church was not entirely unfavourable. True his interests were partly political and he had no wish to have closer ecclesiastical relationships than on his own terms as an amateur theologian and upholder of the divine right of kings. But there was a Roman Catholic queen and the king himself was what we should call a 'high Anglican': his ecclesiology found a central place for the Roman Church. In his first speech to Parliament James said:

I acknowledge the Roman Church to be our mother church, although defiled with some infirmities and corruptions.

If Rome would be able to lay aside these errors he would be willing to compromise and negotiate a union. In a later letter to Prince Charles he wrote:

. . . I am not a Monsieur who can shift his religion as easily as he can shift his shirt, when he cometh for tennis. . . . And as for myself, if that were yet the question, I would with all my heart give my consent that the Bishop of Rome should have the first seat. I being a western king, would go with the Patriarch of the West. And for his temporal principality over the Signiory of Rome, I do not quarrel with it neither; let him, in God's name, be primus episcopus inter omnes episcopos et princeps episcoporum, so it be no otherwise but as St. Peter was princeps apostolorum.[1]

Many factors, however, led to the rapid worsening of the prospects at the beginning of James's reign. All through the latter years of Elizabeth the puritan influence in parliament had been growing. Catholic (and foreign) brides were sought for both James's sons. Queen Anne's efforts to obtain the hand of the Spanish Infanta for Prince Henry[2] were known and resented. But the King's vacillation with regard to his Roman Catholic subjects caused dismay. It was discontent under this heading which led to the Gunpowder Plot of 1605. The adverse effect of this disastrous attempt at assassination, lamented as much by James's Roman Catholic subjects as by anyone else,

[1] March 1623. Quoted in *The Years of Siege*, Philip Caraman, Longmans, 1966, p. 122.
[2] James's eldest son, and heir, who died before his father.

cannot be exaggerated. It cast its long shadow over any subsequent attempts at conciliation for over 200 years. Folk memories are very long, and Guy Fawkes passed into the national ritual memory. It is not surprising that the plot gave rise immediately to reprisals and to further penal legislation.[1]

The 1606 Act enforced upon all recusants an Oath of Allegiance, which denounced as heretical the doctrine of papal supremacy. James maintained that his aims were political. But the Pope and Cardinal Bellarmine[2] interpreted it differently and complained that to take the oath was 'not so much to swear allegiance to the King as to abjure allegiance to the Vicar of Christ'. As a result of the ill reception of the Oath in catholic circles and because of a number of pamphlets circulated at the instigation of Bellarmine, James entered into a period of theological publication in answer to him.[3]

Another interesting episode of this kind in James's reign came later, in 1622, as the result of the proselytising activities of the Jesuits, and in particular of one named Fisher. During a period of clemency in which Roman priests in England were enjoying a measure of immunity, corresponding with the wooing of the Spanish Infanta as bride for James's surviving son,[4] the King became alarmed at the conversion to the Roman Church of the Countess of Buckingham and was afraid for the future of the Marquis himself, one of his closest confidants. Accordingly a series of questions was prepared (by Prince Charles) and a confrontation was staged in which the arguments of the two sides were deployed.[5] The champion of the Anglican side was the newly-consecrated Bishop of St. David's

---

[1] 3 and 4 Jac. 1. Cap V (1606) 'to prevent and avoid dangers which may grow by popist recusants'.

[2] Cardinal Robert Bellarmine, 1542–1621. Theologian and controversialist. Entered Jesuit Order 1560. Professor of Theology, Louvain 1570. Canonised 1930.

[3] There were four chief works: 'The Apology', 1608; 'The Premonition', 1609 (in which the King expressed the hope that a Council would be called); 'The Declaration concerning Vortius' and a 'Remonstrance for the right of Kings'.

[4] The future Charles I.

[5] *A Relation of the Conference between William Laud and Mr. Fisher the Jesuit*, by William, Archbishop of Canterbury (ed. C. H. Simpkinson), Macmillan, 1901.

(William Laud). There is a robust objectivity on both sides of the argument (which is well worth reading) and could be a model for all such discussion. Most of all it does not shirk the difficulty, which some subsequent (and even contemporary) dialogues have done, that both sides honestly believed the other to be in error.

Meanwhile the general attitude of the relations between the Church of Rome and the Church of England was being affected by the progress of two dynastic marriages. First, Princess Elizabeth James' daughter, had married in 1613 the Elector Palatine who in 1618 allied himself with the Bohemian rebels and started the 30 years' war. Secondly, and partly consequently upon it, came James' attempt to secure the hand of the Spanish Infanta for his son Charles. This proposition suited the policies of Spain and the Pope who saw in it possibilities for the relief of Roman Catholics in England and even of the conversion of the Prince. But the King's inability to repeal the laws made by an increasingly puritan Parliament were imperfectly understood abroad, and although Prince Charles went to Spain and exchanged letters with Pope Gregory XV,[1] the marriage did not materialise and Charles married Henrietta Maria, daughter of Henry IV of France, shortly after his accession to the throne.

James died in March 1625; he had kept in front of him, notionally at least, the ideal of the union of Christians. But he had estranged the puritans and set the House of Stuart on the course which was to lead it to disaster. William Forbes, Bishop of Edinburgh, paid him the following tribute:

But without detracting anything from the praises of that most serene and never sufficiently to be praised prince James VI, who, though he had nothing more at heart than the wish to bring about a pious peace and concord among Christian Churches, never was able to obtain or give effect to what he so greatly desired, in consequence of the morose

[1] The Prince's letter dated 20th April 1623 gives his own religious position very clearly. Pope Urban VIII (Maffeo Barberini) also wrote to Prince Charles and James I on 15th October 1623: quoted in Dodd's *History of England* (ed. M. A. Tierney), Charles Dolman, 1843, Vol. V, pp. 454-7; Charles's letter: Vol. II, Part V, Book III, pp. 441-3.

and quarrelsome dispositions of a number of would-be theologians.[1]

In 1634 we find a priest in Rome with a pseudonym of Mr. William Price, drawing up a memorandum that:

> wise King James [was moved] . . . to desire a national cardinal by whose means he might have such correspondence with Rome and such intelligence thence of the general affairs of Christendom, as might according to the various condition thereof, direct him to steer his course. Certainly that wise Prince well knows how diligently the ancient Princes his predecessors nourished a strict correspondence and league betwixt this state and Rome, and this, not only out of devotion, but as esteeming it safe and beneficial in other temporary respects.[2]

[1] 'Considerationes Modestae et Pacificae Controversiarum de Justificatione, Purgatorio, Invocatione Sanctorum Christo Mediatore et Eucharistia', William Forbes, Bishop of Edinburgh, died 1634. Published 1658, p. 97.

[2] *State Papers collected by Edward, earl of Clarendon commencing from the year MDCXXI*, Oxford, 1767, Vol. I, p. 133.

3

EARLY EMISSARIES

Charles, after his accession, found the regulation of the Queen's household no easy problem. And one of the causes contributory to his difficulties with Parliament was undoubtedly the obligation he was known to feel to be tolerant of Roman Catholics as part of the cost of domestic peace. Although opposition to Roman Catholics was growing in the House of Commons, the fact that Charles made no use of Parliament for ten years from 1629 to 1639 made their lot easier. But as the King's influence waned and the power of Parliament grew the situation gradually worsened.

Meanwhile Anglican/Roman Catholic relationships were represented by a series of agents and go-betweens in both directions. The Stuart monarchs never completely lost sight of the ideal of the one Church, whose unity should be restored, nor did the popes resign hope that the English, through their sovereign, should be drawn back into the papal fold. In 1633 Sir Robert Douglas began to reside in Rome as the Queen's agent, though with the full knowledge and approval of the King, who hoped through him to reach an understanding with the Pope. Douglas said that his interests were purely spiritual, though Cardinal del Bagno[1] told Cardinal Barberini[2] that the Palatine question[3] must surely also be involved. Douglas petitioned the Pope for an English cardinal, both to represent the Vatican and to regulate the tangled affairs of the Roman

[1] Former Nuncio at Brussels.　　　　　　　　[2] Secretary of State.
[3] See above p. 27. There can be no doubt that the papal agents were suffered so long as they were in the hope that the Pope's help might be forthcoming over the issue of the Palatinate.

Catholic community in England. Although no cardinal was sent, there appeared on the scene in England a series of papal agents, who came for a variety of reasons and from different backgrounds, whose presence and activities are not without interest.

The first of them was Dom Leander a Sancto Martino, president of the English congregation of the Benedictines and Prior of Douai, who crossed the channel by royal permit with orders from the holy see to report on the state of Roman Catholic affairs in England. His name in the world had been Jack Jones, alias Scudamore, born in 1575 in Breconshire and educated at St. John's College, Oxford, where he had been a contemporary of Laud. Secretary of State Windebank wrote to Leander at Douai:

> His Majesty hath commanded me to let you know that he hath given you leave to repair hither into England to see your friends and kindred, whensoever you shall see fit, and that it shall be lawful for you to stay and remain here (by virtue of His Majesty's said permission) without trouble or danger of the laws.[1]

On arrival in England he went to see Laud at Croydon (he spoke of the ancient friendship between 'My Lord's Grace and me'[2]) before going to see his friends in Wales. He wrote to Rome to Cardinal Bentivoglio on 12th July 1634 and showed Windebank, with whom he was obviously very intimate, the letter.[3]

On 15th November 1634 Leander wrote at length to the Pope and to Cardinal Barberini. On 8th and 16th December[4] Leander commented that the Court at Rome was not well informed on the situation in England nor on the nature of the Anglican Church, which was unlike the Protestant churches on the continent. He listed the points of agreement between the Anglican and Roman Catholic churches and he classified the differences.

---

[1] 1st December 1633, Clarendon State Papers, Vol. I, p. 72.
[2] ibid., p. 128.
[3] ibid., pp. 129–33. All letters from Leander to officials at Rome were endorsed by Windebank.
[4] ibid., pp. 169–70, 180–2, 185–207.

He explained further that the supremacy claimed by the King in the Oath (of allegiance) was a temporal supremacy only. He came out eventually in favour of Roman Catholics taking the Oath and hoped that Rome would compromise. To do otherwise would only vex the large numbers of moderate men whose end was to please both God and the King.

Leander seems to have been in touch with a group of Anglicans, headed by Laud, who wanted reunion, but he eventually got into considerable trouble with Rome for his own views. In 1635 Leander wrote to Windebank[1] asking him to intercede for him to the King to let him stay in England; he was ill and the wrath of Rome was upon him for his opinions. He eventually died in England under the protection of the King and Laud, his old undergraduate friend, lamented by Anglicans and Roman Catholics alike. His main limitation was that he did not fully realise how far the King was bound by Parliament, this being a mistake common to most of these early enthusiasts for union who were not acquainted with the nature of the English constitution. The matter of the Oath of allegiance was one of the main stumbling blocks in Anglican/Roman Catholic relationships for the next century and a half. On the one hand the Papacy would not withdraw its opposition to the Oath since it virtually denied the papal dispensing power. On the other hand, no change could be made in the Oath by kings or ecclesiastics without the sanction of a very antagonistic and increasingly puritan English Parliament. But in spite of these limitations the name of Dom Leander, Scudamore or plain Jack Jones should be inscribed in a place of honour among those of the 'go-betweens' who have attempted, in unpromising times, to keep alive the prospect of the reunion of the churches.

It was at this period that there occurred the strange rumour of the offer of a cardinal's hat to Laud. There is an entry in his diary[2] for Sunday, 4th August 1633 which reads:

News came to the court of the Lord Archbishop of Canterbury's death: and the king resolved presently to give it to me. That very morning at Greenwich there came one to me,

---

[1] 1st October 1635, Clarendon State Papers, Vol. I, p. 331.
[2] 'The History of the Troubles and Tryal of William Laud wrote by himself', London, MDCXCV, p. 49.

seriously, that offered me to be a cardinal, and that avowed
ability to perform it. I went presently to the King and
acquainted him both with the thing and the person.

On Saturday, 17th August of the same year, Laud records:

I had a serious offer made to me to be a cardinal. . . . I
acquainted His Majesty with it. But my answer again was
that somewhat dwelt within me which would not suffer that,
till Rome were other than it is.

The origin of this strange episode is not known. We hear no
more of it. There have been those who speculated whether
Dom Leander was at the root of it. But he didn't arrive in
England till the following year, though it is possible that he
may have been using an agent. He had indeed been very close
to Laud when they were undergraduates.

At the time when Leander was writing to Rome, the Pope,
on the advice of Cardinal Barberini, decided to send Gregorio
Panzani from the Chiesa Nuova to England as an agent so
that 'he could come to a true knowledge of the differences
between the clergy and the regulars'. Before leaving he had an
interview with Urban VIII who hoped for the King's conversion, but fear for his nephews, the young Princes Palatine,
champions of Protestantism, was thought to weigh against
any moves towards Rome. Panzani also saw Cardinal del
Bagno, who was not hopeful on the conversion of the King, and
told him to avoid the use of the term 'Protestant' which would
annoy the Archbishop of Canterbury (Laud), who was inclined
to be friendly and might be further persuaded by suggestions of
promotion to the purple. He thought English Catholics were
sensitive to the Jesuits, who were too clever for them.

Panzani arrived in London on 15th December 1634,[1] and
went first to the Queen with his letter from Barberini. She
said she would try to obtain ease for Roman Catholics. She
advised him to be cautious, to carry on his business with
secrecy, and above all not to meddle in State affairs. Panzani
mentioned in a letter to Barberini that although Roman Catholics

---

[1] His memoirs translated and edited by the English secular priest Joseph
Berington in 1793 (Birmingham, Swinney & Walkes) are the chief source
for his exploits in England.

had many enemies in England, the court party were very moderate. He commented on evidence of catholic practices in the Church of England, such as Gregorian chant, universities reading the Fathers, the use of Confession, and the beautifying of churches, and said that many wished for reunion. Berington commented that Laud and others were currently charged with a design of introducing popery by these means, and that the nation was anti-monarchy and anti-papal. The Laudian party were not friends to Rome so much as enemies to the Puritans.

Panzani later established friendly relations both with the King and with Windebank, the Secretary of State, who told him that the King was sympathetic to Urban VIII, but recommended that the Papal Brief on the Oath be recalled or moderated. Panzani replied that the King should meet the Pope half-way by making the oath more agreeable to the humours of the See of Rome. At this point Berington interpolated: 'How well does the word humours explain the whole policy of the Roman Court in censuring the Oath.' Panzani was later himself to be much censured for entering into discussions about the Oath, and Barberini told him he had exceeded his commission. Panzani and Windebank resolved to propose to the Queen and the Cardinal a dialogue between Rome and England: it was also suggested that the conversations be held in France; or that learned French or Spanish theologians be invited to England for talks. Barberini was against any conferences—there were to be no discussions of dogmatic truth, no suggestions of the slightest doubt to be expressed, nor for Catholics to question articles of faith—only causes of present lack of unity could be spoken of.

Later Windebank told Panzani that 'if we had neither Jesuits nor Puritans in England I am confident an union might be easily effected'. All moderate men in Church and State, he said, thirsted after a union: the Church of Rome would have to give up three things—Communion in one kind, the Latin Liturgy and the celibacy of the clergy. The Oath of allegiance was a grave problem as the King must rely on the loyalty of his subjects. Panzani also had conversations with Lord (Francis) Cottington[1] who observed that 'there is a great alteration in the

---

[1] Secretary to Charles while Prince of Wales. Clerk to Council, etc.

enemies of the Church of Rome. Formerly the word Rome could
not be pronounced without horror and detestation; but now
we are grown more mannerly'. Cottington and Windebank
were in favour of any scheme 'the design of which was to make
an experiment, how far the two churches could be brought
towards an union'.

Another person who contributed a link to the chain was
Richard Montague, Bishop of Chichester from 1628,[1] who met
Panzani at least three times and spoke about reunion.[2]

Panzani was recalled to Rome in 1637, though his replace-
ment arrived in the previous year, so that there was a period of
overlapping. He had clearly overplayed his hand in England
and had reported more on the mind and state of the court
party than on the general situation in the country. His replace-
ment, in the summer of 1636, was George Con, a Scotsman.
Con became particularly friendly with the King and spent much
time discussing religious questions with him, evidently to their
mutual enjoyment. His despatches, preserved in the Barberini
collection in the Vatican Library, contain comments on the
nature of the conversations. Although Charles gave Con every
encouragement to treat the possibility of improving relationships seriously, he was entirely realistic in revealing his own
Anglican position as these quotations from Con's despatches
clearly show:

> The King said to me that many things seemed to be held in
> France which resembled the beliefs of England. I added that
> in questions which had not been defined as matters of faith,
> and even in some which had, there was room for diversity of
> opinion . . . and that to a certain extent his Majesty was able
> to embrace such opinions as were to his taste within the
> liberties of the Catholic Church. . . . Then the King said
> to me 'George, I tell you in all honesty that you people hold
> opinions which cannot be swallowed, and if you must go on

[1] He had been impeached in James's reign before the House of Commons
for a work entitled 'Appello Caesarem' in which he attempted a reconciliation of the two Churches, but the intervention of the King prevented the
impeachment from reaching the Upper House.
[2] *Memoirs of Panzani*, Berington, p. 238.

writing books about heretics not keeping the faith and calling us heretics, of course you will lose us. . . .[1]

Con likewise was perfectly straightforward with the King:

> I asked Charles to think about the love of Christ and what evils resulted to mankind and to the church as a result of schism . . . The King said that he regretted this . . . but the Church of Rome was too proud and obstinate in certain matters, such as defending the Council of Trent. I said that the Council of Trent was mainly about the reform of manners and customs . . . and that there were matters of doctrine which were still open to discussion. I appealed to him to appoint a commission of well-intentioned persons to have such a discussion, and the pope would do the same. Then he would see what a benevolent mother the Church of Rome really was. His Majesty put his hand on my shoulder and said that it was not yet time for this, and that people were not ready for it.[2]

In this last sentiment Laud had also concurred. The Archbishop had shown himself interested. in getting closer to Rome but said openly that neither he nor His Majesty could do so because of the distress it would cause the puritans.[3]

Another prominent figure in the development of these relationships was Christopher Davenport, whose name in religion was Franciscus a Sancta Clara, and who returned from Douai to become the Queen's Chaplain. He threw himself wholeheartedly into formulating actual proposals for reunion, and was in constant contact with Laud and with John Cosin later Bishop of Durham and Bishop Montague of Chichester. He was convinced that he and his Anglican friends agreed more and differed less than was commonly supposed. He wrote a treatise on Justification, 'Deus, Natura, Gratia', to which he later appended a commentary on the 39 Articles.[4] He attempted to reconcile them with Roman doctrine to illustrate

---

[1] 29th Sept. 1636, Vatican Archives, B.L. 8639, 130. (Translation from the Italian.)
[2] Vatican Archives, B.L. 8640, 184. (Translation from the Italian.)
[3] ibid., 337.
[4] Dedicated to Charles I. Reprinted with a commentary by F. G. Lee, 1865. See Bibliography.

the general thesis that nothing stood between the two churches except unnecessary barriers of prejudice. The book seems to have been well received at court, to have been moderately approved by the Laudian party and, of course, to have been totally rejected by the puritans. The last of the papal agents, in succession to Panzani and Con, was Mgr. Carlo Rossetti. He remained only long enough to witness the immense deterioration in the King's fortunes and the closing in of the puritan influence from Parliament.

As already mentioned, in addition to these agents from the Romewards direction, there were also those who were sent from the Queen as unofficial agents to the Vatican, by consent of the King, who mostly did their best to encourage a better understanding. Among these we may note Sir Arthur Brett. He was instructed not to try to negotiate for a bishop for the Roman Catholic community in England; to encourage the Pope to reconsider the formulation of the Oath so as to make life more tolerable for his adherents; and to put a brake on the activity of the Jesuits.[1]

Brett died in March 1636, and was succeeded by another Roman Catholic, Sir William Hamilton. Hamilton was well received by Pope Urban, so much so that he felt able to concern himself with the question of the appointment of an English cardinal, and even to suppose that he might be considered for the post himself. Thomas Gage, one of the many surreptitious agents between the Court and the Vatican, reported in 1640:

> At the same time, whilst I was at Rome, I understood of another great business concerning England. . . . This was to create one of the English nation cardinal, that so the conversion of England, what by the assistance of William Laud, what by the power of a higher person, and what by the authority of the said cardinal, might be more fully and earnestly plotted and endeavoured.[2]

All these relationships and dealings represent the climax of such matters, and the closest points of contact for a long time to

[1] 28th October 1635. *State Papers, collected by Edward, earl of Clarendon*, Vol. I, pp. 354–7.
[2] *Years of Siege*, Caraman, pp. 131–2.

come. In this, as in the rest of their affairs, the King and the court party had been wantonly closing their eyes to the rising tide of national disapproval. The net was closing round the King and his supporters. Laud had already begun to sense the rising antagonism and was anxious to resume a certain degree of persecution of the Roman Catholics if only to keep up appearances. Anti-Popish riots began to be staged. John Pym was railing against Laud in Parliament and attacking him among other things for attempting reunion negotiations with Rome, which increasingly took on the proportions of treachery. It was widely known how far Laud's attempts to deal with Rome had gone. Even Rome itself had been informed that Laud was playing a dangerous game. Thomas Gage reported that:

> Little discourse could be had in Rome except that Arch-bishop William Laud had his part and share in it. The Jesuit began highly to praise the Arch-Prelate for his moderate carriage towards Papists and priests, boasting of the free access which one Simons, alias Flood, a Jesuit, had unto him at all hours, and in all occasions. . . . . 'But the now Archbishop', said he, 'is not only favourable to us there, but here desireth to make daily demonstrations of his great affection to this our Court and Church, which he showed not long since in sending a Common-Prayer book, which he had composed for the Church of Scotland, to be first viewed and approved of by our Pope and Cardinals'.[1]

When Laud was eventually impeached in 1641 the list of charges included those of 'wishing to establish a new religion', 'corresponding with Rome' and 'treating with the Pope's men in England'. The last of the papal agents, at the insistence of Parliament, returned in July 1641.

Even more provocative and disastrous consequences of Charles' and Henrietta's dealings with the Vatican were still to show themselves. In 1641 there was a rising in Ireland of dispossessed tenants against the protestant occupants. The Queen petitioned the Pope for assistance, and Charles made the great mistake of not restraining her. (An attempt had already been made to raise a loan from the Pope at the time of the

---

[1] Report of Thomas Gage 1640, quoted. ibid., 130–1.

Scottish war of 1640.[1]) The matter went so far as the drawing
up of a treaty which it was hoped might implement the papal
desire to assist the Irish 'rebels'. It was in fact signed by the
Cardinal Secretary of State on behalf of the Pope and agreed
to by Sir Kenelm Digby acting on behalf of the Queen. There
was not the remotest hope of its succeeding, whereas the
knowledge of its existence exacerbated even further Charles's
increasingly numerous opponents. He gave himself up to the
Scots at Newark in May 1646. By that time he had actually
signed a letter to Pope Urban approving the treaty. But the
Pope realised that it was now useless to treat with Charles: his
particular view of kingship was doomed; his promises of
toleration for Roman Catholics in England could never be
implemented.

King Charles's confession on the scaffold showed him as a
loyal Anglican to the end. 'I die in the Christian faith, according
to the profession of the Church of England, as the same was
left me by my father of blessed memory.' But in trying to further
his good relations with the rest of Christendom (at least that
part of it which retained allegiance to Rome) he had followed
misguided policies; and the inter-church situation was much less
favourable than when he came to the throne. How steadily the
tide of opposition had risen can be seen from numerous examples, both from the Statute Book and elsewhere.[2]

From the point of view of toleration, if not of understanding,
the period of the Commonwealth comes as a surprise. Many
misconceptions about this period previously held have been
dispelled by recent scholarship. The immense complexity of the
sects and the cross-currents of contemporary religious opinions
need not concern us here, but the general principle which
emerges is that the Independents, whose influence predominated

---

[1] Urban had told Hamilton that he would be prepared to get Charles
out of his financial difficulties. See correspondence of papal agent Rossetti
and Barberini, P.R.O.

[2] Resolutions on Religion drawn up by a sub-committee of the House of
Commons 24th February 1628, IV, *Constitutional Documents*, S. R. Gardiner,
OUP, 1947, pp. 78–82.

'The Root and Branch Petition 1640', Sections 10 and 11, Gardiner,
pp. 139–40.

'The Grand Remonstrance 1641', 63 II, Gardiner, p. 216.

The 19 Propositions presented to the King at York from both Houses of
Parliament, 1st June 1642, 7, Gardiner, p. 252.

under Cromwell, were more tolerant than the Presbyterians and that this was therefore a period of comparative tranquillity for the Roman Catholics. In fact there is evidence that the more extreme sectarians even thought that the Independents had Popish leanings. The ordinance of 1650, for example, easing the penalties for non-attendance at parish churches, benefited Roman Catholics as well as other 'non-conformists', and so could be misconstrued. In 1655 there was a proclamation against English subjects going to foreign chapels. In this Cardinal Mazarin interceded on behalf of the Roman Catholics, to which Cromwell replied that he had already plucked many from the raging fire of persecution which tyrannised over their consciences and arbitrarily encroached upon their estates, and that he hoped to do more as opportunity offered. The French ambassador reported that the Roman Catholics were more leniently treated than under any other regime up to that time.

On the whole therefore Cromwell's boast that 'I meddle not with any man's conscience' seems allowable, though of course it was to be understood that conscientious scruples were not allowed to be a screen for sedition. Only two priests were put to death during the Commonwealth, the later of whom, John Southworth, is reported to have said on the scaffold at Tyburn: 'If any man work against this government now established, let him suffer.' The Roman Catholic historian Berington, to whom reference has already been made, observes that:

> to conciliate the affections of all was the obvious policy of the Protectorate [and] I have little doubt, had providence indulged him with a larger span of life that the whole nation would tranquilly have submitted to a control, the wisdom of which Europe viewed with envy.[1]

Of the fortunes of relationships between Anglicans and Roman Catholics during the Commonwealth there is not much to be said, though we might perhaps take notice of a quotation from Dr. John Bramhall (later Archbishop of Armagh) who in 1656 wrote:

> If I have any byasse, it hath been desire of peace which our

[1] *Memoirs of Panzani*, Berington, Supplement, p. 299. This contrasts strangely, of course, with Cromwell's atrocities in Ireland.

4

RESTORATION TO THE WAKE
CORRESPONDENCE

The end of the Commonwealth and the return of the Stuarts, monarchy, episcopacy and all, opened up a new and complicated chapter in the history of Roman/Anglican relationships. Three new circumstances at least contributed to the complications. The first was the part played by Scotland; the second was the fact that the new king and his family had spent much of the intervening time in France; and the third that the Church of England was now going to become more and more torn by the influence of the victors and vanquished at the Savoy Conference.[1]

The execution of the Stuart King had appalled the population of Scotland. Within a week of the execution of his father Charles II was proclaimed in Edinburgh. He escaped from the battlefields of Scotland via England to exile in France, and there the seeds of his future development were sown.

After the flight from the battle of Worcester Charles entered into negotiations with Pope Innocent X. These were conducted from the Roman end by the General of the Augustinians, who said he was authorised to do so. There is a record of Edward Hyde's[2] correspondence with the Vatican in which the King was represented as being ready to favour his catholic subjects if

[1] Conference which sat at Savoy in the Strand, London, 15th April–24th July 1661 to review the Book of Common Prayer; consisted of 12 bishops, 12 presbyterian divines and 9 assessors from each party.

[2] An adviser to Charles I: in exile 1646. Lord Chancellor 1658. Raised to peerage as Lord Hyde 1660; Earl of Clarendon 1661.

the Pope supported his reinstatement. The Pope answered that Charles must first avow himself a Roman Catholic.[1] To this the King was not prepared to commit himself, knowing that in doing so he would have alienated the strong protestant sentiments of the English people and perhaps even have rendered impossible his return to the throne. After the death of Innocent X similar negotiations were carried on with his successor Alexander VII through the medium of two German princes.[2] Charles promised that in return for aid in retrieving his throne he would save his Roman Catholic subjects from their disabilities and treat them on the same footing as other dissenters. These negotiations bore little fruit. With respect to the future it was entirely fortunate that Charles returned to the throne in the most satisfactory possible way, by general acclamation.

Charles' relationships with the Roman Catholic Church were much as his father's had been. That he eventually became a Roman Catholic on his death-bed is only of minor importance to the general scheme of this enquiry. Innocent XI, who by that time was Pope, was sceptical about his conversion, though James II sent him papers in the late King's hand. In a letter of 7th June 1685, the Pope wrote to James that:

he hoped he had obtained the Divine Mercy.[3]

The reign began with general declarations of tolerance on the part of the King. In the Declaration of Breda before his return from exile Charles had promised indemnity for all except those whom Parliament should exclude; and 'liberty for tender consciences'. But England was not ready for toleration, if that was intended to include Roman Catholics, and the net soon began to be drawn tighter. On 26th December 1662 Charles issued a proclamation alluding to his promises made in the Declaration of Breda, establishing the Church of England once more by the Act of Uniformity and announcing his own intention of asking Parliament to agree to recognise his royal prerogative of dispensation from penal restrictions (which he evidently intended to use in favour of Roman Catholics). This

[1] State Papers, Vol. iii, p. 291, quoted in *History of England principally in the seventeenth century*, Leopold von Ranke, Oxford, Clarendon Press, 1875, Vol. III, p. 396.
[2] ibid.
[3] Roman Correspondence B.M. No. 15, 396.

Parliament declined to do, and the bill was defeated in Committee.

From this point the history of the reign of Charles II follows the general pattern of thirty years before as if no lessons had been learnt. Unable to exercise his royal will in co-operation with Parliament, he tried to do it independently. Having made the secret treaty of Dover in 1670 with Louis XIV, Charles began to feel free to make some gestures of toleration which he hoped would secure him the loyalty of most sections of his people. The Declaration of Indulgence of 1672 confirmed the Church of England as the 'basis, rule and standard of the general and public word of God' but at the same time abrogated the application of existing penal laws against both Roman Catholics and Puritans. This gesture of ambivalent toleration was too much for the Church and the Nation. The following year Charles challenged the Parliament openly with his royal prerogative: but the challenge failed and Parliament asserted again that no laws could be abrogated by royal privilege—only by parliamentary enactment. So determined was the House of Commons to assert its rights that it followed up this victory with the Test Act (1673), which required that all office-holders should make a declaration against the doctrine of Transubstantiation and receive Holy Communion in the Established Church: so firmly was the door shut against progress in toleration. Nevertheless Charles allowed his ministers to commit him in suggesting the possibilities of reunion with the Roman See. In the year 1672 M. Colbert de Croissy, French Ambassador in London, addressed a Memoir on the state of affairs in England to his master Louis XIV, urging the Grand Monarch to give generous financial aid to Charles both for the prosecution of the Dutch war and to help re-establish communion with the see of Rome:

> Your Majesty knows that the principal motive which has engaged the King of England to make a close union of friendship and interest with you is the protection which your Majesty gives to all friends and allies, of which protection he has always hoped to feel the powerful effects in the execution of his design of changing the present state of religion in England for a better, and of establishing his authority so as

to be able to retain his subjects in the obedience which they owe to him. . . . This Minister [Arlington][1] has proposed to me . . . that your Majesty should have the kindness to instruct the Duke d'Estrées to support the requests which will be made of the Pope in the King of England's name by the ecclesiastic whom he sends to Rome, among others a request for the sacrament in both kinds as a favour to the English who desire this concession in order to become converts and a request for permission to say the mass in the vulgar tongue, giving me to understand that if the Holy See would so far condescend, most of the Bishops and, following this example, almost all the Protestants of England, would reunite themselves to the Roman Church.[2]

It can be seen from this how far the Cabal[3] was from understanding the real nature of the situation. So far from there being any possibility of persuading the English people generally back to communion with the see of Rome their spontaneous prejudices were in the direction of blaming Rome for any public disaster. Roman Catholics were suspected in some quarters of being concerned in the fire of London of 1666. The episode of Titus Oates[4] added further fuel to the flames of public prejudice. As a result of the public panic which arose from it some thirty-five people, including seven Jesuits, were put to death for various allegedly 'treasonable' crimes. The same wave of passion led to the execution of Oliver Plunkett, Roman Catholic Archbishop of Armagh, who was accused of plotting to bring a French army to Ireland. One direct consequence of this national hysteria was to open up the whole question of the succession. The advent to the throne of the Duke of York (a known Roman Catholic) was looked upon with the greatest fear, and eyes were already turning in the direction of the Prince of Orange. The Earl of Shaftesbury made definite attempts to have James excluded from the throne. These, however, were failures, and on 6th February 1685, King James II became King of England.

[1] Sir Henry Bennet, afterwards Lord Arlington, Secretary of State 1662.
[2] Quoted in *A Life of Anthony Ashley Cooper, 1st Earl of Shaftesbury*, W. D. Christie, Macmillan, 1871, Vol. 2, App. 2.
[3] Charles II's ministers; so called from the first letters of their names: Clifford, Ashley, Buckingham, Arlington, Lauderdale.
[4] Son of an Anabaptist minister who inflamed public opinion by spreading tales of alleged Roman Catholic plots.

From the moment of his accession it could be said that the reign, from the point of view of Roman Catholic understanding, was destined to be a failure. He still held, and acted upon, the Stuart theories of kingly prerogatives. He put Roman Catholics into official positions at Court and other institutions such as the Colleges of Oxford and Cambridge. A Jesuit was sworn of the Privy Council.[1] These actions neither Parliament nor people were yet ready to tolerate. A wall of prejudice was built higher by the arrival in England of a Papal Nuncio, Fernando Dadda, Archbishop of Amalfi, of whom the Roman Catholic historian Berington records that he:

> habited in his robes and preceded by a crossbearer, with the sound of musical instruments and train of priests, monks and friars . . . went to [Windsor] castle, where the King received them. The multitude with amazement viewed this unusual spectacle at which the profane smiled and wise men shook their heads.[2]

James then turned to a policy of universal toleration, intending in this way to bring in justice for his fellow-religionists by a side-wind. In 1687 he issued a new Declaration of Indulgence, more thorough-going than that of Charles. By it he hoped to appease the protestant non-conformists and to gain their support. In effect he only succeeded in antagonising even further the members of the Established Church. On 7th May 1688 he issued a second declaration, hoping it might meet with a more favourable reception. This was followed up by an order in council requiring that it be read on two successive Sundays in every parish church. William Sancroft, Archbishop of Canterbury, and six other bishops, presented a mild appeal to the King asking that the order be withdrawn, on the safe constitutional ground (as they saw it to be) that the claimed dispensing power was contrary to the law. The seven bishops were imprisoned in the Tower of London amidst popular indignation. The trial became in effect a constitutional trial of James himself. The bishops were acquitted, but the real verdict was against the King. Alarm was further aroused by the birth on 20th June of a male heir to the throne.

---

[1] Fr. Petre, s.j. [2] *Memoirs of Panzani*, Berington, Supplement pp. 351-2.

The Stuart reigns had been lost opportunities from the point of view of Anglican/Roman Catholic understanding on the wider scale. But once again the ultimate aim of reunion for Christendom was not left 'without witness'. Throughout the reigns of Charles and James, as in the time of the Commonwealth, and in spite of the rising tide of protestant objection there was never wanting a succession of visionaries who looked beyond the present. Those whom the Church of England calls the 'Caroline divines', whose writings have formed the main corpus of classical Anglican divinity were on the whole too much occupied with the rescue of the deposit of faith from what they believed to be its perversions on either side, whether protestant or Roman. Their general tone is therefore polemical, but among their writings can be seen evidence that in their hearts and prayers there were wider sympathies and deeper longings. For example, Dr. Heylyn, friend and chaplain of Laud, who died in 1662, but whose life of Laud, entitled *Cyprianus Anglicus*, was not published till 1668, contained in the Preface[1] a remarkable passage on the theme of Christian union.

Even in 1688 when the indignation against James II and his Roman Catholic advisers was at its height Dr. Thomas Smith (1638–1710), a fellow of Magdalen College, Oxford, who had been expelled from his Fellowship by the Roman Catholic President, could publish a book on reunion in which he said 'O happy, O blessed O glorious day, in which all these confusions, which no good man can think of without great disorder of mind, shall be removed, and all who worship the same crucified Saviour shall unite in brotherly love, charity and communion'.[2]

Translations of some of the spiritual works of the continental writers of the Counter-Reformation were appearing in England,[3] although acknowledgment of their work was sometimes rather grudging.

[1] pp. 39, 40.
[2] *A Pacifick Discourse of the Causes and Remedies of the Differences about Religion*, London, 1688, p. 33 (quoted in *English Church Life*, J. Wickham Legg, Longmans Green, 1914, p. 410). English translation of his *De Causis et Remediis Dissidiorum*, Oxford, 1675.
[3] Notably Francis de Sales.

The books of their divines upon Devotional and practical subjects have met with as favourable reception among us as if the Authors had been of a better religion.[1]

There were incidental disasters in the Revolution of 1688 and the advent of the House of Orange which made new difficulties for the kind of understanding on which any hopes of reunion might be built. The first was the resignation of the non-jurors. They were those churchmen whose consciences would not allow them to take the oaths of allegiance to William and Mary because they felt themselves to be already under allegiance to James II. The tragedy of this separation was that they took with them out of a position of influence in the Church a large number of people who were among the most comprehending, leaving the field clear for the broad-church men, bigots and sheer place-seekers. Among the bishops were Ken[2] and Turner,[3] both of outstanding ability. From their position of independence they thought and prayed and wrote. They kept alive what is conveniently described as the 'catholic' tradition in the Church of England. They stressed its continuity with patristic Christendom rather than its indebtedness to the Reformation. By their uncomprehending contemporaries they were therefore thought of as pro-papal: this impression was understandably encouraged by the fact that they appeared to support the catholic King in exile. But they were in fact anti-papal in their thinking and writing.

The other sad consequence of William III's arrival was a further injustice perpetrated on the long-suffering people of Ireland. The exiled King James, with the aid of the French King, landed in the south of Ireland (March 1689), and immediately found support. The protestant minority were beleaguered in certain fortified cities. To their rescue William came, and James was routed at the Battle of the Boyne. This event has intensified one of the sharpest antagonisms of human

---

[1] William Nicholls in a prefixed memorandum 'on the rise and progress of Spiritual Books in the Romish Church'. *An introduction to a Devout Life* by Francis Sales, Bennet & Sprint, 1701.
[2] Thomas Ken, 1637–1711. Bishop of Bath and Wells.
[3] Francis Turner, 1638?–1700. Bishop of Ely.

history, which continues till this day.[1] In the aftermath the harsher counsels of William's ministers prevailed. The population of Ireland settled down to servitude and injustice, and to oppression by the English ascendancy, the memory of which entered into the depths of the Irish spirit.

At the death, without surviving issue, of Queen Anne in 1714, there was a small group in favour of restoring the Jacobite line. They were largely Tory squires and 'high churchmen' like Atterbury, Bishop of Rochester, who believed that adequate safeguards could be secured from Prince James Edward[2] for the Church in the future. But a very large majority of British people were against it. The succession passed to the House of Hanover.

The Hanoverian kings were unattractive and alien, and did not easily command loyalty. This gave additional impetus to the minority who conceived it still to be worth while continuing resistance. The Jacobite plots went on, but did the cause of religious unity no good at all. They seemed to justify the hesitations of those who wanted to keep the Roman Catholic community firmly down. The Established Church continued to be understood as a necessary part and support of the constitution itself.

In 1716, a year after the first rising, a move came from Rome to try to solve the problem of the Oath of Allegiance, always a basic difficulty in these relationships. It had been signified to Clement XI that the English Roman Catholics 'by persevering in their opposition to the established government exposed to ruin the cause of religion and their own domestic concerns'. The Pope commanded a declaration to be written by the Nuncio in Brussels, which was in due course sent to the English Roman Catholic bishops. It read:

I swear and promise a true and universal submission to King George; and that I will attempt nothing to disturb the peace and tranquillity of the realm: moreover I declare that

[1] A portrait at Stormont indicates that protestant Dutch William had moral support from the Pope, who was ready to oppose the designs of the King of France; but contemporary comment suggests that this was a 'vulgar error'.

[2] The 'Old Pretender', son of James II and Mary of Modena, 1688–1766.

I will neither sue for nor accept any dispensation from this oath.

In 1718 there were negotiations between some of the leading Roman Catholic families, such as the Stonors, the Blunts and the Howards, representing those who were prepared to sign such an oath, and certain Members of Parliament. But they failed because of the insistence of an 'ultramontane' element among the Roman Catholics themselves who were glancing backwards at the alleged papal deposing power, and because of exaggerated fears on the government side of possible papal threats to the Constitution. In 1719 a committee for the regulation of these negotiations was formed under Dr. Strickland, later Bishop of Namur, but it failed to be effective for the same general reasons.

On the Anglican side a remarkable ecumenical figure emerged in the early eighteenth century, all the more so because he was not only isolated, but also became Archbishop of Canterbury. This was William Wake. The whole episode of Archbishop Wake's correspondence with the Church of France is of the greatest importance in any historical survey of Anglican/Roman Catholic relations. But it has been brilliantly and exhaustively described by Dr. Norman Sykes, late Dean of Winchester, whose monumental work[1] is one of the most notable fruits of ecclesiastical historical research in this century. The project for union drawn up by the Sorbonne doctors for discussion between themselves and the Archbishop will have but brief mention here, out of all proportion to its significance. Only the fuller treatment by Dr. Sykes can do it justice: any other account can merely be a précis of it.

Wake was born in 1657. In 1682 after study at Oxford and ordination, he accompanied, as chaplain, Viscount Preston, envoy extraordinary to the court of Louis XIV of France and remained there for three years. He became acquainted with several of the Sorbonne doctors, secular priests in Paris and clerical librarians as well as several Protestant ministers. He attended the service of many different churches. His character is seen to emerge as containing initiative, application and an

---

[1] *William Wake, Archbishop of Canterbury 1657–1737*, Norman Sykes, CUP, 1957, 2 vols. In particular Chapters I and IV.

exceptional capacity for hard work. Although only 28 years old he entered into a dialogue with Bossuet,[1] and in 1685 he wrote (among others) a commentary on Bossuet's 'Exposition of the Doctrine of the Catholic Church', in which he gave a picture of the teaching of the Church of England and described what he saw as the chief grounds of divergence:

> ... We have showed that the very grounds of our difference is that you require us to believe and practice such things as the holy Scripture forbids us and the Primitive Church never knew.[2]

While he accused the Roman Church of innovation, he also criticised Anglican lack of discipline in the matter of confession and penance and concluded by emphasising the extent of beliefs held in common. There existed ground, he considered, for mutual charity and for the cultivation of a spirit of unity in the bond of peace.[3]

There remained as the greatest barrier to union the Papacy. He protested against the power, which he said:

> has of late been pretended to when other differences shall be agreed and the true bonds set to his [the Pope's] pretences, we shall be content to yield him whatsoever authority the ancient councils of the Primitive Church have acknowledged, and the Holy Fathers have always taught the faithful to give him.

In conclusion he wrote:

> We do confess the Church of Rome to be a part of the true Church, ... and we do with all our heart desire a union with her and in effect do shew it as far as we are able by retaining whatever we can of the same doctrines and practices with her.[4]

On leaving Paris in 1685 Wake described what he had come to admire in the Roman Church and also some defects. He proceeded rather slowly up the ecclesiastical ladder as he

---

[1] Jacques Benigne Bossuet, 1627–1704. Bishop of Condom 1669; Meaux 1681.
[2] *William Wake* . . . Sykes, Vol. I, p. 31.　　　　　　　　　　[3] ibid.
[4] *William Wake* . . . Sykes, Vol. I, p. 19.

had displeased James II with his outspoken writings. After the accession of Queen Anne he was consecrated Bishop of Lincoln in 1704. On 17th December 1715 he became 82nd Archbishop of Canterbury.

On 11th December 1717 William Beauvoir, English Chaplain in Paris and holder of the post Wake had occupied so fruitfully 30 years before, wrote to the Archbishop. He told him of the appeal of four French bishops against the bull 'Unigenitus';[1] that the Archbishop of Paris, Cardinal de Noailles, was against it, and described a meal he had had with Du Pin[2] and some other doctors of the Sorbonne:

> They talked as if the whole kingdom was to appeal to the future general council . . . they wished for an union with the Church of England as the most effectual means to unite all the western churches. Dr. Du Pin desired me to give his duty to your Grace,[3]

and he sent him some copies of some of Du Pin's writings which the author wanted him to have. The correspondence then opened up on the French side. Dr. Du Pin addressed a letter to Wake via Beauvoir saying that he wished most earnestly some way might be found for the English and French churches to enter into union:

> we are not so entirely different from each other in most matters that we could not be mutually reconciled. And I would that all Christians might be under one fold under one supreme Shepherd, even the Lord Jesus Christ our Saviour. This has the chief place in my prayers and for so good a work I would lay down my life.[4]

In his covering letter, sending this on to Wake, Beauvoir said how overjoyed Du Pin had been with a message from the Archbishop.

---

[1] A papal bull against Jansenism (a religious revival of an ascetic and puritan type then rife in France; the following of Cornelius Jansen, 1585–1638, Bishop of Ypres).

[2] Dr. Louis Du Pin, famous for his *Nouvelle Bibliothèque des Auteurs Ecclésiastiques* of which 35 volumes were published (more were to follow).

[3] *William Wake*, p. 255.

[4] ibid., p. 258.

I think myself in duty bound, my lord, to tell your Grace that he heartily wishes a union between the Gallican church and ours and that he is actually composing a project of such a union.[1]

He went on to say that he had given Du Pin a book of Common Prayer in French, to which the 39 Articles were attached. When Wake himself began to write he took up the position which he had adopted with Bossuet 30 years before. He stressed the adherence of the Church of England to the three Creeds, to the traditional three-fold ministry and to the possession of an unbroken episcopal succession.

He ended:

I certainly, so long as I live, shall never cease to seek those things which belong to peace, and even if in no other way, at least with a mind eager for concord, to hold Catholic communion with all true believers in Christ.[2]

That unity must be based on agreement in the fundamentals of faith, with agreement to differ on other issues both of faith and practice Wake felt very emphatically. He wrote to Beauvoir:

In the meantime so far are they right, to distinguish matters of doctrine from matters of order and discipline, in which national churches may vary without breaking the unity of the Catholic Church. But then they should in points of doctrine too distinguish fundamentals in which all ought to agree from others of lesser moment in which error or difference may be tolerated. And I am much mistaken if they must not at last come to the creeds of the first four General Councils if ever they mean to restore peace to the Church.[3]

The correspondence continued on both sides throughout the spring and summer of 1718. In March Dr. Girardin[4] made an oration to the Doctors of the Sorbonne preparing them for the treatise for union which was being written by Dr. Du Pin. A copy was sent to Wake. He encouraged the Doctors to proceed with a plan which had been formed for drawing a line of distinction between the essentials and non-essentials of the faith.

[1] *William Wake*, p. 258.
[2] ibid., p. 260.
[3] ibid., p. 263.
[4] Dr. Patrick Piers Girardin.

He said that such a course would satisfy the members of the Church of England who did not hold all papal decisions to be articles of faith.

Wake replied to Girardin, as usual approving the recognition of the difference between fundamentals and non-essentials, and contending that this was the indispensable basis of any projected union. But he was realistic in his comment to the English chaplain. Neither the men of the court nor Cardinal de Noailles 'would come into any such project as your good doctors seem to hope for. They will not utterly break with the court of Rome and the princes which will continue in the interests of it, and till that is done, nothing can be done in point of doctrine.'[1]

On 7th August 1718 Du Pin sent Wake his project of union. He called it a Commonitorium, based on his evaluation of Anglican belief. Although Du Pin's project showed a considerable spirit of concession to Anglican principles, Wake was not all that impressed with it. His own conception of union was not in terms of uniformity, but of unity in diversity; and he did not approve of the Frenchman's decisions on what was fundamental. Above all Wake was mistrustful of the assurance on the minimising of the papal power. During the autumn letters continued to flow, mainly on the subject of the Papacy and the position of English bishops. Wake thought it might be a useful lever with Cardinal de Noailles to inform him:

> what authority the Archbishop of Canterbury has gotten by the Reformation.[2]

Du Pin sought to reassure Wake on the subject of the Papacy and in December said that the Gallican Church was proposing to limit papal power and allow a mere primacy of honour. In January 1719 Wake replied that if this were really the case, most Anglicans would agree. But at this critical stage the civil power began to intervene. Knowledge of the correspondence had reached the authorities. An official negotiation for the union of the two Churches was assumed. Du Pin's letters were seized. The correspondence continued for two further months, and on

[1] *William Wake*, p. 263.   [2] ibid., p. 279.

3rd April Du Pin sent his last letter to Wake, thanking him for books on the English episcopal succession. He professed himself so satisfied that if agreement could be reached on doctrine, the question of the ministry would be no barrier to union. His enemies had interrupted the correspondence, but he was resolved to continue his efforts to achieve unity. Wake replied on 1st May:

> I had believed that the time had come in which, having shaken off the yoke of papal tyranny, you might have joined with us in the same communion.[1]

The courier to Paris was delayed with the letter and when it arrived Du Pin had already died on 6th June. Some letters continued with Girardin,[2] but the heart had gone out of the matter. Wake had put before the Frenchmen the fact that in England it was the civil power which eventually took the initiative and came to grips with the Papacy. In France there was no one of sufficient power to do so; the Regent, the Duke of Orleans, was in a precarious position; Cardinal de Noailles vacillated between loyalty to France and to Rome. The causes of the failure of the exchanges are clear and illuminating. The first was its limited representation. What was being proposed was not union between Anglicans and another whole Church, but with a breakaway part of it. Wake was negotiating with dissidents and not with authorised representatives. A handful of doctors at the Sorbonne (even if supported at a distance by the primate of France) did not command the allegiance of the whole Roman Catholic Church. Neither did an Archbishop of Canterbury in his private capacity represent the Church of England.

Wake was acting alone and on his own authority. He never divulged the letters to any of his brethren and wrote every item himself, not trusting even a secretary, because he knew he would not have support if the correspondence leaked out. (The Malines conversations, two centuries later, were to suffer from the same disadvantages, as being the affair of a minority.) The

---

[1] *William Wake*, p. 294.

[2] They had in fact been corresponding for 10 years and Girardin had made a visit to England.

Archbishop's views were perfectly consistent over many years. He thought the disunity of Christendom a scandal and he wanted to promote union not only with Rome, but also with protestants. He supposed that it would be possible to arrive at an agreement on what were the fundamental beliefs necessary for salvation and to differ on others less important. The basis on which union could take place would be the common creeds, the threefold ministry and the episcopal succession.

The second criticism that can be levelled at the Wake episode was that in the attempt to be irenical it minimised some of the differences in doctrine. There was no attempt to come to a basic agreement on the nature of authority in the Church, but only to agree to differ on the matter of the Papacy. The same can be said to a lesser degree of the sacraments and the ministry. Had the correspondence not been cut short, it is possible that greater accommodation might have been reached. There was however a prophetic anticipation of the course which future attempts at reconciliation would one day take: Wake believed that there were 'gradations' of doctrine as between those which were necessary for salvation, those which were necessary for effective ecclesiastical communion and those which could be held as matters of interpretation at will. (Two centuries were to pass before that idea was to be pursued in earnest.) It must be remembered also that Wake was dealing with a Roman Catholic Church that was much nearer to the English Church, technically speaking, than she now is. Between those times and ours stand the First Vatican Council, the definition of the two Marian dogmas of the Immaculate Conception and the Assumption, the unhappy condemnation of Anglican Orders and the large Irish immigration into England and Scotland. Wake was living in a world in which none of these events had had their impact upon the relations between the Churches.

But Wake's last letter to Du Pin might have been written today. He suggested that union would come not when one man had persuaded another to his point of view, but when both men were seeking to discover the mind of Christ.

One consequence of the correspondence between Wake and the Sorbonne was the appearance on the scene of a canon of the Augustinian abbey of St. Geneviève near Paris, Pierre François le Courayer.[1] Courayer had taken a lively interest in certain pamphlets in French written against the validity of Anglican ordinations. He began by accepting the thesis that these ordinations were invalid, but took note that there were considerable inaccuracies of fact in current literature on the subject, and wrote to Wake for information. He held that the Church of England was in schism but had certain qualities of catholicity.

In 1721 Courayer wrote his 'Dissertation on the Validity of the Ordinations of the English',[2] in which he handled the subject of eucharistic sacrifice. He maintained the sufficiency of the ordinal of Edward VI, and while admitting that 'the validity of the ordinations of the English is altogether independent of what they may think of the Sacrifice' he denied that the Church of England had, as a church, rejected that doctrine. His works were condemned and soon suppressed by authority, and he was threatened with excommunication if he did not retract. He escaped to England, encouraged by Wake;[3] and this might never have happened had not Bishop Atterbury,[4] who had been living in France, helped him in his plan. Courayer was given a triumphant welcome on his arrival at Greenwich in January 1728, a guest of the nobility and the friend of prelates. He never pretended to become an Anglican, but lived and died a French priest of Roman obedience, though his doctrinal views underwent some changes. Courayer eventually received £100 a year pension from public funds. In 1733 he delivered a Latin oration in the Sheldonian Theatre, and aroused bitter remarks from those who disliked his praise of the Church of England. He was made an Oxford honorary D.D.[5] Queen Caroline, patroness of literary talent, doubled his pension. Courayer became popular at Court, and he is said to have spent one

---

[1] See *William Wake*, Sykes; also *Church Quarterly Review*, April–July 1883, Vol. XVI, Art. IV; *Reunion* Vol. V, No. 31, June 1944, H. R. T. Brandreth.

[2] Not published till 1723 owing to problems of censorship.

[3] With whom he had corresponded since 23rd July 1721.

[4] Francis Atterbury, 1662–1732. Bishop of Rochester and Dean of Westminster 1713. Deprived of offices and exiled 1723 for alleged complicity in Jacobite plot.

[5] When Cardinal Augustin Bea was accorded this honour in 1969 he was wrongly believed in many quarters to have been the first Roman Catholic recipient.

evening a week with the Princesses Amelia and Caroline, when the King would often join them.

Courayer had deliberately taken up a position towards the Church of England from which he never wavered. He admitted and defended his catholicity but was not satisfied with the relationship between the catholic church in general and Rome. When he was in England he attended Anglican services and often spoke in praise of the prayer book. Every day he said his breviary and went on studying theology. In 1744 Courayer published an examination of the defects of Roman Catholic theology and of the means for its reform. In 1763 overtures were made for getting him back to France:[1] his Superior at S. Geneviève sent a message which never reached him, then 82, and after he had lived in England for 40 years. He was buried aged 95 in the cloisters of Westminster Abbey, and in his will professed that he died 'a member of the Catholic Church, but without approving of many of the opinions and superstitions which have been introduced into the Romish Church and taught in their schools and seminaries, and which they have insisted on as articles of faith, though to him they appeared to be not only not founded in truth, but also to be highly improbable'.

A crop of pamphlets was produced during the eighteenth century which illustrated the kind of sniping warfare which went on among churchmen who were trying to weigh up the consequences of greater or less co-operation or understanding in respect of the Roman Catholic Church. A study of them has been made by J. Wickham Legg.[2] Some promoted schemes for union, notably 'An Essay towards a proposal for Catholic Communion'.[3] Others attacked High Churchmen for their thoughts of a reunion with the Church of France.

The dominant figure of the English religious scene during the eighteenth century was John Wesley; and it was not possible

---

[1] His career may be compared with Marco Antonio de Dominis formerly Archbishop of Spalato (1566–1624) who resigned his office and came to England, was Dean of Windsor, but returned to Italy in 1622.

[2] *English Church Life, 1660–1833*. Longmans Green, 1914.

[3] By 'A Minister of the Church of England', 1704. Reprinted Rivingtons, 1879 (ed. H. N. Oxenham).

that he should have pursued his way and achieved his purposes without coming face to face with the Roman Catholic Church. That he did so under the circumstances of an intensive evangelical campaign made it unlikely that he would look with sympathy on those particular emphases for which the Church of Rome was supposed to stand. In fact he felt himself forced to the conclusion that characteristic Roman doctrines on grace, conversion and the sacraments were harmful to the basic truths of the Christian faith. He also felt that she was unreliable in matters of contractual morality because of the unrepealed canon of the Council of Constance that 'no faith is to be kept with heretics'.[1] In addition he saw a supposed lack of 'holiness':

> They found out another way to get to heaven without holiness. In the room of them they substituted penances, pilgrimages, praying to saints and angels and, above all these, masses for the dead, absolution by a priest and extreme unction.[2]

Yet there is something more perceptive than the ordinary run of prejudice in his assessment of the situation, and an element of objective judgment in some of his comments. In the following extract from the *Journal*, for example, he makes the telling point that even if a 'papist' is in danger of mortal error, the unbeliever is much more so:

> Upon this occasion I could not but reflect on the many advices I had received, to beware of the increase of Popery; but not one (that I remember) to beware of the increase of infidelity.[3]

Wesley's experience shows up the bigotry of his contemporaries by the fact that even such moderation as that of the last quotation exposed him to the suspicion of being himself a Papist in disguise. Wesley's famous 'Letter to a Roman Catholic' of 18th July 1749 is too well known to need quotation here. Suffice it to observe that there is a deep feeling for mutual

[1] *Cf.* his letter to the Printer of the *Public Advertiser*; *The Works of John Wesley*, Zondervan Publishing House, Michigan, 1958–1959. Vol. X, p. 160.

[2] *A Blow at the Root, or Christ stabbed in the House of His Friends*, 1762.

[3] *Journal*, 25th May 1737.

understanding in its opening sentence which is all too rare in the religious controversies of the time.

Like most Englishmen of the eighteenth century Wesley would have joined in any cry that was raised against the Church of Rome on doctrinal grounds; yet he had another side to his teaching which was not without its significance. He had too clear a mind to join in the general conviction of Dissenters that Rome was apostate. In this, as in many other matters, he remained a priest of the Anglican obedience. He freely exhibited his lifelong interest in catholic piety and devotion. Moreover, as he made plain in his sermon 'Of the Church' he was quite persuaded of the authenticity of the Church of Rome, that it possessed the living substance of the true church and a residue of the authentic gospel. As might be expected, he was against all persecution of catholics on grounds of their religion, and was quite prepared to remove their restrictions provided they kept the public peace. It can perhaps be said that in the 'Letter to a Roman Catholic' he attempts the formulation of an agreed rule of faith, totally inadequate in its theological content, yet worthy of note as indicating that he foresaw the necessity of such a discussion before there could be any hope of reconciliation. At this point it is perhaps worth recording Macaulay's celebrated dictum:

Put Ignatius Loyola at Oxford. He is certain to become the head of a formidable schism. Place John Wesley at Rome. He is certain to be the first General of a new society devoted to the interest and honour of the Church.[1]

Various sources give a picture of Roman Catholic life during this century. Despite the continuance of penal legislation the clauses against saying Mass were rarely put into force. J.P.'s did not use their right of enforcing the Oath of Allegiance except in times of trouble and rebellion. Generally speaking, Roman Catholicism[2] was centred round the big country houses with their private chaplains, so that it was the landed

[1] From a review of a new translation of L. von Ranke's *History of the Popes* in Lord Macaulay's *Essays*, Travellers' Library, Vol. 19. Longmans 1851, p. 35.

[2] *State and Behaviour of English Catholics from the Revolution to 1780*, Joseph Berington, London, F. Faulder, 1780, p. 160.

gentry who kept their religion going. Thomas Weld of Lulworth Castle, for example, had Fr. Jean Nichole Grou, s.j. to
live with him. He was a friend of George III, and the King and
Queen made several visits to Lulworth from Weymouth when
they were on holiday. It was against the law to build a Roman
Catholic chapel, so the King told him to build a family mau-
soleum.[1] Defoe, writing of his journeys from Durham,[2] found
the cathedral city full of Roman Catholics 'not withstanding
the residence of so many dignified protestant clergy' (Defoe was
a dissenter). At St. Winefred's Well in Flintshire he wrote:
'The Saint is equally propitious to Protestants and Catholics.
Several Catholic priests attend here . . . no body takes notice of
it or enquires where one goes or has been gone.'[3]

There were other reasons why Roman Catholics stayed
apart and remained a separate community. Their bishops, the
Vicars Apostolic (who were four in number since the days of
James II—in four districts—London, Western, Northern and
Midland—each generally with a co-adjutor) were against
mixing, especially Bishop Walmesley of the Western District.
He was against the repeal of the embargo on Roman Catholics
going into the Army or Navy, just as Manning in the next
century was to forbid Roman Catholics going to Oxford or
Cambridge, and for the same reason; that he thought they
would lose their faith.

At the same time there would appear to have been some
contacts, and mixed marriages seem to have been tolerated on
the Roman Catholic side. Marie Rowlands writes:[4]

Bishop Stonor, authoritarian though he was on most subjects,
declared when consulted on a case arising in his own family,
that mixed marriages were 'sometimes advisable, sometimes
allowable and in many more cases tolerable'. He reminded his
correspondents that the Church 'does not like them', but he
thought that they could not be absolutely forbidden. He
went further and added that in his opinion even the promise

[1] *Lulworth and the Welds*, Joan Berkeley, Blackmore Press, 1971.
[2] *A Tour through the Island of Great Britain*, Rivingtons, 1778, Vol. III, p.
224.
[3] ibid., pp. 329, 330.
[4] 'Education and Piety of Catholics in Staffordshire in the 18th century',
Recusant History, Vol. 10, No. 2, April 1969.

that the children will be educated as catholics could not be 'insisted upon'.[1]

In saying this he was 200 years ahead of his time.

During the last decades of the eighteenth century, therefore, the spirit of anti-Romanism was still alive and relationships were very limited. Berington was scathing in his criticism of the catholic community and its internal disruptions; more particularly did he blame the religious orders and the Roman Church government for this continued isolation from political and social life.[2] Just as there were bigots on the side of the persecuting majority, no doubt there were diehards among the injured few. But the beginnings of the end of total intolerance were about to be seen. A broad movement in human thought, which swept men on the continent into such upheavals as the French Revolution, was not without its impact in England. Roman Catholics woke up and stirred themselves; and towards them some Englishmen began to develop a conscience.

[1] Birmingham Archdiocese Archives 356 and A. 42. John Talbot Stonor, born 1678, grandson of 11th Earl of Shrewsbury. Vicar Apostolic of Midland District, 1715–1756.

[2] *Memoirs of Panzani*, Berington, Supplement conclusion, pp. 451–73.

5
THE PENAL LAWS RELAXED

When at last the catholic body[1] took steps to organise itself and looked for means whereby to lighten its burdens, the initiative was mainly in the hands of laymen. The Vicars Apostolic lagged behind, particularly after 1789, when they thought that laymen had gone too far. Some peers and Members of Parliament who belonged to the Established Church began to help them, and the weight of penal legislation against Roman Catholics gradually lifted.

The beginnings of this movement came in 1778 when, on a petition of Roman Catholic peers and commoners to the King, Sir George Savile[2] on 14th May brought in a bill for the relief of Roman Catholics[3] which passed both Houses. The relief was very slight: upon taking an oath of allegiance to the house of Hanover some disabilities were to be removed such as the forfeiture of children educated abroad to protestant next of kin and the disqualification from holding acquired property. The Bishop of Peterborough, Dr. John Hinchliffe, set what was to be the pattern for speeches on this subject during the next 50 years of debate: religious oppression was unjust, but there were political dangers consequent upon allowing civil rights to Papists:

I am not so ignorant of the genius of popery as not to know it

[1] The detailed account of this episode is mainly to be found in two sources: *The Dawn of Catholic Revival in England*, B. Ward, 2 vols., Longmans, 1909; *Historical Memoirs of English Catholics*, 4 vols., Charles Butler, John Murray, 1822.

[2] 8th baronet (1726–1784). M.P. for Yorkshire, 1759–1783.

[3] To repeal 11 and 12 William III for the future preventing of growth of Popery. Parl. Hist. of England, *Hansard*, Vol. XIX, pp. 1137–9.

is a very difficult matter to consider its religious principles altogether distinct from that political superstructure which has been raised upon them: and to the support of which I cannot but fear, that should occasion offer, they might still be made too subservient. Any alteration therefore, in those laws which the wisdom of parliament has thought necessary, from time to time, for the preservation of our church and state, ought not to be made without due deliberation.[1]

This minor piece of legislation was greeted by many petitions against Roman Catholics instigated by the Protestant Association, composed mainly of dissenters, and headed by Lord George Gordon (member for Ludgershall). Following a petition against Popery from Rochester,[2] he remarked that it was a pity that so few clergy had signed it, since Popery was making great strides to extirpate Protestantism: a massacre was likely.

It is hard to see the influences against which the complaints were made as other than imaginary, and the reasons for the movement which led to the Gordon riots on 2nd June 1780 are equally difficult to define.[3] But the incident showed the strength of the mob, and in the ensuing brawl 456 were killed and wounded. Lord George Gordon was acquitted from the charge of High Treason; he became a Jew and eventually died in prison.

The Roman Catholic community took its first step towards better organisation in 1782 with the formation of the English Roman Catholic Committee, appointed in the first place for five years and re-appointed and re-formed many times. Its first members were laymen such as Lord Stourton, Lord Petre, John (later Sir John) Throckmorton, Thomas Stapleton and Thomas Hornyold; some clerics joined later. Their most urgent wish was for 'proper' bishops rather than mere Vicars Apostolic. Charles Butler,[4] the first Roman Catholic barrister since the reign of James II, was made secretary and became a considerable driving force in the movement. In December 1783

[1] 25th May 1778. ibid., pp. 1143–5.
[2] 11th April 1780. ibid., Vol. XXI, pp. 386–8.
[3] *Reign of George III*, J. Steven Watson, OUP, 1960, p. 236.
[4] 1752–1832. Roman Catholic lawyer, educated at Douai; Lincolns Inn 1775.

William Pitt[1] had formed his first administration and after
1784 he was in a strong position in Parliament. The Catholic
Committee thereupon seized its opportunity. A memorial was
presented to Pitt and on 9th May 1784 members reported that
they had met the Prime Minister on the repeal question. The
Government wanted authentic evidence of the opinion of the
catholic clergy and universities on papal dispensing power.
To meet Pitt's requirements three questions were sent to each of
the universities of Salamanca, Louvain, Douai, Alcala and the
Sorbonne. Had the Pope any civil authority in England?
Could he dispense His Majesty's subjects from their oath of
allegiance? Was there any principle in the tenets of the
catholic faith by which catholics were justified in not keeping
faith with heretics? All the universities answered in the
negative to all questions.

Lord Stanhope's[2] bill of 1788 was designed to liberate
people of several descriptions from the penalties of non-
conformity, by which means he felt he might avoid the prejudice which undoubtedly existed against Roman Catholics,
and increase the chance of success of his measure. To give it
more weight he also framed a Protestation, a series of statements
of what Roman Catholics did *not* believe, so as to assure Members of Parliament that it would be safe to grant the concessions.
The draft Stanhope sent to Lord Petre for consideration by
the Catholic Committee.[3] Some alterations were made and the
Protestation was then given to the Vicars Apostolic.[4] All the
bishops signed it (although they disliked the way it had been
forced on them) and in doing so said that it was wrong to impute
certain doctrines to them: they did not believe that the Pope
held power to release subjects from their allegiance to George
III their lawful king; no obedience was due to the Pope or to a
General Council should they be required to take up arms

[1] 1759–1806. Second son of 1st Earl of Chatham; Prime Minister at 25.
[2] Charles Stanhope, Lord Mahon, later 3rd Earl Stanhope, 1753–1816,
an eccentric radical peer.
[3] 17th December 1788.
[4] Dr. James Talbot of the London District; Dr. Thomas Talbot of the
Midland District; Dr. Charles Walmesley of the Western District; Dr.
Matthew Gibson of the Northern District. It would seem interesting to note
in passing, in view of the turn that events were due to take on the matter of
Anglican consecrations, that some of the Vicars Apostolic and their co-
adjutors were at this period consecrated by one bishop only.

against the government; 'we acknowledge no infallibility'; the Pope could not dispense oaths, nor might Pope or priest pardon perjury, rebellion or high treason; a firm resolution to avoid future guilt and atonement to God and an injured neighbour, were indispensable requisites to forgiveness; it was not true that faith need not be kept with heretics.

The Protestation was signed by almost all Roman Catholic clergy and laity of note.[1] It was laid before Parliament with a new petition and, Lord Stanhope's bill having failed, led swiftly to the preparation of a fresh Roman Catholic relief bill.[2] The lay members acted quickly and decisively. Since the King had just recovered from his illness, an official address of congratulation was proposed and Lord Petre arranged a solemn mass of thanksgiving. (Bishop James Talbot complained that he was not allowed to attend the meeting.) A proposal for a new oath of allegiance, based on the Protestation, was also made. The Vicars Apostolic summoned to a synod by Walmesley[3] deplored the new form. The Catholic Committee went further and adopted the name Protesting Catholic Dissenters, thinking it would favour their cause: the new oath, they considered, was no different from that in the Protestation. This matter of the oath of allegiance had long held up the improvement of the lot of Roman Catholics in England: they now admitted that the condemnation of the oath of 1606 by Pope Paul V had been excessive:

> by some unaccountable blunder, the illustrious Bellarmine . . . confounded an oath of political allegiance with the oath against acknowledging any spiritual primacy in the successor of St. Peter.[4]

The re-opening of the issue of the oath caused a ferment among Roman Catholics, as it had always done. The Lancashire clergy were against it: the clergy of Staffordshire agreed with the Committee. But the relief bill went ahead and was brought into

---

[1] About 240 priests and 1,250 laymen.
[2] 21st March 1789.
[3] Charles Walmesley, o.s.b. Born Wigan, Lancs., 1722, educated at Douai and Paris. Co-adjutor Western District 1756. Vicar Apostolic Western District 1770. Died 1797.
[4] *The Dawn of Catholic Revival in England*, Ward, Vol. I. p. 182.

the house on 21st February 1791. It was still very modest in its provisions; so much so that Burke[1] was able to ridicule those who feared danger to the State, and the bill had its third reading on 20th April. By the time it reached the Lords it appeared that the Roman Catholic bishops had been caught unawares, having not known the bill was so far advanced. They felt they must get some modification of the oath, also of the title 'Protesting Catholic Dissenters'. Some peers proved friends of the Vicars Apostolic, as also did some of the Anglican bishops to whom they appealed to use their influence. The Revd. John Milner[2] of the Winchester Mission (later Vicar Apostolic of the Midland District) wrote to the Bishops of Hereford and Salisbury, giving those parts of the oath considered most objectionable: Bishop Walmesley wrote to the Archbishop of Canterbury (John Moore). Bishop Berington[3] and Bishop Douglass[4] (the new Vicar Apostolic of the London District) wrote to Samuel Horsley, Bishop of St. David's, asking for help and putting the case for a revised oath. The speech of the Bishop of St. David's in the Lords on 31st March 1791[5] proved decisive. He had, he said, an abhorrence of penal legislation and a feeling of charity towards Roman Catholics: the opinions which separated the Roman Catholics of the day from the communion of the Church of England were not of a dangerous complexion nor subversive of civil government. But he went on to say:

My lords, with all this charity for Roman Catholics, with these sentiments of the inexpediency of the penal laws, I must still disapprove of the bill which is now offered for a second reading. . . . I object to the bill that it is insufficient to its own purpose; my lords I quarrel with the bill for the partiality of its operation.

The bill, he said, relieved only those Roman Catholics who took the oath. It was a well-known fact that there were Roman

---

[1] Edmund Burke, 1729–97. Son of an Irish Attorney; ed Dublin. M.P. 1765–94.

[2] Born John Miller, 1752–1826.

[3] Charles Berington, 1748–98, ed. Douai and Paris, Co-adjutor Midland District. Vicar Apostolic Midland District 1795.

[4] 1743–1812, ed. Douai and Valladolid.

[5] Parl. Hist. of England, *Hansard*, Vol. XXIX, pp. 668–9.

Catholics who scrupled at the terms in which the oath was drawn. They were willing to swear allegiance to the King and renounce the Pope's authority in civil and temporal matters, not keeping faith with heretics and the murdering of heretics, etc., but to the deposing doctrine they would not apply the epithet of impious, unchristian and damnable; they thought the doctrine false rather than damnable and scrupled on account of tender memory for their forbears; the 1778 oath should be sufficient. The speech made a great impression and Bishop Douglass, though sensitive to the exposure of Roman Catholic divisions, wrote to the Archbishops of Canterbury and York, Dr. Horsley and others, saying that four amendments were needed if the old oath were to remain, but that the Irish oath of 1774 would be acceptable. On 3rd June 1791 the House of Lords sat as a Committee on the bill: the Bishop of St. David's moved that the oath be expunged and that the oath taken by Roman Catholics in Ireland, with slight modifications, be substituted. The bill was read for the third time[1] and received the Royal Assent:[2] it came into effect a fortnight later. On 24th June 1791, therefore it became lawful once more to celebrate the Roman mass openly in England, the 232nd anniversary of its prohibition under Queen Elizabeth.

The new element in the situation was the communication between Anglican and Roman Catholic bishops. Had this been able to continue and the attitude of such as Horsley been maintained, catholic emancipation might have been achieved more quickly. But three factors prevented it: first, most members of the Anglican bench were not of Horsley's mind: secondly, the internal problems of party government affected the measures it was able to achieve, and thirdly, the divisions among the Roman Catholic body itself became magnified—in particular the tension between the lay people and their bishops increased. The question of the choice and appointment of the Vicars Apostolic was specially acute.

In the London District the local cause was strengthened by a pamphlet by a leading member of the Committee, John Throckmorton, entitled 'A letter addressed to the Catholic clergy of England on the appointment of Bishops by laymen':

---

[1] 7th June 1791.   [2] 10th June 1791.

not three names should be submitted to the Holy See, but only one: the election of a bishop would not be valid unless he were acclaimed by the voice of the people. He concluded that Bishop Walmesley and Bishop Thomas Talbot were bishops without the powers of the keys. The remedy was that the clergy should now elect them, not as Vicars Apostolic but as real bishops.

> you in conjunction with the laity of your respective districts assemble, and choose for your Bishops the persons who now, by a lamentable abuse, preside over you, in virtue of an authority delegated to them by a foreign Prelate, who has no pretensions to exercise such an act of power. They are Bishops of Sees where they have no faithful, you are bodies of Faithful without Bishops. By the laws of the Church they may be elected by you for Pastors; they will not fail to accept the office. They are now aliens, you will make them Englishmen; they are dependent, you will make them free; they are foreign emissaries, you will transform them into English bishops; they must rejoice in the change.[1]

The Catholic Committee was encountering so much opposition, that at the Annual General Meeting of 1792 it decided not to seek re-appointment. As an alternative some members formed themselves into the Cisalpine Club, which continued the policy of working towards better ecclesiastical organisation, especially for parish priests. From 1792 to 1808 Roman Catholics had no effective rallying point in England, but on 23rd May 1808 an Association was started which became the Catholic Board in 1813. From that time onwards the question of emancipation for the Catholic community was at the mercy of several bodies who had not made up their minds which way they were going to act: the political parties for whom the issue was one of state policy; the Church of England which was anxious about its own survival and the rising tide of liberalism within its ranks; the Roman Catholic community itself which was uncertain what price it was prepared to pay, figuratively speaking, for its freedom. As so often in English affairs expediency decided the issue.

Chief among the intractable problems for English politicians was that of Ireland with its predominantly Roman Catholic

[1] *The Dawn of Catholic Revival in England*, Ward, Vol. I, p. 227.

population. Irish issues dominated Anglican/Roman Catholic relations at the time (and are still of great moment). The treatment of Ireland by successive English governments over 300 years was to have serious repercussions. Opportunities for helping Ireland economically continued to be callously missed and Irish trade and industry was suppressed and discouraged, lest it should threaten English interests. Parliamentary debates tell the depressing story of economic pressure on one commodity after another. The only light which penetrated the gloom was produced by the concern of those Members who tried to bring the facts to public notice. One[1] explained that the Irish woollen trade had been ruined by England: Ireland had been prevented from selling wool to any other country; and to England only at her own price. It was the same with linen. The Linen Trade Bounty[2] was to be removed on linens for export under 7d. a yard at once and gradually on finer ones as well. A question was asked as to how this would effect the growing Irish linen industry in the west and figures were sought since it had been stated in 1822 that the removal of the bounty would be destructive to the infant trade. The reply came[3] that 40,000 Irishmen had been thrown out of work by the removal of the bounties; the Chancellor of the Exchequer said later[4] that bounties were not in the real interest of Ireland. (At least they kept the population alive.) A debate on the duty on glass going into Ireland[5] provoked a statement that the tax had put it beyond the power of the Irish poor to buy glass for their windows—most cottages had only one—since the price had been doubled. A debate[6] in 1824 on Banking establishments in Ireland resulted in an Act which hindered the formation of banking companies at a time when capital for investment was the country's greatest need.

In the House of Lords Irish questions fared no better. In the spring of 1822 a severe scarcity of provisions in Ireland was reported. The Earl of Liverpool said he was against relief: 'Nothing could be more improper than the interference of

[1] Dennis Brown, 6th June 1823. *Hansard*, Parliamentary Debates, Vol. NS IX, p. 803. [2] 26th February 1824. ibid., Vol. NS X, p. 452.
[3] 12th March 1824. ibid., p. 943.
[4] 22nd March 1824. ibid., p. 1309.
[5] 2nd March 1829. ibid., Vol. NS XX, p. 661.
[6] 7th May 1824. ibid., Vol. NS XI, p. 786.

Government with the subsistence of the country.'[1] Such interference was far more likely to cause famine than to help. Others favoured relief, but were outvoted.[2] Evidence of distress accumulated; the Earl of Darnley described the failure of the whole potato crop;[3] Lord King said[4] that a million people were in a state of absolute starvation. The Irish Poor Employment Act proposed to lay out £50,000 to give employment, but that sum was far too small. Lord Liverpool said he was prepared to accept a bill, though it was objectionable in principle:

> The general principle acted upon in England was to leave public works, such as roads, to individual or joint speculation, it being well understood, that under such a system, individuals were induced, for the sake of their own interest, to a careful superintendence; and a more economical expenditure of money in consequence took place.[5]

While relationships between Anglicans and the Roman Catholic population of Ireland were being permanently impaired by selfish economic theory, there were several other factors which destroyed confidence, two of which were religious, namely education and Church organisation in Ireland; the others were the presence of British troops in certain areas to keep the peace, and the dreaded evictions.[6] Government money paid more, proportionately, for the education of Anglicans than of the Roman Catholic population. More detrimental still was the organisation of the established Church of Ireland[7] with 22 bishops and archbishops, 33 deans and 102 dignitaries, together with about 1,290 incumbents, for a body of 490,000 faithful. To these clergy improverished Roman Catholic peasants were required to pay tithes. During the course of one of many debates on the Church establishment[8] the Hon. E. G. S. Stanley[9] (Member for Stockbridge) summed up the situation:

---

[1] 29th April 1822. *Hansard* Vol. NS VII, p. 141.
[2] 17 votes for relief, 35 votes against it.
[3] 10th May 1822. ibid., pp. 470–1.   [4] 23rd May 1822. ibid., p. 726.
[5] ibid., p. 727.
[6] *The Great Hunger*, C. Woodham Smith, Hamish Hamilton, 1962, p. 24.
[7] Figures are for 1823.
[8] 6th May 1824. *Hansard*, Vol. NS XI, p. 562.
[9] Later 14th Earl of Derby.

No man who had not seen the interior of an Irish peasant's cabin could form any conception of the misery and wretchedness which were there to be found. He wished most earnestly that the means might be afforded of raising the peasantry of Ireland from their present degraded condition, of removing from their minds that callow indifference to misery which a long acquaintance with suffering had impressed upon their characters . . . [He believed that] the four great evils under which Ireland laboured were the want of a resident gentry, the want of capital, the want of employment and the want of education.

All these four wants, he was ready to assert, would be materially increased by diminishing the income of the clergy. The opposite point of view was taken by William Plunkett (member for Dublin University) who deprecated taking away the revenues of the clergy of the Established Church to give them to Roman Catholics. It was important neither to encroach on their property nor on their sacred duties; the right to property, whether public or private, must not be interfered with. It was necessary that there should be not only an established church, but that it should be richly endowed and its dignitaries enabled to take their stations with the nobles of the land. A further complaint from Members during the course of debates on Ireland was that the Irish poor were swarming into England and degrading the English poor to the same level as themselves. The Irish poor did indeed swarm into England and America during the first half of the nineteenth century, bringing with them memories of what they had suffered at the hands of the clergy and government of the Establishment. These bitter experiences had been burned into their minds; they lasted for generations, and the heat of them, compounded of politics and religion, is still aflame in Ulster.

This melancholy recital could go on indefinitely. What Members of Parliament thought and did affected Anglican/Roman Catholic relations at that time more than is the case today, since had they not been at least nominal Anglicans[1] they would not have been in the legislature.

---

[1] The Test Act (requiring all holders of office to take the Anglican Sacrament) was not repealed until 1829.

Catholic Emancipation, that is the lifting of the laws against Roman Catholic participation in political life, was only one of the elements in a very complex situation. Pitt had intended that it should follow the Union of 1800. He had hoped to achieve the Union and then afterwards to persuade his Cabinet to accept emancipation, but he failed to carry his colleagues with him. More important still, in 1801 the King[1] himself came out against emancipation. His mental instability was evident again and he became convinced that to allow civil rights to Catholics would be against his Coronation oath; he also felt it must bring about the ruin of the Church of England. The King was able to be obstinate because he had now found an alternative to Pitt in Henry Addington.[2] In January 1801 Pitt went out of office after 17 years and the King asked Addington to form a government. Pitt had misjudged the political climate on catholic emancipation, and now that England was at war with France it was not reasonable or patriotic to break up the government on the emancipation issue.

Concerted government policy on this issue was now missing. After the death of Pitt in 1806 came a 'Ministry of all the Talents' under Lord Grenville which could not command united action: Pitt's followers were in opposition. A new government under Portland in 1807 was no more united, since it included such men as Spencer Perceval, fervently against Emancipation on the one hand and Castlereagh,[3] who wanted to fulfil the promises made at the Union on the other: also George Canning,[4] whose volatile personality made some of his colleagues unwilling to work with him. But Roman Catholics continued to petition and there were some answering voices in Parliament. Henry Grattan (Member for Dublin) moved for a Committee of the House of Commons again in 1810,[5] but after an immensely long debate there were still 213 Noes to 109 Ayes. A solution to the emancipation question was required which would be considered safe in England and yet acceptable

---

[1] George III.
[2] 1st Viscount Sidmouth, 1757–1844.
[3] Robert Stewart, Viscount Castlereagh, Marquis of Londonderry, 1769–1822. Foreign Secretary 1812–1822.
[4] 1770–1827. Foreign Secretary 1796 and again 1807.
[5] 18th May 1810. *Hansard*, Vol. os XVII, p. 17.

to the Irish. One proposal, as will be seen in the next chapter, was to give full civil rights to Roman Catholics on condition that the King should have a veto on the appointment of their bishops if a candidate were considered likely to be loyal. A similar system was granted under Napoleon in France. At one time it looked as if this concession would be acceptable, but the discussions which ranged between Rome, London and Dublin covered six years and the whole matter eventually involved more than English politics.

6
'CATHOLIC EMANCIPATION'

At the French Revolution many clergy escaped from France
into other countries, and particularly into England.

It was calculated that there arrived about 8,000 priests,
three archbishops and sixteen bishops. The Abbé Barruel,
writing in his *Histoire du Clergé pendant la revolution Françoise*
commented upon the arrival of some of the refugee clergy on
English shores by saying that:

> 'Every vessel that arrived with a cargo of these exiles seems
> to have been foreseen by the English through an instinct of
> benevolence. They flocked to the landing places to offer us a
> lodging or refreshment. Fifty, a hundred of us arrived at a
> time. They seemed more concerned for us than we were for
> ourselves. . . .[1]

Certainly the Abbé was making the most of the English support
in gratitude for what had been done, but it would seem that a
significant part of the English public were prepared to be
generous to the distressed Frenchmen. Subscriptions were asked
for and relief was organised. A Committee was formed, which
included the Bishops of London (Beilby Porteous) and Durham
(Shute Barrington). A letter was sent to the Archbishops of
Canterbury and York, and by them to the other bishops. This
was read in all parish churches and subsequently a house to
house collection raised £41,304. Many opened their doors to
the refugees and had them to live in their homes. These events

---

[1] *The History of the Clergy during the French Revolution*, Augustin Barruel. A
work dedicated to the English nation. English translation, 3rd edition
revised. Dublin, H. Fitzpatrick, 1795, pp. 324–9.

had their influence both on the English Church and on the English Roman Catholic community. Anglicans and Dissenters became interested in the religious practice of the émigrés, whereas the English Roman Catholics, who had been practising their religion during penal times, were found to be austere by comparison. The émigrés were less inhibited and their chapels were open for all to see. Contacts then made bore fruit many years later. For example Canon Oakeley[1] in the *Contemporary Review* for June 1879[2] speaks of the exchange between a group of French priests and the future Bishop Lloyd:

'The priests who sought shelter in this country from the horrors of the great French Revolution were in the habit of reciting their Office together in the building since known as the Somers Town Catholic Chapel, and soon attracted the compassion and respect of persons in the neighbourhood, who were naturally edified by observing how cheerily these holy exiles could sing the Lord's Song in a strange land.

Among those who became acquainted with them was the Rev. Charles Lloyd, for some years Regius Professor of Divinity at Oxford and Bishop of that See.

In 1826, or thereabouts, Dr. Lloyd began a course of Lectures with a private class of divinity students on the History of the Anglican Prayer Book and the sources from which many of the contents are derived.

Among the students who attended the Lectures were Mr. Newman, Mr. Robert Wilberforce, Mr. Hurrell Froude and myself. I distinctly remember Dr. Lloyd telling us that his knowledge of the Roman Breviary, of which such extensive use is made in the composition of the Prayer Book, was gained in his youth from the French refugee Priests at Somers Town.[3]

In his later years Newman spoke of the experience in his youth of meeting a French priest who showed him a crucifix, and

[1] Frederick Oakeley, 1802–1880. Tractarian Fellow of Balliol. Became Roman Catholic 1845.
[2] p. 469.
[3] Bishop Lloyd referred to his dealings with the French clergy in his speech in the House of Lords, 2nd April 1829. *Hansard*, Vol. NS XXI, p. 79.

Ambrose Phillipps de Lisle[1] recalled conversations with an émigré priest whose outlook made a deep impression upon him as a boy.[2]

The French republic was proclaimed on 2nd September 1792 and by 8th February 1793 Great Britain and France were at war. The British navy in the Mediterranean lost the port of Toulon and had to find other anchorages and places for victualling. In 1796 Spain joined France and declared war on England, as the Dutch had already done. The Directory made Napoleon Commander of the French army in Italy; he crossed the Alps and advanced into Tuscany and invaded the States of the Church. Thus it became of mutual benefit for the English government and the Pope to draw closer together. Envoys were sent to London and Rome; and as the result of the opportunities that were now open, a correspondence and conversations began to develop on a much wider front involving many people in both capitals.

In 1792 the British choice of an envoy fell upon John (later Sir John) Coxe Hippisley,[3] who had undertaken some English diplomatic work during an earlier residence in Italy in the years 1779 and 1780 and who, although an Anglican, had a wide circle of acquaintances at the Vatican. Hippisley's influence in the relations between the two courts during the next decade was to be profound; and it was his pressure on the Pope that led to the appointment of the Scotsman Mgr. Erskine, a relative of the Earls of Mar and Kellie and protégé of Henry, Cardinal Duke of York, as a papal envoy in London. There were some doubts how he would be received, but since the emigrés had been well treated and the Pope was being generous over the matter of the provisioning of British ships, it was decided to despatch Erskine to England, and he left Rome on 4th October 1793.[4] Hippisley had evidence that closer

---

[1] (1809–1878) Leicestershire Squire. Became Roman Catholic aged 15.

[2] *Life and Letters of Ambrose Phillipps de Lisle*, E. S. Purcell, Macmillan, 1900, pp. 4–5.

[3] 1748–1825. Political writer and ardent enthusiast for Catholic emancipation. Oxford. Inner Temple 1766. Called to Bar 1771; Bencher 1803. M.P. 1790–1796 and 1802–1819. Created Baronet 1796.

[4] Probably as the result of the visit in February 1772 of the Duke of Gloucester (brother of George III) to Rome and reception by Pope Clement XIV, the Pope sent Mgr. Caprara, Nuncio in Cologne, to England to look at conditions. The report which came back said that old prejudices were

relationships would be welcome on several accounts. The English government was pressing him to let the Pope see the necessity of supporting resistance against the French, and Edmund Burke had written:

> If the thing depended on me I should certainly enter upon diplomatic correspondence with the Court of Rome, in a much more open and legitimate manner than has been hitherto attempted. If we refuse it, the bigotry will be on our side and most certainly not on that of H.H. Our natural alienation has produced, I am convinced, great evil and prevented much good.[1]

Hippisley sent this letter straight to the Cardinal Secretary of State, Cardinal de Zelada, together with an extract from another letter from the Bishop of Winchester (Brownlow North),[2] half-brother of the former Prime Minister:

> The establishment of relations between Great Britain and the pope is most desirable, especially at a time when the piety, humility and liberality of Pius VI presents him to us as a prince whose friendship is an honour and those political or private engagements are characterised by virtue, sincerity and goodness of heart.[3]

In this memorandum to the Cardinal Secretary Hippisley described how he had paved the way for Erskine's reception in England. He had written to the Prince of Wales, Prince Augustus Duke of Sussex (who had lived in Rome and was known by Erskine and the then Pope), the Lord Chancellor, Lord Grenville,[4] William Windham,[5] Edmund Burke and to many other Members of Parliament.

dying. (*Diplomazia Pontificia nel secolo* XIX, Vol. 4; P. Ilario Rinieri, Rome *Civilta Cattolica*, 1904, p. 145.)

[1] From Vatican Archives, published in *Great Britain and the Holy See 1792–1806*. Aidan Gasquet, Rome, 1919; included in his volume on *Monastic Life in the Middle Ages*, G. Bell, 1922, and p. 276 in that volume.

[2] 1741–1820. Elder son of 1st Earl of Guilford. Fellow of All Souls 1763. Dean of Canterbury 1770. Bishop of Coventry and Lichfield 1771; Worcester 1774; Winchester 1781.

[3] Gasquet, op. cit., p. 276. Sent to Cardinal Zelada 23rd November 1793.

[4] William Wyndham, Lord Grenville, 1759–1834. Foreign Secretary 1791–1801; after 1801 in favour of Catholic Emancipation.

[5] William Windham 1750–1810. Disciple of Burke; Secretary at War 1794–1801.

Once the mission of Mgr. Erskine had been determined upon I took every measure possible to anticipate any difficulties which might arise. The first and greatest obstacle which could be foreseen, was the prejudice of the lower classes of the people in general and of the sectaries in particular.

He went on to say that he feared that the greatest opposition to the appearance of Mgr. Erskine in England would come from the Roman Catholic side, and especially from their bishops, at the arrival of an envoy from the Pope who might try and exercise authority over them. It appears that Bishop Douglass, Vicar Apostolic of the London district, had written to Rome to say that if a papal envoy were to be appointed to England he would be content to be so named.

It has been stated[1] that the Vicar Apostolic of the London district was not told of Erskine's departure, but in Hippisley's papers there is a copy sent to the English agent by Propaganda Fide[2] of a letter to Mgr. Douglass asking for his assistance in London for the papal envoy. It is clear that the views of the English Roman Catholic body were very divided. Erskine, writing back to Rome on 19th December 1793 (he arrived in London on 13th November) said that Mgr. Douglass had tried to prevent him coming. He was fêted by certain laymen, but the clergy were unenthusiastic, and Lord Petre complained in a letter to Hippisley of 'the attitude of certain ecclesiastics'. Erskine eventually had conversations with Burke, Pitt, Windham, the Lord Chancellor, etc., and was present at the opening of Parliament on 22nd January 1794, at a place in the House of Lords near the King. He was presented to the King on the same day, listed officially as 'Envoy Extraordinary from His Holiness the Pope', and to the Queen on the following day. He also met the Prince of Wales. In the communications which were exchanged the object of the mission was said to be to thank the British government for the favours shown to the French emigrés and English Catholic subjects: the letters which passed between Windham, Hippisley and the Pope (despite the Statute of Praemunire[3] still in force) stressed the benefits of

[1] *The Dawn of Catholic revival*, Ward, Vol. II, p. 39.
[2] The Vatican department which then dealt with English affairs.
[3] 1352. Designed to protect the Crown. Forbade communication with the Papacy. Penalties involved forfeiture of property.

these improved relations. In his history of the French clergy referred to above Abbé Barruel made the most of these contacts, when he wrote:

> By a wonderful effect of Providence the French clergy have been the happy cause of drawing together the Holy See and England which for more than two centuries had had no sort of communication. [This was not strictly true.] The truly magnanimous way in which the court and all classes of the British nation has acted towards these ecclesiastics was quickly brought to the attention of the Common Father of the Faithful.

Hippisley's part in the rapprochement was emphasised:

> In this way the barriers were broken and the dividing wall that had so long separated Rome from London was, if not wholly overthrown, at least passed over without difficulty, a mutual confidence was established and the two powers came to understand that they had one object of mutual interest.[1]

It would be realistic to remember that the Pope was anxious for the port of Antibes and to regain Avignon and Venaissin and that Admiral Hood needed more meat and grain for the British Mediterranean fleet (for which Hippisley wrote to the Cardinal Secretary of State on 23rd June 1794). But although driven together on both sides by self-interest, there is no doubt that Englishmen were nearer the Papacy and ordinary Roman Catholics than they had been for a long time.

Sir John Hippisley left Rome in 1796 on account of his health,[2] but he continued to take a deep interest in Roman Catholic affairs and as a Member of Parliament to speak to good effect in the debates on catholic emancipation: he also corresponded at length with members of the Roman Curia. In fact it was through his letters to Cardinal Borgia that events were set in motion which ended in a pension of £4,000 per annum being granted by the British government to Henry,

---

[1] In the Preface.
[2] He was succeeded as English Envoy in Rome by Thomas Jackson, British plenipotentiary to the Court of the King of Sardinia.

Cardinal Duke of York, grandson of James II.[1] He had fallen on bad times, had been deprived of his stipend since the French occupation of Rome in the winter of 1797 and was living in exile in Venice. Hippisley suggested that Cardinal Borgia should prepare a letter setting out the predicament of the Cardinal Duke of York which could be shown to George III and his government. This Cardinal Borgia did on 14th September 1799,[2] referring to 'the friendship with which you honoured me'. Antonio, Archbishop of Siena, wrote also in support. The correspondence was sent to Pitt who placed it before George III and it was not long before payments began to be made to the Cardinal of York through Coutts' bank.[3]

In a similar manner George III also pensioned provisionally Mgr. Erskine who had been deprived of his income on the French occupation of Rome. The Pope suffered too and became a prisoner of the French. On 16th March 1798 Pius VI sent Erskine a long letter from Siena describing his plight and Erskine in turn asked the King and British government to rescue the Pontiff.[4] But nothing was achieved and the Pope died a prisoner at Valence on 29th August 1799. A new Pope (Cardinal Chiarimonti) was elected by a conclave in Venice on 14th March 1800 with the title Pius VII. Meanwhile the French had withdrawn from Rome: Nelson with a frigate and four ships of the line with 3,000 Neapolitan soldiers on board lay off Leghorn and the city surrendered to Captain Trowbridge, Commander of H.M.S. *Culloden* from Civita Vecchia. The Pope re-entered Rome on 5th July 1800 and in September a concordat was negotiated between Napoleon and the Pope, which was signed by the Cardinal Secretary of State Consalvi[5] in Paris on 3rd July 1801.

[1] Born 1725. Younger son of 'Old Pretender'. Bishop of Frascati. Succeeded brother Charles Edward as *de jure* King of Great Britain, France and Ireland under title Henry IX. Died 1807.

[2] Stuart Papers, British Museum Add. 34639 f.6.

[3] This whole episode is dealt with in detail in the 'Relations of Henry, Cardinal Duke of York with the British Government', Walter W. Seton, *Transactions of the Royal Historical Society*, fourth series, Vol. II, London, 1919.

[4] See letters in the Vatican Archives from the Cardinal Dean to Lord Nelson and Lord Grenville of 18th December 1798 when the Pope was in the Certosa of Florence.

[5] Ercole Consalvi. Born 8th June 1757 of noble family. Prisoner of French 1798. Secretary to Conclave 1799. Secretary of State 1800. Made Cardinal deacon but never ordained to priesthood.

To return to England: Mgr. Erskine was made a Cardinal in petto,[1] on 14th February 1801, but the appointment was not made known in England in case it should lead to public abuse, although he told Pitt and the King who asked him, on a court occasion, why he was not in his robes. The end of the year saw Erskine's withdrawal to Rome. It is not easy to assess his usefulness during his eight-year mission either to his own superiors or to Englishmen. He made certain insignificant contacts in London and Oxford, but he had difficulties with his Roman Catholic brethren who resented his presence in England. Differences of opinion between clergy and laity made his path even more thorny. 'He has given himself over to the Cisalpines' was one criticism, but on the other hand Hippisley heard that Erskine had persuaded Lord Petre to see Mgr. Douglass which he had not done for a long time, and tried to stop Throckmorton writing pamphlets, which he had promised to do. At the very least his presence in London was a sign that communication between England and Rome was regarded as desirable.[2]

The French occupied Rome again in 1808 and another Pope found himself a prisoner in France. There had been a plan to evacuate him from the Quirinal Palace by night on to a British frigate lying at Fiumicino, but the Pope refused, and later in June 1812 while Pius VII was at Savona, the Admiralty had a rescue operation planned. But this was forestalled by Napoleon who moved the Pontiff to Fontainebleau. On the temporary defeat of Napoleon the allies met in Paris in May 1814 where a treaty was to be negotiated with the restored French monarchy. Consalvi, Cardinal Secretary of State, took the opportunity to journey to the French capital to seek support for the matter which was at the forefront of papal politics, the regaining of the Pope's lost States. He spoke with some of the sovereigns and ministers who were shortly to attend the Congress of Vienna where the map of Europe was to be redrawn, and decided to travel with them to London, where he arrived on 10th June 1814. Anti-Papal feeling had declined and there was much of mutual interest to discuss, including civil rights for English and

---

[1] Secretly: literally 'in the (Pope's) breast'.

[2] For further information on this mission see 'Memoirs of Cardinal Erskine, Papal Envoy to the Court of George III', W. Mozière Brady. *Anglo-Roman Papers*, Paisley, 1890.

Irish Roman Catholics, the international slave trade, the intrigues of Joachim Murat[1] in Italy, Princess Caroline (the estranged wife of the Prince Regent) and her travels to Italy and the possibility of a concordat between England and the Holy See. Consalvi had been a close friend of Henry Cardinal Duke of York. He had been named in his will, and he had arranged for some of the late cardinal's treasures and papers to be transferred to the Prince Regent through Castlereagh. He was well received in England where he spent 26 days and had conversations with Castlereagh and the Prince Regent. The arrival of Consalvi returns us to the English domestic scene and the matter of legislation for the relief of Roman Catholics.

During the spring of 1813 Henry Grattan, Member for Dublin continued to press for a committee of the House on Roman Catholic claims. At last on 2nd March, after numerous all-night sittings and hours of debate, Grattan achieved a majority for his motion (264 for and 224 against). During the amendment stage of the bill it was proposed that Roman Catholics should not be admitted as Members of the House of Commons: Grattan urged that the House had nothing to lose from a small infusion of Roman Catholics. The clause was lost by four votes on 24th May and since, as Ponsonby[2] said, the bill without the clause was neither worthy of acceptance by the Roman Catholics nor of the further support of the friends of concession, it was abandoned. One of the problems was that catholic emancipation was not the united official policy of any cabinet, despite the disposition of such as Castlereagh and Canning in its favour. Many peers looked upon the granting of political rights for men who were not members of the established church as the height of folly, notably Lord Liverpool (Prime Minister from 1812), and most of the bishops, who seemed to see the Armada sailing up the channel and to hear the crackling of the fires of Smithfield during every debate.

It was said that the Catholics acknowledged a jurisdiction in a foreign power: this jurisdiction was claimed to be confined to spiritual and ecclesiastical matters, but it was impossible to separate civil from ecclesiastical power. (Contemporary papal

[1] Napoleon's brother-in-law, who assumed kingship of Naples.
[2] George Ponsonby, 1755–1817. M.P. for Tavistock. Son of Speaker of Irish parliament.

policy in trying to regain the lost territories and restate the doctrine of Temporal Power, was ironically taking up the same argument.)

Thus the Archbishop of Canterbury (Charles Manners Sutton[1]) had said that whereas the Irish Roman Catholics had received all manner of toleration, now they wanted power. How far was this consistent with the safety of the established church? Toleration was a virtue that grew naturally out of a sense of security and could not exist for a moment where danger was apprehended. On the same day the Bishop of St. Asaph[2] spoke of alleged usurpation of spiritual power. There was a dreadful abuse of power by the Roman Catholic bishops in Ireland, the use of excommunication. 'Nothing of political power and influence can be conceded to the Roman Catholics in Ireland beyond what they already enjoy unless their hierarchy can be reduced to a less offensive form and checked in the monstrous abuse of their spiritual authority.' If this were done he would be prepared to go to a committee.

The only member of the bench who took a contrary view consistently over the years of debate was Henry Bathurst, Bishop of Norwich. The Irish had due cause, he said,[3] to complain of the restrictive statutes as harsh, oppressive, unnecessary and unmerited. It was true, he said, that the present clergy of the Church of England were hostile in the main. Was it not also true that there were exceptions? Even if many people opposed Roman Catholic claims, it did not matter:

considering the nature of the question and how very little competent, generally speaking, men of studious recluse habits are to form a right judgment of great complicated and comprehensive political topics.

But it was impossible to say that those who 'dissent from us are grossly igorant or wilfully perverse: that they are not fit to be trusted, either in civil or in military situations of high responsibility: nor even to be believed upon their oaths'. Bishop Bathurst's view showed a liberality considered equally dangerous

---

[1] 13th May 1805. *Hansard*, Vol. os IV, pp. 775–8.
[2] ibid., pp. 794–804.
[3] 18th June 1811. *Hansard*, Vol. os XX, p. 667.

by the exclusive Church of Rome and by the fearful Church of England.

In June 1816[1] he returned to his theme. In his opinion it was the duty, as it was the criterion, of a Christian bishop to conciliate not to divide, to allay not to exasperate religious differences:

> the only way to secure permanently the existence of any establishment, civil or ecclesiastical was to evince liberal and conciliatory conduct to those who differed from us, and to lay its foundation in the love, affection and esteem of all within its influence. This was the true bulwark of our church .... A Christian spirit could never endanger a Christian establishment.

In 1817 the Bishop of Norwich was provoked by the Bishop of Llandaff, Dr. Herbert Marsh,[2] who said that the question was not one of religious liberty—they had that—but of political power. The fetters which bound Roman Catholics to a foreign prince made them obedient to the Pope when they should be obedient to the King. Dr. Bathurst did not agree:[3] the Catholics of Ireland and of England also, he said, had for more than a century displayed a moderation, a forbearance, a meek endurance of ill, which would have done credit to any of the primitive martyrs.

The Roman Catholic body were not unmindful of Bishop Bathurst's concern for them, for on 24th April 1819 at the meeting of the Board of English Catholics it was moved that 'as a small token of the veneration and gratitude due from every Catholic in the British Empire to the Rt. Revd. Dr. Henry Bathurst, Lord Bishop of Norwich, Mr. Turnerelli should be requested to execute a bust in marble of that illustrious and venerable prelate, in order that the same might be placed in the British Catholic board room'. Subscriptions were taken up, 'one guinea each only in order that an opportunity might be afforded to a greater number of individuals, to evince their

---

[1] 21st June 1816. *Hansard*, Vol. os XXXIV, pp. 1253-4.
[2] 16th May 1817. *Hansard*, Vol. os XXXVI, p. 614.
[3] ibid., p. 624.

affection and respect towards a prelate, so eminently deserving the character of a Christian bishop'.[1]

One of the issues of the abandoned bill of 1813 had been the question of the veto.[2] The chief source of alarm was the support by Roman Catholics of the Holy See, and for the government to have some voice in naming bishops was considered protection against a candidate who might put his loyalty to pope before his loyalty to king. In 1799 the Irish prelates had been in favour of the veto and they kept to this decision, and to an agreement to receive a salary from the State until 1808 when a declaration of Irish bishops found the veto unacceptable.[3] Immediately the 1813 Relief Bill was lost, the Catholic Board met and expelled Dr. John Milner,[4] Vicar Apostolic of the Midland District, for circulating a memorial against it. Roman Catholic opinion was divided into two camps: those with Milner, which included most of the Irish bishops; and the others who followed the Committee of the Catholic Board; these included the Roman Catholic nobles, as well as Bishop Poynter,[5] and many of the clergy, who were in favour of an arrangement with the British government. (During the parliamentary debates opponents of Catholic relief made the most of these divisions in the Catholic ranks.) Bishop Poynter felt he should go to Rome to seek the opinion of the Holy See.

In the spring of 1814 affairs in Rome were in a turmoil; the Pope himself was at Fontainebleau. On 16th February 1814 the Vice-Prefect of Propaganda Fide, Mgr. Quarantotti (under whose jurisdiction the English Roman bishops lay) sent them a Rescript[6] giving approval to the Relief Bill of 1813 and appealing to Bishop Poynter to help the Holy Father to regain his territories: 'Catholics ought with satisfaction and gratitude

[1] *Historical Memoirs of the English Catholics*, Charles Butler, Vol. IV, p. 281.
[2] By which the Crown could prevent the appointment of men thought to be disloyal, as Roman Catholic bishops.
[3] *Historical Memoirs. . .*, Butler, Vol. IV, pp. 151–5.
[4] First agreed with veto, then against it. Expelled from Catholic Board and excluded from meeting of Vicars Apostolic in Durham, October 1813.
[5] William Poynter, born Hants. 1762, educated at Douai; in France during Revolution. Co-adjutor London District 1803. Vicar Apostolic 1812–1827. In favour of the veto.
[6] *Historical Memoirs. . .*, Butler, Vol. IV, pp. 518–23 for copy of Rescript.

to accept and embrace the law which was proposed last year for their emancipation in the form which your Lordship has laid it before us.'[1] The English bishops received the Rescript by April. All except Milner were prepared to accept it. In Ireland the bishops met at Maynooth on 25th May 1814 to protest against the Rescript and delegated Dr. Murray, co-adjutor Bishop of Dublin, and Milner to be their agents in Rome to negotiate its recall. Milner had already left and Poynter went via Paris where he saw Castlereagh and Consalvi.[2] Pius VII had been released from captivity by Napoleon on 22nd January and on 24th May made a triumphal entry into Rome. Murray and Milner saw the Pope at once and according to their evidence (although this was denied later by Charles Butler) Pius said that Quarantotti should not have written the Rescript without the authority of the Holy See. Meanwhile the Board of English Catholics sent an address of congratulation to the Pope on his restoration and gave thanks for the Rescript which they said they had received 'with unspeakable joy'. Charles Butler, in correspondence with Castlereagh, spoke deprecatingly of the Irish attitude and that of Milner, 'the worst enemy of the Roman Catholic cause in the present times'.[3]

It was at this point that Consalvi entered England and formed a friendship with Castlereagh (Foreign Secretary since 1812) which was to continue until Castlereagh's death in 1822. In a long letter to Consalvi in London the Pope urged him to present the case both for the return of the papal territories and for the relief of English Roman Catholic citizens. This Castlereagh understood from their three meetings. At the longest of these on 4th July the Foreign Secretary raised the question of Roman Catholic claims and also the possibility of the exchange of negotiators between the two courts. A chargé d'affaires of the

[1] *Cardinal Consalvi and Anglo-Papal Relations, 1814–24*, J. T. Ellis, Catholic University of America Press, Washington D.C., 1942. For the whole question in greater detail this book is invaluable.

[2] Consalvi in a despatch from Paris, 6th June 1814 (Rinieri, op. cit., p. 367), related that Poynter was also charged by the British government to find out in Rome whether the Italian States wanted to be united under one king.

[3] For more information about the cross-currents between Bishop Milner and the Catholic Board see Butler's *Historical Memoirs*, Vol. IV, p. 530, also *Annals of the Catholic Hierachy in England and Scotland, 1585–1876* by W. Mozière Brady, London, J. M. Stark 1883.

Holy See could be admitted in London and a British subject of similar standing sent to Rome. This was a proposition which had been mooted several times earlier by Hippisley and Edmund Burke. Castlereagh told the Cardinal that the government would not press the Roman Catholics beyond the limits of their consciences, but the emancipation question could not be solved without a guarantee of their continued loyalty and the harmless nature of their correspondence with Rôme. The three government requirements were an oath of allegiance to uphold the British constitution, a voice in the naming of bishops and the power to put aside correspondence of the Holy See with Roman Catholics in England.

Three days before the last interview[1] with Castlereagh Consalvi was received in full regalia[2] by the Prince Regent at a public audience with some Anglican bishops. After greeting him warmly the Prince bade him withdraw for a private talk of about half an hour. He spoke of his personal admiration for Pius VII (who had secured much support in England after his sufferings at the hands of Napoleon). They spoke together about the emancipation question but the Regent did not commit himself to expressing his views. On the subject of the papal states the Prince agreed to support the Pope at the forthcoming congress. Consalvi reported effusively to Pacca on the interview:

> Io fui introdotto dal Regio Principe. E qui mi è impossibile, assolutamente impossibile, di riferire in un modo, che corrisponda alla cosa i sentimenti, la bontà, la cortesia, la premura, l'interesse e sopratutto la vera effusione del cuore, che dal principio fino alla fine distinsero questa udienza.[3]

Consalvi pressed the Vatican to come as close as possible to the British government's three points: emancipation to Roman Catholics would be given in return; other governments had similar arrangements with no concessions to Rome. But he must be told what was in the mind of the Pope before he reached Vienna.[4]

---

[1] Consalvi's despatch to Cardinal Pacca of 4th July 1814 giving full details of the interview, Rinieri, op. cit., pp. 155–7. Bartolomeo Pacca was Assistant Secretary of State to Consalvi.
[2] 'accolto in abito cardinalizio'.
[3] Rinieri, op. cit., pp. 131–8.
[4] ibid., pp. 170–3.

When the Congregation gave their ruling it was to the effect that concession was to be allowed on two points, but not on the question of the communications of the Holy See. No concordat was possible. Consalvi had been too accommodating during his time in England. He was told he might continue to negotiate with Castlereagh and the two men met from time to time in Vienna. But meanwhile the news of their meetings had reached Ireland where it was felt that a bargain was being struck and control over the Roman Church in Ireland was being traded for help in the return of the papal states.

In the spring of 1815 Napoleon escaped from Elba and the forces of Murat were at the gates of Rome. At this point a colleague of Castlereagh, Edward Cooke, his chief of staff, under the guise of ill-health, either genuine or assumed, decided to have a holiday in Italy. When he arrived in Rome (then a notoriously unhealthy city) he reopened the question for an understanding between the two governments and help for English Roman Catholics. At a papal audience Cooke suggested the appointment of a chargé d'affaires at the two courts. The Pope felt that the appointment of the respective ministers should be made public. In a letter to Castlereagh[1] Cooke said he felt he could solve the catholic question and get the necessary concessions: he was deep in discussion with Poynter, whose ideas had struck him favourably.

Threatened by Neapolitan troops the Pope fled to Genoa with Milner and Poynter in tow. Poynter eventually left with a letter from Cardinal Litta[2] and a statement as to concessions in return for emancipation. Castlereagh returned from Vienna to London[3] where he wrote to Cooke: the Cabinet was divided on the Roman Catholic question: nothing officially could be done on a concordat, but if some leading Roman Catholics could intercede with their own government for the sanction of the principles in Grattan's bill, then it must be done. Two years before the Catholics had failed to accept the bill, despite

[1] 13th April 1815, *Correspondence of Castlereagh*, C. W. Vane, John Murray 1848–53 Vol. X, pp. 308–9.
[2] Prefect of Propaganda *Historical Memoirs . . .*, Butler, Vol. IV, pp. 531–6 for copy of letter dated 26th April 1815.
[3] Consalvi left Vienna on 18th June 1815, having achieved almost all he set out to do in the restoration of the papal states.

official opinion in favour of it. Cooke was to make matters clear in Rome. The Catholics ought to take the initative and make their views clear:

> there exists every friendly feeling to the Pope's interest in this Government, quite as much, I think, among the opponents as amongst the friends to the question of emancipation: but they will not relish anything like a new system and the religionists in the country would be very likely to cry out if my friend Consalvi's red stockings were seen too often at Carleton House (sic).

> Upon the whole, I should wish you to advise the Court of Rome to be content for the present with receiving hints and suggestions from the government, as to the means of being of use: but that they should determine to act ostensibly through and upon their own body, till the feeling here is better prepared for a direct intercourse on the part of the State with the See of Rome.[1]

After the battle of Waterloo the Pope returned to Rome, and on 4th September he delivered an allocution to the sacred college in which he thanked the British government for help in the restoration of the greater part of the papal domains and mentioned particularly the vigorous support of the Prince Regent.

Irish opposition from now on was greatly to impede the work of the catholic emancipation pressure group. At a meeting of the Catholic Board in Ireland in August 1815 Richard Hayes, a Franciscan, was appointed to go to Rome to persuade the Pope of the danger of any further dealings with England; he spent two years there, but achieved little owing to the influence of Consalvi who eventually secured his eviction. On 1st February 1816 the Pope wrote to the Irish bishops:[2] he spoke of the help given to him by the British in regaining his territories and told them that he could not deny to the government rights which other governments already possessed. Consalvi made another attempt in 1816 to reopen discussions which might lead to an agreement and Castlereagh replied on 22nd January 1817:

[1] 14th June 1815, *Correspondence of Castlereagh*, Vol. X, pp. 375-8.
[2] *Historical Memoirs* . . ., Butler, Vol. IV., pp. 536-48 for copy of letter.

In the present state of our laws there are difficulties and delicacies to be observed, but I trust that nothing will impede the mutual desire between the two states to render to each other genuine and reciprocal acts of Kindness.[1]

During 1817 and 1818 contact continued between them, and the Holy See also made moves to improve relationships: for example Pius VII asked Propaganda Fide[2] to rebuke Milner for the language of some articles he had published.[3]

During the years since the 1813 bill numerous petitions for emancipation had been received by both Houses including an interesting plea from both protestants and Roman Catholics of Ireland presented by Sir John Newport (Member for Waterford) on 24th June 1814[4] against the Society of Orangemen. After 120 years the victors should not still be allowed to triumph over the vanquished. In May 1816 Lord Castlereagh told the Regent that his ministers were not prepared to act. That stalwart protagonist of emancipation, Henry Grattan, Member for Dublin, died in June 1820, and was buried in Westminster Abbey; 'the charity boys of all the catholic schools of London were present and behaved with a seriousness which affected every beholder'.[5] But in the spring of 1821 William Plunkett brought forward a new bill and the House of Commons went into Committee on 2nd March. Differences of opinion between Roman Catholics were still rife, and Bishop Poynter tried to win some amendments through discussion with parliamentary leaders. A Roman Catholic fear that he was not in favour at Rome and might be removed inspired a letter to the Pope which evinced the reply that Poynter was in fact held in papal esteem.[6]

On 2nd April 1821 the Roman Catholic Disability Removal bill was read for the third time and passed by a majority of

---

[1] *The Foreign Policy of Castlereagh*, C. K. Webster, G. Bell, 1934 Vol. II, p. 113.

[2] 29th April 1820.

[3] *Catholic Emancipation and the Progress of the Catholic Church in the British Isles 1771–1820*, W. J. S. Amhurst, Kegan Paul, 1886, Vol. II, p. 333. Consalvi was no doubt behind this.

[4] *Hansard*, Vol. os XXVIII. . . pp. 245–6.

[5] *Historical Memoirs*. . ., Butler, Vol. IV, p. 393.

[6] In 1806 the Irish bishops tried to get Milner exchanged with Poynter for the London District, but Propanganda Fide would not play, although in 1808 Milner was given a dispensation to live out of his District (*Annals of the Catholic Hierarchy*, p. 226).

nineteen (216 Ayes and 197 Noes). In the Upper House it was read for the first time on 3rd April and for the second on 16th April. The bill was in two parts: the first dealt with the admission of Roman Catholics to almost all the offices of the state: the second regulated their dealings with the see of Rome. The question of the Roman church becoming the established church of Ireland was raised, and whether Roman Catholic claims could be satisfied without this. During the course of a long debate the Bishop of London (William Howley) said that as he was against the bill it became now his duty to state his conscientious objections. He was pleased to grant full freedom of worship to the Roman Catholic body, but not political power, because of a sincere apprehension for the safety of the established church. The greatest stumbling block was the unlimited submission to a foreign authority, an authority which assumed unlimited dominion over consciences, excluding from them all exercise of their own reason regarding all matters of religion. 'The protestant made no such reservation—his salvo was with his God, while that of the Catholic was alone with his Church, as a fixed rule and imperative measure of duty'.[1] The Bishop of Chester (Charles James Blomfield) made identical points.

The attempts of the Bishop of Norwich to redress the balance were of no avail. Dr. Bathurst said he had never acted as a party man and conceived that a bishop ought not to act in that House but where religious matters were involved. He would then ask what was the Church which it was proposed to secure by disabilities and penalties? No one could venture to say that it was that Church of which the law-giver and head had declared that his kingdom 'was not of this world'.[2] Most peers were unmoved and the Bishop of St. Asaph the next day spoke even more strongly:

> Every encouragement of the papal power is a diminutive of the authority of the Crown. . . . My lords my objections to the bill are endless.[3]

[1] 16th April 1821. *Hansard*, Vol. NS V, pp. 241–5.
[2] ibid., pp. 256–7.
[3] 17th April 1821. ibid., pp. 279–81.

The bill was thrown out by a majority of 39—'non-contents' included fifteen English bishops, four Welsh bishops, one Irish archbishop and three Irish bishops: neither of the English archbishops was present. 'Contents' included the Bishops of Norwich and Rochester.

Lord Castlereagh died in 1822 and was succeeded as Foreign Secretary by Canning, who shared his views on the catholic question, but had not corresponded directly with Roman Catholic priests or laymen; in fact from his utterances in parliamentary debates he seems to have been nervous of the operation of the statute of Praemunire.[1] During a debate on the well-worn subject,[2] he referred to the year when he entered office (1822–1823) in which there was a letter from the Pope (Leo XII) to the King announcing his elevation to the papal throne, as well as a complimentary letter from Consalvi to the Foreign Secretary. Canning had asked the opinion of law officers whether he would be liable to Praemunire if he replied. They had answered that under the Act 5 Eliz. Cap. 1 sec. 12 anyone allowing the jurisdiction of the See of Rome in this realm was subject to Praemunire, and an answer to a letter might be so interpreted as a sanction to these claims to authority. Canning had not therefore corresponded with the Pope: he wanted to make it clear to 'that venerable person' that the omission was dictated by no intentional want of respect, but to correspond with the Pope was to put himself in jeopardy.

The Prince Regent inherited his father's intransigence over the emancipation question,[3] and his inhibitions on account of the Coronation Oath. As King he refused to consider eminent clergy for bishoprics if their views did not lead them to oppose catholic emancipation.[4] But at the same time he was friendly to Consalvi, supported the Pope over the question of the restoration of the territories and in fact, unlike Canning, had no reservations about writing to both Consalvi and the Pope himself over a long period. He and his Roman Catholic first wife, Mrs. Fitzherbert, were generous to the French émigrés and

[1] See 17th April 1821. *Hansard*, Vol. NS V, p. 78 n.

[2] 6th March 1827, *Hansard*, vol. NS XVI, p. 1000 *et seq.*

[3] Realisation of the public dislike may have encouraged him to adopt a popular attitude.

[4] *The Victorian Church*, Vol. I, Owen Chadwick, Adam and Charles Black, 1966, pp. 12–13.

although he may have felt piqued at the Pope's reception of his second and estranged wife, Caroline, when she was living in Italy, this did not prevent his writing to the Pontiff. Pius VII himself wrote to the Regent to thank him for having placed the Fleet at his disposal in the spring of 1816; and when a British squadron helped to free some Christian captives held by Muslims, the Pope wrote again.[1] Castlereagh helped the Pope to recover some of the Vatican art treasures removed by Napoleon to the Louvre. The British ship *Abundance* sailed with the precious objects from the port of Antwerp at the expense to the British government of 200,000 francs for transporting them from Paris to Rome. On 6th July 1816 Pius wrote to thank the Regent; and on 9th December the Prince replied with gratitude for a 'temple and cup in Rosso Antico'.[2] There was also a present for Castlereagh. A number[3] of further letters passed between them during the Regency; and on 29th April 1820[4] George wrote thanking the Pope for his letter of congratulation upon his accession to the throne. This correspondence is notable because so many people suppose that all communication of this sort ended with the Reformation and that it has only recently been resumed.

More important still was the commissioning by the Regent of the portraits of Pius VII and Consalvi by Sir Thomas Lawrence. Sir Thomas arrived in Rome in May 1819 where he became a firm friend of Consalvi.[5] The paintings now hang in the Waterloo Gallery at Windsor Castle. Pius became ill in the summer of 1823 and the Duchess of Devonshire, who lived in Rome, wrote to tell George IV, as he then was:

> Your majesty has always expressed so great an interest about His Holiness that I flatter myself that these few lines . . . may be acceptable to you, tho' alas their contents are of a melancholy nature.[6]

[1] 23rd September 1816. *La Civiltà Cattolica*, Vol. III, 1923, pp. 398–9.
[2] *Letters of George IV, 1812–1820*, ed. A. Aspinall, CUP, 1938, Vol. II, pp. 181–2.
[3] ibid., Vol. II, pp. 194, 199, 243.
[4] ibid., Vol. II, p. 327.
[5] Sir Thomas, writing to Sir William Knighton (Keeper of Privy Purse) on 11th November 1823 commented on Consalvi's distinguished qualities and affection for the person of the King. ibid., Vol. III, p. 40.
[6] ibid., Vol. III, p. 6. 8th July 1823.

On 20th August 1823 Pius VII died aged 81,[1] and Consalvi on 24th January 1824. The Duke of Devonshire had written to tell the King of Consalvi's state of health;[2] George IV wrote to the Cardinal to thank him for his continued interest and kindness on questions which concerned this country. But the letter arrived too late. He left legacies to English friends, the Duchess of Devonshire and members of Castlereagh's family; but within his own circle Consalvi was less influential. His attempts to reform the papal government, for which he worked out a project, were frustrated by reactionary fellow-cardinals. He sought to secularise the administration and to introduce laymen into official positions, but bishops and cardinals retained their power.[3] Had Consalvi been given a hearing the problems which beset this hierarchical government in the succeeding half-century would not have been so serious.

The communications that passed between Rome and London in regard to the return of the Jesuit order are of no particular significance to this history,[4] and it is necessary to return once again to the House of Commons. Canning introduced a motion for the repeal of the act of Charles II banning Roman Catholic peers from sitting and voting in the House of Lords, which passed its third reading on 17th May 1822. In the Upper House the bill failed by a majority of 42 which included the Archbishops of Canterbury and Dublin and 16 other bishops. The Bishop of Norwich (Bathurst) alone on the bench voted for the measure. There was every reason for Members to feel confused. On 11th May 1824 Canning asserted that the catholic question must be faced and would make its way, though the government was divided. George Tierney (member for Knaresborough) replied:

> Suppose it were carried here, it would, in all probability, be rejected by the other House. . . . Placed behind so good a leader as the Archbishop of Canterbury, a place-man would naturally think he was safe in all questions respecting Church

---

[1] He broke his femur in a fall in his study and died a few days later.
[2] ibid., Vol. III, p. 41. 20th November 1823.
[3] See E. E. Y. Hales, *Revolution and Papacy*, p. 262.
[4] They can be read in detail in J. T. Ellis, *Cardinal Consalvi and Anglo–Papal Relations*. Eyre and Spottiswood, 1965.

matters. How must it be then when he saw the Archbishop of York and seven other bishops enlisted on the same side?[1]

The following year yet another relief bill was introduced on 23rd March 1825 by Sir Francis Burdett (Member for Westminster). It received its third reading on 2nd May and passed to the Lords with a majority of 21, where it was rejected on 17th May by a majority of 48. The Bishop of Chester reflected on the evils which Roman Catholicism had inflicted on Europe. Moreover, dangerous legislation about tithes had passed the Irish House of Commons at the time of the Union: there was danger to church property if 20–30 Roman Catholic Members entered the House now. The terrible state of Ireland, unlike any other country in Europe, must be corrected by other measures, social, legal and economic.[2] Lord King expressed himself strongly on the subject of such utterances by the spiritual peers when on 7th March of the same year he said:

How far these reverend gentlemen ought thus to meddle with politics I will not now discuss: but they always seemed to take part in them. . . . As these reverend gentlemen bestirred themselves so much to find fault where they had no business, I think it would be but right to bring them back from where they had gone to where they ought to be.[3]

The record of parliamentary debates gives evidence that the situation in Ireland was deteriorating even further. The eloquence of the reformers knew no bounds, especially when describing the maintenance of the Anglican Church in Ireland by the Roman Catholic poor. On 9th March 1826 the Earl of Darnley compared the Irish situation with the emancipation of slaves: the House was concerning itself on another subject:

in which a certain portion of the community took a great interest: namely those measures which were adopted for ameliorating the condition of the slaves . . . of the West Indies. In fact the condition of the slaves in those islands was not, in many cases, so bad as the condition of the Irish poor. . . . He hoped their Lordships would feel as much

[1] *Hansard*, Vol. NS XI p. 722.
[2] *Hansard*, Vol. NS XIII, pp. 727–8.
[3] *Hansard*, Vol. NS XII, p. 936.

sympathy for the peasantry of Ireland, as they did for the slaves of the West Indies.[1]

However the Irish were forming an organised resistance, and what was more important, they had a leader in Daniel O'Connell[2] who was pressing for home rule for Ireland. In fact it was this inflammable situation which finally brought about catholic emancipation. It eventually seemed as if emancipation were less dangerous a prospect than civil war, at least so it appeared to such as Bishop Lloyd of Oxford.[3] The need for troops, he said, and the poverty and discontent of the country proved how impossible it was to maintain a permanent system of exclusion. The only thing to do was to let matters take their course and rely on Providence to bring light out of darkness and order out of anarchy: this was not necessarily the best road, but it was inevitable.[4] Another telling point against anti-emancipationists was that in Europe 100 million people were living freely without such exclusive laws. There were no laws against Dissenters in France, the Netherlands, Germany or Austria. 'If their lordships persisted in withholding their concurrence' said Lord Clifden on 8th February 1827[5] 'they would become a laughing stock. 380 men from Bedlam could not behave worse than their lordships.'

In the final round of this interminable struggle for catholic civil rights the central question became the nature of the securities which were to be offered and which were thought necessary for the maintanance of peace and the status quo in Church and State. First the Irish franchise was reduced and then in the spring of 1829 Peel,[6] who had so far opposed the catholic claims, changed his mind in the face of the serious Irish situation and introduced a relief bill into the House of Commons. During the course of a very long debate the divisions in the Cabinet became apparent. How many Roman Catholics would be returned if the measure went through? Did the

---

[1] *Hansard*, Vol. NS XIV, pp. 1200–1.
[2] Daniel O'Connell 1775–1847. Leader of the Irish Catholic Committee since 1808.
[3] *The Victorian Church*, Chadwick, Vol. I, p. 11.
[4] 2nd April 1829, *Hansard*, Vol. NS XXI, p. 79.
[5] *Hansard*, Vol. NS XVI, p. 407.
[6] Sir Robert Peel, 1st Bart. 1750–1830.

King's Coronation Oath stand in the way? Which offices was it safe to open to Roman Catholics? Many Members persisted in opposing the measure vigorously to the end. Thomas Greene (Member for Lancaster) expressed his conviction that the measure for emancipation if granted would cause the immediate destruction of the Church of Ireland, and that the destruction of that church would inevitably lead to the destruction of the established Church of England.[1] There was no form of religion in the world so little favourable to liberty as the Roman Catholic religion, said Sir Richard Vynyan.[2]

The third reading of the bill in the Commons on 30th March resulted in a majority of 178. In the Lords the bill had the expected stormy passage. Some asked for delay: others refused it; there was no need for further lengthy thought on this issue. The Bishop of St. Davids (John Jenkinson[3]) felt that the time had come to grant catholic emancipation, and he thought that the admission of Roman Catholics to civil privileges would tend to strengthen the establishment by uniting all parties in attachment to the constitution. The Bishop of Oxford (already quoted) felt the pressure of events in Ireland and this persuaded him that the measure should be adopted. It had been said that by admitting Roman Catholics to Parliament a political union was being made with idolatry: this had brought him intense anxiety and agony of mind and alarmed his conscience. But he had come to the conclusion that not all Papists were idolators. 'My lords I shall accept the bill'.[4] The overriding fear among the bishops was that they supposed that members of the Roman Church were committed to the overthrow of Anglicanism once political power was in their hands: pureness of religious doctrine and practice were in jeopardy. One way of counteracting this view was to minimise the power of Rome, if not its intentions. Lord Goderich[5] had put this very clearly on 9th June 1828:[6]

> ... the times are changed—a different feeling has spread itself throughout Europe: and though some noble lords may

[1] 27th March 1829, *Hansard*, Vol. NS XX, p. 1499.
[2] ibid., p. 1518.
[3] 2nd April 1829, *Hansard*, Vol. NS XXI, p. 41.   [4] ibid., pp. 75–9.
[5] Frederick John Robinson, Viscount Goderich, 1782–1859. Later 1st Earl of Ripon.
[6] *Hansard*, Vol. NS XIX, p. 1182.

consider the pope is as formidable now as he was in the earlier periods of the Christian Church, the real fact is, that the Church of Rome, as it was in former times no longer exists. . .
. . . I therefore say that the pope of these days is not the pope of former days: and I will further say (though I may be twitted for the phrase), that this is owing to the march of intellect.

There is no doubt that such opinions carried weight, except with such diehards as the Bishop of Bath and Wells (Dr. George Law) for whom the strength of his convictions made it impossible for him to come to terms with civil relief for catholics. Although largely inaudible, and therefore perhaps less influential, he was heard to say that the tenets of the Roman Catholic religion were totally and diametrically opposed to 'our own' and opposed in such a hostile manner as to render the grant of political power to Roman Catholics exceedingly dangerous.[1] Peers had frightened their wives and daughters about the power of the Pope and Popery, said another.[2] But despite such warnings the bill passed its third reading on 10th April 1829 with a majority of 104 (213 for and 109 against).[3] Twenty bishops voted against the measure and ten in favour. Those in favour were the Bishops of Chester, Derry, Kildare, Llandaff, Lichfield, Oxford, Rochester, St. Davids, Winchester, and that old stalwart the Bishop of Norwich, by proxy. The King accepted the bill with the greatest reluctance and, it is said that he wept as he signed it. That he did so at all has been attributed to the fact that his Prime Minister, the Duke of Wellington, who had steered the bill through the Lords, threatened to resign, and George IV could not have found another Minister to form a government. The details of the securities demanded by the bill are out of place here, since this is a history of relationships and attitudes, but they proved to be minimal, in order that the operation of the Act should not find Roman Catholics starting their political future with a sense of grievance. The oath to be taken by all Roman Catholic Members of Parliament was based on the 1791 oath, giving them

[1] 10th April 1829. *Hansard*, Vol. NS XXI, p. 677.
[2] Lord de Dunstanville, 7th April 1829. ibid., p. 471.
[3] ibid., pp. 693–7.

a separate oath in which they swore not to subvert the present church establishment of Great Britain. There was some doubt in Roman Catholic circles whether the oath was acceptable, but Pius VIII, in an audience granted to Bishop Baines, Vicar Apostolic of the Western District on 4th May 1829, said he could not approve the oath but neither could he condemn it.

The anticipated Roman Catholic landslide which caused so much fear never came: the election of 1830 returned only eight Irish catholic members to the House of Commons. It is difficult not to ridicule in retrospect the sense of insecurity which held up the measure for so long. Moreover, as Professor Chadwick[1] suggests, the majorities in Parliament did not reflect the feelings of the nation as a whole, which (despite some well-wishers) was indifferent or hostile to emancipation. In the end it was expediency and lack of political alternative, rather than principle, which won the day.

[1] *The Victorian Church*, Vol. I, p. 17.

7
THE 'CATHOLIC QUESTION'

The last chapter reviewed the opinions and public utterances of officials, particularly of the bench of bishops, to the 'catholic question.' A look at the attitudes of the lower clergy and of the laity of the two churches to each other will show whether, at this stage, among views on equal political rights for all, there are traces of a deeper charity towards members of another Christian body, and even a desire for unity between them.

One of the major sources of opinion on catholic emancipation is the record of petitions contained in the printed parliamentary debates.[1] 226 petitions were addressed by secular bodies to the House of Commons against further relief for catholics, between the years 1805 and 1828; these originated from a very large number of counties and towns, the universities of Oxford and Cambridge and such diverse parties as 113,000 householders of London, the Gentlemen of Wiltshire, the nobility of Kent, the magistrates of Bolton-le-Moor, the Bailiffs of Ipswich and groups of inhabitants, from Penzance to South Shields: they also included bodies of protestant dissenters from various parts and a group of French protestant refugees.

Petitions from religious bodies numbered 68 during the same period. These comprised the Deans and Chapters of ten Cathedrals—Exeter, Chester, Carlisle, St. Davids, Rochester, Worcester, Salisbury, Ely, Hereford and Gloucester. Petitions came also from the archdeacons and clergy of Berks, Winchester, St. Albans, East Riding, Suffolk, Salisbury, Middlesex,

---

[1] See the volumes of *Hansard* for this period: there is an index for the early years, but the lack of a complete index makes detailed reference very difficult.

Northampton, etc., and from numerous groups of clerics, from Norfolk, Huddersfield, Merioneth, Chichester, etc. On the other hand there were 140 petitions to the House of Commons during the same period in favour of emancipation. Although many of these had their origins among Roman Catholic groups, the 'inhabitants' of some large towns such as Exeter, Colchester, Bristol, Liverpool, Shrewsbury, Chesterfield, Glasgow, Nottingham, Birmingham and Leeds, the portmen of Ipswich, 6,000 people in York, 8,000 protestants in London, protestant dissenters in Liverpool and in the capital, sent in petitions in the Roman Catholic cause. Other groups included Sergeants and Barristers of the English bar, and 'some clergymen of Norfolk'. It looks as though opinion in the urban areas was more kindly disposed towards toleration than in the country. This tendency was also shown in the petitions in favour of civil rights sent to the House of Lords.[1] These numbered 48 and included some members of Oxford and Cambridge universities, the Archdeacons of Norwich and Sudbury and the Revd. John Pike-Jones, curate of North Bovey, Devon. Members of the established church who could regard the catholic question without fear or prejudice were much in the minority, and were regarded as eccentric and unreliable in their time.

Chief among the 'eccentrics' on the Anglican side who favoured toleration towards Catholics was the Revd. Sydney Smith,[2] Canon of St. Paul's Cathedral. Renowned for the brilliance of his wit and the kindness of his heart, Sydney Smith defied popular outrage and threw preferment to the winds by his writings in favour of toleration and against restrictive legislation of all kinds. Particularly did he criticize English policy in Ireland. The English, he said in his characteristic manner, were permanently bedridden with Erinphobia. The moment the very name of Ireland was mentioned, the English seemed to bid adieu to common feeling, common prudence and common sense, and to act with the barbarity of tyrants and the fatuity of idiots. So he exclaimed in a series of pamphlets which were published anonymously as letters from one Peter Plymley to his brother Abraham, a country clergyman. 'If our ancestors had excluded people with red hair from

[1] These do not include petitions also sent to the House of Commons.
[2] 1771–1845.

the House of Commons', he wrote 'I have often thought .... of the throes and convulsions it would occasion to restore them to their natural rights. What mobs and riots would it produce.'[1] On Sydney Smith's death some further unpublished writings were found among his papers in which came the question—why was England not represented at the Vatican? 'If ever a nation exhibited symptoms of downright madness or utter stupidity', so he summed up the matter in the Preface to his *Works*, 'we conceive these symptoms may be easily recognised in the conduct of this country upon the Catholic question.' Smith acted as he did not because he went out towards the views of the Roman Catholics, but because he believed that they should not be victimized for holding them.

'Persecution is the extreme of folly and can have no other tendency than to make those turbulent who would be otherwise peaceful.' The Revd. Rowland Hill[2] replied to Charles Butler's 'Appeal to the Protestants of Great Britain and Ireland'[3] in these words, and echoed, though with less wit, the sentiments of Sydney Smith. 'To make people act contrary to their religious sentiments is only compelling them to be hypocrites, and must be very injurious to the moral interests of mankind'. Rowland Hill shared Sydney Smith's practical view, that on the grounds of expediency the policy being pursued was foolish in the extreme and would cure nothing. One circumstance was unaccountable, he said, that so many Roman Catholics should make such large declarations in favour of candour and liberality towards what they call their protestant brethren, while the Church of England appeared the most hostile to their present claims. He was forced to admit that where the Roman Catholic Church prevailed, the spirit of intolerance was too often to be found, but this did not prevent him taking the argument a step further. The religion of Christ was the religion of love 'and they certainly are the best Christians, however denominated, whose faith produces the best fruits. It is impossible that we

[1] *The letters of Peter Plymley to his brother Abraham who lives in the country*, Intro. G. C. Heseltine, J. M. Dent, 1929, p. 38.
[2] 1744–1833. 6th son of Sir Rowland Hill, Bart., of Shropshire; ed Shrewsbury, Eton and St. John's College, Cambridge.
[3] Published 5th February 1813, *Works of Charles Butler*, Vol. IV, London, 1817, pp. 310–38.

should hate each other if we love God. To love God is to love holiness. Love therefore is the fulfilling of the law.'

The details of Rowland Hill's career show that, as with Sydney Smith, his chances of preferment were inhibited by the nature of his utterances; which nevertheless continued both in content and regularity. He took part in several religious and philanthropic movements of the time, as well as in treating Catholics as fellow Christians, with whom all 'shall throw away every sword but that sword of the spirit which is the word of God'.

Charles Butler had been anxious to point out that it was wrong to argue that the grievances of Roman Catholics were small, or that emancipation would bring no real benefit to the State. He emphasised the loyalty of Roman Catholics to the Crown and held that though they admitted the spiritual supremacy of the Pope, they denied him a temporal authority. If they had been wrong he said, let them say to a protestant: 'Brother . . . we have been in the wrong, let us learn wisdom from them, let us no more upbraid one another with our common failings: let us forget and forgive, bury all our past animosities in oblivion, shake hands and be friends.' Was the differences between the two Churches really as great as was generally thought? He listed the similarities. 'And after all, is the Reunion of the Roman Catholic and Protestant Churches absolutely impossible? Bossuet, the glory of the Catholic Church and her ablest champion, thought it was not.'

These sentiments were taken up in the year 1818 by a divine of the established church, Samuel Wix, Vicar of St. Bartholomew the Less in London, who during the course of a lengthy pamphlet[1] suggested that a Council be held in which the Church of England and the Church of Rome might reconcile their differences and come to a union. He was realistic in his initial approach, starting with the bland statement that: 'It is well known how unprepared the majority of Protestants will be to receive our proposal towards an union between themselves and the Roman Catholics.' Nevertheless he proposed that a Council

[1] 'Reflections concerning the expediency of a Council of the Church of England and the Church of Rome with a view to accommodate religious differences and to promote the unity of religion in the bond of peace', Samuel Wix, A.M., F.R.S.A., London, Rivington, 1818.

should be called 'in a spirit of candid concession: in a humble disposition to renounce whatever opinions or practices, after sincere prayer to the Almighty, and charitable consultation, shall appear erroneous'. Again, with realism, Wix admitted that to attempt to unite in one common religious body would be as absurd as it was unscriptural: 'absurd because it would affect to accomplish what the knowlege of the human heart and all experience prove never can be generally accomplished, namely a sincere union between persons of discordant professions of Christianity; and unscriptural because we are exhorted "earnestly to contend for the Faith, which was once delivered to the saints" '. It was our duty, therefore, to ascertain what that Faith was, and to ascertain what was the belief of those Christians who lived immediately after the Apostolic age and who, therefore, must have known from an acquaintance with customs and expressions then existing, much better than at later times it was possible to pretend to know, the intentions of the writers of the New Testament. A general council or assembly of Christians of the visible Church should be called together in which all the leading articles of difference might be candidly considered, dispassionately compared with early opinion and uncorrupted tradition, and mutual concessions made. Here Wix departed from his realism: would that the solution to the problem of disunity had been capable of being resolved after this fashion. The Church of England he felt 'she being the great reformed Church in Apostolic succession should propose to the Church of Rome . . . whether some plan might not be devised to accommodate their religious differences. The Church of Rome might, perhaps, relax in what the Church of England considers her fundamental errors, and the Church of England might incline a little more than she does to some of the favourite opinions or practices of the Roman Church, which are not unscriptural.' Wix then outlined what were, to his Anglican mind, the errors of the Roman Church, 'But here surely, if a proper Christian temper on both sides were cultivated, mutual advances to conciliation might be made.'

The Revd. William Harness,[1] of St. Pancras Parochial Chapel in Regent Square, also went so far as to suggest that a

---

[1] Formerly of Christ's College, Cambridge.

union could take place between the Churches of England and Rome. Preaching in two sermons in 1829 which were quoted and commented upon (very critically) in the *Christian Review* he said:

> There are many points of contact. The difficulties of this work are not so considerable as the bigoted of either side would represent, or the ignorant are led to imagine . . . Nothing but the spirit of humility and charity in the negotiating parties is required to secure that blessing on their endeavours which the peace-maker may always hope for . . . By the reunion of all Episcopal Churches . . . we should also be gainers in charity, the richest treasure our Christian can ever gain.[1]

Here was the crux of the matter put plainly: some exceptional members of each communion saw beyond the particular interpretation of the faith developed by their own traditions, with its limitations, to a wider view. This they did largely because the promptings of charity and hatred of schism were stronger than their fears of error. The majority were genuinely apprehensive of conciliation because it might involve compromising truth and condoning error; might jeopardise salvation and risk the loss of personal integrity.[2] It has taken another 150 years for the representatives of the two Christian Churches *as a whole* to be willing to take the risks involved in the search for union which was mooted so long ago.

On the Roman Catholic side there were also some protagonists, though few, for reconciliation: most of their apologists favoured a return of the prodigal to the Roman Church as she stood. An exception was Dr. James Warren Doyle, Roman Catholic Bishop of Kildare and Leighlin, who in 1822 was in correspondence with Archbishop William Magee of Dublin. Magee had complained that the Romans by their attachment to the word 'Catholic' excluded from the pale of the Church all those to whom they refused participation in that name. But

---

[1] *Christian Review*, 1829, pp. 44–5.
[2] John Jebb 1775–1833, Bishop of Limerick 1822–1833 was on most friendly terms with his Roman Catholic neighbours; but he made no overtures for reunion and was opposed to political power for Roman Catholics.

Dr. Doyle said that Roman Catholics believed as others: 'We consider that whoever is baptized is incorporated into Christ and has no "damnation in him", and that if he retain the Grace of that first adoption pure and unsullied until death, he enters heaven—no matter to what sect or denomination of Christians while on earth, he may have belonged.' On 13th May 1824 the bishop addressed a letter[1] to a Member of Parliament, Alexander Robertson, Member for Grampound, who on 6th May of the same year had made a speech in the House of Commons[2] urging the union of the churches in Ireland, which he considered perfectly feasible. A certain amount of confusion has arisen over this letter and some commentators[3] have thought that it was addressed to Frederick John Robinson, Chancellor of the Exchequer,[4] but this is not the case. Bishop Doyle wrote:

The union of the Churches, however, which you have had the singular merit of suggesting to the Commons of the U.K. would together and at once effect a total change in the dispositions of men; it would bring all classes to co-operate jealously in promoting the prosperity of Ireland and in securing for ever her allegiance to the British Throne.

The time is favourable, for the Government is powerful and at peace; the Pope is powerless and anxious to conciliate; the Irish Catholics are wearied and fatigued exceedingly desirous of repose; the Established religion is almost frittered away, and the Monarchy, a thing unprecedented in a Christian State, is left in one country, with only the staff of the Church, to use the expression of Mr. Hume, and in the other with less than a moiety of the people attached to the Hierarchy.

The Clergy without, I believe, an exception would make every possible sacrifice to effect a Union; I myself would most cheerfully and without fee, pension, emolument or hope, resign the office which I hold, if by doing so I could in any

---

[1] From Carlow. Published W. Battersby & Co., Dublin, 1824.
[2] *Hansard*, Vol. ns XI, p. 568.
[3] *Life, Times and Correspondence of Bishop Doyle*, W. J. Fitzpatrick, 2 vols., J. Duffy, Dublin, 1861.
[4] Afterwards Lord Ripon, see p. 97.

way contribute to the union of my brethren and the happiness of my country. . . . it appears to me that there is no essential difference between Catholics and Protestants; the existing diversity of opinion arises, in most cases, from certain forms of words which admit of satisfactory explanation or from the ignorance or misconceptions which ancient prejudice and ill-will produce and strengthen, but which could be removed; they are pride and points of honour which keep us divided on many subjects, not a love of Christian humility, charity and truth.[1]

He asked that Mr. Robertson would again call the attention of Parliament to the consideration of this important subject.

A further proposal from the Roman side 'for the reconciliation of the Protestant and Roman Catholic Churches' came from an individual who signed himself 'an Irish parish priest' and was brought to public notice through the pages of the *Dublin University Magazine* of 1841.[2] The editors expressed themselves pleased to print the anonymous communication, not from any belief that it could lead to any important results, but on account of its author, who represented a great contrast to the majority of his brethren. The anonymous writer said he was a parish priest or Roman Catholic pastor of a country parish far removed from the metropolis, 'but whether north, south, east or west, I am not at present disposed to tell'. He spoke of regular meetings with his clerical neighbours and discussions of matters of Church and State: for some months their meetings had been systematic, with rules by which they were regulated and assemblies on certain days. The subjects chosen had included the doctrine of the Puseyites and the view was taken that this could be interpreted as a move towards the Roman Catholic Church. This led in turn to the suggestion that this step towards a general reconciliation ought to be encouraged and that it would be most desirable if their Church could do something towards the union of all in the profession of one faith: the present was an excellent opportunity. Some resolutions had been approved: that the Protestant and Roman Catholic religions agreed in all the fundamental articles of the

---

[1] *An Eirenicon of the eighteenth-century*, (ed. H. N. Oxenham). Rivingtons, 1879. Appendix A has a copy of the letter.
[2] No. CVI, Vol. XVIII, October 1841.

Christian faith and that the differences of these churches were in many cases more apparent than real: and the particular points of belief on which they really disagreed were really but few. It appeared that there was a disposition on the part of some of the most distinguished amongst the Protestant divines to come to a better understanding and, if properly encouraged, perhaps to a final adjustment of religious differences. Such a settlement should be promoted and if possible secured. This could never be done except through a spirit of Christian charity and because this spirit had been manifested by certain Anglican divines, they implored pontiff and prelates to show a like feeling by such concessions and salutary reforms 'as would at once befit the times in which we live and invite to peace and union our dissenting brethren'.

> Our object [said they] is, if possible, to procure an amalgamation of the two great rival churches, by inducing the members of our own communion to go forward as far as they can to meet those of a different way of thinking who have already advanced some steps to join them. How is this to be done? By concession on the part of the Roman Catholic Church and the adoption by her of some rational schemes. . . . Friendly colloquies and mutual negotiations, in the proper quarters, will do much for the purpose we contemplate.

Three further 'letters from a parish priest' appeared in the *Dublin University Magazine* in November and December 1841 and February 1842 in which it was maintained that support and a correspondence had been results of the articles. Since, however, among the reforms which were suggested for the Roman Church the lifting of the ban on clerical marriage stood high up on the list, the scheme did not stand a chance at that moment, and was soon lost in oblivion.

The foregoing were all examples of thinking which was against the popular trend. Up and down the country meetings were being held in protest against what were held to be the Roman Church's misinterpretation of the faith. On six days in February and March 1834, for example, discussions were held at the Roman Catholic College of Downside between the protagonists of the Roman Catholic and established Churches under the aegis of the Reformation Society.[1] Again, Ann, Mrs. Capper, daughter of the Revd. Isaac Saunders, vicar of St. Andrew's-by-the-Wardrobe in the City of London, wrote to her unmarried sister, Jane Caroline, from her home in Cheltenham on 23rd August 1830:

> And now I must tell you about the Discussion Meetings that have taken place here. I suppose you heard what I told Mama about it . . . How long they will continue no one knows. The papists declare they won't give way—5 days they have been on the rule of faith repeating the same objections that have been answered over and over again.[2]

The fact that discussions were taking place was a step forward; and that they should not be merely polemical was being urged by at least some church leaders. Shute Barrington,[3] for 57 years a bishop and for 35 of them Bishop of Durham and a noted evangelical, wrote in a Charge to his clergy in 1806.

> The Romanists and the Dissenters from our Church, afford us an example of zeal and union, and perseverance, which well deserves our imitation. In recommending zeal, it may appear needless for me to caution you against want of charity towards those who do not belong to our communion. Our defect lies more in lukewarmness and indifference, than in bitterness of spirit. Be zealous then in the discharge of your duty; but be charitable. Charity is certainly not incompatible with the most active zeal against erroneous and defective institutions.[4]

In his Charge of 1810 this same prelate had extended his views to cause him to consider the grounds of union between the Churches of England and Rome. He had made his own position clear in his introductory letter to the clergy on 14th April of that year when he wrote:

[1] Discussions, published J. G. & F. Rivington, St. Paul's Churchyard, 1836.

[2] From the collection of manuscript letters of her great-great-aunt in the possession of Mrs. A. J. M. Saint.

[3] 1734–1826. Youngest son of first Viscount Barrington. Bishop of Llandaff 1769; Salisbury 1782; Durham 1791.

[4] *Sermons, Charges and Tracts*, Shute, Bishop of Durham, London, 1811, p. 342.

I am far from being of opinion that no one can be saved within the pale of the Church of Rome; but I do think that any one who lives in habits of idolatory. . . is in a dangerous state.

I have also to add that I use the term Papist or Romanist, not as a reproach, but in assertion of our own right, because the acknowledgement of the term *Catholic* as appropriate to the Church of Rome, and in opposition to Protestant, is an implied exclusion of ourselves from the Catholic Church, in which of course we cannot acquiesce.

In the 1810 Charge Bishop Barrington described how he saw in the contemporary circumstances of Europe better grounds of hope for a successful issue to an investigation of the differences which separated the two Churches than at any former period. 'With this view and these hopes I continue to exact my humble efforts in the great cause of Charity and Truth'.

May that Gracious Saviour [he continued] who has left us with the record of his Gospel his own anxious prayer for the union of his disciples, promote and prosper the blessed work of CATHOLIC UNION, and for this purpose may he divest the minds of both Protestants and Papists of all prejudice and passion, of all indirect and uncandid views and of every feeling contrary to the spirit of the Gospel.[1]

Here was a man still seeing truth in terms of his own interpretation of the faith, but willing to undertake mutual exchange of views and to envisage a union between the two churches as desirable and even eventually possible. These tentative suggestions, although few and ill-received by the churches at large at this period, were to be taken up and developed into reunion movements by certain individuals of the generation which followed. They received no great encouragement even then. In fact they suffered opposition, which successfully put an end to the aspirations of the enthusiasts for reunion for another hundred years. But the desire to come closer together and the initiative to canalize these hopes into a working group can be seen in a study of the personalities concerned.

[1] op. cit., p. 445.

8

THE OXFORD MEN

With the birth of the 'Oxford Movement' the whole matter of the relationships between the Roman Catholic Church and the Church of England entered a new and more hopeful phase. Yet the pedigree of the Oxford Movement is to be found in the evangelical revival of the previous century. The understanding of Anglican Church history, if not the course of history itself, has been obscured by those who think of movements of the Holy Spirit which are merely diverse as if they were opposed. Spiritual revival in any form has always been resisted by the complacent lethargic church. Wesley and the Evangelicals were so scandalised by the formalities of 'established' religion that they went all the more enthusiastically in search of an inspiration which they felt could not be found in a valley of dry bones. By the 1820s the evangelical inspiration had either cooled off, or led some to secede from the Church or been canalised into small areas where it turned in upon itself and lost its widest influence. The early Oxford fathers also found themselves in search of an inspiration and opposed to a barren, 'established' form of religion which did not seem able to discern between the proper functions of Church and State.

Thus it is that resemblances between the two movements, in spite of contrasting superficial appearances, can easily be traced. The fact that they were both refugees from formalism in search of holiness, under very different circumstances, is a stronger mutual characteristic than the variety of expression which their respective searches took on. Newman, still under the influence of an evangelical upbringing, first appeared in the

III

public eye by writing letters to the *Record* on the subject of church reform. The *Tract*, with which the Oxford Movement is so closely associated in the common mind, is itself a legacy from the evangelical tradition.

The Oxford Movement was the Church of England's response to the external hostile forces which were ranged against it at the beginning of the nineteenth century. The evangelical inspiration of the previous century was heavily biased towards concern with the salvation of individuals rather than with the preservation of institutions, no matter how sacred. That was another reason why those who were moved by the nineteenth-century spiritual revival had to look elsewhere for their leadership. When they found that it was not coming from the leaders of the Church as formally constituted they organised themselves into groups to propagate their spiritual aims. The main carry-over from the evangelical tradition to the Oxford Movement was a concern that the Church should show more conspicuously the characteristic notes of 'holiness' and 'apostolicity'. The pursuit of these ideals led their thoughts on, by a natural train of development, to the other two characteristic notes of the Church, 'catholicity' and 'oneness'.

We see the last traces of the alliance in the condemnation by both the evangelicals and the new Movement of Dr. Hampden, appointed Regius Professor of Divinity on the nomination of Melbourne. Hampden had delivered the Bampton Lectures in 1832 in which he seemed to have thrown doubts on the creeds and their authority.

The spirit of secular liberalism let loose in the wake of the French Revolution was another force which indirectly called the Oxford Movement into existence. This had found expression in the natural revulsion felt by thinking people against the idleness and corruption of church dignitaries. This in its turn was traceable to the subservience of the Church to the State, which by its control of the appointment of dignitaries had tended to discourage 'enthusiasm' and to promote those clerics who were least likely to trouble the waters either of politics or of religion. When however the left wing of the political world saw itself called to effect changes in the Church (particularly financial ones) even those clerics who, like the first members of the Oxford Movement, agreed that the Church was in need of reforms, found themselves not able to subscribe to the idea that the State should reform the Church ab extra.

Thus it was that the Movement felt called to seek first principles in the whole question of the Church and its place in the world. As far as relations with the Church of Rome were concerned there was no help there, and nobody at the outset could have thought it possible that she should have come into the picture at all. The first members would all have agreed that whatever the Church was or should be, it should not be what Rome had become, a centralised bureaucracy under the despotic rule of the Pope. In England, they held, the Roman Catholic Church was schismatic, an intruder. For many of the Tractarians the passing of Catholic Emancipation was a turning point, for it showed them most vividly what the main shape of their own uneasiness was to be. Their duty was then to claim for the Church of England the true name of catholic, which meant that it must claim the right to make decisions concerning its own future independently of the State. But the catholicism so claimed would not exactly correspond with that of Rome. Protestantism, on the other hand, with its disastrous tendency to join forces with the State against the independence of the Church, was equally to be avoided.

Under these circumstances it is not surprising that the Movement began to think of the Church as a Via Media, a term which in those days served a useful purpose. But to anyone who used it then, or who uses it now, it is important to insist that it is a rule of thumb invented ad hoc to describe a situation as it was in one point of history: it is easy enough to see how when misused it can be magnified into the status of a philosophy. It then becomes the banner of a colourless churchmanship and the enemy of zeal. The phrase neatly described the position in which the English Church at that time was meant to stand, in defence of the genuine catholic tradition of the Church, free from Roman 'errors' on one side and protestant excesses on the other. So far from this being a negative position in current discussion, it was conceived from the first as one which must have a positive programme of attack—attack meant to assail the enemies who were bearing down on the Church from two sides at once.

The incident which set the Movement on an active course was

the proposed suppression of some of the Irish bishoprics in the Irish Church bill of 1833. This raised the Church and State issue, which led to Keble's Assize Sermon,[1] to the famous meeting in Hadleigh Rectory, and so to the Tracts.

The 'Advertisement' to the First Edition of the Assize Sermon included the following passage:

> ... The Legislature of England and Ireland (the members of which are not even bound to profess beliefs in the Atonement), this body has virtually usurped the commission of those whom our Saviour entrusted with at least one voice in making ecclesiastical laws, on matters wholly or partly spiritual. The same legislature has also ratified, to its full extent, this principle,—that the Apostolical Church in this realm is henceforth only to stand, in the eye of the State, as one among many, depending, for any pre-eminence she may still appear to retain, merely upon the accident of her having a strong party in the country. ...
>
> What answer can we make henceforth to the partisans of the bishop of Rome, when they taunt us with being a mere Parliament Church? And how, consistently with our present relations to the State, can even the doctrinal purity and integrity of the MOST SACRED ORDER be preserved? ...

These words sounded like a direct challenge to a duel. The purpose of the campaign was in general to make the English Church aware of its true nature and to re-establish its confidence in itself and so to brace it to maintain its rights and status in a secularising world. The first tract, by Newman himself, was on 'Thoughts on the Ministerial Commission': it raised immediately the question of the Apostolical Succession, which it claimed for the Ministry of the English Church. Side by side with the writing of the Tracts went a number of other activities which gave an effective intellectual and devotional solidity to the movement. Chief among them were the pastoral zeal of the members themselves, particularly of Keble; the new type of preaching and catechetical instruction of which the most famous example was that of Newman at the University Church of Oxford; an elaborate and systematic exploration of the Fathers which was undertaken by their scholars; and a

[1] 14th July 1833, in St. Mary's, Oxford.

flowering of devotional poetry such as the 'Christian Year' of Keble and the 'Lyra Apostolica' of Newman. The Movement achieved considerable success in its early years, chiefly by the accession of influential members. Of these the most famous was E. B. Pusey, Regius Professor of Hebrew, from whom eventually the Movement took one of its chief nicknames.

The Movement did not start out with any particular intentions in any direction towards what we now call 'shades of churchmanship', higher or lower or anything in between. Its aim was to make the Church of England what it essentially was called to be, and perhaps even to clarify or develop what that vocation was. As over against the 'evangelical excess' it felt obliged to stress the emphasis which then was called Arminian.[1] As over against the State it stood for the independence and 'catholic' authority of the Church. As over against the Latitudinarian concept of church membership then prevailing Dr. Pusey felt moved to write some masterly Tracts on Baptism, three of them, not pleading a special 'slant' on it, but just stating objectively what it had always been taken to be, and what for membership of the Church, were the implications of it. It was inevitable that right at the outset the reformers would have to take up a position vis-à-vis the Church of Rome. Newman had been abroad, mainly in Italy, with Hurrell Froude at the beginning of the Movement and returned with his position quite clear. In 1836 he delivered a series of lectures in St. Mary's at Oxford on 'Romanism and Popular Protestantism'. In them he drew a distinction between what was Catholic and what was Roman, but found himself already speaking objectively, if critically, of the Church of Rome and even saying things in its favour. This, in that particular generation, was a rare occurrence. The same year Mgr. Nicholas Wiseman,[2] recently arrived from Rome, entered the lists against the Oxford men by delivering in London a series of lectures on the Doctrines and Practices of the Roman Catholic Church. This issue was brought further forward into the public gaze by the

[1] i.e. in the following of the Dutch theologian Arminius (1560–1609). By this time it was a term loosely given to theologians who reacted away from Calvinism.

[2] 1802–1865. 1840 Co-adjutor Midland District; President of Oscott. Cardinal Archbishop of Westminster 1850.

publication, in 1838, of the *Remains* of Hurrell Froude, who had recently died. The *Remains* were in fact an intimate diary, not suitable for publication, and it is not surprising that its appearance caused dismay and set back the fortunes of the Movement. The harm consisted in criticisms of the Reformation of the sixteenth century, then sacrosanct in most Anglican minds. Hurrell Froude had said, for example, 'I am becoming less and less a son of the Reformation'[1] and 'The Reformation was a limb badly set; it must be broken again to be righted.'[2] Whatever were the rights and wrongs of the matter, the publication of such sentiments so early in the history of the Movement inevitably gave rise to misunderstandings. By 20th May 1838, when the effect of the Froude *Remains* had been added to the general impression created by the Tracts, Dr. Faussett, Lady Margaret Professor, said in a university sermon:

> To affirm that these persons are strictly Papists, or that within certain limits of their own devising they are not actually opposed to the corruptions and the Communion of Rome, would I believe, be as uncharitable as it is untrue. But who shall venture to pronounce them safe and consistent members of the Church of England? and who shall question the obvious tendency of their views to Popery itself?[3]

It is true that no advance in ecumenical understanding would be possible until the Reformation and the Council of Trent could both be regarded objectively as climacterics of history which were past, But prudence might have shown that at that early stage it was still the time for patient rebuilding on old foundations, and not for demolition. S. L. Ollard, in his *Short History of the Oxford Movement*[4] describes the *Remains* as a 'quarry to which every protestant controversialist has gone for stones to throw at the Oxford Movement'. The reaction which their publication provoked in Oxford led among other things to the erection by public subscription of the Martyrs' Memorial.

[1] *Remains*, London, J. G. & F. Rivington, 1838, Vol. I, p. 336.
[2] ibid., p. 433
[3] *History of the Romeward Movement in the Church of England 1833–64*, Walter Walsh, James Nisbet, 1900. p. 100.
[4] Mowbrays, 1915.

Liddon records[1] that Pusey subscribed to the Memorial, not only because it was politic that he should do so, but as a sincere believer that the English Church should honour the martyrs of its Reformation.

The very success of the Movement had also begun to make it enemies. The main chronicle of the Movement from one of its chief participants is that of Dr. R. W. Church[2] who recorded that:

From the end of 1835, or the beginning of 1836, the world outside of Oxford began to be alive to the force and the rapid growth of this new and, to the world at large, not very intelligible movement. The ideas which had laid hold so powerfully on a number of leading minds in the University, began to work with a spell, which seemed to many inexplicable, on others unconnected with them. This rapidity of expansion, viewed as a feature of a party, was noticed on all sides, by enemies no less than friends.[3]

The principal charge on the bill of indictment was to be that the Movement was pushing the Church of England in a Romeward direction—as though that could be assumed without argument to be a condemnation of everything it said and did. Considering the circumstances in which the Movement was called into being, that of an alleged trespass by the State on the liberties of the Church, and the immediate need to define the nature and extent of the Church, it was inevitable that the 'Roman Question' should appear at an early stage. When the Tracts began it was an aim of their publication to cut the ground from under the papal claims by recourse to the history and doctrines of the early centuries of the Church's life. An advertisement to Volume I of the Tracts, published in 1834, claimed that

nothing but these neglected doctrines, faithfully preached, will repress the extension of Popery, for which the ever-multiplying divisions of the religious world are clearly preparing the way.

---

[1] *Life of E. B. Pusey*, H. P. Liddon, Longmans Green, 1893, Vol. 2, pp. 64–76.

[2] Richard William Church, 1815–1890. Fellow of Oriel College, 1838. Dean of St. Paul's 1871.

[3] *The Oxford Movement 1833–45*, R. W. Church, Macmillan, 1891, p. 171.

Newman wrote in 1835:

> The controversy with the Romanists has overtaken us 'like a
> summer's cloud'. We find ourselves in various parts of the
> country preparing for it, yet, when we look back, we cannot
> trace the steps by which we arrived at our present position.
> We do not recollect what our feelings were this time last year
> on the subject; what was the state of our apprehensions and
> anticipations. All we know is, that here we are, from long
> security ignorant why we are not Roman Catholics, and they
> on the other side are said to be spreading and strengthening
> on all sides of us, vaunting of their success, real or apparent,
> and taunting us with our inability to argue with them.[1]

Newman had begun with a strong distaste for Roman Catholicism, a distaste which was confirmed by his visits abroad in
Roman Catholic countries. His main contribution to the
development of relationships between the two bodies during his
Anglican days was to make many Anglicans view the Roman
question objectively, to represent it as it was, to speak and
write calmly about the Roman Church without fear or favour,
and to banish bigotry and prejudice from their consideration of
it. It was part of the exercise to examine the Roman Catholic
objections to Anglican claims and formularies and to refute
them.

But we must now turn our attention to two developments
which had profound effects on the progress of relationships.
The first of these was the evolution of Newman's own attitude
to Rome and the second was the change which came over the
Oxford Movement after his eventual departure from it.

In 'Romanism and Popular Protestantism' Newman had
traced his development from those early days when, to him, the
Pope was Anti-Christ. Even after the beginnings of the Movement Newman had found himself taking up a less sympathetic
attitude on the Roman question than, for example, Hurrell
Froude. Newman's reading was wider and his thought deeper;
and steeped as he was in the writings of the Anglican divines of
the two previous centuries and of the Fathers, his estimate of
the teachings of nineteenth-century Rome was unfavourable.
Nevertheless, though she was undoubtedly in serious error she

[1] Tract 71.

was still the de facto channel of God's word and of his grace to most of Christendom, and as such entitled to great respect.

The main thrust of Newman's case against Rome was on Infallibility—34 years, that was, before Infallibility was infallibly defined by the First Vatican Council. In his examination of the Roman case and his demonstration of its weaknesses he was objective enough to admit also the weaknesses of the Anglican notion of authority. Yet it is not possible to find in his writings explicitly stated the hoped-for conclusion (now widely recognised) that in a divided church there is no possibility of a satisfactory definition of authority, let alone of infallibility.

In the summer of 1839 Newman undertook a study of the Monophysites, which he found unsettled his confidence in his Anglican position. The position of the Church of Rome, he began to believe, was the same now as it was in the fifth century. In this he was making an unreal abstraction of the juridical from the other aspects of her existence. For the lex orandi is indeed the lex credendi; and that the mystical, liturgical and catechetical content of her doctrinal position had expanded since beyond recognition he seemed to ignore from that time on. Later in the same year an article in the *Dublin Review* by Wiseman, in which the author compared the position of the Anglicans vis-à-vis the Papacy to that of the Donatists, caused him to be further unsettled, in fact gave him 'a stomach-ache'.[1] He even allowed himself to be disturbed by St. Augustine's phrase 'Securus iudicat orbis terrarum', speaking of the Donatist situation, as if that could have parallel application in the situation of a seriously divided Christendom.

Newman's crisis was however precipitated by his writing of Tract 90, in which he went to great lengths to show that the 39 Articles of the Church of England were capable of a 'catholic' interpretation, and that Rome had not seriously deviated from the catholic faith in the definitions of the Council of Trent. One of the objects of writing the Tract had been to dissuade those who were contemplating secession to Rome, such as W. G. Ward[2] and Frederick Oakeley, from doing so. The

[1] *Letters and Correspondence of J. H. Newman*, Anne Mozley, 2 vols., Longmans, 1898, Vol. II, p. 286.

[2] William George Ward, 1812–1882. Fellow of Balliol. Author of *Ideal of a Christian Church*. Roman Catholic 1845. Married; therefore did not become a priest. Taught at St. Edmund's Ware. 1863–1878 editor of *Dublin Review*.

effect of the Tract was immediate, and catastrophic, and the sequence of events too familiar to need more than bare mention here. First a group of four tutors (including a future Archbishop of Canterbury), then the Heads of Houses, declared their disapproval. Censure by the University was prevented by the veto of the Proctors, one of whom was R. W. Church. Cumulative opposition soon became evident, and ultimately led to episcopal censure. Newman undertook to discontinue the Tracts and withdrew from his ministry at the University Church to Littlemore. Blow upon blow then seemed to fall on the Movement. Dr. Pusey was condemned by the University without a hearing and suspended from preaching for two years for a sermon on 'The Holy Eucharist as a comfort to the Penitent'. Then came the proposals for a Jerusalem bishopric— a scheme whereby a see was to be set up in Jerusalem, to be occupied alternately by an Anglican and a Lutheran, without formal proposals for union, with the implication that the Anglican churches had no convictions concerning theology or ministry to distinguish them from Lutherans. Meanwhile the episcopal censure of the Tracts gathered momentum. It was perhaps this which brought Newman to the parting of the ways. For the position which he had upheld from the start of the Movement was that the Church of England, if left to itself and allowed to exercise its sovereign rights, would show itself to be genuinely inclusive of catholicism as well as upholding the true principles of the Protestant Reformation. Newman had subsequently considered himself as holding on, as a sort of penance, in a church which was indeed separated from the centre of catholic communion, preparing the ground for a wider reformed catholicism until it should be right and opportune for it to return whence it came. In 1839 he had written to his friend Frederick Rogers:

> Well, then, once more; as those who sin after Baptism cannot at once return to their full privileges, yet are not without hope, so a Church which has broken away from the centre of unity is not at liberty at once to return, yet is not nothing. May she not put herself into a state of penance? Are not her children best fulfilling their duty to her—not by leaving her, but by promoting her return, and not

thinking that they have a right to rush into such higher state as communion with the centre of unity might give them. If the Church Catholic, indeed, has actually commanded their return to her at once, that is another matter; but this she cannot have done without pronouncing their present Church good for nothing, which I do not suppose Rome has done of us. In all this, which I did not mean to have inflicted on you, I assume, on the one hand, that Rome is right; on the other, that we are not bound by uncatholic subscriptions.[1]

But now that the bishops of the Church of England (including the comparatively sympathetic Dr. Bagot, his own bishop) had turned against him, the pattern of his loyalties took on a very different shape, for the misunderstanding was severe.[2]

Staggering under these blows Newman began seriously to examine his position again, to see whether he had in fact been wrong in his premises all the time. Yet even at this late stage he wrote to the Bishop of Oxford in these terms:

They find in what I have written no abuse, at least I trust not, of the individual Roman Catholic, nor of the Church of Rome, viewed abstractedly as a Church. I cannot speak against the Church of Rome, viewed in her formal character, as a true Church, since she is 'built upon the foundation of the Apostles and Prophets, Jesus Christ Himself being the Chief Corner Stone'. Nor can I speak against her private members, numbers of whom, I trust, are God's people, in the way to Heaven, and one with us in heart, though not in profession. But what I have spoken, and do strongly speak against, is that energetic system and engrossing influence in the Church by which it acts towards us, and meets our eyes, like a cloud filling it, to the eclipse of all that is holy, whether in its ordinances or its members. This system I have called, in what I have written, Romanism or Popery. . . . I wish from my heart we and they were one; but we cannot, without a sin, sacrifice truth to peace; and, in the words of Archbishop

---

[1] *Letters and Correspondence of J. H. Newman*, Vol. II, p. 288.
[2] See *The Judgment of the Bishops*, W. S. Bricknell, Oxford, 1845, pp. 81, 85, 537, 547, 550, 559.

Laud, 'till Rome be other than it is', we must be estranged from her.[1]

He then undertook a study of Athanasius, and once again was impressed by the magisterial position of Rome. He set himself to work out a theory of the development of doctrine; and it was in the course of this that he was carried well across the bridge between Canterbury and Rome: and by the time he reached the end of the study he found himself in effect on the other side. From that time onwards it was a matter of removing remaining obstacles which, with that new tool available, he was not long in doing. Fr. Dominic Barberi, a Passionist, was at hand to give Newman that sense of holiness which he had hitherto found lacking in the Church of Rome; and it was at his hands that Newman was received into that communion, in October 1845.

Of the times which succeeded the defection of Newman from the Church of England there is again no better witness than Dean Church whose chronicle of the Movement concludes:

> All the world knows that it was not, in fact, killed or even much arrested by the shock of 1845. But after 1845, its field was at least as much out of Oxford as in it. As long as Mr. Newman remained, Oxford was necessarily its centre, necessarily, even after he had seemed to withdraw from it. When he left his place vacant, the direction of it was not removed from Oxford, but it was largely shared by men in London and the country. It ceased to be strongly and prominently academical. . . .[2]

Besides Newman, both before and after him, a number of Anglicans went over to Rome for a variety of reasons, patent and hidden, cogent and incoherent. When it is considered how unsympathetically the Oxford reformers were treated both by their own university and by the state-controlled authority of the Established Church it is remarkable that there were not more migrations. Looking at the future ecumenical movement as it was eventually to be revealed, it is easier to admire those who in

[1] A Letter to the Bishop of Oxford on the Occasion of No. 90 in the series called Tracts for the Times, Oxford 1841, pp. 20, 21.
[2] *Oxford Movement*, R. W. Church, p. 351.

the mid-century crisis stuck to their loyalties than those who indulged their personal search for security by 'going over'.

One of the aims of the Movement was certainly to bring about the union of Christians; and in the course of an examination of the prospects it was seen first that the compatibility of the doctrine of the Church of England with the mainstream of Roman doctrine had been understated, and the differences exaggerated. Moreover she seemed to have a function to perform in helping to complete the Reformation in the Roman Church which had only been begun in the procrastinating council of the sixteenth century. For the most part the Anglican reformers of the nineteenth century, returning to their sources for assurance, continued in their certainty that though the Church of England held a very large portion of the catholic inheritance of Christendom in common with Rome, Rome had gone into error in certain fundamental matters from which the English Church had struggled free. Struggled, indeed, and under the very harassing conditions of the sixteenth century; though the struggle for freedom had left its mark on the Church of England as on the other protestant churches, all of whom still stood in need of further reform. With this assessment only a minority of the Oxford reformers disagreed; of those some came eventually to the conclusion that Rome had been right all the time. The Church of England was sadly misusing these new powerful resources which the Holy Spirit was putting at her disposal. As she had turned her back on those promptings in the eighteenth century in rejecting Wesley, so she was doing again in the nineteenth in the case of the Oxford men.

The unreformed University of Oxford also contributed much to the discomfiture of these reformers. Dean Church lamented that:

> the good Heads [of colleges] ate and drank, and only cared in an obscure sort of way for these things.[1]

The University of Oxford, a much too independent clerical corporation, an *imperium in imperio*, was able, unchecked, to let loose its full force to denigrate and, had it been possible, to overthrow, the Tractarians. The successors of those who in the

[1] 11th November 1886. To the Warden of Keble. *Life and Letters of Dean Church* (Ed. Mary Church), Macmillan, 1894, p. 322.

previous century had ridiculed and exiled those whom they
nicknamed the 'Methodists', to the impoverishment of the
Church, now did the same with the 'Puseyites'.

The battering which the Oxford fathers took from their
University and from the Church gave rise in them to the
reactions of which we have spoken above. By the nature of the
case they were bereft of leadership. Those bishops who might
have been expected to support them, as we have seen, felt
obliged to yield to majorities, and only gave them clandestine
encouragement. The Movement therefore lacked the effective
guidance it should have had in an episcopal church. Newman,
himself no natural strategist, had been their leader while he
lasted; but the other giants of the Movement, Keble and Pusey
in particular, singularly lacked the charisma of government.
And Newman was quite unable to keep his followers in check
and was guilty of many miscalculations. Few would doubt now
that the whole episode of Tract 90 represented such a mis-
calculation, an excess of zeal which a sober judgment, the
quality which makes good statesmen and generals, would have
controlled. That the Church was in need of reform, that it
needed reminding of its catholic heritage, that that heritage
could be sought in the Scriptures and the Fathers and perhaps
by an objective reconsideration of the sixteenth century reform
in conjunction with the Council of Trent; even that the 39
Articles could be subjected to careful revision—this programme
could have gained a wide hearing. But that the 39 Articles as
they were could be interpreted in a sense which allowed most
of the doctrines of the Council of Trent to be believed within
the Church of England, was more than that Church could be
expected to swallow. The enthusiasm of overstatement led on,
not unnaturally, to suspicions of duplicity. When the reformers
went on to declare, rightly, that the English Church would be
well advised to pay attention to those parts of the catholic
heritage which Rome had preserved and the Church of
England had compromised or lost, they had even fewer
hearers. The confidence of England was lost.

It is not easy to classify in detail the attitude of the Oxford
men towards questions of union. Several studies have been
made on it.[1] After the secession of Newman there was clearly a

[1] e.g. H. R. T. Brandreth, *Ecumenical Ideals of the Oxford Movement*,

debate in the ranks of the Tractarians about their relations to the Church of Rome. Pusey, Keble and Marriott steered the Movement on its main course, which was to be away from the old-style polemics and towards a conception of the union of Christendom which put Rome at its centre as a matter of course while at the same time submitting to careful scrutiny those differences of doctrine which still stood as obstacles. This policy led Pusey along the path of the Eirenicons until the definitions of the First Vatican Council seemed to empty the project of all hope.

The three Eirenicons, as the name implies, were conceived by Pusey as attempts to increase understanding and advance the cause of union. The first of these was a reply to an open letter of Manning[1] entitled *The Working of the Holy Spirit in the Church of England*.[2] This was one of the strongest attacks ever penned against the Church of England. It concluded that:

> The Church of England, so far from being a barrier against infidelity, must be recognised as the mother of all the intellectual and spiritual aberrations which now cover the face of England.

Pusey's answer, the first Eirenicon,[3] tried to set forward the Church of England as a means of restoring visible unity on the grounds that it was able to steer a course between opposing tendencies to exaggeration. But it contained, for all its eirenical pretensions, a great deal about errors, and especially about the recently-defined doctrine of the Immaculate Conception.[4] Newman found the letter too polemical for his taste and said of it that:

> You discharge your olive branch as if from a catapult.[5]

Partly by way of removing the impression of hostility which the SPCK, 1947; secondly, an unpublished doctoral thesis of R. H. Greenfield. 'The Attitude of the Tractarians to the Roman Catholic Church 1833–50', in the Bodleian Library, to be seen by permission of Dr. Greenfield, to whom the author is indebted.

[1] See p. 126 n. 4 below.

[2] *A letter to the Revd. E. B. Pusey*, by H. E. Manning, London, Longmans, 1864.

[3] A letter to the author of the *Christian Year*, Oxford, 1865.

[4] See pp. 184–7.

[5] *A letter to the Revd. E. B. Pusey on his recent Eirenicon by the Revd. J. H. Newman, D.D.*, London, Longmans, 1866.

first Eirenicon had given, Pusey wrote a second[1] in 1869 setting out in greater detail, though with no less emphasis, the criticisms on Roman practice with regard to the Blessed Virgin Mary. He tried particularly hard to show that no disrespect was intended to Our Lord's mother, but that a special place was assigned in Anglican formularies for the commemoration of her part in the gospel narratives.

Pusey finished a second letter to Newman, which was his third Eirenicon, in November 1869, published in 1870,[2] a document of 350 pages, carrying further the examination of Roman practice. The Vatican Council then intervened to put an end, as far as Pusey was concerned, to future hopes of useful discussion, and the title of future editions of the Eirenicon was changed.

The Oxford Movement had seriously challenged the assumption that the Church of England was entirely protestant, claiming for it firmly an unbroken heritage in catholic Christendom. It had done this by a reappraisal of the Reformation and by a deliberate attempt to re-enthrone the classical apologists of the golden Caroline era. Newman, in his appreciation of the veteran President of Magdalen had said that Dr. Routh had been

> reserved to report to a forgetful generation what was the theology of their fathers.

All this had been grist to the ecumenical mill. The unsympathetic efforts of the state-allied Anglican establishment to reassert the Protestant ascendancy only served to convince more people of the rightness of the Tractarians' case. This was to be reinforced by the episode of the Gorham judgment in 1850.[3] The Oxford men, further, took the line of appeal to the Scriptures and to the Fathers. This appeal led on, in the case of Henry Manning[4] and a few others to a verdict in favour of

[1] First letter to the Revd. J. H. Newman. In explanation, chiefly in regard to the reverential love due to the ever-blessed Theotokos and the doctrine of her Immaculate Conception. Oxford, 1869.

[2] *Is Healthful Reunion Impossible. A second letter to the very Revd. J. H. Newman.* Oxford, 1870.

[3] See p. 132 below.

[4] Henry Edward Manning, 1808–1892. Ordained 1832; married 1833; wife died two years later. Archdeacon of Chichester 1840. Became Roman Catholic 1851.

submission to Rome. Yet the large majority of those concerned, including the best of the scholars among them, were not involved in this migration; and continued within the English Church to make their point that an appeal to the Fathers established, broadly speaking, the position of the Church of England as it was, and certainly her position as it could be after a few necessary reforms.

This appeal to antiquity left open the question of authority, of how to judge the issues which had arisen since the era of the Fathers was closed and since the Church had existed in a state of division. Newman's doctrine of Development, conceived in his last days in the English Church, served as a dangerous weapon in the hands of Roman Catholic theologians and became, from an Anglican point of view, his own undoing. The main stream of Anglican scholarship, which in those days was massive, rejected it. From the point of view of eventual ecumenical understanding the whole subject still remains on the agenda as unfinished business: but even those who believe it to be inadmissible must acknowledge that it was a brave essay on the road to the truth. Thus it can be said that although the Oxford men had suffered many setbacks and left many questions unresolved their searchings had not been in vain. They had rescued Anglican/Roman Catholic relations from the political scrap-heap and set them in their proper place. They had opened up a debate which has developed greatly since their day, which has resolved many problems and given hope and encouragement for the solution of those which still remain.

The characteristics of the next era of the Movement were first that the inspiration of it spread from Oxford into the provinces; and second that the interest of the participants became no longer principally academic but pastoral, liturgical and ceremonial. The move into the provinces, and particularly into the industrial cities of the north, was a development much to be welcomed. The gospel message itself was not to be a mere matter for theology, but the backbone of human life. And so the Tractarian movement was no longer to be observed only in the pulpit of St. Mary's, Oxford, but could now be seen at work, and at effective, exemplary evangelistic work, in the slums of east London or Leeds. But there were circumstances in the life of the Church of England which prevented even this

movement of the Spirit from conferring its full benefit. The
pattern of failure in the consequences of the Evangelical revival
was to be repeated, but in a different form. For although the
eighteenth-century movement had also made an immense impact
on the Church generally, so its effectiveness was limited by being
confined to certain centres. Because of the corrupt system
of patronage of benefices the evangelicals, first in order to
establish themselves and then in order to ensure 'continuity of
their ministry, had bought up and put in the hands of patronage
trusts the advowsons of many influential parishes. The patronage so acquired was limited to clergy of a certain type of
spirituality, and the influence of the movement was correspondingly decreased, to the impoverishment of the Church
as a whole. The same kind of destiny awaited the Oxford
Movement in its later stages, although the stages of development were different in detail. When the second generation of
Tractarians moved out into the unevangelised suburbs of
England's large cities they founded new parishes, being generally debarred from ministering in most established areas. Here
again, as in the case of the Evangelicals before them, they
created inevitably distinctive parishes or districts, and as the
Tractarians began to evolve more and more in liturgy and
ceremonial in their own enclaves their influence decreased,
again to the impoverishment of the whole Church. This
unhappy development was to prove an increasingly obstinate
stumbling block in the way of Roman Catholic/Anglican
understanding. For it gave rise to a situation in which the
English Church was polarised into two rather uncommunicative
groups; so that it was the 'High Church' men, generally
speaking, even when they had no intention of submission, who
looked longingly to Rome as the undisputed champion of
catholic Christendom, while the 'Low Church' men continued
to emphasise the seriousness of the Roman aberrations from the
fundamentals of the faith and to deride and oppose any
attempts to make approaches to them. This same situation made
difficulties also on the Roman side. They were unable to
resist the temptation to make propaganda out of it, for, understandably enough, it was difficult for them to take seriously a
Church so ill-disciplined as to present what looked like two
fronts to the world. And although in the course of the next

century they exaggerated the gravity of the situation in the English Church (for in spite of appearances the Church of England had only one set of official beliefs, and one liturgy), it must be admitted that the large number of individual conversions to Rome in the first half of the twentieth century was very largely traceable to this reprehensible defect among the Anglicans. This situation has continued and in a measure still exists. But it has been considerably alleviated by recent liturgical developments (among other things) in the Church of England, and its effect as a stimulus to defection has been neutralised at last by the emergence in the Roman Church itself of the same polarities in the wake of the Second Vatican Council. Now a certain pluriformity is recognised on both sides as a sign of healthy freedom to grow. But in its Anglican form (in which it manifested a defect in discipline) it has in the past created a barrier to development within the Church of England herself and *a fortiori* has created a bar to understanding with the Roman Church. It is one of the many evil legacies of the rigid Establishment of the Church of England, against which the first Tractarians raised their voice, and which is still among the number of her unresolved problems. This feature of Anglican life did much harm, for the second time in two centuries, to the general health of the Church and to the normal growth of good relationships. All the estates of the realm, from the monarchy to *Punch*, were mobilised to resist what the verdict of history now recognises as promptings of the Spirit. Prime Minister Lord John Russell wrote to the Queen:

> The matter to create national alarm is, as your Majesty says, the growth of Roman Catholic doctrine within the bosom of the Church. Dr. Arnold said very truly, 'I look upon a Roman Catholic as an enemy in his uniform. I look upon a Tractarian as an enemy disguised, as a spy'. It would be very wrong to do as the Bishop of Oxford proposed, and confer the patronage of the Crown on any of the Tractarians.[1]

And to his successor Lord Aberdeen the Prince Consort wrote suggesting:

> that a system of marked disfavour should be adopted and

[1] 25th October 1850. *Queen Victoria's Early Letters* (ed. John Raymond), B. T. Batsford, 1963, p. 177.

steadily persevered in towards those who promulgate 'principles likely to disturb the peace of the Church'; even the most active, ambitious, and talented of the High Church party are not likely long to hold principles which permanently excluded them from preferment.[1]

In spite of the sullen opposition of the powerful in the Established Church, many conceived another vision, that of enjoying the fruits of catholic doctrine, liturgy and spirituality within the framework of the Church of England as she existed. Yet some of those who did not migrate to Rome dealt the Movement an even more deadly blow from within by deciding that they would continue in the Church of England as an interim measure while professing the whole of Roman Catholic belief (and often teaching it) until such time as reunion were possible. Of all solutions to the problem this has proved to be the least satisfactory: it has perplexed both sides and brought enlightenment to neither.

This kind of ecclesiastical schizophrenia, fortunately, was the affliction of only a small minority, some of whom, including Ward himself, eventually also went over to Rome; though there has always been a small group in the Church of England ever since, who have tried to walk the same ecclesiastical tightrope. They have tended to be an embarrassment in both camps and can be said to have hindered, rather than to have promoted, the growth of understanding. The majority of the Tractarians set themselves, however, patiently to reintroduce certain long-lost catholic emphases, ideas and practices to places and to people where they had been lost or forgotten. The debate among the academics went on. Pusey and Keble stood firm; and the torch, in the University of Oxford at least, was handed on to Pusey and to J. B. Mozley. Of the migrations Dean Church later said:

> With all the terrible losses of 1845, I am not sure that without them we should have done as well as we have. They awed people and made them think, and gave time for the latent strength of the Church to grow quietly.[2]

[1] *Life of Samuel Wilberforce*, R. G. Wilberforce, John Murray, 1881, Vol. II, p. 169.
[2] 23rd May 1877. To the Warden of Keble. *Life and Letters*, Church, p. 260.

Of Mozley Mr. Gladstone said that he:

> combined the clear form of Cardinal Newman with the profundity of Bishop Butler.[1]

The most spectacular and influential growth in the Movement was to be seen, as has already been mentioned, in the parish churches of the land, in such places as it was allowed to exist at all. Churches were renovated and reseated, daily services reinstituted, frequent celebrations of the Eucharist introduced and a resurgence of liturgy, ritual, devotion and all forms of art and architecture was to be observed. Here again, with the well-meant intention of emphasising the catholicity (instead of, or as well as, the protestant relationships) of the English Church, there was a disastrous tendency to use the Church of Rome in its most garish Latin, and therefore un-English, manifestations as a model. The interiors of churches, the shape of vestments, gestures, devotions and music were in some places uncritically copied from Roman models until in certain cases it was impossible to tell whether a particular church was in communion with Rome or Canterbury. This regrettable development of one wing of the Oxford Movement again undoubtedly hindered the progress of understanding with Rome, the very thing it was hoped to promote. As has been said, it mystified the Roman Catholics themselves. The unfortunate Pusey was of course supposed to countenance, if not actually to be the origin of, every single thing which happened in the Oxford Movement, particularly by people outside England. Pope Pius IX in an interview with A. P. Stanley (afterwards Dean of Westminster) is reported to have said:

> You know Pusey. When you meet him give him this message from me, that I compare him to a bell, which always sounds to invite the faithful to Church, and itself always remains outside.[2]

If this blatant copying of Rome gave rise to misunderstanding among Roman Catholics, it did so much more among the Anglicans themselves. In the midst of such turmoil the leaders of the Movement were under obligation to develop its

[1] Quoted *Commonwealth*, p. 52 (February 1908).
[2] *Life and Letters of Dean Stanley*, Rowland E. Prothero, Nelson, 1909, p. 456.

original inspiration by working out a policy whereby it could be contained within the existing framework of the Church of England. And this they manfully attempted to do. They could still command a certain degree of approval for the more sober of their planned developments, and that often in high places. Notably Gladstone himself was a known supporter. When the Privy Council judgment on the Gorham[1] case shook the sensitivities of the English Church, it was to Gladstone that Archdeacon Manning betook himself for comfort and encouragement. Gladstone is said to have exclaimed: 'The Church of England has gone unless it releases itself by some authoritative act.' Blomfield, the Bishop of London, though he had been critical of the Romanising tendencies of some members of the Movement, actually moved in the House of Lords a bill to transfer to the Upper House of Convocation the powers of the Judicial Committee of the Privy Council as the final court of Appeal in matters of doctrine. This even received the support of the Archbishop of Canterbury. Though the bill was defeated it needs to be remembered as a great pioneering step in setting the Church of England's house in order preparatory to making her polity acceptable not only to the Roman Church but also to the diverse non-conformist bodies with whom she would soon be called upon to enter into new relationships.

The process of introducing the new aspects of catholic life which were being revived in the Church of England was very complicated. There were also many theological questions to be dealt with. Pusey, tired of the endless difficulties, tried to encourage an attitude of benevolent neutrality with regard to the Roman Church. He advocated laying aside, for the time being at least, reference to the errors which he and the majority of those under the influence of the Movement believed her still to hold. This was the period of formation of the church unions 'for the defences of the principles of the Church of England' all over the country. One of those principles, he asserted, was that they should concentrate on domestic reforms without entering into any unnecessary comparisons with other churches, still less

---

[1] The Judicial Committee of the Privy Council had overturned a decision of the Bishop of Exeter (Phillpotts) refusing to institute the Revd. G. C. Gorham to a benefice on grounds of defective teaching on baptismal regeneration 1850.

into contentious argument. It was possible to live the full catholic life and receive the fulness of the apostolic faith within the Church of England, and the task now was to show how that could best be done. The immediate tasks were more practical than academic. As at the time of the Reformation there was little point in discussing the theology of Justification as long as the Church was selling pardons for gold, so in the nineteenth century it was not possible to sustain enthusiasm for a debate on whether the fulness of truth and authority lay with the English Church until she appeared to show more evidence that it did. We have already referred to high level attempts to improve the relationships between the State and the Church, so that the Church's sovereign authority should at least look a little more like that of the Lord. But there were so many other departments of her life which needed overhaul which have already been referred to, new music, tidy churches, regular services, zealous pastoral visitation, renewed missionary enterprise, new standards of devotion and the reawakening of the ascetical side of religion. These were all features of the revival. This happy progress was a stage in the general preparation of the Church for newer and wider relationships, especially with the Church of Rome. The transformation was such that it is not possible to exaggerate it.

The impetus given to this movement by the Oxford reformers soon reached the larger part of the clergy and laity, until people who had no thought of themselves as heirs of the Tractarians were in fact enjoying the hymns revived by such as J. M. Neale and the general doctrinal and devotional inheritance of the Oxford men.

But the Movement did more than help to repolish the outward appearance of the Church of England or call to mind her forgotten teachings. It also introduced into the Church practices and devotions which had in fact lapsed entirely since the divisions of the sixteenth century, particularly by the revival of the Religious Life and the wider respect paid to the Sacrament of the Eucharist. Both of these things were of course cardinal to a better understanding with the Roman Catholic Church, and these represent the first-fruits of a closer contact with her. As far back as 1841 Pusey had been able to write to Newman that:

A young lady is purposing today to take a holy vow of
celibacy. . . . She hopes to receive the Holy Communion . . .
as being part of her self-devotion. . . . You will know her by
her being dressed in white with an ivory cross.[1]

From that time onwards there was an abundant flowering of
communities for women, both 'active' and 'mixed'. Eventually
the same stimulus brought forth its first enclosed contemplative
order, the 'Society of the Love of God', at Fairacres,
Oxford. Many of these have become world famous, and it is not
our business to chronicle here either their foundations or their
achievements, but only to record that by their very existence
they have been a witness to the fact that the Holy Spirit is able
to bring forth such fruits in answer to prayer.

Communities for men appeared later. The names of Cowley,
Mirfield and Kelham have become familiar throughout the
Anglican communion: they each adapted the standard rules
to their own Anglican need or have worked out ther own
Anglican spirituality. One community established itself openly
on the Benedictine rule, and after an uncertain start which
involved a considerable number of them on the island of
Caldey in South Wales going over to Rome, settled down first
at Pershore and then at Nashdom to work out the rule of St.
Benedict as applied to the Anglican situation. Another group
took vows on the Franciscan pattern, and the Anglican Society
of St. Francis has flourished widely and rapidly. It has so far
succeeded in keeping itself reasonably close to the original
pattern of the life of the Poverello. We mention these communities under the heading of the Oxford Movement, for it was
the inspiration of that movement that gave them birth. Their
significance as agents in the repair of the breach of the sixteenth
century can hardly be exaggerated. For not only does their
existence bear witness to the recovery of the ascetical dimension
of Christian discipleship, but they have also been instruments,
both corporately and individually, in making effective contacts
with the Roman Church as opportunity has begun slowly to
arise. For where official hierarchies were remote and un-
friendly, the Roman religious orders, enjoying as they do a
certain independence from episcopal jurisdiction, were able to

[1] *Life of E. B. Pusey*, Liddon, Vol. III, p. 10.

creep out surreptitiously into an ecumenical no-man's-land to shake hands with their fellow religious. In doing so they witnessed to the importance of a certain degree of presbyterian autonomy even in the Roman Church and so prepared in practice the ground for the reshaping of hierarchical structures which was to be one of the tasks of the Second Vatican Council.

Yet the introduction of necessary and laudable reforms went its usual unhappy way. Those in authority (and that in the Church of England meant not only the bishops, but the squirearchy, the trusts and corporations and colleges) who saw in it an implied rebuke of their own neglect, opposed the reasonable development of the whole Movement. The introduction of surplices, hymn-books, and of the simplest improvements in piety and good order was opposed with vigour and vindictive reprisals, leading up to judicial prosecution. The whole story is one of the distasteful episodes of Anglican history. It is only fair to say that the supreme judicial tribunal of the land, the Judicial Committee of the Privy Council, which was appealed to more than once, did in some important cases save victims of this persecution and establish the right of the church to a reasonable freedom.

At a deeper level the Oxford men were responsible for a substantial deepening in the Anglican understanding of the sacramental life. The use of sacramental confession, authorised under certain circumstances by the Prayer Book itself, was reintroduced, both the practice and the doctrine. Those who encouraged it were subjected to opposition, to espionage in certain cases, and to infamous misrepresentation on moral grounds. The Eucharist, which had been reduced in previous centuries to the status of an 'occasional office' was more frequently celebrated and many zealous spirits, hoping to promote thereby a closer identification of the Church of England with Rome attempted the introduction of the whole gamut of Roman Catholic eucharistic doctrine, the Real Presence, the sacrifice of the Mass, and even transubstantiation. Here again, perhaps, it was the inadequacy of Anglican formulas and the conservatism which would not undertake to provide anything better which can be said to be primarily responsible for the quarrels which followed. In this field of doctrine and devotion also, however, a general *consensus fidelium*

9

A ROMAN CATHOLIC HIERARCHY
IS ESTABLISHED

A critical period in the relationships between Anglicans and
Roman Catholics in England came in 1850 with the establishment of the Roman Catholic hierarchy. There is a sense in
which this was inevitable. The Anglican Church regarded
herself as the catholic church in England, and the achievement
of a greater degree of efficiency by a rival body, if the Roman
Catholic bishops were to be so regarded, which they were, was
bound at that time to be seen as a threat. On the other hand a
period of calmer co-existence and increased charity was being
experienced and there was little expectation that the reaction in
England would be as ferocious and hysterical as it turned out to
be. The Roman body had been lulled into a sense of false
security, and they would seem to have been amply justified in
their belief that to replace the vicars apostolic in England with
'ordinary' bishops would not be greeted with any particular
alarm. The public utterances of English politicians gave them
this expectation in the years preceding 1850. In July 1845 in the
House of Commons Lord John Russell, as Prime Minister, said
that with reference to the law forbidding catholic bishops from
holding the titles of English sees, 'he believed they might repeal
these disabling clauses which prevented a Roman Catholic
bishop assuming a title held by a Bishop of the Established
Church'.[1]

On 17th August 1848, during the debate on the bill for

[1] *Hansard*, 3rd series, Vol. LXXXII, p. 290.

permitting Diplomatic Relations with Rome, Lord John said that there were two alternatives: either there must be some reciprocal arrangements with the Pope or else he must be considered free to exercise spiritual authority over the minds of Roman Catholics in other countries and communicate with them.[1] In the event the Roman Catholic community were to take the liberalism of a liberal Prime Minister for granted, and it was found wanting (a fact that his political opponents were not slow to point out).[2] Moreover, the English envoy sent to Rome in 1847, Lord Minto, was apprised of the intention of the Holy See to set up a hierarchy in England. As late as August 1850 Wiseman visited the Prime Minister shortly before leaving for Rome to receive his red hat[3] and although the subject of their conversation is not recorded, it seems likely that the Roman jurisdiction in England was discussed. That there was to be this change to ordinary jurisdiction had been mooted in various newspapers for some years without much comment.

In the event it was a very long transaction, covering about 23 years. And nobody could accuse the Holy See of precipitate action. The matter was carefully deliberated, ironically enough, partly to avoid conflict with the English law. The very caution and delay contributed to the situation that arose when the Roman Catholic sees eventually were set up. For by 1850 the religious climate in England, and the international political scene, had changed for the worse. Had the hierarchy been restored in say 1847, without undue publicity and with a discreet leader, and the change represented as a matter of internal organisation of interest only to the Roman body, it would probably have passed without widespread notice. But the timing of 1850 was unfortunate, the setting unpromising, and the manner in which the promulgation of the hierarchy was made known disastrous, for which the personality of the new Archbishop of Westminster must be held responsible.

Roused by all these factors, the nation gave the new hierarchy a poor reception, so much so that the Queen (who was not noticeably sympathetic to Roman Catholics) wrote to her

[1] *Hansard*, 3rd series, Vol. CI, p. 220.
[2] Disraeli's letter to the Lord Lieutenant of Buckinghamshire, 8th November 1850.
[3] He arrived in Rome on 5th September 1850.

aunt the Duchess of Gloucester on 12th December 1850 from
Windsor Castle:

> ... I much regret the unchristian and intolerant spirit
> exhibited by many people at the public meetings. I cannot
> bear to hear the violent abuse of the catholic religion, which
> is so painful and cruel towards the many good and innocent
> Roman Catholics. However, we must hope and trust this
> excitement will soon cease and that the wholesome effect of it
> on our own Church will be the lasting result of it.[1]

The administration of the Roman Catholic community in
England was overdue for change by the middle of the nineteenth century. The eight vicars apostolic in their districts had
insufficient authority, organisation, buildings, means and so on.
Nor was the relationship between bishops and laity always well-
defined. Ullathorne[2] described[3] how a scheme drawn up by a
layman for the creation of 16 bishops in England was also going
the rounds in Rome.

The reasons for these administrative problems are plain: the
Roman body of the 1840s–1850s bore little resemblance to that
of the mid-eighteenth century with its scattered great houses
where the remaining Roman Catholic gentry practised their
religion with their chaplains and the country people round
their estates. The Roman Church in England had in the meantime been joined by two new groups, one large and one small,
both highly significant: the Irish and the Oxford converts.
Between them they were to create a situation which was
temporarily of great complexity, for their presence aggravated
the situation between Anglicans and Roman Catholics, and
caused divisions in the Roman body itself.

The Irish, mainly labourers, who entered England in such
large numbers after 1840, were the victims of English mal-
administration in Ireland. Starvation, unemployment, poor
education, drove them across the Irish sea in search of the
means of subsistence.[4] The Irish situation, which had always

---

[1] *Queen Victoria's Early Letters* (ed. John Raymond), p. 179.
[2] William Bernard Ullathorne, 1806–1889. Vicar Apostolic of Western
District 1846, Central District 1848. Bishop of Birmingham 1850.
[3] *From Cabin Boy to Archbishop.* Burns Oates, 1941, pp. 279–83.
[4] *The English Catholics* (ed. G. Beck), Burns Oates, 1950, says that the
1851 census showed 519,959 people in England who were Irish by birth.

been bad,[1] became desperate as the result of the failure of the
potato crop in the early 1840s, when thousands died in the
famine. Those who came were not likely to be sympathetic to
their new countryfolk and their religion. They settled mainly in
the towns of the north and created pastoral problems for their
bishops, social problems for the Roman Catholic community,
and economic problems for their English neighbours whom
they undercut on the wage market, since any money was
better than none.

The Oxford converts were small in number by comparison.
Having been the cause of division in the Church they had left
which could not contain them with their new vision, they moved
on to cause dissension in the Church in which they found their
new home. They were better educated than most of their
fellow Roman Catholics to whom the Universities of Oxford
and Cambridge were closed and who went to foreign or small
English schools. Also the converts imbibed to a great extent
(and one of the exceptions was Newman) the new Roman
devotions and style of worship and religious setting introduced
by Wiseman and the Italian missionaries who came to England
under his aegis. When Faber[2] began to write the *Lives of the
Modern Saints* he was cautioned by Ullathorne and inhibited
from finishing the work which was considered excessive and
likely to cause offence. Those Anglicans who were dedicated to
the status quo blamed Rome as the source of the changes which
were finding their way into the Church of England. And much
of the new ceremonial, ecclesiastical attire and expansive modes
of religious expression also caused offence among the 'old
catholics' with their more austere traditions. A much quoted
example is Dr. Lingard[3] who objected to the carrying of the
Cross or Crucifix in processions and was distressed at the
introduction of the practice of sprinkling congregations with
holy water.[4] Wiseman was criticised by some of his colleagues
clergy and people not only for these innovations, as they were

[1] See Chapter 5, pp. 68–71.
[2] Frederick William Faber, 1814–1863. Scholar and Fellow of University
College, Oxford. Became Roman Catholic November 1845. Oratorian
1848. Superior of London House.
[3] Vice-Principal of Ushaw.
[4] *Life and Letters of John Lingard*, M. Haile and E. Bonney, Herbert &
Daniel, 1912, p. 306.

seen to be, and his closeness to the Oxford converts, but for his flamboyant style of life, his lack of administrative skill and facility for running into debt: his Roman training was regarded with suspicion by a community whom he considered as 'barely emerging from the catacombs'. Differing attitudes towards the policy of O'Connell in Ireland were also a divisive factor among the English Roman body. 'We are so dreadfully disunited (I mean we English Catholics)' wrote Ambrose de Lisle to Cardinal Acton.[1]

Nor did the international situation help to provide a calm passage for the introduction of the hierarchy. The Austrian threat to the papal states caused the new Pope Pius IX to look towards the English government for support. In 1847 English opinion saw Pius in a liberal role and there was expectation that he would make changes in the administration of the territory under his control in a liberal direction. Wiseman, who had been in Rome, was charged to bring back a memorandum for the Prime Minister from the Pope asking for assistance and a diplomatic mission. Wiseman saw Lord Palmerston on 13th September 1847, and Palmerston acted swiftly, for this suited his purpose of flying a liberal flag in Italy and of seeking aid to subdue the Irish clergy. On 16th September Lord Minto[2] was appointed by the Queen to Switzerland, Sardinia and Tuscany on an extraordinary mission in the capacity of one of Her Majesty's Ministers; from Florence he was to proceed to Rome.[3]

In 1831–1832 the governments of Austria, France, Russia and Great Britain had most urgently advised the Pope to make some general changes and improvements. The reigning Pope had not reached the full extent of the requirements; the Papacy did not endear itself to the powers by the fact that all government positions in the papal states were held by clerics.

The despatch of Lord Minto to Italy was largely concerned with interfering with the Pope's administration of his papal dominions. On this account and the Pontiff's allegation that Minto was allying himself with the revolutionary elements in Italy, the mission was not a success and relationships were less happy than heretofore. In the meantime *The Times* newspaper

---

[1] *Life and Letters of Ambrose Phillipps de Lisle*, E. S. Purcell, Vol. I, p. 238.
[2] Father-in-law to Lord John Russell.   [3] P.R.O. F.O. 44.1.

had reacted instantaneously to the rumours of diplomatic exchanges and on 15th September 1847 had pointed out that it was still illegal to negotiate or conduct business with Rome. The government brought in the Diplomatic Relations with Rome bill in the following year (which has already been referred to) and this received the Royal Assent on 4th September 1848. An amendment added in the Lords precluded the reception of an envoy from the Pope should he be an ecclesiastic, and another amendment failed to give the Pope the title which Roman custom decreed; so the Act was unilateral and prevented an embassy being sent to England. *The Times* on 20th July 1848 printed an appeal to the Commons by 3,500 names, mainly archdeacons and other clergy of the Church of England, against the bill for legalising diplomatic relations with Rome because the petitioners, looking at

the acts and language of the present Pope are convinced that he is as fully resolved to advance the dominion, uphold the false doctrines, encourage the idolatrous practices of the Church of Rome, and put down all persons and societies opposed to it, as any of his predecessors have ever been. . . .

During the autumn of 1848 the incendiary political situation in Rome burst into flames. The revolutionary forces under Mazzini and Garibaldi seized possession of the city. In November the Pope fled to Gaeta where he took with him the sympathies of many nations.

The Pope was offered asylum on British territory in Malta, but he chose to remain on Italian soil. On 4th December 1848 he had addressed a letter to the Most Serene and Potent Sovereign Victoria, the Illustrious Queen of England, in which he spoke of his exiled plight and the 'cruel difficulties' by which he was pressed by the 'nefarious conspiracy of abandoned and turbulent men', that God . . . 'may unite you with us in perfect charity'.[1]

Queen Victoria, in what has been described as the first letter from an English Sovereign to a Pope since the Reformation, (which it certainly was not) replied in January 1849.[2] In it

[1] *Queen Victoria's Early Letters*, pp. 153–6. (From originals in Vatican Archives.)

[2] ibid., pp. 154–5 (also in Vatican Archives). And see chapters 2 and 6 for letters of James I and George IV.

she expressed to 'Most Eminent Sir' her sympathies on his predicament.

She asked the Pope to believe that it would afford her real pleasure to be able in any degree to contribute to a result so much to be desired, and she was happy to assure the Pope of her sincere friendship and of the unfeigned respect and esteem which she entertained for his person and character.

But the hopes of a more liberal policy in the government of the papal territories were soon to be dashed on 20th April 1849 by the allocution 'Quibus Quantisque', issued from Gaeta. In this denunciatory document the Pope made plain what he felt about the revolutionaries and the so-called will of the people; that he intended to be master in his own household; a liberal regime was not suitable at the present time; no free institutions were promised on his return to Rome, which he achieved with the help of French troops in April 1850. The sympathy which had flowed towards him from England turned to scorn when it was decided that here was no liberal Pope, but an autocrat; as some of the Mazzini refugees who reached England with tales of papal intransigence said—a tyrant. 'The Society of the Friends of Italy' was formed to promote Italian independence and political and religious liberty. The cynical might say that it was strange that such a high degree of religious liberty was not considered desirable at home. Englishmen began to see the Papacy in opposition to the aspirations of the Italian people and followed the course of the Risorgimento with interest and sympathy.

Such was the backcloth against which the transformation of the vicariates in England into sees was achieved. And, as has been said, the deliberations were slow and cautious. The English bishops were under a cloud for failure to keep in close touch with the Holy See: the Pope, who did not feel the vicars apostolic had shown enough enterprise, divided the districts, and created more bishops. This was not achieved until 1840 (partly due to the lack of speed with which the vicars apostolic answered letters), when eight districts took the place of the original four; the powers of the religious orders were strengthened, to the resentment of the vicariate. Mgr. Acton,[1] the chief consultant in Rome on English affairs, maintained

[1] Later Cardinal.

that the English vicars apostolic could not sufficiently be relied upon to bear the responsibilities of 'ordinary' bishops in view of their independence from the Holy See, their disunity and the resistant spirit they had shown. He also took part with Wiseman in the move to send Italian Passionists as missionaries to England.

At their spring meeting in May 1848 the bishops agreed, on a suggestion from Dr. Grant, Rector of the English College, that one of their number should go to Rome. Laymen and priests were making touble there for the English bishops and it was important that someone should represent the urgency for a new administration. Ullathorne, as the chosen representative, left England almost immediately and travelled to Paris, which he found in the throes of revolution. He arrived in Rome on 26th May and left only just in time to avoid that revolution, which broke out at the end of July. The initiative and documentation which led to the eventual establishment of the English Roman Catholic hierarchy were largely the work of Ullathorne during his weeks in Rome. He discovered that there were two matters which were holding up the promulgation: one was the legal factor, the question of titles for the new sees and the transfer of ecclesiastical property, both in accordance with the English law: the second was, who should be the first Archbishop of Westminster. According to Ullathorne great trouble was being taken to avoid a clash with the law and therefore to avoid using ancient titles, and the liabilities of the Emancipation Act of 1829. On the other hand, he wrote:

There is a party which teaches that the Church has never condemned the Anglican establishment or Church and that the latter is a living branch of the Church Catholic, and that she has the apostolic succession. If then we avoid all the titles held by our ancient Bishops, even when there are evident reasons for taking them, and that in all cases, we shall give force to the notion that the Holy See dares not touch a sister church (and one on equality with that of Rome, to use their expressions) and that Rome thus confesses the Apostolicity of their ministers and their communion. The importance of avoiding this impression, especially as entertained by the

Puseyites, has appeared a strong reason to some of the Bishops.[1]

The question of Catholic ecclesiastical property and the transfer of it legally from a vicar apostolic to a diocesan bishop was one which taxed the Roman authorities and made more delays. The Member of Parliament for Devonport, John Romilly,[2] had offered to introduce a Catholic Trust bill into the House of Commons and the English bishops asked the guidance of Rome on its clauses. Through the machinations of laymen to Propaganda Fide, said Ullathorne, no answer was forthcoming and 'Romilly, disgusted at the lack of Catholic support, let the matter drop'.[3]

Finally one outstanding question remained. Who should be leader of the new hierarchy? The eventual choice of Rome was that Bishop Walsh, Vicar Apostolic of the Central District, should be the first Archbishop. Ullathorne pointed out his age and infirmities and that he had asked to be allowed to resign, but his seniority and the manner in which his colleagues had deferred to him were considered of primary importance. A letter came from England that Walsh was dying, but Mgr. Barnabo Secretary of Propaganda Fide, announced 'whether living or dead he shall be the first Archbishop of Westminster'. Wiseman was to be his co-adjutor. No words of Ullathorne could shift the decision. Finally the Pope gave Ullathorne an assurance that the hierarchy would be established as soon as possible.

Ullathorne left Rome to the sights and sounds of the incipient revolution. What he did not hear were the bells of Rome ringing 'Turn again, Ullathorne twice (almost) Archbishop of Westminster'.[4] For Bishop Walsh died in the following year and by the time the revolution was past and the Pope back in the city, a new candidate had to be found. Bishop Wiseman, summoned to Rome in July 1850, wrote sadly to Ullathorne

[1] *From Cabin Boy to Archbishop*, pp. 266–7.

[2] Later Solicitor-General.

[3] A similar bill was introduced by T. Chisholm Anstey in 1847 (*Hansard*, Vol. XCV, p. 211) when it was pointed out that Mr. Romilly's bill had been withdrawn on finding it was 'so much opposed to by the wishes of the persons it was intended to benefit.'

[4] Ullathorne was undoubtedly one of the possible candidates as Wiseman's successor in 1865.

that he feared that his total separation from England for ever was about to take place. It seems certain that he knew he was to be offered a cardinal's hat and a place in the Curia. Calling upon Ullathorne subsequently in Birmingham, Wiseman explained that the Holy Father had said that he would provide his successor in London. The future cardinal added that for certain reasons he felt that Ullathorne might be that person. Ullathorne disclaimed the possibility and ended the description of the episode with the prophetic words 'I have no doubt but that he had completely bent his mind on returning to England if he could accomplish it.'[1]

How right he was. When Wiseman reached Rome in September he persuaded the Pope to allow him to return to England despite the reports against him which had been received in Italy. Suggestions in favour of Wiseman had also been sent, notably from the Canadian Sulpician Abbé Quiblier with whose argument the Pope was said to be struck. Certainly Wiseman was a prelate of gifts: his lectures in England over fifteen years had been a considerable success: he had promoted many religious orders and had presence and charm. Moreover he had learning which was highly favoured by the Curia who made constant references to this desirable quality in candidates for English bishoprics. He was an Englishman, but trained in Salamanca and Rome and he could be relied upon to strengthen the ties between England and the Holy See. It having been decided to make Wiseman a Cardinal at once and to send him back to England, the establishment of the hierarchy became urgent. The Brief, already prepared and long awaited, was at last promulgated on 29th September 1850.

It is interesting to speculate upon the outcome had Ullathorne (and not Wiseman) been the first or even second Archbishop of Westminster. Certainly there would have been no pastoral from the Flaminian Gate to stir up public opinion and the Church of England so violently against the new Roman hierarchy. Ullathorne was representative of the old-style bishop of the English vicariates who ministered pastorally in the back streets of towns on small means and resources, sometimes to die of disease and spent with over-work. Mgr. (later

---

[1] *From Cabin Boy to Archbishop*, p. 293.

Cardinal) Vaughan, writing to Wiseman on 22nd February 1862[1] described Ullathorne as 'Anglican and Gallican in the strongest way', but this was only meant pejoratively and there is no record that Ullathorne ever had any but the most formal contact with Anglican bishops or clergy: it is unlikely since a cultural as well as a denominational chasm existed between them. It was not upon Ullathorne, with his personal experience of mission to Australian convicts or the organisation of urban parishes, with his rough speech and practical ability, that the choice fell, but upon Wiseman who had greater scholarship and presence. The fact that he assumed the role of Prince Bishop, much more akin to the contemporary scholarly and princely bishops of the Church of England, added more fuel to the inflammable situation.

Wiseman's pastoral letter of 7th October 1850 from the Flaminian Gate of Rome, and its effect, is well known. Its excessively exuberant and tactless tones can only be explained by Wiseman's joy at the prospect of returning unexpectedly to his native land and having in his own person been the instrument through whom the Roman Catholic hierarchy was at long last being established.

Unfortunately absent at the court of Austria while they were being read, he sent these words ahead to England; a country now antagonistic to the policy of the new Pope, a Church rent by the Gorham judgment and a spate of conversions, and suspicious of so-called Romish tendencies in her midst:

> ... the greatest of blessings has just been bestowed on our country, by the restoration of its true Catholic hierarchical government, in communion with the See of Peter.... we govern and shall continue to govern, the counties of Middlesex, Hertford and Essex, as Ordinary thereof, and those of Surrey, Sussex, Kent, Berkshire and Hampshire ... as Administrator with Ordinary jurisdiction.[2]

Wiseman was a somewhat arrogant man by nature, and he

---

[1] *Henry Edward Manning, His Life and Labours*, Shane Leslie, Burns Oates, 1921, p. 491.
[2] 7th October 1850, *Out of the Flaminian Gate*, T. Hooker, 1850.

was overcome by the importance of his new position. On his visit to England in 1835 he had written:[1]

> I intend to quarter myself upon such of the nobility and gentry of these realms as can sufficiently appreciate such an honour.

He had a penchant for pageantry, livery and elaborate cere-monial which was alien to his compatriots, except in exercises of the armed forces or the monarchy. The English were at fault in taking him seriously; they regarded his claims as real threats. Chief among those who roused the nation along these lines was *The Times* newspaper, which spoke in derogatory tones about the establishment of the Roman Catholic hierarchy throughout the months of October and November 1850.

Our concern is with the effect of what was happening on specifically Anglican opinion. Anglican comment in the news-papers, and views expressed at the numerous meetings of clergy and churchpeople, took three main forms. First there was outrage that the Pope seemed to be claiming exclusive rights which ignored the existing Church in England. Typical of this manifestation was the letter presented by the bishops to the Queen.

> . . . This our country, whose church being a true branch of Christ's Holy Catholic Church, in which the true Word of God is preached and the Sacraments are duly ministered according to God's ordinances, is treated by the Bishop of Rome as having been a heathen land, and is congratulated on its restoration, after an interval of 300 years to a place among the Churches of Christendom.[2]

Second it was claimed that through the exercise of the Pope's spiritual authority over the consciences of men, there was a possibility of corruption of dogma; third, a challenge had been presented to the constitution and monarchy. These accusations of usurpation and contested allegiance had been heard before in the seventeenth century over the Oath con-

---

[1] To Monckton Milnes. *Life and Times of Cardinal Wiseman*, Wilfred Ward, Longmans, 1897, p. 215.

[2] 'Address and Protest of the Archbishops and Bishops of the Church of England (except the Bishops of Exeter and St. Davids)'.

troversy, and were to be heard again after the definitions of Vatican I. They were representative (but not exclusively so since Gladstone was later to raise the allegiance question) of nationalistic elements in the Church who were alarmed by the Tractarians' attitude towards the State and sheltered behind the establishment and the Gorham judgment.

The Prime Minister, Lord John Russell, having received a letter of alarm from his friend Bishop Maltby of Durham, rushed ill-advisedly into print and his reply, which was published on 7th November 1850, stirred up great indignation. He could not resist using the event in his case against the Tractarians:

> What alarms me more is that clergymen of our own Church who have subscribed the 39 articles . . . have been leading their flocks step by step nearer the precipice. [He listed their so-called offences] all these things are pointed out by clergymen of the Church of England as worthy of adoption, and are now openly reprehended by the Bishop of London in his charge to the clergy of his diocese.

This was indeed so, for Dr. Blomfield had directed his archdeacons to visit all churches and chapels 'in which it was alleged that Romish ceremonies are practised and to report to him every case in which any ceremonies or forms are used not authorised by the rubric, nor sanctioned by established custom'.

It was, as might be expected, Bishop Ullathorne who sprang to the rescue after the furore caused by Wiseman's Pastoral. His comment from his autobiography gives his own point of view:[1]

> After all the solicitude exhibited by the Roman cardinals in discussing the hierarchy, the subsequent policy demanded in its promulgation undoubtedly was that it should have been done as quietly and as much within our own circle as possible. Unhappily the opposite course was adopted, which defeated all the precautions that had inspired the Roman congregations and the Pope.

[1] *From Cabin Boy to Archbishop*, p. 296.

In Wiseman's continued absence (he did not arrive in England until 11th November) Ullathorne wrote a letter to *The Times* on 22nd October in which he pointed out that the bull concerned an internal matter of church administration and there was no intention to rule the English people. The Anglican newspaper the *Guardian* commented upon his efforts in the edition of 30th October:[1]

> Dr. Ullathorne writes to deprecate the public anger: the transaction, he urges, is simply between the Pope and 'his own subjects here'—a reorganisation of the machinery for the spiritual superintendence of the sect. But how does this modest language comport with the pretentious Pastoral 'given out of the Flaminian Gate at Rome' in which Cardinal Wiseman informs his flock that 'at present, and till such time as the Holy See shall think fit otherwise to provide, we govern and shall continue to govern, the counties of Middlesex, Hertford and Essex . . . .' All this, it is true, is an empty and ridiculous assumption: so far Dr. Ullathorne is quite right, but an assumption it is, . . . that there cannot be two Churches, although there may be many sects on the same soil: and to ask whether the English Church is still, as it formerly was, the National Church in the eye of the law? If not, let us note the change in her position.

After Lord John Russell's letter to the Bishop of Durham, Ullathorne went to London and rebuked Wiseman's vicar-general for allowing the Pastoral to be read in Roman Catholic Churches[2] (albeit on the Cardinal's instructions). Having got that off his chest, he began to compose an explanatory pamphlet on the whole episode. At this point Wiseman reached England and at once took over Ullathorne's material and in a matter of a few days produced his celebrated 'Appeal to the English People'.[3] Now in more reasonable and reasoned lines he showed a surer grasp of the situation. Although the storm was not over, it began to abate. He maintained that the Pastoral was meant only for the faithful, that the bull was concerned purely with a

---

[1] The *Guardian*, 30th October 1850, No. 253, p. 757.
[2] It was read on Sunday, 13th October.
[3] An 'Appeal to the reason and good feeling of the English people on the subject of the Catholic Hierarchy', published 20th November 1850.

change of internal organisation and that no reaction had been anticipated since there were already Roman Catholic bishops in the Colonies. Moreover prominent men had been made aware of the intentions of Rome and had expressed sympathy rather than surprise or alarm.

Wiseman's Appeal was on the whole well received and although not the only cause for it, the tide of antagonism began to turn. Lord John Russell had overstepped the mark, his colleagues did not support him, and the incongruity of the illiberality of liberal opinion was recognised. A few more reasonable voices made themselves heard. A correspondent to the *Guardian* wrote that the real danger to the Church of England was not Rome

> who neither has, nor can have any real power or influence in England over the mass of people, but in exact proportion to the failure of the catholic character of the Church of England. Let us Bishops, clergy and people do and suffer for the catholic faith. And we need not concern ourselves about the Cardinal Archbishop of Westminster.[1]

The Bishop of Exeter[2] counselled prudence and to avoid giving offence:

> Whether you shall in your pulpits deal frequently with the matters in controversy between the two churches is a question which cannot be answered in the same way to all. Generally speaking, where Roman error is not endeavouring to insinuate itself I should advise you to abstain from dealing with it. Where it is, be cautious how you deal with it. Inform yourself well on the points in dispute and, till you have done this, beware of hazarding your own credit, the honour of your Church and the faith of your people by crude and hasty disputation.[3]

Gladstone acknowledged that the language used in the Pope's Brief and in Wiseman's Pastoral had been 'not only unfortunate but of a vaunting and boastful description', but asked 'was it

[1] Letter to the *Guardian*, 30th October 1850, from G. A. Denison.
[2] Henry Phillpotts.
[3] 'Reply to the Addresses of the clergy of the Archdeaconry of Exeter on the recent Romish Aggression', Lord Bishop of Exeter. Chapter House, 18th November 1850. London, Joseph Masters, p. 11.

just to pass a proscribing Act affecting our Roman Catholic fellow-countrymen on account of language for which they were not responsible'?[1]

An open letter in reply to Lord John Russell criticised the Prime Minister's attitude towards abuses in the Church of Rome, when there existed offensive practices in the Church of England, such as those concerning the election and consecration of bishops.[2]

Such views were far from typical but they were written. And despite the hysteria, anxiety and rioting, burning of effigies of the Pope and Cardinal Wiseman, and raised voices at public meetings, the excitement eventually spent itself and left some sense of shame. As for the future and the way in which members of the Church of England were to live with the newly con-stituted Roman body, another correspondent in the *Guardian* gave a pointer:

> With regard to the claim set up by Cardinal Wiseman that all baptised persons should submit to him, I fear the only answer is that our Bishops must set up a like claim. It is a necessary consequence of the lamentable divisions of Christen-dom, that each body is forced to set up an exclusive claim of this kind.[3]

And so it had to be: two jurisdictions existing side by side, until such time as the scandal of it forced a re-examination of the causes of division, in search of a more edifying solution. In the meanwhile the same correspondent suggested that there were members of the Roman Catholic community in England who were not happy with the change of status of their bishops:

> But with regard to our brethren of the Church of Rome

[1] 25th March 1851, House of Commons, *Hansard*, Vol. CXV, p. 568, No mention has been made of that damp squib the Ecclesiastical Titles bill which was introduced into Parliament on 7th February 1851 and passed six months later. Many Anglicans were against it, notably Gladstone, and the fine of £100 for assuming the title of an English see was never exacted.

[2] 'A letter to Lord John Russell upon the late appointment of a Cardinal and Bishops of the Church of Rome into dioceses in these countries'. Kensington, 17th November 1850. John Perceval.

[3] F. H. Dickson to the *Guardian*, 1st November 1860, the *Guardian*, 6th November 1850, p. 797.

themselves, and the prospects which the times hold out to them, I should very much deprecate any thing like persecution. Those who know more than I do of them say that there are seeds of division among them, and different schools forming, which do not always hold the most moderate language with regard to each other. Far be it from me to rejoice in divisions, but I do rejoice when I see men thinking for themselves and using the learning and freedom of the day to correct their own faith by Holy Scriptures and Christian antiquity. [1]

The timing of the establishment of their hierarchy was a considerable surprise to many Roman Catholics in England. As already described, it had been a long while in the accomplishing and was precipitated by Wiseman's unexpected appointment. Lord Shrewsbury, virtually leader of the English Catholics, wrote to Ambrose de Lisle from Naples:

It was, I fear, and every one thinks, very ill-judged of Cardinal Wiseman to return as Cardinal. It was enough for him to be Archbishop of Westminster. It was I fancy all his own doing, for certainly the Pope intended him to remain at Rome. It has added to the excitement very considerably. As to the Hierarchy, I am anxious to know how it is to affect the lower clergy. If they do not get their rights, they have been scurvily treated. How came the good Pope to say it had been solicited by the Laity? How or when was that done? I have no recollection of anything of the sort. I am sure I would never have asked it without being assured that the inferiors would enjoy their rights as well as the bishops. Pray tell me about this. It is a hard case to put the responsibility upon us when (as far as I know) we have had nothing to do with it . . . [2]

Some Roman Catholic peers disassociated themselves from the action of the Papacy. Lord Beaumont, for example, took the extreme view held in common with arch-patriots of other confessions, that the bull threatened the constitution:

The Pope, by his ill-advised measures, has placed the

[1] F. H. Dickson to the *Guardian*, 1st November 1860, the *Guardian*, 6th November 1850, p. 797.
[2] 25th November 1850. *Life and Letters of Ambrose Phillipps de Lisle*, E. S. Purcell, Vol. I, p. 327.

Roman Catholics in this country in a position where they must either break from Rome, or violate their allegiance to the constitution of these realms: they must either consider the Papal Bull as null and void, or assert the right of a foreign prince to create, by his sovereign authority, English titles, and to erect English bishoprics. To send a bishop to Beverley for the spiritual direction of the Roman Catholic clergy in Yorkshire, and to erect a see of Beverley, are two very different things . . .[1]

The Duke of Norfolk thought likewise and in writing to agree with Lord Beaumont's views said that ultramontane opinions were 'totally incompatible with allegiance to our sovereign and with our constitution'.[2] He left the Roman Catholic Church, made his Communion as an Anglican and was only reconciled with the Church of his upbringing on his death-bed. English Roman Catholic opinion divided into two camps over the restoration issue. On the whole the 'old catholic' families, country gentry and nobility were against the change. They had been through the fire in penal times and had emerged independent and formed in the ways which they had carved out for themselves with sacrifice and endurance. Moreover, in spite of foreign education and persecution by Englishmen, they remained very English. Rome was abroad; Wiseman almost a foreigner who was introducing strange foreign customs. The old vicars apostolic had been close to them in what had been almost a family: dependence upon a foreign court and obedience to a foreign sovereign threatened liberty. Some of the more educated priests such as Lingard, Tierney[3] and Dr Rock[4] also raised some opposition. It is a measure of the basic loyalty within the Roman Catholic Church (which has shown most particularly in times of crisis and is one of her most shining characteristics) that she was able to carry her critical English members into the new era of history. Newman, as might be

[1] Lord Beaumont to Lord Zetland, Dublin, 20th November 1850.
[2] Duke of Norfolk to Lord Beaumont, Arundel Castle, 28th November 1850.
[3] Mark Aloysius Tierney, 1795–1865. Priest at Arundel. Editor of *Dodd's Church History*.
[4] Daniel Rock. Chaplain to Earl of Shrewsbury.

expected, saw that the main problem was to fill the new sees[1] satisfactorily.

> ... We are not ripe ourselves for a Hierarchy. Now they have one, they can't fill up the sees, positively can't. ...
> We want seminaries far more than sees. We want education, *view*, combination, organisation. I don't see the lie of things down here, but I am really inclined to think our game is to turn black, silent and sulky: to suspend the use of those titles which the Bishops cannot really lose—to appoint Vicars General, locum tenentes, to the sees not filled up. ... The great difficulty to this plan would be the Cardinal's status, would it not?[2]

Ambrose de Lisle, who had a more international outlook than some of his milieu, did not view the restoration of the hierarchy so apprehensively. He wrote with enthusiasm to Cardinal Wiseman, offering his most dutiful homage of respect and congratulations,[3] and he saw the new pattern as a help rather than a hindrance to his life's ambition, which was to see Christian unity in England.

He also wrote an open letter to Lord John Russell and one to Lord Shrewsbury who, although unenthusiastic about the new hierarchy, returned to England from Rome in order to support the bishops.

Certainly some of the outcry was irrational and hysterical. But the whole episode called up conflicting loyalties in an age before men had begun seriously to doubt the merits of patriotism. When a national church in support of a national sovereign and constitution was for most Englishmen so sacred, agents of a foreign power promoting what seemed to be false doctrines appeared to present a serious threat. (This was particularly acute in view of growing elements within the English Church who were pursuing a similar and therefore supposedly treacherous line.) That this conflict of loyalties was felt also by members of the English Roman Catholic body, is evident, and

---

[1] The appointments to the new sees were not all made until the summer of 1851.

[2] Letter to J. M. Capes, 18th February 1851. *Letters and Diaries of J. H. Newman*, Vol. XIV, p. 213, ed. C. S. Dessain and U. F. Blehl, Nelson, 1963.

[3] 13th November 1850, from original in Westminster Cathedral Archives.

it was to take a stronger Archbishop of Westminster than Wiseman to unite them firmly together and strengthen their dependence upon the Holy See. By that move, achieved during the Archiepiscopate of Cardinal Manning, English Roman Catholics were to lose a further measure of what they held in common with Anglicans; relations between the two communions would become yet more difficult.

But before this stiffening process took hold there was a series of attempts to bring Anglicans and Roman Catholics closer together. Some of these were visionary and unrealistic, even on occasion ludicrous (such as the Order of Corporate Reunion), but they were undertaken with faith and represent the good intentions and brave hearts of their promoters and are therefore worthy of notice in these pages.

10

REUNION AND THE VICTORIANS

Whether any of the contacts between Anglicans and Roman Catholics during the nineteenth century can properly be described as Reunion Movements is doubtful; certainly not in the sense in which the term is used today. The most that can be claimed for them is that they were attempts on the part of a few individuals, the same individuals in the main throughout the period, to set up such communication between their two churches as might eventually make reunion possible. Some of the participants had their own view of how this could come to be: others had no set formulas. Such Anglican enthusiasts for reunion as there were, and this must be seen all along as a very small minority, fell into the latter category. On the Roman Catholic side, reunion was seen as involving the 'reabsorption' of Anglicans into the only true Church, that is the Church under the authority of the Holy See. There was nothing new in this. What was unusual was that although almost all the adjustments were required to be made on the Anglican side, certain fresh approaches were made to particular bodies of Anglicans; vague terms were sometimes offered and a certain tenderness shown to secure and to mitigate the necessary submission.

Those Roman Catholics who favoured reunion showed two blind spots. The first derived partly from the fact that this was a time of concern for minutiae. (Heated letters were exchanged on the essential nature of candles or processions; and the shape of a chasuble, even the cut of a pair of trousers, were of religious significance.) The Oxford Movement wrought visible changes in the appearance of the Church of England, but it was not appreciated how far she still remained away from the Roman standpoint. This misapprehension enabled the central authorities at Rome correctly to accuse English and continental promoters of reunion of not understanding the Church of England, and to refer them back to the Roman Catholic hierarchy in England. Particularly after 1865, this hierarchy understood very well the ways in which they differed from the Anglicans, but they were not interested in the reasons for the differences, nor in their great and deep similarities. Secondly, reunion, as seen in the guise of an erring daughter returning at last to her mother, showed lack of realism, for the parent had altered in the period of division. The church headed by Pius IX which Englishmen were being exhorted to rejoin was not the Church they had left in the sixteenth century, either doctrinally or in organisation. Reluctance to embrace nineteenth-century Roman Catholicism on the part of the Tractarians was seen by such as Lord Shrewsbury to be insincerity, since they were already enjoying many catholic practices. But it was their catholicity which they quoted as the cause of their conscientious unwillingness to reject their own traditions.

The new and frequently used term 'corporate reunion' added confusion. In the minds of some it simply meant secession in very large numbers. For others it had a different connotation: the re-joining of bodies of separated Christians according to some plan. Amidst the meetings, the discussions, the schemes, the exchange of letters, and bedevilling them all, was the issue of individual conversions. Should they continue despite the talk of reunion on a broader canvas? Would attempts to achieve reunion prevent conversions, and if so, should all such endeavours for reunion therefore stop? These questions were raised throughout these years and not only were a complication, but eventually brought the whole matter to a halt. There seems no doubt that individual changes of allegiance in the nineteenth century hindered the progress of the reunion of the churches. Had men with a wider vision been able to remain within their own frontiers and to work from inside towards deeper understanding of other interpretations and traditions, neither side would have become so rigid and antipathetic. But the Roman teaching that there was no salvation outside the Church of Rome was a powerful persuasive to the waverer, and compromise, toleration, adaptation and adjustment were alien and unacceptable concepts to both parties. Where the two bodies could have edified each other, there was bigotry and prejudice. Rome had a strong, but sometimes naive sense of the supernatural:[1] contemporary Anglicanism had a neurotic terror of superstition.[2] While both remained apart these traits hardened; they prevented understanding when they might have become correctives to each other.

There were three periods when the subject of reunion came to the fore. The first was in the years 1840–1845 when there occurred meetings and correspondence, which came to an end on the Anglican side when it was felt that Roman Catholics were thinking solely in terms of individual conversions. The formation of the Association for the Promotion of the Unity of Christendom in 1857 marks the beginning of the second period; this ends in 1864 when the Holy Office instructed the Roman Catholic members to leave the Association, and its history becomes of no further interest to this study. The third period covers the years 1875–1880 with the uniat scheme of Presbyter Anglicanus[3] and the curious affair of the Order of Corporate Reunion. The friendship of Lord Halifax and the Abbé Portal; the events of 1894–1896 which led to the enquiry into Anglican Orders; the international contacts between Pusey, A. P. Forbes, the Bishop of Brechin, and other Anglicans with the Belgian Jesuit, Victor De Buck and some French bishops, might have been described here. But as they form part of larger subjects, the bull 'Apostolicae Curae' on the one hand and the First Vatican Council on the other, they find their place in Chapters 11 and 12.

Throughout the period there were friendships and letters

[1] Lord Shrewsbury, de Lisle and Bishop Ullathorne went at various times to see miraculous virgins in the Tirol, the Estatica of Caldaro, etc. Newman went to Loreto.

[2] The future Archbishop of Canterbury, A. C. Tait, writing in his diary from Perugia on 29th July 1845 and commenting on a religious festival: 'The scene was indeed like the worship of some heathen deity. This surely is anti-Christ'. From his *Life*, by T. R. Davidson and W. Benham, Macmillan 1891, Vol. I, p. 125. Archbishop Benson made similar remarks in his diary from Florence in 1894. *Life of E. W. Benson*, A. C. Benson, Macmillan, 1900, Vol. II, pp. 563–7.

[3] Pseudonym of the Revd. Edmund S. Grindle, Vicar of St. Paul's, Brighton.

between individuals across frontiers, and athough these were mainly on a social and intellectual level, in the case of the communications between the Acton, Gladstone and de Lisle[1] families, the commons interest in religious questions meant that some of the exchange was devoted to these issues.

The first character in the reunion drama must be the future Cardinal Wiseman who, although not an ecumenist in the modern sense, had a deep interest in what was happening among the Anglicans at Oxford, tried to cultivate them and visualised their place in the great catholic revival which he felt he had been called to lead. He was, therefore, a good deal more liberal in his attitude than any of his successors.[2] His part begins with the visit of Newman and Hurrell Froude in 1833 when they went to Rome with an introduction. Wiseman was then Rector of the English College.[3] He was greatly struck with their outlook and description of the 'wonderful movement then commenced in England'. Fifteen years later he wrote[4] 'From that hour . . . I watched with intense interest and love the Movement of which I then caught the first glimpse. My studies changed their course, the bent of my mind was altered, in the strong desire to co-operate with the new mercies of providence'. Wiseman had already received visits from several religious thinkers in France; Lacordaire, Lamennais and Montalembert who appealed to him to lead a great catholic revival in England,[5] and also from two young Englishmen, converts to Roman Catholicism, Ambrose de Lisle and George Spencer.[6]

---

[1] Ambrose Lisle Phillipps changed his names to Phillipps de Lisle in 1862, but he is referred to in the second style for the whole of this work in the interests of clarity.

[2] Fr. J. Derek Holmes of Ushaw College points out in *One in Christ*, 1972, No. 1, Vol. VIII, p. 57 that Fr. Vincent McNabb wrote an article based on Wiseman's 'Letter on Catholic Unity' in 1924. Permission to publish was refused by Cardinal Bourne as it seemed as if the expressions used in 1841 might at that point be 'mischievous and misleading'.

[3] p. 115.

[4] *Essays on Various Subjects*, Cardinal Wiseman, Charles Dolman, 1853, Vol. II, p. 94n.

[5] *Cardinal Wiseman*, Denis Gwynn, Denis Browne & Nolan, Dublin, 1929, p. 40.

[6] 1799–1864. Son of 2nd Earl Spencer. Ordained 1824. Became Roman Catholic 1830. Passionist 1847 with name Ignatius of St. Paul.

Three further personalities must here enter the story. The first of these, Lord Shrewsbury, did not share Wiseman's enthusiasm for the Tractarians; the second and third, Ambrose de Lisle and A. W. Pugin[1] were almost the only other Roman Catholics who did. Lord Shrewsbury, as leader of the English Roman Catholic community and a prime mover in the revival movement, failed to see the significance of the Oxford men because he distrusted them, and was unsure of their good faith. 'Anglicans' he wrote to de Lisle[2] . . . 'said to themselves . . . we must needs seek Truth, but we must find her at home.' They were pre-determined 'to find right in England and wrong in Rome'. He thought they sought to 'mend themselves, but when that amendment comes in contact with their position (and that position in their interest) their zeal dies and they come to a full stop'. de Lisle remonstrated with Lord Shrewsbury over several years and at great length on the Tractarians' behalf and if there is a hero in the piece, it is he. Visionary in the extreme, un-realistic even, but indefatigable despite countless disappoint-ments and rebuffs, especially from his own communion, de Lisle laboured for reunion for fifty years, conscious, as few other men were, of the scandal of disunity and believing that, if God were with him, it mattered not who was against him. In 1838 he had joined with George Spencer in promoting a Crusade of Prayer for the conversion of England, had travelled Europe for its support, and had run up against trouble from the vicars apostolic. Now he was to become with Pugin the intermediary between Bishop Wiseman and the Oxford men. 'Your plan for converting England is an idle dream', he wrote to Shrewsbury.[3] 'If then you really desire England's conversion, you must adopt my plan, which is a practical one, and which is already hailed in a friendly way by a very large party in the Church of England, both clergy and laity.' de Lisle's optimism and overstatement were as abundant as his enthusiasm.

[1] Augustus Welby Pugin, 1812–1852. Architect; pioneer of Gothic revival. Became Roman Catholic 1835.

[2] *Life and Letters of Ambrose Phillipps de Lisle*, E. S. Purcell, Vol. I, pp. 276–7. The Letters and papers of Ambrose de Lisle were destroyed during the 1940s and the library sold. The authors acknowledge their considerable indebtedness to the present Squire de Lisle who is attempting to reassemble the collection with a tenacity worthy of his great-grandfather.

[3] *Life and Letters of Ambrose Phillipps de Lisle*, E. S. Purcell, Vol. I, p. ix.

Pugin shared de Lisle's love for all things gothic, and his obsessional mediaevalism dictated his designs both artistic and ecumenical. It is not easy to take his extravagant views and dramatic tendencies entirely seriously, but since so many more stable men showed no interest whatsoever in these burning questions, the field was left wide open for personalities such as his. He saw the Oxford men as trying to re-introduce a style of worship prevalent in the Middle Ages with plain chant and a monastic ethos in dark gothic churches and vowed that here was a manifestation of pure religion. Members of his own Church who followed different architectural, liturgical and artistic patterns and who did not see catholic revival as gothic revival he considered beyond the pale. He wrote to de Lisle:[1] 'I now almost despair. I do indeed . . . . the present state of things is quite lamentable and were it not for the Oxford men, I should quite despair.' At times de Lisle found Pugin cause for some anxiety and he wrote to Shrewsbury[2] that he wished Pugin would not talk against the Jesuits so much when in Oxford, where he had found a number of congenial acquaintances. In fact Pugin, who had made his headquarters at Oscott with Wiseman, played his only significant role as a go-between. He became a link between the English catholics and the Oxford school by his visits to that university. In February and October 1840, he became greatly excited by what a body of Anglicans there were thinking and doing, and he formed an acquaintance with J. R. Bloxam,[3] Fellow of Magdalen College, and other Tractarians. Bloxam had been Newman's curate from 1836 until 1840, when the illness of his father caused him to resign. An incident during this ministry illustrates the temper of the times. Bloxam had made a visit to Alton Towers, home of Lord Shrewsbury in 1839, and had attended Mass, the family having filed into the chapel when he was there saying Morning Prayer. A correspondent (the Revd. W. Dodsworth) wrote to Newman that it had been reported to him that Bloxam had bowed his head at the elevation. Newman replied on 19th

[1] From Ramsgate, 18th December 1840. *Life and Letters of Ambrose Phillipps de Lisle*, E. S. Purcell, Vol. II, p. 214.
[2] 23rd Sunday after Pentecost (23rd October) 1842. ibid., Vol. I, p. 259.
[3] John Rouse Bloxham, 1807–1891. Liturgist; originator of ceremonial revival in Church of England.

November 1839.[1] Bloxam had assured him he had taken no
part in the service and had not changed his position, but this did
not prevent Newman from referring to the matter as 'a very
unpleasant occurrence'. The affair was reported to the Bishop
of Oxford, who also wrote (twice) to Newman. This indicates
some of the problems of mid-nineteenth-century ecumenists
and why there were so few.

Six months after Bloxam left his curacy, in the autumn of
1840, he went, at an introduction from Dr. Rock, to see the
Trappist Monastery which Ambrose de Lisle had founded at
Charnwood on his estate in Leicestershire. The two men had a
short conversation outdoors and, on 25th January 1841, de
Lisle followed up the encounter with an immensely long
letter[2] in which he confided to Bloxam his hopes and fears for
corporate reunion in England. This was the beginning of a
voluminous correspondence which continued between the two
men for the following nine months. de Lisle reflected on the
many ties which already bound them together and of the
'truly catholick' spirit he had seen exhibited in the recent
writings of Oxford men. 'Surely God cannot intend such souls
to be much longer divided from the rest of his catholick children.' Some learned continental theologians agreed with him.
He was himself labouring 'to soften down the asperities which
exist on our side, and which I candidly acknowledge display
but too often in Catholic writers amongst us a spirit . . .
unworthy of Christian charity'.

de Lisle's main theme concerned the difference between a
Church and a Rite: he said it was no new thing for catholics of
different rites to live together in the same country. He himself
had accepted the Roman rite seventeen years ago, having for
several years before regarded himself as a catholic, while
following the modern Anglican rite. He hoped that the day

[1] *Newman and Bloxam. An Oxford Friendship*, R. D. Middleton, OUP, 1947,
pp. 55–8.
  [2] MS Magdalen College Library. Ambrose de Lisle has been badly
served by a very indifferent biography by E. S. Purcell, the chronology of
which is lamentable, and some of the recipients of letters inaccurate. The
letters exchanged between Bloxam and de Lisle are preserved in the
Library of Magdalen College, Oxford, and were transcribed into a manuscript entitled 'Reunion' by Bloxam, but never published. Wherever possible,
reference is made to the version of a letter which is contained in that collection.

would dawn when Anglicans could be united with the Holy See while yet retaining their own ancient Sarum rite, and many of their own traditions.

Bloxam, startled, but delighted, replied in a short note[1] in which he said it would give him great pleasure to receive de Lisle with college hospitality whenever he wanted to visit Oxford. Letters passed thick and fast between Bloxam and de Lisle; in the background was Newman, whose comments, at first anonymous, were relayed to de Lisle. de Lisle said[2] he felt convinced that it was necessary to take immediate steps because of the present favourable disposition on the part of the Anglican Church. At this early stage he recommended that the Anglican clergy should not make any communication or proposal whatsoever to any authority of the catholic church on the continent or elsewhere

> and as for the English Roman Catholick body, I put them wholly out of the question. It would be most injudicious for the Anglican Church to negotiate anything with them (when I come to Oxford I will explain more at large my meaning on this head). . . .

de Lisle[3] told Bloxam that Wiseman was writing to him continually 'for I am always overwhelmed with anxiety about this glorious affair' and 'he completely enters into all my views'.

> Our gaining Bishop Wiseman is an immense point. He is decidedly one of the first men in Europe. He will do all in his power to promote the reunion, for which he would gladly give his life. . . .

In a later note to Bloxam[4] de Lisle sent some extracts from a letter he had received from Wiseman dated 1st April.

> Let us have an influx of new blood, let us have but a small number of such men as write in the Tracts, so imbued with the spirit of the Early Church, so desirous to revive the image of the ancient Fathers . . . and we shall be speedily

[1] 9th February 1841. MS Magdalen College Library.
[2] 22nd February 1841, ibid.
[3] 29th March 1841, ibid.
[4] 5th April 1841, ibid.

reformed, and England quickly converted. I am ready to acknowledge that, in all things, except the happiness of possessing the Truth, and being in communion with God's true Church and enjoying the advantages and blessings that flow thence, we are their inferiors. . . . if the Oxford Divines entered the Church we must be ready to fall into the shade, and take up our position in the background. . . . I will willingly yield to them place, and honour, if God's good service require it. I will be a cooperator under the greater zeal and learning and abilities of a new leader. Depend upon it they do not know their own strength.

Bloxam hoped de Lisle would stay with him at Magdalen for a week after Easter 1841, but the communications being sent through Bloxam from Newman[1] were far from heartening:

This I feel most strongly and I cannot conceal it viz. that while Rome is what she is, union is impossible—that we too must change I do not deny. Rome must change first of all in her spirit. I must see more sanctity in her than I do at present. Alas I see no marks of sanctity—or if any they are chiefly confined to converts from us. . . . I do verily think that, with all our sins, there is more sanctity in the Church of England and Ireland, than in the Roman Catholic bodies in the same countries.

Again, on 2nd March, he continued, that although de Lisle's letters breathed a beautiful spirit, to any one who came to him with a proposal of negotiations for the reconciliation of the Church of England to the Holy See, his answer must be to direct him to his bishop: he ended with some very harsh words about Rome. Paradoxically, Newman's attitude to de Lisle's advances was a good deal more rigid than Bloxam's, yet it was Bloxam who was to remain in the Church of England and Newman who was to leave. Bloxam forwarded Newman's letter with the comment that although its contents were on the whole painful to read, it must not prevent the visit of one who did not come as a negotiator, 'but with whom they had much sympathy and who was greatly respected and admired for his exertions'.

[1] Enclosed with Bloxam's letter of 25th February 1841. MS Magdalen College Library.

In March 1841 the furore following the publication of Tract 90 made Bloxam think it wise to postpone de Lisle's visit, but the correspondence continued and letters were exchanged also between de Lisle and Newman. They may well have been encouraged by Wiseman who was so anxious to make Newman's acquaintance that he obviously suggested compromises[1] to de Lisle which he might otherwise not have made, in order to secure this end. By April Bloxam thought it safe to reopen the invitation to Oxford and de Lisle came on 30th April. He stayed not at Magdalen, but at the Angel Inn, and met a number of Tractarians and visited some churches. On his return he went straight to Oscott to report to Wiseman and painted a glowing picture of the Oxford men and their interest in reunion. Writing to Bloxam[2] he said that Wiseman now understood the position and was to write to Rome hoping for an answer recommending as conciliatory a tone as possible towards Anglicans and a request for reform 'within the English Catholicks according to the Holy Maxims of the Church'. Wiseman himself wrote to de Lisle on the feast of St. Stanislaus (7th May) confirming that this was in his mind and saying that he thought he ought to go to Rome to ask the Pope what instructions he had for his dealings with the Oxford men. He was obviously hoping for some concessions, reform or mildness. de Lisle on his part wrote to Shrewsbury and, pointing out his expectations from the Tractarians, besought the peer to use his influence in Rome against any precipitate action in that quarter.

Urge at Rome the necessity of immense prudence and forbearance to do everything to encourage, nothing to damp; not to call upon these men to quit their own communion in order to join ours, but to proceed on courageously with their holy and glorious intention of reconciling their Church to ours: remember this involves the reconciliation of the Kingdom, of the aristocracy, with all its wealth and power, of the Nation. A false step would spoil all, would produce a

[1] *Cardinal Wiseman*, Denis Gwynn, p. 119.
[2] 15th and 18th May 1841. MS Magdalen College Library.

Protestant reaction and would defeat the hopes of the Holy See for another century.[1]

While he was thinking in these terms de Lisle was caught in a dilemma: Wiseman reminded him that it was not safe for Anglican souls to stay where they were: Bloxam was suspicious of conversions and the rumours about certain individuals who were threatening to leave the Church of England. Poor de Lisle described his 'battling for your church which I find dreadfully uphill work';[2] he also spoke of Wiseman's dismay on receipt of a letter from Newman regretting Wiseman's vindication of invocations of the Blessed Virgin Mary.[3] Bloxam found that de Lisle wanted to move too quickly:[4] there was a steady feeling of the want of unity and hardly a Sunday without an allusion to it in the university sermons. 'Devout men are praying for it on all sides.' An inconsiderate step on the part of individuals would give a complete triumph to the opposite party in the Church. Reunion might not come in their lifetime, but they would be more than recompensed if they had helped to pave the way. 'Let us in both churches be content for a while to act upon each other for good, if I may venture to say so, and strive to rival each other in the pure and holy marks of true catholic Christianity and why should we despair of God's mercy in His own good time. . . .' Those who at the present time 'hastily forsake their Church for another, they will do irreparable mischief to the great cause for which we are labouring'. de Lisle had feared delay because he thought the catholic-minded clergy might leave the Church of England. 'I firmly believe that if a proper scheme of reunion were set before the whole body of your clergy and bishops no man amongst them that has the slightest claims either to piety or good sense could possibly resist it.'[5] Newman quickly sent de Lisle his reactions.[6] He did not expect the reunion of the churches in his time.

---

[1] Sabbato in Albis, 17th April 1841, *Life and Letters of Ambrose Phillipps de Lisle*, E. S. Purcell, Vol. I, p. 217.
[2] To Bloxam, 5th June 1841, MS Magdalen College Library.
[3] *Life and Times of Cardinal Wiseman*, W. Ward, Vol. 1, p. 393.
[4] Bloxam to de Lisle, 27th June 1841. MS Magdalen College Library.
[5] de Lisle to Bloxham, 25th June 1841, ibid.
[6] 28th June 1841. From the draft sent by Newman to Bloxam on 1st July. ibid.

I have discouraged the notion of all sudden proceedings with a view to it. I must ask your leave to repeat on this occasion most distinctly, that I cannot be a party to any agitation; but mean to remain quiet in my own place, and to do all I can to make others take the same course.

This, I conceive to be my single duty; but over and above this paramount consideration, I believe it to be the wisest and most expedient course for the eventual unity of the Church Catholic. I will not attempt to reap before the sowing. I will not set my teeth on edge with sour grapes.

I know it is quite within the range of possibilities that one or another of our members should go over to your communion; though I trust it will not be the case as regards the individuals you specify. However, if such an event were to happen, it would be a greater misfortune to you than a grief to us. If there is one thing calculated more than another to extinguish all hope of a better understanding between Rome and England, by discrediting us with our own people and rendering us suspicious of yourselves, it would be the conversion by you of some of our members. If your friends wish to put a gulf between themselves and us, let them make converts, but not else. . . .

On St. Matthew's day 1841 (21st September) Wiseman's *Letter on Catholic Unity* was published in the form of an open letter to Lord Shrewsbury.[1] In it he described the current state of religious division in England and the Tractarian revolt: the Oxford divines had an approximation of catholic practices and doctrines, were dissatisfied with the system of the Anglican Church and the State connection, and some yearned for catholic unity. The Church of Christ had a paramount duty to heal schism, not to be deterred by past failures, nor by present difficulties, nor by future sufferings, but 'to begin at once and to persevere energetically in such measures as *directly* tend to the work of religious reunion: not to say that the time is not yet come, but to hasten it forward'. Mischief must be undone and obstacles removed to bring people back to kinder, juster,

[1] *A Letter on Catholic Unity* addressed to the Rt. Hon. the Earl of Shrewsbury by Nicholas, Bishop of Melipotamus, London. Charles Dolman, 1841.

truer views between Roman Catholic and Anglican. Roman Catholics had been misjudged in the past and their true character had not been shown. It was the duty of Roman Catholics to explain and defend phrases used in popular devotion; not to be harsh or sarcastic; not to attempt to defend local malpractices, but acknowledge them; to lament deficiencies, and to offer explanations. Bloxam thought the letter useful.[1] de Lisle renewed Wiseman's invitation to Richard Waldo Sibthorpe, a Fellow of Magdalen;[2] there was an ordination at Oscott on the 28th: would Sibthorpe like to see it? Newman did all he could to prevent his going (Sibthorpe had a traumatic early history) but he went, and returned to Oxford 'looking worn and agitated and no longer a member of the Church of England'.[3] Bloxam was disturbed by what had happened and wrote to de Lisle to all intents and purposes closing the correspondence.[4] This was not how he conceived a movement for reunion.

> It appeared to me that your expectations were raised to see a number of members of our Church leave it, and that in a short time, and betake themselves to your Communion. . . . I speak candidly when I tell you that however desirous I may be of reunion I have never yet felt the slightest conviction that it is my own individual duty to leave the Church of England, and my repugnance to the notion is so great that I must decline any discussion of it. . . . I am well satisfied that things are upon the whole working for good, and will continue to do so, if we look only to God's will that we may follow it, and pray for guidance that we may know what that will is. . .

A few letters passed between Bloxam and de Lisle in later years, and they met again, but there was no further discussion on reunion. de Lisle and Wiseman continued to be in touch with a number of the Oxford men and there were individual conversions, including that of Newman himself in 1845. But

[1] Bloxam to de Lisle, 12th October 1841. MS Magdalen College Library.

[2] 1792–1879. Became Roman Catholic October 1842. Returned to Church of England 1843. Became Roman Catholic again 1865. Roman Catholic and Anglican burial services at his request.

[3] J. R. Bloxam, the *Magdalen College Register*, Vol. IV, the *Demies*, p. 224, quoted in *An Oxford Friendship*, R. D. Middleton, p. 160.

[4] Bloxham to de Lisle, 31st October 1841. MS Magdalen College Library.

it was with a small band of close friends that he went and not, as Wiseman had hoped, as the leader of a large corporate movement towards the Church of Rome. After this, and largely because of it, reunion was seen as a question of secession and this section of the history of moves towards unity in the nineteenth century was over.

One of de Lisle's problems in his plans for reunion was the diversity in the Church of England. To expect the whole body to consider union with Rome was clearly impossible, since the wing which was most sympathetic to the debt which the Anglican Church owed to the Reformation could be relied upon to be positively antagonistic. He therefore sought to impress the 'catholic-minded' members and hoped that they would be strong enough to influence and carry the remainder. In doing so he first over-estimated the size and strength of the 'catholic' party and secondly misunderstood the basis of their desire for reunion, which was not an enthusiasm for submission to the authority of the Holy See, as she then was. The extent of their loyalty to their own communion became clearer to him. 'The Oxford men', he wrote to Lord Shrewsbury, 'have no thoughts of quitting the English Church.'[1]

When in 1857 de Lisle began again in pursuit of his goal, if indeed he had ever stopped, it was with another and less formulated plan for reunion. 'The time is not come for that', he wrote to George Spencer,[2] 'all we dwell upon is the importance of unity in the fold of Jesus Christ, and in encouraging a deep study of Christian antiquity, and of that blessed Primitive Church before the unity of Christ's Church was broken by any large or durable secession'. de Lisle had found some new Anglican allies, the two most considerable of which were Dr. Frederick George Lee[3] and Alexander Penrose Forbes,[4] Bishop of Brechin in the Episcopalian Church of Scotland.

In December of 1856 Dr. Lee founded an Anglican periodical

---

[1] 23rd Sunday after Pentecost (23rd October) 1842. *Life and Letters of Ambrose Phillipps de Lisle*, E. S. Purcell, Vol. I. p. 258.

[2] 25th February 1860. ibid., Vol. I, p. 185.

[3] 1822–1902, theological writer: most of his life vicar of All Saints', Lambeth. Became a Roman Catholic on his death bed.

[4] Born Edinburgh, 16th June 1817. Indian Civil Service 1836–1839. Oxford 1840–1844. Deacon: Trinity 1844. Bishop of Brechin 1857. Died 8th October 1875.

named *The Union*[1] which was devoted to advocating the corporate reunion of the Church of England with the Holy See.

de Lisle wrote some letters to *The Union* in the spring of 1857 and was severely rebuked by some of his brethren. But he was still undaunted and being in touch once again with a group of Anglicans who were keenly interested in the reunion question, entered another phase of activity whilst living partly in this world, partly in the world to come, and partly in a world of fantasy. He wrote to Newman that summer[2]

> Now it having been officially intimated to me, who, as you know, have for very many years cherished the hope that by means of a Reunion of Churches the great breach of the 16th century might be healed, that there was now a powerful Party in the Established Church ready to take definite steps towards the realisation of such a measure, I was induced in the early part of the year to write the letters which appeared in *The Union*, and when subsequently these letters occasioned a strong outburst of remonstrance in some of the organs of the Catholic body, I felt we could take no further step, until we had ascertained from the voice of authority how far we could with safety proceed on our course.

In his letter to Cardinal Barnabo, Cardinal Prefect of the Propaganda Fide,[3] de Lisle estimated a 'powerful party in the Established Church' as containing 2,000 priests and ten bishops who were joined together in a desire for reunion with the Holy See. The pages of his letter showed many other examples of similar wishful thinking. Simultaneously de Lisle had written a pamphlet of 70 pages, *On the Future Unity of Christendom*. In it he insinuated that there were three great denominations of Christians; the Catholics, the Greeks and the Anglicans. He proposed a congress at Paris of theologians from 'the three churches' who should in concert 'lay down certain preliminaries that might serve as a basis for further operations'. The congress would lead to the calling of an ecumenical council to heal differences and restore unity.

[1] Succeeded 1862 by the *Union Review*.
[2] 2nd July 1857. From original in Birmingham Oratory.
[3] 18th May 1857. *Life and Letters of Ambrose Phillips de Lisle*, E. S. Purcell, Vol. I, pp. 375–8.

On 4th July the leaders of the reunion movement met in London and pledged themselves to a series of resolutions which de Lisle was to convey to the Holy See. They determined not to rest until the two churches were reunited.

Cardinal Barnabo replied to de Lisle's letter[1] but he also wrote one to Wiseman asking for his comments. Wiseman wrote a very full reply;[2] de Lisle, he said, was quite mistaken about the number of Anglicans who were enthusiastic: he was wrong about the Bishops of Oxford and Exeter, and his pamphlet made many errors. The greatest of these, Wiseman said, spoke of 'the three great denominations of Christians' as though they were all equal and could treat of religious union upon a footing of equality. It would not be possible for the heterodox and schismatical bishops of England and Greece to take part as Fathers of the Council. On the contrary, they must stand outside the door, and sue for absolution and pardon, and bow. Barnabo wrote de Lisle[3] a severe letter telling him that no unity was possible which in the slightest degree questioned the office of the Roman Pontiff as Vicar of Christ and Supreme Head of Christ's Church or left the slightest shade of error. de Lisle was immediately conciliatory and replied with meekness,[4] but also with convincing if lengthy arguments. He denied hotly having implied that the question of reunion was discussed as between equal parties: '. . . yet in considering the question of the restoration of unity between us, it is obvious that I must do so rather from their point of view than from my own.' If Cardinal Barnabo wished him to abandon the work he had begun, one word would suffice: 'and in giving up great and thankless labour, I shall at the same time be setting myself free from the most unfounded calumnies of my enemies'. The Cardinal seems to have been mollified by these words, at least temporarily. Wiseman also, rather strangely, did no more; he had made his points, from his angle very important ones, and he allowed de Lisle and other Roman Catholics to carry on. He was diabetic and his strength was spent (factors which were to be

[1] 8th June 1857. *Life and Letters of Ambrose Phillipps de Lisle*, E. S. Purcell, Vol. I, pp. 378–9.

[2] *Life and Times of Cardinal Wiseman*, W. Ward, Vol. II, p. 429.

[3] 17th August 1857. *Life and Letters of Ambrose Phillipps de Lisle*, Vol. I, pp. 380–1.

[4] 31st August 1857. ibid., pp. 381–4.

important in the history of English Roman Catholicism, because they put greater power into the hands of Manning). de Lisle was therefore free to take part with Lee, Lord Glasgow, the Bishop of Brechin and others in the formation of the Association for Promoting the Unity of Christendom. This took place on 8th September 1857 at Lee's Chambers in Danes Lane, the Strand, in London. Thirty-four members were enrolled at once[1] and the membership has been calculated to have risen to about 8,000 by 1864.[2] The Association was for united prayer that visible unity might be restored to Christendom. The manifesto describing the Association made it clear that no principles were required to be compromised. The appeal was made to all 'who while lamenting the divisions among Christians, look forward to their healing, mainly by a corporate reunion of those three great bodies which claim for themselves the inheritance of the priesthood and the name of catholic'. The only obligation was the daily use of a short form of prayer, taken from the Roman Mass, together with one 'Our Father' and in the case of priests, the offering of one Mass at least once in three months for this intention. As Bishop Clifford of Clifton (who was a member of the Association) wrote later[3] he understood the object to be 'to get people to pray for unity without any view being expressed by the Association as to how this end was to be attained. So that Catholics prayed for Unity in the only way in which they could pray, viz. that those who were not united to the centre of Unity might become united'.

One of the Anglican secretaries of the Association, the Revd. George Nugee,[4] was received in audience by Pope Pius IX and described the movement. In his letter[5] to the *Weekly Register* he commented on 'the heartiness of the Holy Father's commendation'. The exact expression by which he sought to convey his cordial statement was 'Mio interno sentimento voluntario'. Mgr. Talbot[6] had been present. 'I

---

[1] The original list of those present was left by F. G. Lee to Pusey House, Oxford, where it now is.

[2] Of these 1,070 were said to be Roman Catholics (including a number of foreigners), 300 Orthodox and the remainder Anglican.

[3] *Life and Times of Bishop Ullathorne*, Cuthbert Butler, Burns Oates, 1926, Vol. I, p. 348.

[4] Vicar of Wymering, Cosham, Portsmouth.

[5] 19th and 26th November 1864.   [6] Canon of St Peter's.

shall not easily forget the zeal he evinced during that interview in urging the claims of the Association for the Unity of Christendom on the Holy Father'. A letter from de Lisle to Wiseman[1] seeking to introduce Nugee to the Cardinal also spoke of the incident:

> he laid before His Holiness the general plan for the Reconciliation in a conversation of great interest, and the Pope expressed his great delight and gave him his Blessing for the success of the work—on the same occasion he presented to the Pope the Mother Superior of a Convent of Sisters of Charity . . . and His Holiness gave her his Blessing and expressed his amazement at such an institution having been established in the Church of England.

The causes of the downfall of the A.P.U.C. (as it came to be called) were various.[2] The English hierarchy was already disturbed by the suggestions of the Branch theory, by the thought that the presence of the Reunion Movement would diminish the number of conversions, and by the promptings of the Manning party. At the Bishops' meetings in Low Week of 1864 the A.P.U.C. was discussed and the question of catholics being allowed to remain members was raised. Ullathorne was deputed to write to the Holy See and ask for a ruling. His letter now lies in the Archives of the Propaganda Fide.[3] A free translation from the letter reads as follows:

> This association comprises some English Catholics among whom (it is difficult to believe) one or two bishops. . . . It is pledged to pray for the reunion of the Roman Catholic Church, the Greek Schism and the Anglican Communion, as those who claim to have inherited the Catholic name and priesthood . . so the Anglican sect is tacitly assumed to be part of the catholic church. . . .

Bishop Ullathorne then went on to describe *The Union Review*.

> The editor even suggests that the Catholic Church might profit from some free discussion. . . . As long therefore as this organ of the Association exists, it is a refuge for imprudent

[1] 11th April 1864. Westminster Cathedral Archives.
[2] See *Dr. Lee of Lambeth*, Henry R. T. Brandreth, SPCK, 1951, pp. 90–101.
[3] Written from Birmingham, 26th April 1864, Scritt. Refer, nei Congress: 1864–1866. Anglia 17, No. 156.

catholics who can let their imaginations run to offensive lengths, where episcopal authority cannot reach them.

He therefore submitted two questions to the Sacred Congregation: whether catholics should be allowed to belong to this association; whether priests should give it their co-operation and offer the Holy Sacrifice for this intention. These Archives also contain several letters from Manning about this date. The first,[1] also to Cardinal Barnabo, supported Bishop Ullathorne's letter and emphasised that some catholics attached to the 'Unione' had written articles 'gravemente erronei e scandalosi'. Two other letters from Manning warned the Propaganda Fide against certain individuals.[2] One divulged that the editor

of a Protestant review which calls itself Catholic and is entitled '*L'Unione*' is on his way to Rome to get encouragement for his venture. He is a very wily person and the least indication or recognition of the Anglican Church, its priesthood and catholicity, or that of the Greek Schismatic Church will be much exaggerated and publicised. I ought to apologise to your Eminence for even suggesting how such an apostate should be treated.

The other complained about the ubiquitous Lee again six months later (although nothing has come to light on his Italian visits in that year)

'the Unionisti', with that excellent man Phillipps de Lisle at their head are now sending a further letter to Cardinal Patrizi trying to show that the objects of the society have been misrepresented to the Holy Office. I therefore write to confirm that Bishop Ullathorne's assessment of them was perfectly valid. . . . And since 'Signor' Lee communicated to the English press the fact that he had had a personal blessing from the Pope, I must warn you to be careful of him. He and Signor Nugee, his colleague, are on their way to Rome at the present moment.

[1] Scritt. Refer., nei Congress; 1864–1866. Anglia 17, No. 195. 7th May 1864. Manning wrote in Italian. Quoted are free translations.
[2] ibid. No. 279 dated 10th June 1864 to Barnabo and No. 404 or 416 (the series have two lots of numbering) dated 3rd December 1864 to Mgr. Capalli—both from Bayswater.

Manning's complicity in the ban upon the A.P.U.C., which came in September 1864, is therefore substantiated despite the efforts of the dying Wiseman to protest (in the face of suspicion to the contrary) that Manning had not been involved.[1]

The Holy Office Letter to the English Roman Catholic bishops[2] which condemned the view of their being three Christian communities, also closed the membership of the A.P.U.C. to Roman Catholics.

The requirement that he should cease to be a member of it, was a serious blow to de Lisle. He spent the autumn of 1864 in frantic correspondence; writing to the ailing Wiseman,[3] and to Manning (explaining that what had been implied had never been suggested) and to his colleague Lee,[4] in order to frame a riposte.

Later comments on the A.P.U.C. drama are not without interest; in 1877 E. S. Purcell relayed to de Lisle a conversation he had recently had with Ullathorne on the subject of reunion.[5] The Bishop had maintained that it was by no means condemned in Rome: all that was condemned was the principle involved in the 'communicatio in Divinis'. He had written to Rome at the instigation of the bishops; Cardinal Wiseman, 'having committed himself too deeply in its favour to care to move in the matter'. Purcell remarked that Ullathorne seemed to be more favourable to the movement than Cardinal Manning. These statements must not be taken too seriously, since Purcell was a somewhat erratic witness. Moreover, Ullathorne's later attitude seems strange in view of his letter (50 pages) to his clergy at the time of the Holy Office instruction. Manning's attitude was consistent throughout, although the arguments he used to support the attitude were not always so. As Butler says

[1] *Life and Times of Cardinal Wiseman*, W. Ward, Vol. II, p. 491. Canon Morris, secretary on Wiseman's behalf, wrote to an unidentified correspondent 'that it is not true that the recent letter of the Holy See has been obtained by representations made by Mgr. Manning'. He also denied that the Cardinal had been in disagreement with the ban.

[2] Dated 16th September 1864, signed by Cardinal Patrizi, *Rome and Reunion Papal Pronoucements*, E. C. Messenger, Burns Oates, 1934, pp. 91–5.

[3] Some of the original correspondence at Oblates of St. Charles, St. Mary of the Angels, Moorhouse Road, London, W.2.

[4] Originals in the possession of Squire de Lisle.

[5] From the *Gazette* Office, the Strand, 21st April 1877 (in the possession of Squire de Lisle).

in his *Life of Ullathorne*,[1] Manning's intellect was under the sway of his will. Examples of this indicate also the way in which English Roman Catholicism was changing during the nineteenth century.[2]

de Lisle resigned from the A.P.U.C. as an act of submission to the authority of the Holy See, but under protest and under the impression that a great mistake had been made. From then on, although having withdrawn, he had to defend himself even more strongly from the charges of unorthodoxy and disloyalty and for following a policy which dissuaded individual conversions.[3] Even when finishing Purcell's biography of his father,[4] Edwin de Lisle was forced to defend Ambrose's posthumous reputation by adding a note[5] that as the unity of the Church has not been and cannot be broken, by broken unity Ambrose de Lisle means that 'it is evident that the unity of the Church which remains after a schism is diminished pro tanto, the unity of the remainder is no longer the perfection of the whole'.

In consultation with Lee, de Lisle arranged for a reply to the Holy Office Instruction to be sent to Cardinal Patrizi[6] in the summer of 1865 on behalf of the Anglican clergy.[7] Before it was ready Cardinal Wiseman had died and de Lisle turned to Mgr. Talbot to ask him to lay the Address before the Pope; this he agreed to do. The Address was signed by only 198 clergy of the Church of England and included no one in any senior position.

[1] *Life and Times of Bishop Ullathorne*, Cuthbert Butler, Vol. II, p. 121.

[2] Manning to Talbot, 25th February 1866. *Life of Cardinal Manning*, E. S. Purcell, Macmillan, 1895, Vol. II, p. 322 'Compared with Milner's days, ours are ultramontane: even our Anglicanising Catholics are higher than Milner's colleagues'.

Simpson (editor of the *Rambler*) to V. De Buck s.j., 6th January 1866, records the conversation of Manning to a layman who had said, with reference to some ultramontane view of the Papacy: 'Surely Milner and the Vicars Apostolic at the beginning of the century were of a different opinion from this.' Manning replied 'They thought as I think'. Simpson commented: 'This is all very well to a congregation of Irish hod-men, but it is too insulting to men who can read and remember what they read' (Belgian Jesuit Archives in Brussels), quoted in thesis on V. de Buck by Fr. Jurich, s.j.

[3] Especially in his correspondence with Mgr. Talbot: originals at English College, Rome.

[4] E. S. Purcell died before completing the *Life and Letters of Ambrose Phillipps de Lisle*. [5] ibid., Vol. I, p. 185n.

[6] Prefect of the Holy Office.

[7] *Rome and Reunion*, E. C. Messenger, pp. 95–7.

This must have been a disappointment to its authors.[1] Talbot wrote to Manning in the name of the Holy Office to consult him on the nature of the reply, and Manning sent the kind of answer that might have been expected, on the 18th July.[2] When he went to Rome in the autumn on his appointment as Archbishop of Westminster he had further consultations on the subject. The final reply (8 pages) sent on 8th November 1865[3] owed something to his influence. It did not refer to the recipients by their clerical titles and condemned the branch theory once more: the Church, it said, was always undivided and indivisible and its unity unbroken by schisms and secessions: 'the Church of Christ has never lost her unity, nor ever will lose it. . . .' But it is clear from his correspondence with Talbot that Manning wished that the letter could have been stronger. ('I had hoped for more, but it will do.') Talbot also had his regrets. ('It is not exactly what I should have wished' and 'it has cost me a great deal of trouble and anxiety', 'it is difficult, almost impossible, to make Italians understand the Anglican mind'.[4]) Dom Cuthbert Butler points out[5] that Manning confided to Ullathorne in a letter that 'de Lisle has I fear some letters of the Cardinal [Wiseman] which imply more tolerance of the Union than could be wished'. Manning was anxious to redress the balance. Ullathorne thought the Holy Office reply 'sharp' and Newman considered the members of the A.P.U.C. to have been 'treated cruelly'.[6]

Thus closed another incident in reunion history. Created by a handful of enthusiasts, it was finished by the intervention of another group of individuals, no less enthusiastic, who were pulling in the opposite direction. Although merely restating official policy, they gave to the situation in England a rigidity

[1] Liddon wrote to Lee that he would not sign; it would do no practical good, 'Manning is omnipotent in Rome'. *Dr Lee of Lambeth*, Brandreth, pp. 106–7.

[2] *Life of Cardinal Manning*, E. S. Purcell, Vol. II, p. 281.

[3] Printed as an Appendix to: *The Reunion of Christendom; A Pastoral Letter to the Clergy*, 1866, by Archbishop Manning.

[4] *Life of Cardinal Manning*, E. S. Purcell, Vol. II, pp. 282–4.

[5] *Life and Times of Bishop Ullathorne*, Cuthbert Butler, Vol. I, p. 353.

[6] Newman to de Lisle, 13th February 1865. *The Letters and Diaries of J. H. Newman* (ed. C. S. Dessain), Vol. XXI, p. 415.

peculiarly their own for the next 80 years, and made it increasingly difficult for future English reunionists to manoeuvre within the existing framework, as they had tried to do in the past.

* * * * *

Because of his loyalty to the Holy See de Lisle withdrew publicly from the reunion scene for nearly fifteen years. There is, however, evidence[1] that he continued to have conversations and to attend meetings which concerned the greatest interest of his life. On 27th April 1866[2] the de Lisles joined a group which met in London at the Architectural Union Hall, Conduit Street from 8 p.m. till midnight. (Lee, who opened the meeting, said it had nothing to do with the A.P.U.C. but was merely a group of friends favourable to reunion: since there were 467 present this was stretching a point.) But in the late 1870s the old campaigner made two last bids to further the reunion of Christendom during what remained of his life. 'They will find in me one who will never give in but with my dying breath'[3] he once wrote to Newman. In 1876 Newman answered a letter from de Lisle about a Uniat scheme contained in a pamphlet by Presbyter Anglicanus[4] and dedicated to Cardinal Manning.[5] A following of 500–1,000 clergy and 50,000–100,000 laity was claimed for the proposal by the ever-hopeful de Lisle.[6] Newman was less optimistic. 'It seems to me a plausible scheme, but I am told few will feel inclined towards it of the Ritualists.'[7]

[1] Diaries of his wife Laura (in the possession of Squire de Lisle) show that he continued to invite many people to his home and visit them in this cause.

[2] Laura de Lisle, Diary for 1866. She remarks 'I would not have missed it for anything'.

[3] de Lisle to Newman, 12th August 1857, from original in Birmingham Oratory.

[4] Pseudonym of the Revd. E. S. Grindle, author of two pamphlets on Uniat status for the Church of England: 'Christianity or Erastianism', 1875; 'Do they well to be angry', 1876. London. John Batty. Reviewed in the *Pilot*, 26th April 1876. The movement for an Anglican Uniat church was commented upon in the *Civiltà Cattolica*, V.1.XI, 9th series, for 26th August 1876, p. 640.

[5] Newman to de Lisle, 19th January 1876, *Life and Letters of Ambrose Phillipps de Lisle*, E. S. Purcell, Vol. II, pp. 26–7.

[6] de Lisle to Manning, 12th January 1876. ibid., pp. 23–4.

[7] Newman to de Lisle, 19th January 1876. ibid., pp. 26–7.

In this view he echoed Manning: 'Ritualism in Oxford is, I hear, intensely anti-Catholic. In this form it is like Donatism or the Photian Schism.'[1] Nothing came of the idea and de Lisle turned his mind to the most extraordinary scheme for unity of all, the Order of Corporate Reunion.

On the feast of the Visitation 1877, at dawn, an extraordinary document was read on the steps of St. Paul's Cathedral in London. It was a Pastoral[2] from three (so called) bishops of the Order of Corporate Reunion: F. G. Lee, with the title of 'bishop of Dorchester', T. W. Mossman (an incumbent in the Lincoln diocese) as 'bishop of Selby' and J. T. Seccombe, a doctor from the parish of Terrington St. Clement in Norfolk, who called himself bishop of Caerleon. The document was sent to the Pope and all 'Catholic bishops' and to the English archbishops. A letter to the *Morning Post* on 14th July 1877 announced: 'we bind ourselves together anew under godly obedience and discipline for necessary self-defence for co-operation and for promoting the grand and most necessary work of corporate Reunion, the highest and greatest need of our time'. There is no doubt that de Lisle was deeply involved in the affair.

The intention behind the launching of the enterprise would seem to have been to introduce into the Church of England orders recognised as valid by the Roman and Greek churches and thereby to hasten the day of reunion.

The full story of this fantastic incident has never been told, and since those involved were committed to secrecy so that their knowledge died with them, it is very doubtful whether it ever will be. The first important question is whence did the consecrations derive. The two main sources of information are Henry Brandreth's biography of Lee and an article by Fr. J. H. Crehan s.j. in the *Month*.[3] There is also some correspondence in the *Tablet* for 1908. Brandreth suggests that Seccombe was consecrated first by one of the episcopi vagantes, Julius Ferrete, who arrived in England in 1866[4] and claimed to derive his

[1] Manning to de Lisle, 23rd November 1875. *Life and Letters of Ambrose Phillipps de Lisle*, E. S. Purcell, Vol. II, p. 22.
[2] A copy is extant at Pusey House, Oxford.
[3] 23rd December 1970, pp. 352–8.
[4] Laura de Lisle's Diary, for 15th November 1866 says. 'Julius Ferrete, friend of Nugee arrives' (at Grace Dieu, Leics).

orders from a Jacobite source in Antioch. According to Brand-reth, Lee and Mossman were consecrated in Italy during the summer of 1877, and he involves de Lisle in the arrangements. Lee's second son, Ambrose, was of the opinion that the 'con-secration' of his father took place at sea near Venice.[1] de Lisle had maintained a life-long interest in the Armenian Uniat Mekhitarist monastery on the island of San Lazzaro in the Gulf of Venice and some books given to him by the Monastery have been traced.[2] The visitors' book of this monastery does not contain the names of the three main characters in the drama, but the name of Miss de Lisle (Ambrose's daughter Margaret) appears for 27th May 1877, and this may be of significance.[3]

Another great mystery is to what extent was the scheme known centrally at Rome. de Lisle, writing to Gladstone on 9th July 1877, said that the Pope had now committed himself 'over head and ears to the two points for which I have always agitated through good report and evil report. The first is for the Principle of Corporate Reunion. The second is for the special prayers for the reunion of the Graeco-Russian Church with our Latin Church.'[4] His Chaplain, Fr. Tondini, obtained from Pius IX on 13th May 1877 a formal approval of prayers for the reunion of Anglicans, Eastern Churches and Rome, but what else he achieved is not known and recourse to the Archives of the Vatican has so far yielded nothing. It is significant that the *Civiltà Cattolica* commented thus on 12th April 1878 on Lee's Pastoral[5] 'when a sufficient number of Anglican clergy have

---

[1] Letter of 29th June 1912. The *Month*, December 1970, p. 357 and the *Tablet*, 5th December 1908, p. 894.

[2] In the possession of Squire de Lisle.

[3] Laura de Lisle's diary for 10th May 1877 said that Margaret was pre-sented to Pius IX on this day.

[4] *Life and Letters of Ambrose Phillipps de Lisle*, E. S. Purcell, Vol. II, p. 175.

[5] Vol. VI, 10th Series: Cronaca Contemporanea, 11th–13th April, p. 248. 'L'Ordine della riunione corporativa prosegue alacremente nel suo lavoro, e i suoi ufficiali han dato fuori una lettera pastorale . . . . I tre primarii ufficiali dell' ordine hanno altresi ricevuto la consacrazione episcopale della medesima sorgente; sorgente che, a quanto si afferma, e tale da precludere onninamente la via ad ogni questione intorno alla validità degli Ordine, in tal modo conferiti, venuto che sia il tempo di sottoporre l'affare all'esame della Santa Sede. Ma quando un numero sufficiente di membri del clero anglicano avra di tal guisa tolte di mezzo le

removed by means of this Order the difficulties arising from their own ordinations, the Order hopes to be able to present a request for corporate reunion with the Catholic Church'. Manning and the English Roman Catholic hierarchy were strangely silent upon the subject of the Order,[1] but two Anglican societies, the English Church Union and the Society of the Holy Cross, attacked it and one expelled Lee and the other Mossman from membership.

It only remains to touch briefly on some correspondence which passed between the members of three families at the end of the nineteenth century, two Roman Catholic and one Anglican: Lord Acton and Gladstone wrote copiously to each other:[2] de Lisle and Gladstone did likewise.[3] Gladstone also wrote to de Lisle's daughter Margaret,[4] who became a nun at Mill Hill, and Acton penned long letters to Mary Gladstone,[5] afterwards Mrs. Drew. This correspondence is chiefly remarkable for what it does not say. Many of the letters are on religious themes, yet, except by de Lisle, the subject of reunion was mentioned hardly at all. The correspondents were loyal to their own communions. Acton expected constantly to be excommunicated,[6] but there was no question whatever of his joining another church. The *scandal* of disunity did not seem to affect them. This appears to have been characteristic of the age, and the nineteenth century drew to a close with an impasse: the possibility of reunion was too remote for most people to contemplate it.

difficoltà dipendenti dalla loro ordinazione, l'ordine spera poter presentare la sua istanza per la riunione corporativa con la chiesa cattolica, firmata da un numero di membri così imponente da rendere impossibile alla Santa Sede il disconoscere la gravità e l'importanza del movimento.'

[1] *Dr. Lee of Lambeth*, Brandreth, p. 135.
[2] *Selections from the correspondence of the first Lord Acton* (ed. J. N. Figgis and R. V. Lawrence), Longmans, Green & Co., 1917.
[3] In *Life and Letters of Ambrose Phillips de Lisle*, by E. S. Purcell, and manuscripts in the British Museum.   [4] Originals in Mill Hill Convent.
[5] *Letters of Lord Acton to Mary Gladstone* (ed. Herbert Paul), Macmillan & Co., 1913.
[6] e.g. to Gladstone, 16th December 1874. *Selections from the correspondence of the first Lord Acton* (ed. Figgis and Lawrence), p. 49.

IMMACULATE CONCEPTION, THE SYLLABUS, INFALLIBILITY

It will be seen from Chapter 9 that the establishment of the Roman hierarchy in Britain in 1850 showed up two tendencies in the matter of relationships between the Roman Catholic Church and the Anglicans. This episode was from one point of view an act of acceptance on the part of the British people, who could have prevented it if they had set about seriously to do so. But it did at the same time stir up old memories and put sensitive Protestant consciences on the alert; while for many Roman Catholics it was another embodiment of what was meant to be a permanent estrangement, a deliberate 'No' to the possibility of future accommodation. The worst feature of it, from an ecumenical point of view, was the triumph in the Roman Catholic community for a policy of dependence on Rome. As long as the 'old catholics' had an effective say in the government of the Roman Catholic Church in England there was a temper of moderation in what was said and done. But from the establishment of the hierarchy onwards the centralising ultramontane tendencies in catholicism, beloved of converts and the new Irish immigrants, were bound to prevail.

Unfortunately the international political scene, in so far as it had a bearing on the situation at this time, took a general turn for the worse. The anti-clerical mood in most European nations at the beginning of the century was in some respects a by-product of the French Revolution. Going as it did hand in hand with the extremes of liberal philosophy, it tended to draw Christians together in shelter against the prevailing storm.

Pius IX, who came to the Papacy in 1846, reacted vigorously against the behaviour of his predecessor Gregory XVI. And because he tried to come to terms with the prevailing liberalism then sweeping Italy he attracted some sympathy in England, especially when he was eventually besieged by the revolutionaries in the Quirinal (1848) and had to make his escape to Gaeta.[1] This experience seems to have turned him permanently into a defender of the temporal sovereignty of the Popes in its fullness. From about that time onward his conservatism extended into his theology and his ecclesiology. The rest of Pio Nono's pontificate must be regarded as a disaster from the point of view of the reunion of Christendom. With his back to the wall in the matter of temporal sovereignty he sought to ensure the future influence of the Papacy by means of stronger and stronger definitions of its place in Christian ecclesiology.

From his accession Pius IX was known to have a special devotion to the Blessed Virgin Mary. When therefore he found himself receiving a growing number of requests (especially from France) for the official proclamation of the doctrine of the Immaculate Conception he gave it full encouragement. Although the doctrine had been under discussion for many centuries it was given special impetus at this time by an alleged vision of the Blessed Virgin on the part of a novice, Catherine Laboure, in Paris in 1830. The Pope gave the devotion the right to be officially investigated while still at Gaeta in 1848. Also from Gaeta in 1849 he issued the encyclical 'Ubi primum' asking the prayers and advice of the bishops on the matter. A large majority expressed themselves in favour, though there were those who, like the Archbishop of Paris, gave their opinion that such a doctrine was indefinable and not specifically contained in or implied by Scripture; and some from Germany and other protestant countries who believed any definition to be inopportune. The dogma was, however, solemnly proclaimed on 8th December 1854, and so a further obstacle was set up to future ecumenical relations.

The dogma states that 'from the first moment of her conception the Blessed Virgin Mary was, by the singular grace and privilege of Almighty God, in view of the merits of Jesus Christ, Saviour of Mankind, kept free from all stain of original

---

[1] See Ch. 9 *passim.*

sin'.[1] Many of the great schoolmen, particularly St. Bernard, St. Albert, St. Bonaventure and St. Thomas Aquinas, had declared themselves against it. Its progress into the catholic consciousness, however, had been steady. Sixtus IV had allowed a mass and office in celebration of the belief. Clement XI, in 1708, had even made it a feast of universal obligation. The observance of the Conception as such appears in the Anglican Prayer Book for 8th December, though no provision is made for its observance. But the whole spirit of Anglican theology is contrary to the nature of the Roman definition. The dogma, according to Anglican theologians, was not contained in Scripture, nor is it evidently to be deduced therefrom. It has never been defined by what they would recognise as an ecumenical council, nor is there any danger in not receiving it which might make some such definition necessary. For the future it is to be hoped that it will be allowed to pass into the category of optional devotions and beliefs whose acceptance de fide is not to be required for catholic communion. One Anglican comment on the definition is to be found in a leader of the *Guardian* newspaper:

> Our readers are aware that a large number of Bishops have lately been assembled at Rome for the purpose of putting to the vote the question whether the Roman Catholic Church should add to the articles of faith the opinion of the Immaculate Conception. Means had been taken, with the judicious caution which generally distinguishes the proceedings of the Papacy, to secure by the previous inquiry a nearly unanimous vote, and we learn without surprise that the dissentients were comparatively few. . . . The Archbishop of Paris . . . and the Bishop of Évreux . . . protested against its being adopted without a General Council. . . . The effect of this decision is to adopt in the most solemn manner the principle of development, to exact new terms of communion, and to add to the creed a tenet which most Christians not of the Roman obedience will hesitate to characterise as even a 'pious opinion'! Within that communion it will be received without difficulty; the doctrine (or one which is hardly distinguishable from it) is already accepted pretty univer-

[1] The bull 'Ineffabilis Deus'.

sally, though not as an article of faith, and it is peculiarly
agreeable to the dominant sentiment of modern Romanism.
Yet we may be very sure that even there it is making many
thoughtful men sad and scattering for future generations, if
not for this, seeds of secret disunion and unbelief.[1]

R. W. Church commented:

The dogma is itself an opinion which any one might hold, if
he thinks that there are materials in the world from which to
form an opinion about it. In itself there is not much to object
to it, except its ground—which is absolutely nothing, not even
a tradition, not even a misinterpretation of a dislocated text,
nothing but the merest inferences from suppositions about a
matter of which we know nothing—and its end, which is to
give a new stimulus to a devotion which wanted none. It is
the mode of establishing it, and the system of which it is the
central feature, which make it so important.[2]

Apart from these it is not easy to trace comments or other
evidence of the impact of this promulgation on Anglicans.
Many of the lives of leading churchmen, and quite a number of
standard history books of the period, bear no reference to it in
their index. This may mean that it passed by unnoticed. The
doctrine invited comment both from those who might have
read in it the signs of an unhappy future for ecumenical
relations, and from those concerned with the prospects of
Roman Catholic dogma and the Papacy itself. Mgr Talbot[3]
observed at the time that it was not so much the doctrine itself
but the way in which it was proclaimed which was significant
for the future. A suggestion that the bishops should be associated with the Pope in the promulgation, to give some
appearance of universality to it, was turned down, and the
stage was set, it seemed, for papal dogmatic absolutism. A
century later when Pius XII came to define the analogous
doctrine of the Assumption the same programme was followed:
consultation with the bishops beforehand, but promulgation
sola auctoritate, as in the case of Pio Nono.

[1] 13th December 1854.
[2] A review of Pusey's Eirenicon contributed to *The Times*, Tuesday, 12th
December 1865 printed in *Occasional Papers* (ed. Mary Church), London,
1867, Vol. I.
[3] *Pio Nono*, E. E. Y. Hales, Eyre & Spottiswood, 1956, p. 149.

But the promulgation of the doctrine of the Immaculate Conception in 1854 was only the prelude to a series of events which was to heighten the autocracy of the Papacy and to alienate the rest of Christendom from the Roman Communion. At the time of the Second Vatican Council, when the issues of ecumenical rapprochement were under consideration, it was frequently observed that the task would have been easier 150 years previously, and if the events of the second half of the nineteenth century had never happened. Christian churches were facing the double onslaught of rationalism in thought and liberalism in politics. To these struggles was added for the Church of Rome in particular the attack on the temporal power. The papal states were destined to be swept away as a consequence of successive occupations. But the reactions of the Papacy added to the burdens of those who might have tried to salvage something from the wreck. Certainly the papal indignation against those who had seized or were proposing to seize the temporal possessions carried over into the measures with which the Papacy tried to stem the oncoming tide of secularism.

The details of the campaign against the papal states are not in themselves germane to the purpose of this book, except to note that there were times, and issues, in which the sympathies of the British people were on the side of the Pope. But as usual Britain's variegated interests pulled her in various directions at once. She had long been urging and supporting the idea of a federalist solution of the problems of Italy, in which the Pope would have a dominant role. However, doubts were expressed all over Europe whether there had yet emerged in Italy a middle class which would be able to match the strength of a clergy accustomed to government. And then the emergence of Cavour posed a further problem. Cavour himself had been an ally of the English in the Crimean war, so that at the Paris Conference of 1856 the British delegates found themselves supporting the Piedmontese Kingdom, and so, by implication, going into opposition to the Pope. It must be remembered that 'papal aggression' (as the establishment of the hierarchy was called in many English circles) was only then six years behind. The King of Piedmont went on a visit of goodwill to Paris and London in the autumn of 1855. The crowds in England gave

him a warm welcome under the impression that he was
inaugurating some kind of protestant reform. His attendance at
Mass, it is said, came as a shock.[1]

The policy of Britain seemed to draw her steadily to the side
of the Risorgimento and away from the Pope. As it became
increasingly clear that he was helpless before the rising tide of
Liberalism and reform, so British policy was seen to lie in
keeping in with the nascent nation. A united Italy would be
useful as an ally against France. When, however, the time came
for direct negotiation between the Pope and the liberators of
Italy, ministers advised him to leave Rome and seek refuge in
Malta or elsewhere in the British Dominions. About 1860 there
seems to have been a further hardening of attitude on the part
of Pio Nono. Whatever chance there might have been of wise
counsels prevailing before that date there was certainly none
after it. The temporal power was to be defended to the end as a
sacred patrimony, to be preserved without diminution. Among
the influences in the papal court which told in this direction
one was certainly that of Mgr. Talbot, one of the long succession
of English Roman Catholic 'reactionaries' who were to domin-
ate the Roman scene. The point of no return in the matter of
the papal states was reached in 1861 when on 18th March, in
the encyclical 'Jamdudum cernimus', the Pope threw down the
gauntlet to Cavour and the Piedmontese pretensions and made
it clear that he would never negotiate. From then onwards it was
clear that the Pope must lose and the new united Italian
nation be born. It was only a matter of time.

The importance of these events for the progress of ecumenical
understanding is that for the moment they retarded it severely.
Overwhelmed by what seemed a world-wide conspiracy to
unseat him and to defeat the gospel itself, the Pope became
more and more driven into himself, less and less able to understand or to influence what was going on in the world. It appeared that the only weapons in the papal armoury against this
onslaught were the wholesale condemnation of every new
movement of thought which seemed to tell against religion and
the exaltation of the Church's teaching office, even that of the
Pope himself, as the only sure rock in time of storm.

The problems of the day were indeed the problems of all

[1] Noted in *Pio Nono*, E. E. Y. Hales, p. 186.

the churches. But before examing Pio Nono's solution of them
we might notice how, for example, Archbishop Tait of Canterbury faced the same situation. Tait has already come into this
narrative as one of the 'four tutors' who started the agitation
against Tract 90.[1] He had identified himself with the evangelical
tradition in the Church of England as over against the Oxford
revival. Yet he was no fanatic. And when asked to join the new
protestant Alliance which came into being as a result of the
establishment of the Roman hierarchy he replied, inter alia

> Popery in this country is better met by every Protestant
> clergyman and layman zealously doing his duty in the
> position God has assigned him than by the agitation which
> seems implied in the formation of a Society for the defence of
> Protestantism.[2]

The current philosophical and social problems of the day were
not well understood in the Church of England generally. The
Oxford fathers certainly set out on a course which, had it been
undisturbed, might easily have met the needs and opportunities of the times with a renewed theology and a reformed
church which would have confronted them effectively. The
evangelical wing

> had failed, with a few notable exceptions, to gain touch with
> the intellectual and critical side of the life and conversation of
> educated men. Literature, Science, Philosophy and Art
> were by them regarded as things altogether apart from
> religion. Their view of the antagonism between the Church
> and the world led them to a strange distrust of the higher
> forms of human usefulness and activity. These belonged to
> the world, and the main business of the religious man was
> with religion as a personal matter between himself and his
> God.[3]

The tradition of Arnold had few survivors, so that the Church of
England was not as fortunate, in the middle nineteenth century
as was, for example, the Church in France, in having a firm
tradition of liberal thinking with which to understand and to
confront the secular knowledge of the age.

[1] See p. 120.
[2] *Life of Archbishop Tait,* by Davidson and Benham, Vol. I, p. 184.
[3] 26th January 1852, ibid., Vol. 1, p. 196.

Against this background Tait stood out distinctly. Where the basic truths of religion and the authority of the Bible itself were at stake Tait was not afraid of free enquiry,[1] and in this he was not alone. The publication of *Essays and Reviews* in 1860, though it met with a hostile reception, showed that though the minds of most of those who discussed the issues of the day were set in an obscurantist pattern, there were some, and those in surprisingly high places, who were prepared to face the issues, even if they did not entirely understand them. In the end, however, it drew strong opposition on itself and was synodically condemned in 1864. The coincidence of dates is remarkable, for the notorious 'Syllabus of Errors' was issued in Rome the same year. The date 8th December (the Feast of the Immaculate Conception of the Blessed Virgin Mary) of its promulgation in the encyclical 'Quanta Cura', put it exactly ten years after the declaration of the Marian dogma. One of the principal advocates of its publication was Mgr. Pecci, then Bishop of Perugia, later Pope Leo XIII.

The Syllabus grouped the condemned errors under ten heads:

1. Pantheism, Nationalism and Absolute Rationalism.
2. Moderate Rationalism.
3. Indifferentism and Latitudinarianism.
4. Socialism, Communism, secret societies, Bible societies, Liberal clerical societies.
5. The Rights of the Church.
6. The Church in relation to the State.
7. Natural Ethics and Christian Morality.
8. Christian Marriage.
9. The Pope's Temporal Power.
10. Modern Liberalism.

Some of the propositions were citations of documents and sources already issued, while others were being heard for the first time. All were cast in the form of anathemas; and they ended with the notorious 80th proposition that

> whosoever teaches that the Roman Pontiff can and ought to reconcile and adjust himself with progress, liberalism and modern civilisation . . . let him be anathema.

[1] See his charge to the diocese as Bishop of London, 1862.

However alien these propositions may seem to be to twentieth-century ideas it may be admitted that they have met with more misrepresentation and opposition than they deserved. They are indeed stated and phrased in the worst possible way, inviting a maximum of hostile prejudice. The last proposition, as the most provocative of all, can be taken in illustration. To the eyes and ears of an awakening world it was understood as indicating that the Church of Rome was always and everywhere opposed to progress and 'natural' truth. And it was so understood in many high places, as any French, German or British adviser could have warned the papal curia that it would be. Yet the same caution where fashions in doctrine were concerned could be found in the Archbishop of Canterbury or in any other responsible Christian prelate or pastor. The Church and her officers are frequently expected to adapt themselves and their doctrines to what may easily prove to be temporary currents of thought. But it is clearly the duty of the Church on many occasions to resist such vagaries and not to be 'carried away with every blast of vain doctrine'.

It can further be stated in extenuation of part of the 'Syllabus' that it is written from the limited point of view of the Latin world, and is highly coloured by the unfortunate political situation in which the Pope found himself. Nineteenth-century socialism in Italy meant something quite different from its English counterpart in the middle of the twentieth century. The same is true of Liberalism, which on the continent was almost always anti-clerical. The stark condemnation, off-hand and without exceptions either stated or contemplated, seemed to northern European readers to be a heartless opposition to what were high-principled endeavours for the welfare of mankind.

The Syllabus provoked much misunderstanding and resistance both within the Church of Rome and outside her. It can be regarded as a serious step backwards in the history of ecumenical understanding. In France publication of the encyclical and its annexed Syllabus was actually forbidden at the beginning of 1865, by the Roman hierarchy themselves, though the prohibition was later withdrawn, when they thought that they had made their position clear, and that continued opposition would do greater damage than acquiescence.

Odo Russell,[1] in his despatch on the question to Earl Russell,[2] said that the Syllabus has:

> either placed the Pope at the head of a vast ecclesiastical conspiracy against the principles which govern modern society or it must put the Catholic clergy in opposition to the Vicar of Christ whom they are bound to obey.

During the following month Russell had a private audience with the Pope, whom he had described as being in a state of acute nervous tension. The encyclical and the appended Syllabus were fully discussed. Russell recorded that:

> the principles of the Church are eternal and unchangeable. . . . There is no salvation out of the Roman Church, yet I, the Pope, do think that some Protestants may by the special Grace of God be saved. I mean those Protestants who by peculiar circumstances have never been in a position to know Truth. For those who, like yourself, have lived in Rome at the very fountain of Truth, and have not recognised and accepted it, there can be no salvation.[3]

In England the encyclical was received in stunned surprise, except among the 'ultramontane' party in the Roman Catholic Church itself, which was all the time gaining in strength, and was now firmly in control. There were, however, not a few expressions of dismay among Roman Catholics. Particularly notable was the revolt, as it was understood to be in spite of many disclaimers, of the leading Roman scholar Sir John (later Lord) Acton. It is generally agreed that the Syllabus was a turning point in Acton's life. Until that moment he had felt a strong duty to co-operate as far as possible with the Church authorities. But from this time onward he was a severe critic of the pontificate of Pius IX. Acton found himself increasingly drawn to Gladstone, who as a High Church Anglican in search of all that was best in the Roman Church, and a Liberal to boot, was highly dismayed by the publication of the Syllabus.

The year after the Syllabus occurred another tragedy, as

[1] Diplomat, attached to British mission in Tuscany.

[2] 17th January 1865. P.R.O. 30/22/77. Noel Blakiston, *The Roman Question*, Chapman & Hall, 1962, p. 305. Odo was his nephew.

[3] 13th February 1865, to Earl Russell. F.O. 43/94A, No. 10. Blakiston, op. cit., pp. 306–8.

from the ecumenical point of view we cannot hesitate to call it, in the appointment of Henry Edward Manning to be the head of the Roman Catholic hierarchy in England. Manning's attitude on ecclesiological questions had 'hardened' even further since his defection. On any reckoning a distinguished man and a strong personality, he was bound to be a strong candidate on the death in 1865 of Cardinal Wiseman. But the nomination of the Westminster Cathedral chapter was Errington,[1] a man who commanded a greater following among the Roman Catholics in England. Yet Manning was known to be a strong papalist, and the Pope's nomination fell on him. He was to prove a most loyal son of the Papacy, intolerant to the point of bitterness in his dealings with other Christians, showing a special intransigence towards that part of the Church which had reared him and implacably opposed to anything in the way of union by any method except total submission to the Roman claims. He had in Rome an ally in Mgr. Talbot, who often acted as an independent channel of communication with the Pope. Acting together, as they frequently did, they formed a formidable bastion against any liberalisation of either the doctrinal emphases or the political stances of the Holy See. And they set their faces steadily against the remotest suggestion of an understanding with the rest of Christendom except on their own uncompromising terms. Manning's attack on the English Church,[2] Pusey's Eirenicon to Keble, which drew an answer in Manning's Epiphany Pastoral of 1866, which led in turn to Newman's letter and Pusey's answer, form part of the narrative of Chapter 8. Manning showed determination to follow nothing but the extreme 'ultramontane' line about ecumenism. His intransigence led him to regard Newman as a danger to the Roman Church in England and to oppose the entry of Roman Catholics to Oxford University. 'The English national spirit', he said in that connection, 'is spreading among Catholics and we shall have dangers'.[3] The ascendancy of Manning meant an eclipse

---

[1] George Errington, 1804–1886. Educated at Ushaw and English College, Rome. Bishop of Plymouth 1851. Wiseman's co-adjutor 1855 until removed in 1862.

[2] 'The working of the Holy Spirit in the C. of E.', 1864.

[3] Letter to Talbot, 26th June 1866. *Life of Cardinal Manning*, E. S. Purcell, Vol. II, p. 300.

of ecumenical understanding in England. But it must be admitted that the attitude of Archbishop Tait, and with him of the majority of the Anglican hierarchy, though more sympathetic towards contemporary science and philosophy, was equally obstinate in the other matters at issue with the Church of Rome.

Although the official trends of both sides were thus antagonistic to each other, loftier conceptions could be seen in such visionaries as Newman, who after some years of obscurity, suddenly burst back upon the stage in the middle of the 1860s. The encyclical 'Quanta Cura' and the Syllabus had been a sad event for him and his friends. It was, he said, 'A heavy blow and discouragement to us in England'. Ever since leaving the Church of his baptism he had experienced an increasing estrangement from the hierarchy and the official policies of the Church of Rome, both at the centre and in England. In 1860 Newman was at a low ebb of disappointment and depression about his position. There seemed to be a total rejection of his hopes for educating catholic laity to a deeper understanding of their faith. The central policies of the Church, under the guidance of Pio Nono, tended more and more to absolutism both in doctrine and temporal power, both of which tendencies were alien to Newman's conception of catholicism. He was encouraged by news of a congress at Munich in 1863. The theologian Döllinger[1] expressed himself profoundly dissatisfied with the narrowness of scholastic theology and with the Papacy's growing discouragement of liberal inquiry into matters religious. But the Pope published a brief to the Archbishop of Munich which amounted to a censure; spirits such as Acton and Newman in England felt themselves further discouraged. At this period Kingsley, later canon of Westminister, wrote his ill-advised criticisms of Newman's intellectual integrity which drew from him the 'Apologia',[2] the answer which he and the dominant Broad Church element in the Church of England so richly deserved. The effect of this publication upon the future of relationships was incalculable: it undermined the confidence of many Anglicans and laid the foundation of future conversions. It was the heaviest blow to the self-esteem

[1] J. J. I. von Döllinger, 1799–1890. Bavarian Church Historian.
[2] *Apologia pro Vita Sua*, 1864.

of the Church of England since the Gorham judgment of 1850. It restored Newman's confidence in himself and set him up as a national figure for the rest of his life. It increased his confidence so much that he now felt able to renew contacts with his former Anglican friends, particularly Keble and Church. At this period observers within the Church of England saw that a great struggle was going on within the Roman Church herself, a struggle which in England became typified in the figures of Newman and Acton on the one hand and Manning and the hierarchy on the other. The issues in the struggle became clearer as the decade of the '60s moved on. Newman and his friends stood for the open education of the laity, and some form of their fuller participation in the life of the Church. He thought the education of the catholic laity much more imporant than zeal in making 'converts'. He was accused of making 'no converts, as Manning and Faber have'.

Newman and his friends stood also for a measure of 'liberalising' the doctrines of the Church (in the sense that their expression should not always be in the terms of Thomistic philosophy). They were against the increasing absolutism of Rome, and deplored the tyranny which tried to stifle reasonable enquiry.

> Are they not doing the Holy See a grave disservice who will not let a zealous man defend it in his own way but insist on his doing it their way or not at all.[1]

And they favoured a greater exposure of seminarists to courses of secular education throughout their preparation for ordination. In all these things, of course, they were opposed by the hierarchy, especially by Manning: but they were forerunners of that new spirit which was to show itself in the pontificates of John XXIII and Paul VI and in the proceedings of the Second Vatican Council.

The course of Manning's spiritual development had driven him to see the problem of authority as the keystone of the whole doctrinal edifice. It was for this reason that he was destined to play such an important part in the First Vatican Council.

The Council eventually grew out of the circumstances of its

[1] 24th August 1867. *The Letters and Diaries of John Henry Newman* (ed. C. S. Dessain and T. Gornall), Clarendon Press, Oxford, 1973, Vol. XXIII, p. 319.

age. That can be said in some degree of all the Councils, but there was this additional unpropitious element in the Vatican Council that the Pope of the day and his closest advisers were under the heavy psychological pressure of the loss of the temporal sovereignty. There was accordingly a strong disposition to compensate by bolstering up the spiritual authority. The Church needed to take up some strong position in face of the growing secularism of nineteenth-century philosophy and the misuse by some liberal thinkers of the fruits of scientific discovery (Darwin's *Origin of Species*, e.g., was published in 1859).

The question of papal infallibility, which was to prove the main topic for decision at the Council, and was also destined to drive a further wedge between the Church of Rome and the rest of the Church, had already been widely canvassed. Theologians had begun to take sides in a steadily crystallising debate.

During the years leading up to the Council, while the dogma was maturing in the minds of those who favoured it, alarm was spreading among its opponents. What was at issue was not so much the question of the infallibility of the Pope, still less of the Church, which Roman Catholics accepted in one form or another, but of the need for a definition at all, and of the opportuneness of such a definition at that particular time. But the issue was made one of loyalty or disloyalty, of belief or disbelief by proponents of the dogma. The effect of this whole enterprise on such as Newman and Acton shows up the politics and the background of it all. Newman in particular was manoeuvred by his enemies in England into what was made to look like a 'disloyalist' position. Nobody could have been a more thorough exponent of the claims on the loyalty of catholics, of the deposit of sacred doctrines, and of the position of the Pope in that system. In 1862 he had written, in answer to those who were suggesting that his loyalty was in question:

I have not had one moment's wavering of trust in the Catholic Church ever since I was received into her fold. I hold, and ever have held, that her Sovereign Pontiff is the centre of unity and the Vicar of Christ; and I have ever had, and have still, an unclouded faith in her creed in all its articles; a supreme satisfaction in her worship, discipline, and teaching.[1]

Yet in 1867 Talbot was able to write to Newman:

> . . . a certain school in England have done you much harm by making many believe that you sympathised with their detestable views. You have also been more injured by your friends than your enemies. When I was in England three years ago I heard some of them quoting your name in opposition to the Authority of the Holy See. I remarked that there was a party forming of what are called 'Liberal Catholics' who wished to place you at their head, in reference of professing a filial devotion to the Vicar of Christ and a due veneration for the Chair of St. Peter. . . . .[2]

This was to prove the cause of increasing estrangement between Newman and most of the bishops, an estrangement which was destined to be assuaged only at the very end of Newman's life.

During the '60s the contention over the Infallibility question increased steadily in momentum. One of its leading protagonists was M. Veuillot of the *Univers*, though his exaggerations and censures drew the opposition of many of the French hierarchy, notably Archbishop Darboy of Paris and Dupanloup, Bishop of Orléans. Manning, on the other hand, is said to have made a vow on the feast of St. Peter and St. Paul 1867 in St. Peter's at Rome that he would not rest until the definition had been obtained.

But if we are to offer this picture of Manning as a resolute enemy of any school of theology which might even remotely have an eye on the unity of Christendom, it is only fair to set against it the figure of his Anglican opposite number in the person of Archbishop Tait who from his standpoint adopted an equally uncompromising attitude. In his charge as Bishop of London Tait had said, in 1866:

> We do not forget how desirable it is that Christendom should be one and at peace with itself. We long and pray for this peace and union; but we want no hollow peace, still less a peace which shall be purchased by sacrificing our liberty and

[1] 28th June 1862. Letter to the *Globe*. *Letters and Diaries of John Henry Newman*, Vol. XX, p. 215.   [2] 31st May 1867. ibid., Vol. XXIII, p. 242.

God's truth. Thus we feel ashamed when told of members of our noble Reformed Church going, cap in hand, to seek for some slight recognition from that old usurping power—so unlike the gentle, truth-loving Church of the Apostles, of which it vaunts itself the sole representative—which slew Latimer and Ridley and Cranmer and Hooper in the old time, because they would not surrender God's truth, and which certainly values the pure Gospel now at as low a rate as of old. And we feel some satisfaction in learning how these advances were coldly rejected by the old haughty spirit which they seek in vain to propitiate.

It pains me also deeply to find men labouring, as I noted above, to show that the Church of the Reformation has, after all, by some felicitious accident, escaped from being reformed; that, if we could only see it, there is nothing really Protestant in the Thirty-nine Articles, and nothing really Romish in the Decrees of Trent. If this were so, language must be a still more uncertain vehicle of men's thoughts than all acknowledge it to be.

But, indeed, there is no sign that this mode of making peace with Rome is possible. Rome is too wise, and I think I may say for at least ninety-nine out of every hundred of English Churchmen, that they are too wise also. Archbishop Laud's saying holds true still: that there can be no thought of union with Rome till she becomes other than she is.[1]

This unpromising attitude can also be found in a resolution of the First Lambeth Conference of 1867 which warned Anglicans against

the pretensions to universal sovereignty over God's heritage asserted for the see of Rome and the practical exaltation of the Blessed Virgin Mary as mediator in the place of her Divine Son.

Yet although this kind of leadership on either side (and Manning, though only Archbishop of Westminster, was soon to exert a considerable influence on the Pope and the Council) might have appeared to preclude the possibility of much mutual understanding, the work of reconciliation was going

[1] *Life of Archbishop of Tait*, Davidson and Benham, Vol. I, pp. 484–5.

slowly on in unofficial quarters. And it was to give the visionaries on both sides a hope, at the moment of their greatest
official estrangement, of a possible future embrace. For the
decade preceding the Council showed the Roman Church to be
deeply divided on a main item of ecclesiology, a division which
the eventual conciliar decision was not going to heal. The
divergence which developed, for example, between Newman
and Manning, was only part of the picture. The division ran
right through Europe and through the Roman Catholic
Church, and ended up, as is widely known, on the floor of St.
Peter's. The course of the preparations for the Council was
seen by the party of the 'moderates' (such as Newman and
Acton in England) as a campaign to resist the definition of a
dogma which, though many Catholics already held it as a
general principle, they were certain would suffer distortion if
defined. The anxieties increased as the Council drew on, and
they became feverish in the course of it.

Particularly interesting for our purpose is the evidence of the
discussion having crossed the Anglican border and of its being
the occasion for some special ecumenical encounters.

The exchanges between Newman and Pusey at this period
are well known. Equally important was the correspondence
between Pusey, A. P. Forbes, Bishop of Brechin and a Bollandist
Jesuit Victor De Buck, a Belgian. This present account draws
heavily on a thesis by Fr. Jurich, s.j.[1] De Buck had first made
the acquaintance of English students at Louvain in 1845, where
he specialised in canon law. He was later drawn towards the
study of the history of theology. This introduced him to the
subject of the separation of the English Church. His introduction
to the ecclesiology of the Anglicans was the consideration of the
case of an American Episcopal bishop (Dr. Ives, of North
Carolina) who on changing to the Roman obedience was
excommunicated by the American Episcopal Church. This
very fact, strangely enough, gave De Buck the impression that
the Anglican dioceses were conscious of themselves as a
properly constituted church, with received doctrines, rules and
even a canon law. In excommunicating a schismatic bishop they

[1] 'The Ecumenical Relations of Victor De Buck, s.j. with Anglo-Catholic
leaders on the eve of the First Vatican Council', Preludes 1854–1868.
Université Catholique de Louvain. 1970.

were bearing witness to their belief in the reality of their own jurisdiction. When De Buck turned his attention forward to the future of the Church he found himself hoping for a universal council of Christendom in which 'creditable' Christians such as, in his experience, were the Lutherans and the Anglicans, would take part. His reading of history had shown him how great an opportunity of saving the unity of the Church had been lost by the failure to secure the participation of the Protestants in Trent.

De Buck's interest in matters English was stimulated through his acquaintance with Richard Simpson, editor of the *Rambler*, which was becoming the organ of the liberal catholic movement in England. It was Simpson who sent a copy of Pusey's Eirenicon to De Buck only a few months after its publication. He immediately saw in Pusey's approach to doctrinal questions an open-mindedness allied to relentlessly sound scholarship which he would have liked to have seen at work on the probems facing the Church of Rome—that is to say, a disposition to separate the necessary from the unnecessary, to isolate faith from opinion and to 'minimalise'. This latter point was to feature much in the debates which led up to the definition. It was intended by those who exploited it to be an embodiment of that apostolic principle 'to lay upon you no greater burden than these necessary things':[1] as against the efforts of those who seemed determined to seek out, to define in detail, and to impose upon men's consciences de fide, as many doctrines as they could lay hands on.

In the initial stages of their acquaintance Pusey gave De Buck far too favourable an impression, from a Roman point of view, of the English position, inviting subsequent disillusion. To the editor of the *Weekly Review* Pusey wrote his conviction that the great body of the faith was held by both, and that the Council of Trent demanded nothing which could not be explained to the satisfaction of English churchmen

> We readily recognise [he wrote] the Primacy of the Bishop of Rome; the bearings of that Primacy on other local churches we believe to be a matter of ecclesiastical, not of Divine, law; but neither is there anything in the Supremacy to which we should object.[2]

[1] Acts 15.28.
[2] *Life of E. B. Pusey*, Liddon, Vol. IV, p. 129.

The correspondence between De Buck on the one side and Pusey and Forbes on the other, gradually extended and deepened as the Council drew nearer. De Buck was chosen as theologian to the Jesuit General (Pieter Bieckx), and was sent to Rome. There he proposed that Forbes and some Anglican theologians should be invited to the Council. This project did not mature, and at the end of 1869 De Buck was ordered by Rome to desist. But this episode merits inclusion in the narrative, and the name of De Buck should certainly be inscribed in the list of those who have tried to bridge the gap of separation.

Considerable correspondence was also exchanged between Pusey and Forbes and Darboy (Archbishop of Paris) and Dupanloup (Bishop of Orléans). Bishop Forbes had visited both the Archbishop of Paris and the Bishop of Orléans, and Pusey had called on Dupanloup on a visit to some of the French bishops in 1865. It was clear both to Pusey and to Forbes that the French bishops would welcome some relationship between them and the forthcoming Council. After the Council was formally announced in 1867 Newman repeated the same encouragement to Pusey. This, he said, was his great opportunity

> if a large and strong body of united Anglicans would address the Council, being willing to be reconciled.[1]

At one stage there was some talk of a manifesto going out from some English Anglican bishops in the hope of helping the minority party in the Council, but the suggestion was rejected by Tait. On 8th June the Bishop of Lincoln (Wordsworth) wrote to the Archbishop:

> About ten days ago I received a private letter from Rome stating that some of the Bishops in the Roman Council who apprehend evil results from the promulgation of the dogma of the personal Infallibility of the Bishop of Rome would be very thankful for the moral support of the Anglican Episcopate... and for a protest against the decrees of the Roman Council as not having the true character of an Ecumenical Synod.
>
> I venture to submit to your Grace's consideration, whether

[1] *Life of E. B. Pusey*, Liddon, Vol. IV, p. 148.

the present crisis is not very favourable for the action of the Anglican Episcopate in two respects—(1) With regard to the English public, and (2) in the face of Christendom, as holding a definite and distinct position in maintaining the true Faith and ancient Discipline of the Church; and next, as taking a defensive position against Roman error and usurpation.

The Bishop of Ely[1] has prepared an English protest for the English public, and has sent me a copy of it. In compliance with the request received from the Bishop of Winchester, writing in his own name and that of other Bishops, I have drawn up another manifesto, for the Christian public generally, and I beg leave to submit herein a copy of it to your Grace for your consideration; and I have also sent a copy to the Bishop of Winchester and the Bishop of Ely.

I suppose that the dogma of the Papal Infallibility will be promulgated to the world on the 29th of this month, St. Peter's Day; and I cannot but think that it would be a great and glorious opportunity for the Anglican Episcopate to put forth on the same day a Manifesto to the world in opposition to Romish Error, and in defence of Catholic Truth.[2]

Two days later Tait replied:

I am much obliged to you for letting me see the Manifesto which you have drawn up against the Roman Council. It is with regret that I find myself compelled in this matter to take a different view from one whose opinion naturally commands such high respect. But I cannot, as at present advised, persuade myself that it is desirable for the Episcopate of the English Church to put forward any manifesto. The statements of our Church, as set forth in our Articles and Formularies, respecting the claims of the Church of Rome, are so full and explicit that, as it seems to me, they require neither explanation nor addition. The more dignified, sober, and wise policy for us to adopt, as I think, is to let Rome take her own course. The Church of England has not been addressed by the Pope or the so-called Ecumenical Council on the subject, and I cannot say that I see any necessity for

[1] Harold Browne.
[2] *Life of Archbishop Tait*, Davidson and Benham, Vol. II, pp. 76–7.

our putting forth an address. I fully expect that if the supporters of the claim to Infallibility are left alone, they will do their own cause infinite damage and us a great deal of good.[1]

Forbes was evidently more realistic about the prospects of success with the Council than Pusey. Liddon quotes a revealing remark of Forbes in a letter to Pusey.[2]

You have got more from the Archbishop of Paris than I expected you would get from any R.C. bishop in view of the terrorism of the Jesuits. So far, I see, the Archbishop takes the place of du Pin.[3] The Archbishop and the presbyter have only changed places.

In the Spring of 1868 Forbes visited the Archbishop of Paris on his way to Rome (where, incidentally, he was much discouraged by reactions to his *Explanations to the 39 Articles*). As a result of this visit Archbishop Darboy wrote to Pusey that:

there wouldn't be the slightest difficulty in obtaining what you hope for in your letter, that is to say that a Roman Congregation should pronounce on propositions submitted to it which would represent the maximum of possible concessions from your point of view.[4]

Newman, on the other hand, as has been said above, did not favour individual approaches, and did not think that Rome would pay attention to anything less than a representative group, including some Bishops. Pusey eventually desisted from his plan.

If we had a Cardinal Wiseman now [he wrote to Newman] a great deal might be done in England; but Manning appeals to God to avert such an evil as he thinks organic union to be. . . .

. . . In fact what I wanted is what Bossuet did for the Lutherans. . . . Having got such propositions accepted, I should know where I stood and could set to work.[5]

[1] *Life of Archbishop Tate*, Vol. II, pp. 78–9.
[2] *Life of E. B. Pussey*, Liddon, Vol. IV, p. 153.
[3] See Chap. 4.
[4] 21st March 1863, *Life of E. B. Pusey*, Liddon, Vol. IV, p. 154 (English trans).
[5] Pusey to Newman, September 1868. ibid., p. 157.

Such small prospects as there were of Anglican participation in the Council were completely destroyed by two letters which followed the bull calling the Council together. One summoned the bishops of the East 'who were not in communion with the Holy See', and the other addressed 'Omnibus Protestantibus aliisque Acatholicis' who were summoned to join the one fold. This was taken by all Anglicans and by many inside the Church of Rome herself[1] to be an affront to the bishops of the Church of England and her sister churches, who were thus put lower down in the scale of Roman values than, for example, the Nestorian bishops of the East.

A problem which worried Newman greatly, which he shared with his Anglican friends, was the case of Pope Honorius, who had been formally censured by the Council of Constantinople of 681 for 'Monothelitism'. This would seem to rule out the possibility of the definition, and Newman was anxious to exploit the case against the enthusiasts. This he did not hide from his correspondents.

Another Anglican who became deeply involved in the heartsearchings and the preparations for the Council, and who was very influential in moulding Anglican opinion in respect of it was Odo Russell,[2] nephew of the Foreign Secretary. Although he was technically a private individual and a spectator ab extra as far as the Council was concerned, he was in effect the English representative at the Vatican. His despatches[3] from Rome form one of the chief sources of external comment. Russell had the very greatest difficulty in feeling respect, as distinct from affection, for Pius IX. The Pope's reactions to the gradual approach of the 'liberating' forces and the diminution

[1] e.g. a letter of 9th December, 1869; Ambrose de Lisle to the Bishop of Brechin:

> I deeply regret the blunders committed by the attitude of the Papal Court in the communications with the great Patriarchs of the Eastern Churches, but I regret still more the refusal of the latter to come to the Council. I still hope that the Holy Spirit will move them to come, as also the Bishops of the Anglican Churches, including of course those of Scotland and our Colonies, as of the United States. It is at Rome that the learned men of all the Christian communions should sit before the whole Christian world whether united or not with us, to consider what are those things which they believe to be faulty in our system.' Original at Pusey House, Oxford.

[2] 1st Lord Ampthill 1881.

[3] Public Record Office.

of the temporal power had often been hysterical. Russell believed him to be a mild epileptic. Considering the prejudices and circumstances of the times, he had gone a long way in trying to understand and to sympathise with the difficulties of the Papacy. But as far back as 1860 we find him writing:

There is not a day passed here in Rome where I don't feel the blessings of the Reformation, and I thank God with all my heart that we at home have broken for ever with this infernal papacy.[1]

He had felt unhappy about the appointment of Manning to Westminster, and then had supposed that Manning's known unpopularity with the clergy and the 'old catholics' would neutralise the effects of his extreme zeal in matters of doctrine.

The first hint of the coming Council was given in a despatch of 19th June 1867:

It is said that the Pope in the Consistory to be held on the 26th inst. at the Vatican will intimate the convocation of a general Council of the Roman Church for next year. If this be true, the event is of great importance as it involves a revision of Canon Law and of the decisions of the Council of Trent. Another report is that the doctrine of the individual infallibility of the Pope, which was rejected by the Council of Trent, is now to be proclaimed a dogma by the projected Council. I should scarcely have mentioned this strange report which has long been fondly nourished by Ultra-montane ecclesiastics, had it not now been powerfully advocated by the Jesuits in their last number of *Civiltà Cattolica*.[2]

Russell was a keen observer of the prospects for the Council as they unfolded:

The convocation of this Council is certainly a very popular measure in the Clergy, who flatter themselves generally that they are to have an Ecclesiastical Parliament for the discussion of their local grievances and the promotion of their private interests, whilst the French bishops in particular, who

[1] To Earl Cowley from Rome, 5th December 1860. F.O. 519/205. Blakiston, op. cit., p. 144.
[2] F.O. 43/99B No. 51. Blakiston, op. cit., pp. 344–5.

think the Papal Government too exclusively Italian, hope through their eloquence to obtain office in Rome. And no one seems yet to realise that the Pope merely intends the Council to be a grand ceremony in St. Peter's for his own glorification and the formal confirmation of his Syllabus doctrines, his temporal Dominion and his Ex-Cathedra infallibility. De part et d'autre il-y-aura des surprises! Whatever may be said to the contrary on high Authority, I do not myself believe that any single Bishop or any number of conspiring Bishops can sustain an individual or independent opinion under the paternal wings of the Vatican if the Pope commands obedience. . . .[1]

As the great event drew nearer he seemed to have little doubt what the outcome would be. Russell's despatches make no secret of his antipathies to the strident dogmatism of the Council. This was in part due to his close association with Manning himself, who obtained permission to give weekly reports to the eminent Englishman of the proceedings of the Council. Russell was thus able to report, for example, the strange relationship between the Catholic governments of Europe and the Holy See. They had become exceedingly anxious lest the claims of Pio Nono should succeed in binding upon millions of consciences claims for the temporal power which might compromise the position of their sovereignty. The Pope, on the other hand, despaired of what he regarded as his betrayal by the catholic nations, and even began to look with envy on those countries in which catholic citizens were free to pay their respects to the see of St. Peter without reserve.

Russell was right in drawing the attention of those to whom he was reporting that any intended papal definition might have political consequences. This eventually became clear in England, and a considerable setback in the atmosphere of trust which had led to Catholic Emancipation and the toleration of the new hierarchy was the result of it. Acton, who stationed himself in Rome in the early part of the Council was later to write home to Gladstone:

The Schema bears on politics in many ways, that the Canons,

[1] To the Earl of Clarendon (his father-in-law), 16th December 1868. Clarendon papers c.487. Bodleian Library. Blakiston, op. cit., pp. 354–5.

giving infallible authority to the Pope in all matters needful for the preservation of faith and in questions of morality, give him an arbitrary power of the most unlimited kind in everything with which he chooses to deal. They are entirely in contradiction with the conditions of allegiance which the Catholics formerly accepted in England.[1]

And shortly afterwards he reported that:

A Protest on the question of Papal Infallibility was presented today by certain bishops of the United Kingdom.

They exhort the Legates to pause before they put that doctrine to the vote. They state that the English and Irish Catholics obtained their Emancipation, and the full privileges of citizenship by solemn and repeated declarations that their religion did not teach the dogma now proposed;[2] that these declarations, made by the bishops and permitted by Rome, are in fact the condition under which Catholics are allowed to sit in Parliament and to hold offices of trust and responsibility under the Crown; and that they cannot be overlooked or forgotten by us without dishonour.[3]

The debate on the Faith in Modern Times, which Newman and Acton had so much feared, was brought to an end in April 1870 when the Syllabus of Errors virtually passed into the permanent law and teaching of the Church. The constitution 'Dei Filius' condemned the pantheism, materialism and atheism of the time and then attempted to define the respective functions of Faith and Reason and to state what the relation between them ought to be.

Before the debate on Revelation, Faith and Reason was finished, it was formally announced that the subject of the papal primacy was to be the principal item for the rest of the Council. The matter had been explored at great length in the schools of theology, and much speculation had gone on all over the world as to whether it would be pressed as far as definition. Liberal Roman Catholics, and friends of the Church of Rome beyond her borders, had been hoping for a long time that no

[1] 11th March 1870. *Selections from the Correspondence of the first Lord Acton* (ed. Figgis and Lawrence), p. 109.

[2] See p. 68 above.

[3] 15th March 1870. *Selections from the Correspondence of the first Lord Acton* (ed. Figgis and Lawrence), p. 111.

definition would be attempted; some of even those who were not opposed to the doctrine were of the opinion that its definition was 'inopportune'. They feared the handling it would receive and the extremes to which it might be pushed by its protagonists. Newman was the supreme example in England of those who felt the need of a strong and clear authority in the Church—he had left the Church of England largely because of what he believed to be her lack of it—and for the papal primacy he had a great respect and a deep attachment. But the thought of its exaltation into a dogma of papal infallibility under the aegis of Manning and the 'Ultramontanists' filled him with alarm. 'Non tali auxilio', he wrote 'nec defensoribus istis.'[1]

The Ultramontane party could count on about 500 supporters among the 700 members of the Council. The opponents were divided among those who disapproved of the doctrine entirely, those who approved of it but thought its definition 'inopportune' and those who were prepared to accept it with modifications, particularly that it should be linked with the infallibility of the Holy Spirit speaking through the Church as a whole. At the first vote in July 1870 there were 451 placets, 88 non-placets and 62 'placets juxta modum'.[2] The section on Infallibility eventually read:

> We teach and define that it is a dogma divinely revealed: that the Roman Pontiff, when he speaks ex cathedra, that is, when, in discharge of the office of Pastor and Doctor of all Christians, by virtue of his supreme Apostolic authority, he defines a doctrine regarding faith or morals to be held by the Universal Church, by the divine assistance promised to him in blessed Peter, is possessed of that infallibility with which the divine Redeemer willed that His Church should be endowed for defining doctrine regarding faith or morals: and that therefore such definitions of the Roman Pontiff are irreformable of themselves, and not from the consent of the Church.

[Canon]

But if anyone—which may God avert—presume to contradict this Our definition let him be anathema.[3]

[1] Vergil, *Aeneid* 2.521.
[2] This means approval conditionally on a certain amendment or amendments.　　　　　　　　　　　　　　　　[3] Manning's translation.

The history of the last months of the Council is well known. All possible efforts were made to undermine the opposition, and their loyalty was appealed to in a form which left them no alternative but to go home. The constitution was eventually passed by 533 placets to 2 non-placets. The aged Pope, with the liberation armies at the gates of Rome, had won a complete victory.

In all this history Odo Russell had from the beginning staked his reputation on the likelihood of this result. In March the Earl of Clarendon had written to him that:

> The plot seems to be thickening at Rome and everything tends to prove that the Pope is infallible and Odo the only true prophet.[1]

Clarendon then goes on to make the interesting observation (interesting, that is, as illustrating the reaction of an educated Englishman and Anglican to the definition):

> I agree with you, as I have all along, that this monstrous assault on the reason of mankind is the only chance of mankind being roused to resistance against being insolently thrust back into the darkest periods of church despotism.[2]

When the definition was promulgated, Clarendon was again able to write and congratulate him on the accuracy of his prophecy:

> The moral of the whole tale is that you have been right from the beginning and have steadily maintained against all comers that the Pope would have his own way.[3]

While thus commenting on the excellence of Odo Russell's reporting we might mention the singular episode of the Pope's interview[4] with the Dominican Cardinal Guidi. The Cardinal had made a last-ditch stand in a speech against the definition, and on being rebuked for it by the Pope had tried to show him that tradition was not favourable to papal Infallibility. To this he got the celebrated reply 'La tradizione son Io'.[5] Russell's

---

[1] Earl of Clarendon to Odo Russell, 1st March 1870. F.O. 361/1. Blakiston, op. cit., pp. 398–9
[2] ibid. [3] idem, 30th May, Blakiston, op, cit., p. 437.
[4] On 22nd June. [5] 'I AM tradition.'

final despatch and summing up of the whole affair was sent on
18th July:

> I have the honour to enclose copy of the Constitutio Dog-
> matica adopted by the bishops in the absence of the bishops of
> the opposition and in the presence of the Pope, at the 4th
> public session this morning at the church of St. Peter. Your
> Lordship will perceive that the definition of Papal Infallibility
> dogmatically decreed and promulgated by the Pope and
> Council this day is the strongest and most absolute that words
> can express.
>
> The independence of the Roman Catholic Hierarchy has
> thus been destroyed and the supreme absolutism of Rome at
> last been obtained, established and dogmatized for which the
> Papacy has contended more than one thousand years.[1]

So Odo Russell, and together with him the greater part of
Christendom outside the Church of Rome and some of her own
members within her, saw the Vatican Council definitions as the
ne plus ultra, the extreme, of dogmatic escalation. From the
standpoint of Anglican received tradition alone, for example,
the Church of Rome had in one single enactment exhibited
five deviations from the catholic Christian faith.

(1) She had presumed to define a doctrine without the
    sanction of a fully ecumenical council.
(2) The definition was based on faulty exegesis of the
    Scriptures concerning the relationship of St. Peter to the
    other Apostles.
(3) It assumed that our Lord's promise to St. Peter was
    intended to be continued to the bishops of Rome (always
    supposing that he could rightly be styled the first of them).
(4) In claiming universal, etc., jurisdiction for the Bishop of
    Rome she departed from catholic received tradition about
    the nature of a bishop's office; and
(5) In defining the infallibility of the Pope she departed from
    catholic belief about the teaching office of the Church.

From the point of view of ecumenical understanding it must

---

[1] To Earl of Clarendon, F.O. 43/103. Blakiston, op. cit., pp. 458–9.

have seemed to be the end of all possible hopes, the final barring of the door. Yet the Council had left certain loopholes and unresolved explorations which gave a certain ground for manoeuvre. To begin with, the Council was inconclusive. It was hurried to an unpremeditated end by the political and military circumstances of the city of Rome. No one therefore was able to be certain what modifications or qualifications and subtleties of interpretation the Council might have achieved if it had sat for longer. And then, although the definition did seem from the point of view of the liberal catholics to be the end of the road, it did not in fact completely satisfy even the Ultramontane party. For whereas it made the papal definitions 'irreformable of themselves, and not by consent of the Church' yet it appeared, or could be made to appear, to limit the application of infallibility for those occasions only when, speaking 'ex cathedra', the Pope was defining some matter of faith or morals. The exact application of this doctrine has been widely debated in subsequent years, as has the calculation of the number of those occasions to which it can be said to apply. This was fortunate for the future of ecumenical understanding. But the number of people who were well instructed or subtle enough to take advantage of these possibilities at the time was small.

Anglican reaction to the Council and the definition was of course almost universally unfavourable.[1] It seemed to many that such possibilities as there had been were now precluded for ever. Just before the end of the Council Pusey was writing to Newman:

> I see that there is an anathema proposed against those who do not hold that S. Peter had jurisdiction over the other Apostles, who had equal fullness of inspiration with himself. What a multiplication of minute anathemas! I can only turn away, sick at heart, and say 'Though they curse, yet bless Thou'. . . I fear that these decisions will be a great strain on men's faith. Anti-Christ must come, and everything which tries faith must prepare for his coming. Then those who believe must be driven together; whereas this Council seems to be framed to repel all whom it does not scare.[2]

[1] See Gladstone's pamphlets, for example, The Vatican Decrees in their bearing on *Civil Allegiance; Vaticanism*, John Murray, 1874 and 1875.
[2] 21st May 1870. Pusey to Newman, *Life of E. B. Pusey*, Liddon, Vol. IV, pp. 192–3.

When it was over Pusey, supposing as did many others that the Council would reassemble, wrote to Newman:

> I wonder whether the Council will do anything, on its reassembling, to express the conditions of the Infallibility which it has affirmed. To me some of the lesser cases seemed more irreconcilable with Infallibility than the great case of Honorius. As to Honorius, it seemed to me (as I said) either that Honorius erred as to faith, or that General Councils and Popes bore false witness against him. Still, answers were made. But the errors of Popes as to marriage Bellarmine himself does not defend.
>
> However, I say this, because I am writing to you; I have done what I could, and now have done with controversy and Eirenica.[1]

That Pusey's hopes for future ecumenical understanding was dashed is to be seen from the fact that in later issues of the Third Eirenicon he changed its title from 'Is Healthful Union Possible' to 'Healthful Reunion, as conceived possible before the Vatican Council'. And if Pusey, then what of the rank and file of Anglican Christians? The Lambeth Conference of 1878 declared:

> that the act done by the Bishop of Rome in the Vatican Council in the year 1870—whereby he asserted a supremacy over all men in matters both of faith and morals, on the ground of an assumed infallibility—was an invasion of the attributes of the Lord Jesus Christ.

The Conference of 1888 rejoiced that between the Anglican Communion and the Eastern Churches:

> there exist no bars such as are presented to communion with the Latins by the formulated sanction of the Infallibility of the Church residing in the person of the supreme pontiff, by the doctrine of the Immaculate Conception, and other dogmas imposed by the decrees of papal councils.

and its Committee on Reunion affirmed that:

> under present conditions, it was useless to consider the

[1] 26th August 1870. *Life of E. B. Pusey*, Liddon, Vol. IV.

question of Reunion with our brethren of the Roman Church.

'Manning's Council', as it was described by many, turned out to be a climacteric in ecclesiastical history. With the promulgation of the dogma there came into being a period of even stricter Vatican control of the world-wide church. The discipline and loyalty which the new situation called forth from Roman Catholics drew them more admiration than the dogmas themselves earned misunderstanding. To the surprise of many the Roman Church advanced to the contest with Modernism more adequately armed and in better heart after the Council than before it. In fact she showed herself better able to deal with the crisis than the amorphous forces of Liberal Protestantism; so much so that in the course of the fray she drew many thousands of new converts out of the ranks of the Church of England alone, from among those who despaired at their own leaders' tendency to bow before the contemporary world rather than to stand up to it. But this was achieved in a world where it was still possible to satisfy the unsophisticated with unreason and dogmatic intransigeance. From this point of view Manning, to whom under Pope Pius IX so much of the formative influence of the Council was due, appeared to be one of the saviours of the Papacy and the Roman Church. But in the long run, as her sons in the latter half of the twentieth century now know to their cost, this legacy of rigid papalism succeeded in steering the church towards an era of possible disaster, which it has taken the Second Vatican Council and all the navigations of John XXIII and Paul VI to avoid.

In the course of this narrative, because of its special concern with the escalating dogmatism of the First Vatican Council and its baneful consequences for ecumenical relationships, Manning has largely appeared as the villain of the piece. And in his subsequent dealings with the far greater figure of John Henry Newman, whom he seemed to English opinion to misunderstand and even to persecute, he gave the further impression of being an austere, unsympathetic and passionless ecclesiastic, as pastorally insensitive as it would be conceivable for a cleric to be. This picture, if any still have it of Manning, should certainly be redrawn, not only for truth's sake, but in the name of ecumenical understanding. For he was also celebrated, and to some perhaps far better known, as a man of pastoral feeling for the welfare of the poor, and for social conditions generally— and that, let it be said, when the attitude of many Anglican bishops, with their comfortable endowments and their political advantages, did little to commend the gospel. This trait in Manning dated from the days when as Archdeacon of Chichester he had concerned himself with the sufferings of the agricultural labourers of Sussex. He distinguished himself above all when as Cardinal it was mainly his personal intervention which led to the peaceful solution of a dock strike in the east end of London. This side of Manning's ministry must be reckoned to him for ecumenical good, as it cannot have failed to soften the minds of unprejudiced Englishmen towards the renascent and successful branch of the Church of Rome in their midst. Manning was made Cardinal in 1875, Newman in 1879. In the event many must have reflected on the fact that the two men who did most to mould the Roman Catholic Church at that time and in this land—and indeed far beyond it—had both found their beginnings in the ministry of the Church of England.

The ecumenical situation between the Anglican churches and the Church of Rome at the end of the Council can therefore be summed up as follows. The Roman Church is seen as embracing a new doctrine (new at least in being defined) which had been achieved at the cost of great division. At the best its interpretation was uncertain, awaiting further clarification by the schools of theology; and its implementation was in the hands of administrators and canon lawyers, who were to use it unremittingly to strengthen the Papacy at the expense of the bishops. The Council was unfinished, again at the cost of the bishops, whose relationship to the newly-strengthened Papacy remained uncertain. As for the prospects of the reunion of Christendom to those outside the Roman communion they looked exceedingly bleak. And they were to become yet bleaker, and to remain so until the very eve, a century later, of the Second Vatican Council. Looking back from that very eve, Abbot (later Bishop) Christopher Butler was to write:

It may be regretted that . . . the complementary question about the status and God-given functions of the episcopate as a whole was not answered by the Councils. Such regret may be tempered by the reflection that the time was not yet ripe for a fully balanced view. Perhaps, in the providence of God, this question will be answered by the second Vatican Council, so that the two Councils, taken together, will provide an authoritative picture of the supreme government and magisterium of the Church, which will do justice both to the primacy conferred on Peter and to that 'collegiate' element which is so strongly evidenced by tradition and so rightly cherished by many of our separated brethren. The word ecumenical has taken on a new nuance in the modern movement towards Christian unity.[1]

One of the consequences of the decisions of Vatican I which had a bearing on ecumenical relationships was the schism of Dr. Döllinger, one of the chief antagonists of the Infallibility definition. Although there were many of the German bishops who felt able to submit to the dogma on the grounds that it only applied to doctrines said to have been delivered 'ex cathedra', there was a number of German catholics who could not stretch their consciences that far. In March 1871 Döllinger organised a large-scale protest in Munich. Those who felt bound to separate themselves not, as they said, from the communion of catholic Christendom, but from 'the doctrinal aberrations of the Bishop of Rome' met in congress in Cologne in August 1873. As a result of this meeting they joined forces with the 'Jansenist'[2] Church of Holland, the new body being called from that time onwards 'the Old Catholics'. They rejected 'papal assumptions', decided to use vernacular languages, admitted the marriage of the clergy and made auricular confession voluntary. Anglicans were naturally interested in this reform. The Bishop of Lincoln (Christopher Wordsworth) warmly supported it, as did Bishop Harold Browne of Ely (later of Winchester), and various other Anglican leaders, notably H. P. Liddon, gave it their approval. The Lambeth Conference of 1878 gave the new Church a measure of support and Archbishop Tait gave hospitality in 1882 to two

[1] Preface to *The First Vatican Council*, Dom Cuthbert Butler, Collins and Harvill Press, 1962, p. 6.
[2] See Chapter 4, p. 23.

of their bishops. Relationships have become closer in the course of time. The movement spread to America by the affiliation in 1897 of a group of Polish catholics in the U.S.A. under the title of the Polish National Catholic Church. The title deed of the Old Catholic Churches, agreed upon by the bishops at Bonn in 1889, is the 'Declaration of Utrecht'. They formally recognised Anglican Orders in 1925, and in a concordat agreed upon in Bonn in 1931, they entered into full communion with the Church of England. The very existence of the Old Catholic Churches, small though they are in numbers, had made a contribution to the resumption of relationships with the Church of Rome herself. For as the Anglican Churches stand between the Church of Rome and the Churches of the Protestant Reformation, so the Old Catholics stand in the middle ground between Rome and Canterbury. And they have sometimes played a restraining part in the councils of the Church of England against those who would sell her out too easily in the direction of total protestantism. Her bishops have taken part, from time to time, in the consecration of Anglican bishops, which has been a comfort for those who have a mechanical theory of the transmission of orders, as admitting without doubt the Roman succession into the Anglican stream. It is now generally admitted, for what it is worth, that the 'rectification' (if that be the word) of Anglican ordinations is now largely accomplished through that stream alone: though the majority of Anglican students of the matter are content that the succession is unbroken as it is. The Old Catholic Church, meanwhile, is to be reckoned with as a new factor in the ecumenical problem, and has been a considerable agent for good.

It might have been supposed that the definitions of the Vatican Council had alienated the possibilities of Roman Catholic/Anglican understanding beyond recall. Many believed this, and some few do still believe it. But there was worse to come, and that worse came in the encyclical of 1896, 'Apostolicae Curae', in which Anglican Orders were declared by the Church of Rome to be invalid. By that time Pius IX had given place at Rome to Leo XIII, Archbishop Tait to Edward White Benson at Canterbury and Cardinal Manning to Herbert Vaughan at Westminster.

12

APOSTOLICAE CURAE AND ANGLICAN ORDERS

Leo XIII (formerly Cardinal Pecci) succeeded to the exceptionally long pontificate of Pius IX in 1878. He represented
a considerable change from his predecessor in many matters,
particularly in the relation of the Church to the State and to
the modern world. Besides the encyclical on Anglican orders he
is best remembered for the famous Rerum Novarum of 1891 on
social matters, for 'Providentissimus Deus' of 1893[1] on the
Scriptures and for two documents on ecumenical matters, the
letter 'Ad Anglos' of 1895[2] and the encyclical 'Satis Cognitum'
of 1896[3]. The first gave encouragement to Lord Halifax[4] and
the Abbé Portal:[5] the second was almost a prelude to the letter
Apostolicae Curae. For less sanguine persons they would have
extinguished all hope of ecumenical encounter as being only
benevolent variations on the original theme of union by
unconditional surrender. Halifax, however, was impressed by
the tone of the former which was very generous in its appreciation of the characteristics of the English people and contains
the following passage:

> In these days our thoughts turn with love and hope to the
> English people, observing as we do the frequent and manifest
> works of Divine Grace in their midst; how to some, it is
> plain, the confusion of religious dissensions which divide

[1] *Enchiridion Symbolorum* ed. Denzinger 1941.
[2] Apostolic Letter 'Amantissimae Voluntatis', 14th April 1895. English
version in *Rome and Reunion*, E. C. Messenger, pp. 14–28.
[3] ibid., 31–74.　　　　[4] See p. 222 below.　　　　[5] ibid.

them is a cause of deep concern; how others see clearly the need of some sure defence against the inroad of modern errors which only too readily humour the wishes of fallen nature and depraved reason: how the number of those religious and discreet men, who sincerely labour much for reunion with the Catholic Church, is increasing. We can hardly say how strongly these and other signs quicken the charity of Christ in us, and redoubling our prayers from our inmost soul, we call down a fuller measure of Divine Grace which, poured out on minds so well disposed, may issue in the ardently desired fruit, the fruit, namely that we may all meet into the unity of faith and of the knowledge of the Son of God (Eph. iv.13).[1]

From some points of view these four documents could be understood as moves in a general direction favourable to improvement in relationships; which may explain why the event of 1896 came as the surprise and disappointment it was. 'Rerum Novarum', by its very title, showed that there was a new atmosphere in the Vatican. It reviewed the situation created by the new conditions of the Industrial Revolution and applied to it admittedly traditional catholic teaching, yet in a way which made it appear both inside and outside the Church of Rome as a charter of new liberties and rights for the hard-pressed peoples of Europe. It had a flavour of revolution about it. Acton said of Leo XIII:

I think he is the first Pope who has been wise enough to despair, and has felt that he must begin a new part, and steer by strange stars over an unknown sea.'[2]

'Providentissimus Deus' was an encyclical which took into account the new world of biblical scholarship and archaeology which was now beginning to feature so strongly in theological discussion. Naturally it was in some matters conservative, and could be held to condemn the excesses of such scholars as Loisy. It was subsequently appealed to by both sides in the argument, but Leo's intentions can best be judged by the institution later in his pontificate (1902) of the Biblical Com-

[1] Messenger, op. cit., 23–4.
[2] 25th March 1881, *Letters of Lord Acton to Mary Gladstone* (ed. Herbert Paul).

mission. This has indeed been responsible in its time for the major Roman Catholic errors, as the rest of Christendom holds them to be, on such matters as the decisions on the Mosaic authorship of the Pentateuch and the Synoptic Problem. But it can also be said to be the beginning of that splendid flowering of biblical scholarship which has been the pride of the Church of Rome in the mid-twentieth century, and which in turn has been the seed-bed of all the new attitudes which have made catholic ecumenism possible in our day.

Archbishop Benson, however, later said:

> Portal asked me what I thought of the Pope's encyclical on Scripture, and I was obliged to say that though very beautiful Latin, it was full 50 years behind the present state of actual knowledge, and that I could not have believed that such a paper could have been written now by any theologian.[1]

Whatever may have been the technical objections to 'Ad Anglos', and however regrettable and retrograde its eventual consequences in Apostolicae Curae may have been, there is no doubt that the origins of this movement with Leo XIII were open and benevolent. And in the early stages of its development he appeared to Anglicans to be just that kind of person.

If, from the point of view we are taking, Leo XIII was an improvement on Pius IX, so was Archbishop Benson on his predecessor Tait. Benson had a profound knowledge of patristic studies, and his chief published work was to be a detailed commentary on St. Cyprian. This study led him to a reverence for the proper position of the Church of Rome as the mother church of Christendom in the West; though equally strongly to a rejection of papal claims as they have later been built up, and especially as defined in the First Vatican Council. For his time Benson had a considerable love of beauty, of good order and ceremonial and of the place of music in worship. He was a frequent and enthusiastic visitor to Italy, where he took full opportunity of observing Roman customs and practice in the churches. Where he felt he could give praise, his diary shows, he gave it: notably he found great edification in the Easter Eve celebrations in Florence, and thought of the possibility of

---

[1] *Life of E. W. Benson*, A. C. Benson, Vol. II, p. 593.

their introduction, suitably adapted, into the Church of England. But for the Church of Rome herself, as an (un-reformed) institution, he had little good to say and the possibilities of ecumenical advance in his time were accordingly slight. To a suggestion that he should send the Pope a present on the occasion of his jubilee he brusquely replied:

> I thought I had long since made it sufficiently clear that I would not approach the Pope. But 'is not the hand of Joab with thee in all this'?
>
> We are utterly guiltless of any schism. Till the eleventh year of Elizabeth, when we were as we are now, there was no thought of such a thing. Then we were impiously excommunicated.
>
> It is impossible that your proposed present from me to him should be 'personal'. You yourself say its value would be greatly more significant because the Lambeth Conference is approaching.
>
> It is the Pope's business to eat dust and ashes, not mine to decorate him. Therefore, my dear Mephibosheth, hold thy peace.
>
> Your loving, EDW. CANTUAR.[1]

Benson was personally interested in the Old Catholic movement, as representing a glimmer of a vision of restored non-papal catholicism, but felt bound to maintain an attitude of official caution at the beginning of his archiepiscopate, hoping for further clarification of doctrinal points, waiting for further openness on the part of the Old Catholic bishops and also not being willing to disturb evangelical sentiment in the Church of England by too great a commitment. It was William Dalrymple Maclagan, Archbishop of York, who was the chief Anglican go-between with the Old Catholic movement. In 1887 he undertook a journey in the company of the Bishop of Salisbury (John Wordsworth) to Germany and to Switzerland, after which they drew up a cautious report and presented it to the Lambeth Conference. Maclagan's personal reaction was by no means unsympathetic. To his wife he wrote of his visit:

> Like me, you would have found occasionally les larmes dans

[1] Letter to Canon Mason, 27th November 1887. *Life of E. W. Benson*, Vol. II, p. 586.

les yeux, as visions of a united Christendom floated before one's mind.[1]

But to return to Benson. He was a man less austere than his predecessor Tait, in that he could see more clearly the great strengths of the Church of Rome; yet he was firmly rooted in the ethos of the Anglican Church and was disposed to guide its destinies from the position of a deep scholarship and tenacious loyalty.

The succession of Vaughan to Manning at the head of the Roman Catholic community in England cannot be said to have changed the situation much in regard to ecumenical attitudes. Vaughan, from his background as a member of a traditional catholic family, might have been expected to be a milder and more tolerant prelate than Manning; yet his appointment did not represent much change. In fact he must have absorbed a good deal of Manning's zeal in the course of his association with him, for on most essential points of policy they thought alike, with rigid loyalty to the findings of the Vatican Council, in the aggressive attempt to reclaim England as the 'Dowry of Mary' and in an inability to think of ecumenical relationships in terms other than those of unconditional submission to the one, true Church. Manning's zeal in social questions was replaced by Vaughan's vision and enthusiasm for overseas missions. He was the founder of the College of the Mill Hill fathers.

The investiture of Vaughan with the pallium in 1892 was the occasion of a visit of an Apostolic Delegate (Archbishop Stonor, a member of an old-established catholic family). This occasion not only drew attention to the firmly established position of the new hierarchy but also illustrated the spirit of tolerance which was beginning to show itself in England generally only a short generation after the end of the Vatican Council. It was the first such function in England since the investiture in 1555 of Cardinal Pole, in the reign of Mary Tudor. *The Times* commented:

The historian will observe the proceedings of yesterday as a landmark in the successive attitudes of public opinion

[1] Letter of 12th October 1887. *Archbishop Maclagan*, F. D. How, Wells, Gardner, Darton & Co., London, 1911, p. 256.

towards the Roman Catholic Church and its claims. A generation ago it was almost impossible for a Roman Catholic to sit for an English constituency. A religious function such as that of yesterday would have raised a storm of indignant protest.[1]

Pope Leo XIII, Archbishop Benson and Cardinal Vaughan. These, then, were the responsible administrative heads during the next act of the drama. But the principals were to be the Anglican Lord Halifax and the Abbé Portal. At the time of his meeting with Lord Halifax the Abbé was a teacher in the Seminary at Cahors in France, but left there and went to live in Paris in order to devote himself whole-time to exploiting the opportunities which his acquaintance with Halifax was opening up.

Charles Lindley Wood, Viscount Halifax,[2] travelled many miles and devoted endless energies to the pursuit of a better understanding. But he made many mistakes; and one might suppose that he enjoyed little achievement in his lifetime to set over against much disappointment and positive discouragement. Yet he had great faith, and that faith has been the father of many achievements in our present generation. He was a true son of the Oxford Tractarians from the days of being an undergraduate at Christ Church under Pusey. President of the English Church Union from 1868, he had taken part in the arguments, the struggles and the litigation in which the second generation of Tractarians had become involved. But it was as a result of his meeting the Abbé Portal by chance (if that is the right word) in Madeira in 1890 that he caught the full vision of the unity of the Church, a unity inevitably involving Rome, and a glimpse of possible solutions to its problems.

Apart from the chief sources in the lives of Halifax[3] and the Abbé Portal[4] and in Lord Halifax's *Leo XIII and Anglican Orders*,[5] one of the most interesting contemporary documents is the account of T. A. Lacey (Canon of Worcester),[6] itself well documented, of his stay in Rome with Fr. Puller, s.s.j.e. during

---

[1] 17th August 1892.　　　　　　　　　　　　　　[2] 1839–1934.

[3] *Charles Lindley, Viscount Halifax*, J. G. Lockhart, Vol. I, 1935; II, 1936.

[4] *Mons. Portal*, H. Hemmer (trans. A. T. Macmillan under title *Fernand Portal, Apostle of Unity*, Macmillan, 1961).

[5] Longmans, 1912.　　　　　　　　　　[6] *A Roman Diary*, Longmans, 1910.

the deliberations of the Commission. The position of these two Anglicans in itself was a new feature of ecumenical experiment, and although they had no official status they were in spirit the forerunners of the observers of the Second Vatican Council.[1]

The meeting in Madeira touched off in the mind of Halifax the idea that Christian union might be nearer and more possible than he had previously thought. Through most of his adult life he had tried to make and to keep contacts with catholic clergy on the continent of Europe. He had exchanged letters with the Archbishop of Paris. But it was the fact that the learned Abbé seemed to be so unaware of the doctrinal and liturgical position of the English Church, and the Abbé's pleased surprise at discovering what he learned, that encouraged Halifax to suppose that the dispelling of ignorance was the chief way to ecumenism. In any case it was the starting-point, the sine qua non of progress. The Frenchman was touched by the Anglican peer's enthusiasm and very quickly decided that there was an urgent need to put the question of improved relationships to Rome. He chose the matter of the validity of Anglican Orders as a first point of reference from which, it might be hoped, a start might be made to resolve the other problems at issue. Nearly twenty years later, before the Malines conversations, the Abbé was to write to Cardinal Mercier:

> The question of Holy Orders was chosen as providing a suitable meeting ground for Anglicans and Catholics, where they could discuss, not only the validity of Anglican Orders, but also other problems which separate them. As regards Holy Orders, there was agreement on certain basic principles: the need for uninterrupted transmission: of sufficiency of matter and form, and of an intention to do that which the Church does. I thought there were sufficient points of contact to enable the question to be discussed profitably. It was not really necessary to come to any final decision on the validity of Anglican Orders: that could have been left to the end, after all the other problems had been discussed.[2]

[1] The whole literature of this critical period has taken on a new dimension in our day by the publication of the two volumes of J. J. Hughes. *Absolutely Null and Utterly Void*, Sheed & Ward, 1968; *Stewards of the Lord*, Sheed & Ward, 1970.

[2] 24th January 1921, *Fernand Portal, Apostle of Unity*, trans. A. T. Macmillan, p. 34.

They decided to ignore the important fact that neither of them had the support, let alone the authority, of his own side. They had gone too far too soon, and they had chosen the wrong starting-point. All this is easy to see from after the events, and in no way diminishes the respect due to these pioneers of the cause.

At Portal's suggestion Halifax began, though the Abbé had to finish, a study of Anglican Orders, published in French. The resultant *Les Ordinations Anglicanes*[1] was brought to the notice of the historian Mgr. Duchesne who, after answering certain objections, gave it as his opinion that it would be safe to make it at least a basis of enquiry. By this time both sides were trying to obtain support and to 'sell' their enthusiasm to their respective constituencies.

At Halifax's request Portal made a visit to England in August 1894. He saw, among others, the Bishop of Peterborough (Mandell Creighton),[2] the Archbishops of York (Maclagan) and Canterbury (Benson). The documents of the time illustrate the favourable impression that the intellectual stature of these men made upon him, even if their reserve and caution and fear of consequences of any kind of action were unreassuring. Halifax, recording the meeting with Mandell Creighton, shows the great historian as having an objective approach to the problems of reunion. Talking of the Papacy the bishop had said that:

> he often told his people that they did not understand what they were saying when they talked about the Pope, and that it might be useful for them to remember, when discussing Papal Infallibility that it was an axiom in England that 'the King can do no wrong'.[3]

Of the Archbishop of York Portal records that Maclagan, speaking of his appeal to the Eastern Churches, had said:

> It is impossible not to be touched by the sight of this old man [the Pope], like S. John, making this appeal to the charity of Christians.[4]

[1] Under the pseudonym 'Dalbus'.
[2] 1843–1901. Dixie Professor of Ecclesiastical History. Cambridge 1884. Author of *History of the Papacy* (5 vols).
[3] *Leo XIII and Anglican Orders*, Halifax, p. 98.
[4] *Fernand Portal, Apostle of Unity*, p. 40.

On his return from York the Abbé wrote that:

> I reflected on the strange role I was playing, a role I had not foreseen nor particularly desired. I have never been more sure that we were being used for some great purpose.[1]

But of Benson he was bound to record a great caution. Portal wrote:

> I am puzzled by the Archbishop of Canterbury. He is a holy man and learned, but he seems to think that in his position he must be very cautious, a feeling probably explained by what he said to me in connection with our movement, 'Reverend Sir, we have to remember that many of our fellow churchmen to whom we must be loyal do not agree with us on these matters'.[2]

In saying this the Archbishop had only been stating the obvious. Any attempt at corporate union of the whole body of the Church of England with Rome at that time was entirely out of the question. Such a project would require a long period of mutual co-operation and education, with positive and deliberate attempts to remove bigotry and ignorance on both sides. A clear view of one of the main obstacles to progress, and a warning of what was to come later, was given at this time by Cardinal Vaughan in a speech at Preston, in which he made clear what was to be the attitude of the English Roman Catholic hierarchy. It was a full-scale attack on the Church of England and a denial of any possibility of reunion conceived on terms other than those of total submission. It ended with a particularly offensive description of those who tried to live by 'catholic practices' under the patronage of the Church of England, reminding them that St. Jerome had said that the devil was the Simia Dei, the ape of God. But even this failed to quench the ardour of the French advocates of other methods of Christian behaviour. It was to be demonstrated once again that Christian understanding between Anglicans and Roman Catholics was more easily promoted on foreign soil than at home.

Meanwhile the Abbé had been courting Rome in the persons of Cardinal Rampolla, Secretary of State and then the Pope

[1] *Fernand Portal, Apostle of Unity,* p. 40. [2] ibid.

himself, who had personally summoned him.[1] For the Pope's information Portal seems to have touched on the main difficulties, not excepting the infallibility and other doctrines and the hostile attitude of the English Roman Catholics. But the audience ended on a note of encouragement, the Abbé repeating the Bishop of Peterborough's words:

Let us hope we are assisting at the beginning of great things',

and the Pope, who was then 85, saying:

God grant it: but I am 85. How thankfully should I sing my Nunc Dimittis if I could do anything, even the least thing, to help forward this union'.[2]

Portal had hoped for a direct invitation from the Pope to be sent to the Archbishops of Canterbury and York, but that was not forthcoming and he had to be content with a letter from the Cardinal to Lord Halifax, who thus recorded Portal's last interview with the Pope before leaving Rome. The Pope had on his table *Les Ordinations Anglicanes*.

I have read your work,' said the Pope; 'it is very well done. Cardinal Rampolla has given you his letter; are you satisfied?

'Yes, Holy Father, but your Holiness knows that I should have preferred a letter direct to the Archbishops; the result would have been much more certain.'

'That is possible, but I have seen the Principal of the Scottish Seminary, and talked to him about the Anglicans, and he tells me that the Scottish Presbyterians would be more easily reunited than the Anglicans, because they have no relation with the civil power.'[3]

Meanwhile the situation in England had been deteriorating. Cardinal Vaughan's speech at Preston had shown that relationships were very difficult in any case; but when asked for explanation of the expression 'recognition of the sin of schism' used in that speech he replied that he rejected uncompromisingly the possibility of Anglican orders being valid. More exasperation was caused at this time by the revelation that the

---

[1] *Fernand Portal, Apostle of Unity*, pp. 42–3.
[2] *Leo XIII and Anglican Orders*, Halifax, p. 121.
[3] ibid., p. 122.

Archbishop of Dublin had consecrated a bishop to build up a non-Roman episcopal congregation in Spain. Lord Halifax thought it opportune to write to the Primate of Spain disclaiming this action as contrary to the practice and intention of the Church of England as a constituent part of the Catholic Church. He wrote as President of the English Church Union, without canonical authority and without ascertaining whether in fact a considerable number of members of the Church of England might even have favoured the setting up of a Church to counter what they would have called 'the errors of Romanism' in a country where they were popularly supposed to be at their worst. Cardinal Vaughan, on hearing of the episode, also wrote to the Primate of Spain, reviling Halifax and his sect and accusing him of duplicity. The letter somehow got published and a sharp exchange ensued which further damaged the possibility of improving relationships between Canterbury and Rome. Wiser counsels should have led Halifax to remain silent on this matter, in the knowledge that one result of publicity would be to show naked to Rome the inability of the Anglican provinces to keep in step with one another—in fact the absence of a recognised authority between them.

These encounters made Vaughan keen from his side for an official ruling from Rome about Anglican Orders. Anglican hopes were running high that there might be an official enquiry and that the results of such an enquiry might be not unfavourable to the Anglican cause. Vaughan, on the other hand, had begun to receive ominous reports from Rome. In July 1895 he had received from Merry del Val[1] (later to be the secretary of the Commission) a letter alerting him to his fears.

We were talking over all this, the position of the Ritualists, etc. etc. when Cardinal Rampolla was announced and the H.F. had him introduced at once wishing me to be present, and there began an anxious and rather painful time for me. The Cardinal is an earnest upholder of H. He has to my mind been completely hoodwinked by him and he evidently has no grasp of the situation in England.[2]

[1] 1865–1930. Protegé of Leo XIII who treated him as a son. Diplomatic missions to London, Vienna and Berlin. Archbishop 1900. Cardinal Secretary of State 1903.

[2] 24th July 1895, *Absolutely Null and Utterly Void*, Hughes, p. 296.

In May 1896 Gladstone produced a paper[1] giving his personal reflections on the subject.

> It is to the last degree improbable [he wrote] that a ruler of known wisdom would put in motion the machinery of the Curia for the purpose of widening the breach. . . . If the investigations of the Curia did not lead to a favourable result, wisdom and charity would in any case arrest them at such a point as to prevent their becoming an occasion and a means of embittering religious controversy.[2]

Gladstone little knew the zeal and the determination of Vaughan and his chief assistant, Dom Aidan (later Cardinal) Gasquet in the opposite direction. From the moment of hearing that the Pope was considering a letter to the English archbishops, Vaughan and Gasquet had hurried to Rome and had begun a strong campaign to dissuade him from his objective attitudes (this as early as the beginning of 1895). The success of their persuasion was soon to be visible.

The manoeuvres on both sides ended, then, in the Pope feeling unable to address a letter to the English archbishops but only to circulate a general epistle 'Ad Anglos', in April 1895; and in the archbishops not wishing to compromise themselves in asking for a Roman pronouncement, thereby making it look as though they were uncertain about their orders. But the front-line protagonists on both sides in Rome, strangely enough, were equally strongly in support of the appointment of a Commission, in the certainty that they would gain their respective diagonally opposite objectives. Halifax, Portal and Duchesne were of the opinion that a Commission could not fail to be persuaded by the case as they would present it; Vaughan and Gasquet were equally persuaded to the contrary. They were confident that such an examination would lead to a condemnation, and that a condemnation was urgently needed both for the edification of the Roman Catholic community in England and for the disillusioning of those, whether on the Roman side or the Anglican, who still thought there was any hope for reunion except by total submission. Yet writing of the Epistle 'Ad Anglos' in a Pastoral Letter Archbishop Benson spoke of[3]

---

[1] Entitled a *Soliloquium*.   [2] *A Roman Diary*, Lacey, p. 141.
[3] *Leo XIII and Anglican Orders*, Halifax, pp. 227-8.

the friendly advance made from a foreign Church to the people of England without any reference or regard to the Church of England. We cannot fail to find in it a call to renewed faith in the mission of the Church and commend this call to the thought and prayers of all who loved our Lord. Our divisions are the chief obstacle in the progress of the Gospel and we accept the many expressions of anxiety to be delivered from them as a sign among us of God's purpose at the present time. The Lambeth Conferences of 1878 and 1888 have commended the matter of reunion to the special prayers of all people in preparation of opportunities for further action. The aspiration after reunion is a vast one: it must take account of the East and non-Episcopal bodies at home and abroad; it must also consider the Christianising of Asia and Africa under the most extremely varying circumstances. . . . The Roman Church had not always proved capable of retaining its hold on nations once its own. . . . It had invited the English people into reunion with itself in apparent unconsciousness of the position of the English Church and in that invitation it has paraded methods of worship and rewards of worship repugnant to Teutonic Christianity. We must rejoice in the manifestation of such a spirit of love, but the appeal made was inadequate. Recognition [of the English Church] might have lent a meaning to the mention of reunion. . . . History shows what great duties in view of reunion are being forced upon the Church of England.

The Archbishop of York, speaking at the opening of a Church Congress in Norwich later in 1895, felt able to say that:

Reunion is in the air . . . a voice from Rome has spoken to us; moved by the same desire . . . it breathes from first to last a spirit of fatherly love . . . the supremacy of the Bishop of Rome as understood by St. Gregory in the sixth century or by St. Bernard in the twelfth, was widely different from the idea which is now pressed upon us [by Cardinal Vaughan] . . . a return to the earlier conception is not beyond the bounds of hope. There are deepening evidences of the longing for the reunion of the separated members of Christendom. . . .[1]

---

[1] *Leo XIII and Anglican Orders*, Halifax, p. 230.

Under these circumstances the Commission to examine Anglican Orders was set up in March 1896. It consisted of Cardinal Mazzella, president, Dom Aidan Gasquet, Canon Moyes and Fr. David Fleming[1] (these seemed to be the 'unfavourables'); then Duchesne, Mgr. Gasparri[2] and de Augustinis, s.j., Rector of the Gregorianum ('favourables') with a neutral Spanish Capuchin, Fr. Llevaneras. Fr. Scannell, from England, was also summoned.

The Commission took only a few months to deliberate on what had been discussed for three centuries. They had many documents before them, the most notable of which was the 'De Re Anglicana', drawn up by Canon Lacey.[3] In his memoirs Lacey was insistent that he and Fr. Puller were not in Rome as *promotores causae*, but only to be available for information. This they provided when required, and on occasions procured from Great Britain. The full text of 'De Re Anglicana' and the answer which Moyes and Gasquet felt impelled to write can be read as chapter 8 of the *Roman Diary*.

The main documents which were pressed upon the Commission from the other side were a bull discovered in the Register of Paul IV, unknown to all previous writers on the subject, dealing with the powers delegated to Cardinal Pole for the readmission to the ministry of those ordained in the reign of Edward VI, and previous judgments on Anglican orders in 1704 and in the Gordon case. The zeal and insistence of the English Roman Catholic influences seems to have prevailed quickly, for the deliberations were foreshadowed in June in the encyclical 'Satis Cognitum'. Although this treated of Unity rather than Orders, it must have put the outcome of the Commission beyond doubt. For without examination of basic assumptions about the nature of the Church, it repeated traditional Roman Catholic teaching, in terms not acceptable either to the Orthodox or to the Anglican or Protestant churches. There was entire preoccupation with the external symbols of unity, particularly the succession from Peter, and the office of Peter as treated by Roman Catholic exegesis.

After the Commission had finished, the whole matter was

---

[1] The chief linguist of the team.
[2] Later Cardinal; then Professor of Canon Law in Paris.
[3] *A Roman Diary*, Lacey, p. 195.

referred to a committee of Cardinals, who in turn reported to the Pope. On 19th September the blow fell. In the bull 'Apostolicae Curae' Anglican Orders were declared 'absolutely null and utterly void'. The main grounds of objection were first to the claim to continuity, due to the alleged defects in the rite and in the consecrators in the sixteenth century; and secondly to the intention. In March 1897 the archbishops[1] sent their Responsio.[2]

To the charge of defective intention the Responsio replied first that the general intention was clear beyond doubt both in the Preface to the Ordinal and in the rite itself. To the charge of defective rite the answer was that if the Anglican sixteenth-century omissions (such as the transmission of the vessels, the anointing and the declaration of intention to offer sacrifice of masses etc.) were essential to the efficacy of the rite so as to invalidate it if not present, then all Roman ordinations at any earlier stage, where those elements can be shown to be missing, were invalid also. To the historical objections to the validity of the Edwardine bishops (including the now wholly discredited 'Nag's Head Fable') contrary evidence was alleged; and as the lineal descent of Anglican bishops does not in any case depend only upon them, this soon ceased to be regarded as a valid line of argument. Moreover no attention was given to, nor was there apparently any awareness of, Anglican successions outside England. To the modern generation these contentions may seem irrelevant, and there is growing agreement that a settlement can only be reached by a fundamental re-examination together of the basic theology of holy orders and of the means of their transmission. This is receiving the attention of the Joint International Commission.

One of the worst features of the situation was the exultation of Cardinal Vaughan and the organs of Roman Catholic publicity in England. Shortly before the publication of the bull the *Tablet* had said that:

> the status of the Anglican church is that of a sect in manifest heresy and schism and as such as hateful as the contradictions of Korah, Dathan and Abiram.[3]

[1] By then Frederick Temple at Canterbury.
[2] Appendix 2 in Lacey, *A Roman Diary*, pp. 354–94.
[3] *Leo XIII and Anglican Orders*, Halifax, p. 353n.

Soon after the bull Vaughan was saying in Stoke on Trent:

> The main mass of Anglicans, who are Erastian and Latitudin-
> arians, are in no way affected by the declaration that the
> Anglican Ordinal confers no power to offer sacrifices nor to
> forgive sins.[1]

To Halifax Vaughan went so far as to say:

> I should have thought, from the point of view of piety and
> devotion to our Lord, you and I ought to rejoice to think that
> men have not had the power to profane and dishonour our
> Lord in the Blessed Eucharist during the last three centuries
> which they would have had were their Orders valid. Think of
> how shocking it would be if men were actually producing our
> Lord, not to be honoured and adored, but in truth to be
> disowned and dishonoured by themselves and the people.[2]

The general verdict on the situation was summed up in a
leader in the *Times* on 19th September 1896

> The long and exhaustive study under the Pope's direction
> declaring the Orders conferred by the English Church
> absolutely invalid, will be a shock to well-meaning members
> of the Anglican communion and puts an end to all hope that
> the Pope will smooth the road for reunion of the two churches
> by at least recognising that the Anglican Church exists as a
> Church.[3]

Halifax and Portal exchanged touching letters in the hour of
their defeat and disappointment. Portal wrote to Halifax:

> Our first thought was for you and our friends in England—
> Puller, Lacey, etc. Poor friends, who have been so good, so
> generous, so loyal. There is nothing for it but to bow the
> head and keep silence. I talk to no one. Besides, the blow is so
> heavy and the grief so overwhelming that I am quite
> benumbed.
>
>   May our Lord have pity on us. May He at least grant us
> the consolation of seeing with our own eyes that we have not
> done more harm than good. You and yours have shown too

[1] *Leo XIII and Anglican Orders*, Halifax, p. 368.
[2] 5th October 1896. See *Absolutely Null and Utterly Void*, Hughes, p. 303.
[3] *Leo XIII and Anglican Orders*, Halifax, p. 355.

much faith, too much abnegation, for your praiseworthy deeds and your sacrifices of every kind to be lost. They will help immensely in the salvation of your souls, and also (against all hope I hope) towards reunion.[1]

And Halifax replied to Portal:

Your letter fills my eyes with tears; but it does me inexpressible good. Assuredly it was love of souls that moved us: we did not think of anything else. May something be done to put an end to the divisions among those who love our Lord Jesus Christ—those divisions that keep so many souls far away from Him—so that those who love each other, communicating at the same altars, may love each other more. . . .

We tried to do something which, I believe, God inspired. We have failed, for the moment; but if God wills it, His desire will be accomplished, and if He allows us to be shattered, it may well be because He means to do it Himself. This is no dream. The thing is as certain as ever. There are some bitter things which are worth all the joys of earth, and I prefer, many thousand times, to suffer with you in such a cause, than to triumph with the whole world. Your letter is more precious to me than I can possibly say. Troubles shared are already half assuaged; only I know that if we suffer, you are suffering still more, and it is this thought that hurts me most.[2]

Looked back on from our days the mistakes of this episode can be seen to lead inevitably to the disillusionment. The time was not ripe. There was no question that the Roman Curia could or would come to a conclusion acceptable to Anglicans. Even if it had, it is also certain, alas, that the large majority of Anglicans would not have felt moved to do anything about the opportunities so afforded, nor would any legislation consequent upon it have had the slightest chance of success. That thought by itself should soon have dried the tears. There is something classically tragic about the figure of Halifax, going doggedly on towards an objective which he most firmly believed in, yet carrying the weapons of defeat in his own

[1] 19th September 1896. *Fernand Portal, Apostle of Unity*, p. 75.
[2] 21st September 1896. ibid., p. 76.

knapsack, like a load of unexploded bombs. The only question was which of them would explode first. Portal was, of course, unintentionally deceived by Halifax, though he might have seen some of the difficulties for himself. What must have been the greatest surprise for him were the effective energies of the English Roman hierarchy thrown into the scales against him with a violence he could not have anticipated. Halifax was faced, like heroes of other tragedies have been, with irresolvable dilemmas. It was clearly impossible to make any headway in Anglican/Roman Catholic relationships so long as the half of the Anglican Church was indifferent to the matter and many were against it. Yet to have waited even for a bare majority mandate would have been to have waited for ever; and achievement is to the venturous. And the same was true of official approval by the bishops: Halifax knew, and the Roman Curia knew, that he had not the support of the bench of bishops.

Twenty-six years later we are to see him again, an older, an equally hopeful man, setting out to Malines on the same errand, with the same small prospects of success. But in the era of Apostolicae Curae, largely through his contacts and enthusiasm, a few people started thinking deeply about the whole question of the union of Christendom.

Thus the nineteenth century, for Christian relationships, went out in a mood of estrangement and despair. And worse was yet to come. For the early twentieth century was to add to the causes of separation several deliberate attempts to make it wider and to give it canonical shape. And there was yet another unconciliar dogma to be added to the list. But the vision which had drawn the Viscount and the Abbé into fellowship had captured other hearts as well. The cause of Christian union was for the time being driven underground. But the seed was to sleep and to grow night and day, and in a later chapter we will describe its spring.

13

LOSSES AND GAINS IN THE NINETEENTH CENTURY

The last two chapters have made their way through a succession of events in which the Roman Catholic Church has seemed to be deliberately moving outward from the rest of Christendom, like a receding galaxy, putting distance between itself and the possibility of relationships with any of the other Churches of Christendom. And there was further provocation to come: the worst was yet to be.

But to get a proper perspective of these events we must now turn to the evolution of the Church of England and her sister churches during the same period. The main development in the English Church during the nineteenth century was the emergence of the Oxford Movement. This revival, which was the subject of Chapter 8, did much to reawaken the English Church to the importance of its catholic heritage, and so to draw it nearer in sympathy to the Church of Rome. But the Oxford Movement also raised problems, both within the English Church and outside her, which weighed in the opposite direction. There was first the question whether the Church of England was willing and able to accept the challenge which the new movement put before her. It was the constant claim of the early Tractarians that they brought forward no new doctrines, but were only trying to remind England of the true character of the heritage she had received. But the Tractarian fathers soon found that the Church as a whole, and the Church officially, largely repudiated them. And when in due course they claimed that the 39 Articles could be reconciled with the Council of

235

Trent, it rose up and slew them. This gradually convinced a number of the pioneers that the Anglican formularies and structures could not bear the strain that was being put upon them, and they took what they thought to be the logical step of deserting Canterbury for Rome. Another unfortunate consequence of the Movement in its later stages was the fashion of 'Ritualism'. Some of the third generation of followers supposed that the way to convince themselves and the world at large of the true 'catholic' inheritance of the Church of England was the indiscriminate adoption of all the ritual practices of the Church of Rome. That trend undoubtedly did harm, and in two directions. On the one hand it diverted the attention of those who should really have been engaged on the basic processes of teaching the catholic inheritance of Anglican doctrine and practice into a preoccupation with ritual minutiae which was most unedifying. A characteristic end-product was a form of service of which it used to be said that it had 'Choreography by Fortescue, Libretto by Cranmer'. This in turn not unnaturally set up a violent reaction among the bishops and in the nation at large which resulted in restrictive legislation against the 'ritualists', typified at its worst moment by the trial of Bishop King of Lincoln, himself one of the very best products of the whole Movement, for the mildest of liturgical reforms.[1]

'Ritualism', in its extreme forms, therefore not only failed to convince the Church of its catholic heritage, but drove some of its own extremists into the hands of Rome, where they could more easily satisfy their liturgical longings; it also alienated their fellow-churchmen whose religion did not require such florid expression; and forced into antagonism those who regarded the church and her affairs as in effect a department of state.

Another important development in the history of the Anglican churches during the nineteenth century which was to have ecumenical consequences was the extension of the missions of the Church of England in many different parts of the world. In Africa and Asia, in Australia, New Zealand and Canada, she was either establishing independent provinces of her own nationals or setting up missions which were soon to function as separate provinces. The Lambeth Conferences of bishops increased correspondingly in size and importance.

[1] See pp. 242–3 below.

They had no canonical, but only a moral, authority over the
constituent provinces. The Conference of 1888 was attended by
145 bishops from all over the world. By 1897 separate provinces
were being formed and given their autonomy. By the Conference of 1908 there could be observed the beginnings of a
world-wide vision, with all its implications for Anglican
ecclesiology. 'There is the splendid hope', the Conference of
1908 said in its official statement, 'that from the field of foreign
missions there will be gathered for the enrichment of the
Church's manifold heritage the ample and varied contribution
of the special powers and characteristics belonging to the
several nations of mankind.' This had the double result of
building up the importance of the see of Canterbury and of
allowing Anglican church polity to show what it looked like
when transplanted to another soil. Then, by the gradual
dismemberment of the original structures, new church orders
began to be built up, totally independent of the controls of the
British Parliament, and free to order their life and liturgies
according to new patterns within the general Anglican mould.
The American Anglicans (Protestant Episcopal Church in the
United States of America), deriving both their episcopate and
their liturgical tradition through Scotland, had long been
independent. They, in their turn, sired new missions and
dioceses in the Latin American republics and the Caribbean, so
that by that route the Anglican tradition was translated into
a Spanish and Portuguese-speaking world. In 1869, against a
strong chorus of objections from the English bishops, the
Church of Ireland was disestablished and also became independent of the English Crown. The Church in Wales had to
wait till 1920. All this meant that the Church of England's
self-understanding was (or should have been) modified to suit
her new situation. No longer were the majority of Anglican
dioceses under the canonical authority of the British Crown or
Parliament. But the metropolitan church of England continued
to function as the national church, and a nation which was the
head of a great Empire, as long as that Empire lasted. Nevertheless, for the purpose of relationships with other churches, and
especially with Rome, she became able to slip from under the
charge of being a State Church which was dependent on
Parliamentary sanction and cushioned by endowments. In

Ireland, in Scotland, in the United States and Canada, and in the new dioceses all over the world, this was no longer so.

Although this new development was showing itself all over the world, and was finding its expression in the Lambeth Conferences (from 1867), the influence of the English establishment continued its hold on the Church's life. It undermined the Church's self-respect, opened up in the minds of many members fundamental doubts about its independence as a church and sent converts by the thousand into the arms of Rome and of the protestant denominations. A series of notorious test cases, coming from a variety of causes, all illustrated the same theme. One had been the double appearance of an otherwise rather undistinguished man, Dr. Hampden.[1] Nominated in 1836 by Melbourne to the Regius Professorship of Divinity at Oxford, the appointment was immediately questioned as unsound by a considerable number of people in Oxford, including Richard Bagot, the bishop. Hampden had attracted the notice of the Whigs by his support of certain liberal ideas with regard to subscription to formulas, but parts of his teaching were found to lean excessively towards rationalism beyond what was tolerable in the Church of England, and some of his opinions were condemned by the University. Nevertheless the Prime Minister insisted on going through with the nomination in spite of the opposition of the Archbishop and the Bishop of Oxford. But much greater indignation was aroused when later Lord John Russell insisted on nominating him to the bishopric of Hereford, and the susceptibilities of the whole church were disquieted at the insistence of the Crown's advisers in persisting with their intention. The farce of election by the cathedral chapter under the threat of the Statute of Praemunire was exposed to the public gaze, and the whole system under which the Church of England was subjected to Crown authority gave cause for uneasiness. It was seized upon, of course, by Roman Catholic propagandists to the Church's disadvantage and has continued to this day to be one of the flaws to which the Church of Rome has been able to point as an obstacle to closer relationships. Whatever the rights or wrongs of the two 'Hampden 'scandals' there is no doubt that they did much to harm the self-esteem of the English Church.

[1] See above, Chapter 8.

This reputation had already received rough handling in the first half of the nineteenth century. The long history of inequalities and injustice in the distribution of the Church's endowments had led, amid howls of protest from the more prosperous clergy (particularly the Deans and Chapters of the cathedrals), to the setting up of an Ecclesiastical Commission, which in 1840 removed some (but by no means all) of the financial anomalies in the payment of the clergy. Here again an immense skeleton was let fall out of the ecclesiastical cupboard and some of the grim realities of her life were revealed. These were not only her inability and unwillingness to reform the most flagrant abuses, but the abuses themselves, which showed up considerable numbers of idle and worldly clergy settled in benefices to which they had been appointed for less than the highest reasons, often absentees, less than diligent in their duties, many well endowed and prosperous in the middle of a hard-pressed population. This too was a factor in making difficult any possibilities of understanding with other churches. Many of the Anglican clergy and their families had political and social affiliations which made disagreeable the thought of associating with Dissenters, whether protestant or Roman.

Another provocative event of this period was the inauguration in 1841 of an Anglican bishopric in Jerusalem, the constitution of it being that it should be held alternately by an Anglican and by a Lutheran German. Again it was not only the deed but the manner of its execution which was unsettling. The bishopric was set up mainly at the instigation of the Foreign Office, without adequate consultation of the bishops, more as an act of policy than of ecclesiastical venture. Undertakings had to be given to the Turkish occupation government and to other established Christian churches in the Holy Land that missionary work would not be undertaken except under the most limited circumstances; which made the *raison d'être* of the whole venture exceedingly doubtful. And then it raised doubts about the canonical propriety of alternating with a Luthern bishop whose place in the hierarchical system was so different from that of the Anglicans. The whole project attracted the opposition of the Tractarians. It was one of the matters which unsettled Newman and it gave excellent opportunities, both at the time and later, to cast doubts upon Anglican integrity in the use of the episcopal office.

Perhaps the worst, from an ecumenical point of view, of the disasters of the century was the 'Gorham judgment'. This again highlighted two weaknesses of the English Church and laid her open to misrepresentation and attack. The case has been set out in detail in many places, but its results in brief were three, that:

(a) it appeared legally possible for a priest holding teaching contrary to that of the Church of England (in this case on the question of baptismal regeneration) to be able to minister in the church without hindrance; and

(b) it emphasised the supremacy of the judicial committee of the Privy Council as a final court of appeal in matters touching doctrine; and

(c) it showed the establishment to be a reality in that it was prepared to force a crown nomination, as in the case of Bishop Hampden, on the church against the judgment of the ecclesiastical authority.

We have no reason here to explore the consequences and corollaries of this whole struggle. But we have to record it as an episode which did harm to relationships with the Church of Rome. It gave rise to immediate secessions (notably those of T. W. Allies and Henry Wilberforce) and was no doubt a remote cause of many others. (It undoubtedly contributed to the defection of Manning.) But most harmful of all it weakened the witness of those who had been trying to maintain against appearances that the English Church solidly maintained the chief traditions of 'catholic' truth. The Roman Catholic Church made great use of the episode to question the doctrinal integrity of the Church of England and to caricature it as a mere Department of State. The habit of referring to it exclusively as 'the establishment' gained considerable impetus from this time. From the Gorham judgment onwards we find more and more Roman Catholic propagandists calling in question the validity of Anglican baptisms on the ground that it could not be certain what were the doctrinal intentions of the minister baptising. But as in some other episodes to which we have had occasion to refer, a certain amount of good came out of this evil; for it awakened the consciences of many Anglicans to the need for some measure of self-government for the Church. It led, after painful and tedious efforts to overcome opposition, to the re-establishment of the meetings of the two convocations, Canterbury in 1851, York in 1860 (they had been suspended since 1717). This was at least a token of good faith which enabled the English Church to look its critics in the face. The first emancipation was to lead on to a degree of enfranchisement of the laity, and their eventual incorporation into direct responsibility in church government. After the Enabling Act of 1919 the Church of England in its turn was able to challenge the Church of Rome in the matter of the representation of the laity in the Councils of the Church; and the exchange of ideas and experiences in this matter was one of the many mutual advantages of the Second Vatican Council. At the time of writing the Church of England has recently (1971) acquired herself a measure of synodical government; yet the central problem of the control of church appointments and of liturgical and doctrinal developments, though modified, is still unresolved. The Church of Rome, likewise, is feeling her way slowly and hesitantly towards the enfranchisement of the laity.

As this chapter is a catalogue of those events and tendencies which affected Anglican/Roman understanding, we cannot pass over the development during the century of organised evangelical churchmanship. As we have seen in a previous chapter the genius of the eighteenth-century revival left behind it a considerable mark on the Church in the nineteenth century and many of its most notable products were retained, and flourished, in the Church of England. Yet at the beginning of the century their influence had begun to wane, and though the debt of some of the early Oxford Fathers to them (Newman in particular) was recognised the new movement began to build upon the unfinished constructions of its predecessor. Yet the triumphs, and in the second generation the arrogance and provocation of the successors of the founders, began in the mid-century to elicit a reaction. And then the renascence of the Church of Rome tended to add to evangelical piety what was by no means germane to it, protestant prejudice. And so there came about that unfortunate bi-polarity in the Church of England to which reference[1] has already been made. The existence side by side of 'schools of thought' and varieties of interpretation has more often been a source of strength rather

[1] See p. 128.

than of weakness. But unhappily in the nineteenth century this divergence became institutionalised, and therefore less spontaneous. Thus it was to be seen not in the schools of philosophy and theology where it would have been stimulating, but now in parallel and rival institutions set up one against another. The buying up of advowsons condemned whole areas, whether they wished it or not, to adopt for all future time one 'tendency' or the other; theological colleges which began to flourish in the mid-century, growing up under private patronage, tended to separate the ordinands into party affiliations from the first and so to exaggerate their allegiances; missionary societies, again separately organised under private patronage, went their several ways, offering to their respective victims not the whole conspectus of Anglican divinity but 'catholic' or 'evangelical' salvation, narrowly so conceived. Both sides had their newspapers, their societies and their annual meetings. They were organised to do ecclesiastico-political battle. Such developments led to weakness, to a certain amount of distress among the uncomprehending faithful, and put one further bolt into the propagandistic armoury of the Church of Rome.

But the worst consequence of all this was the ritual trials into which the Church was allowed to drift through her inability to govern herself. Because of the lack of confidence between bishops and many of the clergy and the indignation of the laity at the spectacle of inaction and disorder, resort was eventually had to law; and with disastrous consequences. The most infamous of the ritual trials were those of Mackonochie of St. Alban's, Holborn, in 1867 and of John Purchas in 1869. In both these cases appeal was made to the Privy Council, whose authority in such matters the accused were not willing to recognise. The next stage in the battle was the passing of the Public Worship Regulation Act of 1874 and the consequent imprisonment of a number of priests, particularly Arthur Tooth of St. James', Hatcham. This procedure served no purpose except to demonstrate the helplessness of the Church of England to manage its own affairs, the indiscipline of her clergy and the inadequacy of any workable conception of authority. Even after resort to the civil power was seen to achieve no results the Church Association persisted in its attempts at legal action and brought the eminent Bishop of Lincoln (Edward

King) to trial before the Archbishop of Canterbury's court on an indictment of six counts.[1]

King was condemned on the questions of the mixed chalice and the sign of the Cross, but not on the other counts. The whole action was inept in being directed against one of the most eminent and best-beloved of the bishops; and served this time to demonstrate the inadequacy not only of the civil inhibitions of the Church but of her own liturgical provisions as well. For the ornaments rubric of the Prayer Book was clearly unable to bear the strain of being interpreted for contemporary use. This in turn had the consequence of driving dissident priests not only to contract out of the usual interpretations of 'lawful authority' as residing in the secular courts of the land with their inadequate interpretations of rubrics, but to recognise as morally authoritative the 'catholic liturgical traditions of the Western Church', thus accepting the possibility of total Romanisation of the English Liturgy. A period of indiscipline then ensued. The next step was the appointment in 1904 of a Royal Commision on Ritual Matters appointed 'to inquire into the alleged prevalence of breaches or neglect of the Law relating to the conduct of Divine Service in the Church of England . . . and to make such recommendations as may be deemed requisite for dealing with the aforesaid matters'. The Commission produced a hopeful set of recommendations. It had no option but to report that the existing state of affairs was intolerable and should be reformed. It recommended:

(a) the repealing of the Public Worship Regulation Acts;
(b) the preparation of a new rubric, whose meaning should be clear and unequivocal concerning ornaments and vestments;
(c) the revision of the Church courts;
(d) the discontinuance of certain practices such as Reservation of the elements of the Eucharist, Benediction and the Invocation of Saints.

The spirit of the whole Report was one of promise for the future in that it recognised that 'the law of public worship in

---

[1] The mixed chalice; the eastward position, allowing the singing of Agnus Dei, taking ablutions in public, lighted candles and making the sign of the Cross.

the Church of England is too narrow for the religious life of the present generation. It needlessly condemns much which a great section of church people, including many of her most devoted members, value'. Modern essays in Prayer Book revision can be said to date from the time of that Commission. The fact that revision was being undertaken was an opportunity for closer understanding with the Church of Rome, in whose bosom also great new stirrings were becoming observable in liturgical matters. But as it turned out, the first Anglican attempts at revision were only going to show up the weakness of her canonical machinery and to demonstrate the power of her divisions. A quarter of a century later (1927 and 1928) the fruits of these labours were to be rejected by a Parliament which was no longer the Anglican laity and whose claim to legislate on religious matters at all was hard to justify. The Church of England was going to have to wait a whole half-century before alternative experimental forms of service were going to be put out tentatively under the Prayer Book (Alternative Services) Measure of 1966. But by that time the Church of Rome, as in the classical allegory of the hare and the tortoise, would have awakened from her long Latin slumber and outstripped the still half-Cranmerian Church of England.

This recital of what might have seemed like a random collection of developments and events in the Church of England during the nineteenth century has been intended to act as a counterweight to a similar recital concerning the Church of Rome during the same period in the previous chapter. We felt obliged to describe the latter as a steady progress away from the path of the rest of Christendom, illustrating at official levels a total absence of concern with any future union of Christendom other than that of individual submission to the one true and only Church. This chapter has been intended to convey the impression that the Church of England likewise was going its own insular way, again without any noticeable intention of seeking the union of Christendom, in so far as Rome was part of that concept. There was still no desire on the part of Anglicans for reunion with Rome until she were something other than what she was. But there did not seem to be any evidence that Anglicans were conscious that the reverse was also the case. For besides the usual doctrinal differences and obstacles which

Rome must obviously have felt to exist between themselves and the Church of England there were three preliminary difficulties which forced themselves on her attention. First that there was no real desire on the part of the Anglican body for Christian unity as far as she was concerned; second that the Church of England was so divided internally as to make it difficult for her to be thought of as one entity; and thirdly that her relationship to the State made it difficult for Roman Catholics to take her seriously as a church. No self-respecting church conscious of its sovereign existence as a part of the body of Christ, Rome supposed, could possibly rest content, as the Church of England seemed to do, with such conditions.

The events which we have recorded in this chapter have served to illustrate how difficulties seen from the Roman angle were also aggravated during this period. And these things take on the dimension of tragedy when we consider that the main development of the century, as far as Roman relationships was concerned, was the sympathetic revival which stemmed from the Oxford Fathers. What could be counted gain from that quarter was for the most part converted into loss by the exposures of weakness and incapacity brought about by the other happenings in Anglican church life in that century.

Yet we may end by recalling that in all the major events, in the Vatican Council, in the calamities of the second stage of the Oxford Movement, and even in the catastrophic result of Apostolicae Curae, there were left loose ends and open questions in the minds of visionaries of both sides which the Holy Spirit was to build up into hopes and achievements in the following century.

14

ROME AND CANTERBURY IN THE
EARLY 1900s

The course of the Roman Catholic Church through the first quarter of the twentieth century led to increasing bureaucratic despotism at Rome, to obstinate resistance to the new knowledge of the century, and to a resolute and uniform refusal to have anything to do with other branches of the Church except to convert their members one by one. This at least would be the conclusion drawn from a review of official acts and pronouncements, though as we shall see below, there were stirrings and feelings among the forward-looking which were destined to develop into something quite different by the middle of the century. At the same time there was an admirable increase in missionary activity throughout the world.

Pope Pius X succeeded after the exceptionally long reign of Leo XIII in 1903. Hoping not to be involved in as many political difficulties as his predecessor he made the object of his pontificate 'instaurare omnia in Christo'.[1] Nevertheless he was soon involved in politics when the French Government effected, in 1905, the separation of Church and State, which he attempted in vain to resist by saying that such action was an offence against divine laws and basic human rights.[2]

In Pius X's time (1903–1914) we must notice a series of lamentable judgments put out by the Biblical Commission founded by his predecessor.[3] One of June 1906 confirmed

[1] Encyclical of 4th October 1903.
[2] Encyclical 'Vehementer nos', to the French people, 11th February 1906.   [3] See p. 218 above.

246

the Mosaic authorship of the Pentateuch. In May 1907 the authorship of the fourth gospel was confirmed in the name of the Apostle St. John without any possibility of further discussion. In November 1907 the findings of the Biblical Commission were said to have the force of definitions of doctrine under appropriate conditions and therefore to be binding upon the consciences of all. In 1908 the prophecies of Isaiah were declared to be literally inspired personal vaticinia of the prophet, so as to admit of no possible subsequent collection, collation or arrangement. In 1911 and 1912 decrees were issued which permitted no deviation from the traditional view of the authorship of the three Synoptic gospels or of the chronological relationship between them: and in 1913 complete confirmation was given to the traditional views about the Pauline authorship of the Pastoral Epistles and the Epistle to the Hebrews, 'notwithstanding the arrogant presumption of certain heretical scholars'.[1]

To this must be added the fact that Pius X continued a relentless campaign against the dangers of 'Modernism', thereby collecting under one designation most of the errors enumerated in 1854 by Pius IX in the Syllabus of Errors and canonically condemned in the Vatican Council.[2] He collected the items of the indictment in a very long encyclical[3] of 1907, and later in a *Motu Proprio*[4] set up the 'anti-Modernist oath' which was to be administered to clergy of doubtful orthodoxy.

We should perhaps add here a note about the Catholic 'Modernists'. They were a very varied body of men who, inside the Church of Rome, attempted to apply the findings and insights of contemporary knowledge to the various fields of theology. 'Modernism', on the other hand is a wider term, embracing all the fields of knowledge in which doctrines believed to be contrary to catholic faith were being held and taught, as for example in politics, sociology and the pure sciences. The pedigree of the 'Modernists', strictly so called, traces them principally from France, and from the Institut Catholique in particular, and even from such 'respectable' scholars as Duchesne—though he vigorously dissociated him-

---

[1] Answer of the Biblical Commission, 12th June 1913.
[2] See p. 190.
[3] 'Pascendi dominici gregis', 8th September 1907.
[4] 'Sacrorum antistitum', 1st September 1910.

self from the aberrations of some who had been his pupils. Their impact on the faith came from a number of sources, one of which, perhaps the chief, was that of reaction from the limited syllabus imposed upon students in seminaries; and secondly the influence of critical attitudes to biblical studies which survived all attempts to have them banned and discredited, and perhaps flourished all the more for being so treated. The writings of Renan,[1] particularly a *Life of Jesus*, had put even the hierarchy of France on their guard against possible excesses of liberal scholarship (he had originally been a protégé of Dupanloup). But the most familiar names are those of Loisy,[2] Tyrrell[3] and von Hügel.[4] Loisy had come under the influence of Duchesne and was Professor of Scripture at the Institut. He wrote against the *Wesen des Christentums* of Harnack, seeking to base the doctrines of Christianity not, as Harnack would have it, on the personal authority of the figure of Jesus in the Scriptures, but in a very orthodox manner on the Church's authority in later definitions. But as in doing so he more or less emptied the church of sacraments, and questioned her foundation by Christ himself, he was not surprisingly condemned. George Tyrrell was an English Jesuit, first laicised and then excommunicated, who went off the orthodox lines by way of the gap between the spiritual experiential life as he developed it and the rigid framework of scholastic theology. Baron Friedrich von Hügel had importance as a go-between, and many of the 'Modernists' were kept in touch with one another through him. He was a philosopher and mystic who was deeply moved by the currents of modern thought. What is important, for our purposes, to note is that these men who were formally heretics (the Baron sailed very close to the wind, though he was never excommunicated) all seemed to show (with the possible exception of Loisy) a touching desire to remain loyal to the Church. But there can be no doubt that the chapter of the Modernists and their treatment within the catholic church, the sweeping condemnation of 'Modernism' as if it were one single phenomenon, and then the anti-Modernist oath, did much to unsettle the Roman Catholic lay people, and perhaps to prepare for their revolt in the middle of the twentieth century. Soon after

[1] Joseph Ernest Renan, 1823–1892.   [2] Alfred Loisy, 1857–1940.
[3] George Tyrrell, 1861–1909.   [4] Friedrich von Hügel, 1852–1952.

the appearance of the encyclical 'Pascendi' a letter appeared in *The Times* which said:

> I have been asked to make the following statement on behalf, not only of those who call themselves liberal catholics, but also of many who have hitherto taken no part in the conflict between Modernists and the Pope.
>
> They desire to say that, although they may differ from Father Tyrrell on particular points, they are entirely at one with him in his criticism of the late Encyclical. They regard it as an unprecedented evil that, while one Pope has implied direct approval of the writings of an English Catholic[1] by making him a Cardinal, his successor should reverse the decision by condemning every characteristic proposition for which that writer made himself responsible. . . .[2]

The 'Modernist' phase in the Anglican Communion had caused, and was still to cause, its own travail. We have seen how the impact of the two 'Hampden' cases[3] had given rise to convulsions; and the probings of the *Essays and Reviews* and the 'Lux Mundi' groups had caused considerable stirs in their days, and perhaps permanent unsettlement, in the Church of England, as 'Foundations' (1912) was to do later. Already a clear contrast was appearing as between the Church of Rome and the Anglican. Church, of the exercise of too much authority in the one case and of too little in the other. Yet there were not wanting on both sides those who felt the full impact of modern knowledge on their faith, not as a hostile intrusion from outside, but as a new tie and strength from the original source of all revealed truth. On the Anglican side we should not pass from this topic without mention of the name of Frederick Denison Maurice[4] who from within the Anglican Church attempted a constructive synthesis which helped to confirm many in their faith at a time when many influences were shaking it.

Although from the treatment of Modernism within the Roman Church it might seem that the pontificate of Pius X was entirely reactionary and in a direction away from the possibility of understanding with the rest of Christendom, yet

---

[1] Newman. [2] 2nd November 1907. [3] See p. 238.
[4] 1805–1872. Professor of Theology, King's College London, 1846; Knightsbridge Professor of Moral Philosophy, Cambridge, 1866.

he gave a considerable impetus to the nascent Liturgical Movement by his directions regarding church music and by his advocacy of frequent, even daily, communion.[1] This reform, thought of in the context of a deep eucharistic devotion, was destined to be, whether it was so conceived or not, a revolution in the pattern of Roman Catholic practice in the use of the second dominical sacrament. It was a belated admission into the Roman economy of one of the basic reforms of the sixteenth-century Reformation and so potentially a considerable step forward in mutual understanding. It did not have great immediate effects, because the idea of frequent communion was permissive rather than mandatory. But its potential for good in the future was incalculable: it prepared the way for the new general shape of the eucharist after the Second Vatican Council. Pius X, on the other hand, helped forward the escalation of Marian dogma which was to be a characteristic of Roman Catholic development in the first half of the twentieth century. One of the first acts of his reign had been an encyclical largely devoted to this subject, in which he declared that whereas Christ was our Saviour and the origin of all the benefits of salvation de condigno, Mary could rightly be described as reparatrix de congruo.[2]

It is interesting to note one circumstance of Pius X's attitude in social matters in which, partly under the influence of the powerful Merry del Val, his Cardinal Secretary of State, he found himself driven into opposition against the rising tide of socialism in Europe. The bishop of Bergamo in north Italy, Radini-Tedeschi, had been charged by Leo XIII to keep contact with a movement for social action called 'L'opera dei Congressi.' This he had done with the enthusiastic aid of his young chaplain Angelo Roncalli, later Pope John XXIII. When Pius X peremptorily closed down the movement this came as a shock to the bishop's chaplain, who we now know had found it congenial to his aspirations for the underprivileged citizens of his country.

Pius X died in 1914. He was succeeded by Cardinal della Chiesa under the title of Benedict XV, whose pontificate was largely occupied by the first German war, during which he did

[1] Decree of the Sacred Council, approbante Pio X; 20th December 1905.
[2] Encyclical 'Ad diem', 2nd February 1904.

his best to preserve a dignified neutrality between the belligerent sides. The war itself was a factor in the development of the relationships between the churches, as it led to the mixing-up of nations and groups, and forced upon the churches contacts which they would not otherwise have experienced. That was perhaps more formative for the Church of England than for the Roman Catholic Church. The latter, used to its own inter-national self-understanding (though still content, for the most part, to be Italian-dominated) had not so much to learn; whereas the Church of England, insular by the very circum-stances of its existence, found itself intimately involved in the life of catholic countries where Englishmen were quick to notice the welcome lack of that antagonism in religious matters which was so much a part of their experience of their Roman Catholic neighbours in England.

Two circumstances of the pontificate of Benedict XV bear upon the theme of this book. The first was the establishment, in 1915, of a British Legation to the Vatican.[1] This office, though sometimes treated as a sinecure, has in its time been of inestimable service to the cause of mutual understanding between the churches. It is invariably held by a layman who is not a Roman Catholic, with a Roman Catholic second-in-command. It has afforded an easy meeting place of responsible leaders on both sides under congenial circumstances, often for discussion of purely secular concerns, or of the non-theological factors in religious questions. Never was it better exploited for the good of both sides than during the tenure of Sir Peter Scarlett during the time of the Second Vatican Council, when literally hundreds of prelates were able to meet with Commonwealth and other observers in total freedom from ecclesiastical protocol; and when during the Second World War, in the pontificate of Pius XII, Great Britain and Italy then being enemies, the occupant of the Legation, Sir d'Arcy Osborne, was able to use it to great advantage to keep open the lines of communication between the peoples and the churches. It has been a hope among Roman Catholics that this office

[1] Sir Henry Howard had been despatched to Rome to extend the con-gratulations of King George V to Benedict XV on his accession. The mission was not recalled. (See 'British Diplomatic Relations with the Holy See', Stephen Gaselee, *Dublin Review*, CCIV, January 1939, pp. 1–9.)

would one day be raised to the status of an Embassy; though this has been constantly resisted both by the British Government and by the Church of England, on the grounds that as the Pope has no political concerns in England he has no need of a political respresentative for them, while his relationship with the Roman hierarchy is accomplished by an Apostolic Delegate; and that when formal relationships with the Church of England are resumed they will presumably be directed through the Archbishop of Canterbury. The other relevant event of Benedict XV's pontificate was the encyclical 'Spiritus Paraclitus' of September 1920, which repeated and re-emphasised the doctrines of Leo XIII's 'Providentissimus Deus' (1893) on the inerrancy of Scripture. The new encyclical only served to delay the outbreak of mutual understanding in the right approach to the Scriptures and to confirm the opinions of those who already supposed that effective communication with the Church of Rome on such matters at official levels was impossible.

At this point we cease to follow the fortunes of the Church of Rome and allow the Church of England to leap-frog up to the end of the Great War. During this period we must notice two particular features which bear most strongly on our theme. The first is the gradual emergence of the Ecumenical Movement; and the second is the growing awareness among Anglicans of the Eastern Orthodox and other churches. The impact of both those phenomena on the Anglican mind was the greater because they were seen against the background of a complete absence of official exchange of ideas with the Church of Rome. It was in the context of these two movements together that the Anglican conception of and programme for Christian union gradually emerged and eventually took shape.

Once again we have to avoid any temptation to provide a chronicle of Anglican history, or any kind of consecutive narrative, but only a record of such events as can be said to throw light on the theme of relations with the Church of Rome. Of such events the further expansion of the Lambeth Conferences, and therefore the beginnings of the Anglican Communion as an effective unit, must be given an important place. The first Conference had been called in 1867, through the enthusiasm of the province of Canada and in spite of the unwillingness of the English bishops. The Archbishop of York and five bishops declined to attend. The main achievement of the Conference was a virtual condemnation of the activities of the Bishop of Natal (Colenso). Coming a few years after the furore of the *Essays and Reviews* crisis of 1860[1] the Conference had shown that there was a limit to the divergencies from orthodoxy which the Anglican Communion would tolerate. This was perhaps a reassurance, as far as sympathetic Roman Catholic observers were concerned, about the bona fides of the Anglican Church in the matter of doctrine. Moreover it created an entirely new situation in which the Anglican Church in the world no longer meant the 'state church' of England but something wider and freer, and for the sake of future ecumenical development, more hopeful. The importance of this international dimension of the Anglican churches cannot be overemphasised. Not only was it destined to work a change in the insular Church of England herself, but by the transplanting of Anglican Christianity into foreign soil by way of her missionary activity, new churches were to grow up and make their appearance on the Anglican scene, churches whose outlook had not been distorted by the painful ecclesiastical history of Britain.

The second Lambeth Conference of 1878 had made a first attempt at ecumenical activity, with overtures to the Old Catholics and to the Moravians. But it was the third Conference of 1888 which marked the great watershed in this matter and saw the course of Anglican affairs firmly beginning to be guided towards the notion of the reunion of Christendom. As a result of a Report of the American house of bishops two years previously in Chicago, Lambeth 1888, under the heading, oddly enough, of 'Home Reunion' adopted the famous 'Lambeth Quadrilateral' as 'the basis on which approach might be, under God's blessing, made towards Reunion'. The four headings of the Quadrilateral were:

1. The Holy Scriptures of the Old and New Testaments, as 'containing all things necessary to salvation' and as 'being the rule and ultimate standard of faith'.
2. The Apostles' Creed, as the Baptismal Symbol; and the Nicene Creed, as the sufficient standard of the Christian faith.

[1] See above p. 190.

3. The two Sacraments ordained by Christ himself—Baptism and the Supper of the Lord—ministered with unfailing use of Christ's words of institution and of the elements ordained by him.

4. The Historic Episcopate, locally adapted in the methods of its administration to the varying needs of the nations and peoples called of God into the unity of his Church.

From that beginning the Anglican Churches had felt themselves steadily propelled towards the task of giving shape to what might otherwise have been empty talk about reunion. The visionaries who framed the Quadrilateral certainly had the possibility of Rome in mind, at a time when it would have been hard to commend it as a possibility to the majority of Anglican people, and when the answer of Rome to the practical problems involved was clear enough to everybody except Lord Halifax and his friends. And they were to be made unmistakably clear only seven years later by the decree on Anglican Orders. And of course there was worse to come—the gap was to get wider before it showed signs of narrowing.

As for the rest of Christendom the churches named as being possibly the next to approach were the Scandinavian Churches and 'the Churches of the East'. One of the many benefits which the Oxford Movement had conferred upon the Church of England (which in that context is sometimes forgotten) was a new awareness of the ancient patriarchates of Jerusalem, Alexandria, Antioch, Byzantium, etc.—and who could be unmindful of such great names when thinking of the reintegration of the union of Christendom? J. M. Neale[1] with his *History of the Holy Eastern Church* of 1847, was the pioneer in this field, though William Palmer[2] had been in Russia as early as 1850 having conversations with Khomiakov[3] on matters of mutual ecclesiastical interest. In 1863 the Eastern Churches Association was founded, and in the same year the Bishop of Oxford (Samuel Wilberforce) moved in Convocation that:

His Grace the President be requested to direct the Lower House to appoint a Committee to communicate with the

---

[1] See above p. 133.   [2] Fellow of Magdalen.
[3] Alexis Stepanovich K. (1804–1860), Russian philosophical theologian interested in unity. Also corresponded with Birkbeck.

Committee appointed at a recent Synod of the Bishops and clergy of the United States of America as to Inter-communion with the Russo-Greek Church, and to communicate the result to Convocation at a future Session.

The initiative proved to be unproductive at the time, but as the number of Eastern European immigrants into the U.S.A. has increased, so has the importance of this field for Anglican/Orthodox contacts. The Eastern Churches Association gradually became transmuted into the Anglican and Eastern Orthodox Churches Association, and from the beginning of the twentieth century there has been a steady growth of interest in and contact with the Eastern Churches in which the name of W. J. Birkbeck,[1] a layman, has the place of honour. The result of this long experience has been to open the eyes of Anglicans to the existence of this non-papal catholicism of very great antiquity and prestige. Certain features of Orthodox spirituality and doctrinal method have found a ready echo in Anglican hearts. The Orthodox conception of the great mysteries of the faith as things to be gazed upon, wondered at and lived by, rather than as in the Roman dispensation, to be acutely defined and submitted to close philosophical analysis, was very congenial.

In comparison with Roman frigidity the warm benevolence of Orthodox contacts made a most favourable impression. And though the Orthodox were no more disposed to compromise the faith for the sake of union than Rome (and who would want them to do so?) the tradition of Orthodoxy carried a much lighter doctrinal burden. Since any search for a basis of union must involve going back behind the classical dividing points to primitive agreements, where better could a wandering ecumenist turn than to those whose formularies have remained unrevised since John of Damascus? And as the Orthodox conception of the mysteries found sympathetic hearers in England so did the conception of Sobornost or 'harmony' between the patriarchates seem to throw a new light on possible lines of progress in the problem of authority. This too looked as if it might help remove one of the obstacles to ecumenical understanding. This rediscovery of the Churches of the East, then, must be considered as one of the principal

[1] See Bibliography.

influences on the Anglican churches in these decades. It encouraged them in their search for union and at the same time helped them to see a way past the immobility of Rome until such time as Rome herself was ready to move.

We must also record, as bearing on our main subject, the gradual involvement of the Anglican churches in the movement which led up to the formation of the World Council of Churches. It was originally an American, Bishop Brent of the Philippines, and an Episcopal layman, Robert H. Gardiner, of Boston, Massachusetts who persuaded the General Convention in 1910 to take steps towards summoning a world conference on Faith and Order, to which 'all Christian communions throughout the world' should send representatives.

The plans for such a conference had begun to take shape before the war began, and by 1914 Mr. Gardiner had written to the papal secretary of State, Cardinal Gasparri, to inform him of the proposal, and to invite Roman Catholic participation. The Cardinal wrote declining this; and his reply included the passage:

> The plans of the Roman Pontiffs, their cares and their labours, have always been specially directed to the end that the sole and unique Church which Jesus Christ ordained and sanctified with His divine Blood should be most zealously guarded and maintained, whole, pure and ever abounding in love, and that it should both let its light shine and open wide its door for all who rejoice in the name of man and who desire to gain holiness upon earth and eternal happiness in heaven.
>
> The August Pontiff, therefore, was pleased with your project of examining in a sincere spirit and without prejudice the essential form of the Church [intimam Ecclesiae formam] . . . and He earnestly hopes that under the spell of its native beauty you may settle all disputes and work with prosperous issue to the end that the mystical body of Christ be no longer suffered to be rent and torn.[1]

We shall often meet this situation in which World Council sources, taking the initiative in inviting Rome to ecumenical participation, are rebuffed in documents which refer with monotonous regularity to the theme of return to the one true Church. Non-Roman readers should make efforts to under-

[1] 18th December 1944. Faith and Order Pamphlet No. 30, pp. 12f.

stand, and not too hastily to condemn, this attitude. It being the plain duty of Rome, for the eventual good of all, to preserve her unity intact until such time as she could confidently open her doors, it was understandable that at this stage she should want to see the character and intentions, and some evidence of the theological integrity, of the multitudinous non-Roman denominations before committing herself to discussion with them. In the event the move towards the Faith and Order conferences had to wait until 1920. In their ecumenical exercises Anglicans were being pulled in two directions at once, by a tension which is still not entirely resolved, between those who have wanted to draw them towards the Protestant world and those who have kept their attention firmly fixed on overall union, with Rome included in it. This controversy was aggravated by what is known as the Kikuyu crisis of 1913. In that year an attempt was made to bring about in East Africa a federation of 'protestant missions' in which two Anglican dioceses would be involved. This generated great heat in England and elsewhere and was strongly opposed by the heirs of the Tractarian fathers, strongly championed by Frank Weston, Bishop of Zanzibar. The wisdom and skill of Randall Davidson, Archbishop of Canterbury, managed to avert a crisis, and fortunately the scheme was not proceeded with because of the outbreak of the Great War in 1914. From that year all official schemes for drawing the churches closer together were interrupted, but at the same time the intermixture of nations gave opportunities for international contacts. The very spectacle of mass annihilation perpetrated between civilised and so-called Christian nations also started men thinking about basic questions, in particular the place of the Church in contemporary society. From this time we can trace the emergence of self-reliance among some of the Christian churches in the new world. For the spectacle of those nations which had brought them the gospel of peace and reconciliation themselves engaging upon a process of mutual destruction made it more evident to the new churches that they were already not entirely in the position of learners.

Of events during the war itself we have little, for our purposes, to record, except perhaps the emergence of the 'Life and Liberty Movement' in the Church of England. This movement, which owed much of its inspiration to the leadership of William Temple, was the beginning of thinking and planning for post-war reconstruction, in which it was hoped that the churches would play an effective part. The important thing about it, from the point of view of eventual Anglican/Roman understanding was that it gave expression to a dissatisfaction with the relation of Church and State in England. Although at this stage it could hardly be said that there was ˙a movement towards disestablishment, there was a deep awareness that the whole question of the exercise of authority in doctrine and discipline in life was inhibited by the system in force. The extreme difficulty of initiating, let alone of achieving, liturgical reform, or of organising anything like reasonable canonical discipline among either clergy or laity, was traceable to this defect. Although the Life and Liberty Movement put forward no precise programme of reform, 'Liberty' was at least one of its watchwords. This meant that for the purpose of Anglican/Roman understanding the Anglican, in pointing to the weaknesses of the Roman conception of the Papacy, could at least say, while admitting the weaknesses also of the Anglican practice of authority in England, that this practice was now deliberately under review. The practical outcome of the movement was the legislation which prepared the way for the Enabling Act of December 1919 and the formation of the Church Assembly. This meant a considerable delegation to the Church of powers of government which were formerly vested solely in the Houses of Parliament: though it still remained true that the appointment of the Church's chief officers and final decisions on matters doctrinal and liturgical were still in the hands of the State.

Immediately after the end of the war the churches began to feel a growing compulsion towards the task of Christian union. In May 1919, in particular, the long-planned scheme for reunion among the non-Roman churches in South India took its first step, in a conference held at Tranquebar. This stated the general principle that:

The challenge of the present hour . . . calls us to mourn our past divisions and turn to our Lord Jesus Christ to seek in Him the unity of the Body expressed in one visible Church.

We face together the titanic task of the winning of India for Christ—one-fifth of the human race. Yet, confronted by such an overwhelming responsibility, we find ourselves rendered weak and relatively impotent by our unhappy divisions—divisions for which we were not responsible, and which have been, as it were, imposed upon us from without.[1]

This scheme, involving as it did both the Anglican and Methodist churches as well as branches of the protestant reformed bodies in various combinations, was a hopeful sign for the future, because it showed a general intention to keep the traditional creeds and structures of the Church in the united body, and so to avoid any attempt to create a pan-protestant federation of churches, involvement in which might have prejudiced seriously any future dealings between Rome and Canterbury. Although this represented a good start, the going was slow, and considerable resistance was offered so that the new united church was not actually inaugurated until 1947.

In October 1919 the ecclesiastical interest in the reconstruction of the nations caused a group of representative churchman to come together for the first post-war meeting of the International Committee of the World Alliance for promoting International Friendship through the churches in Holland. The leader of it was the Archbishop of Uppsala (Söderblom) whose name must be honoured wherever the subject of Christian union is under discussion. The Archbishop said openly that he had no hope of co-operation from Rome, and no invitation was issued. But it is interesting to note that at continuation meetings at Paris and Geneva in late 1919 and 1920 respectively Archbishop Davidson refused Anglican participation unless the position of Rome was fully recognised and invitations sent. In this he was supported by Söderblom. It was from this series of meetings that impulses came for the conference in Stockholm in 1925 which in turn gave birth to the Life and Work Movement, and so to the other half of the World Council of Churches.

Close on the heels of these meetings for international fellowship came the sixth Lambeth Conference, in 1920. The bishops assembled under Archbishop Randall Davidson, 252 in number,

[1] *Documents on Christian Unity* (ed. G. K. A. Bell), 1st series, OUP, 1924, p. 278.

issued an encyclical addressed not to churches, but to all Christian people. 'Men of all communions', they said 'began to think of the reunion of Christendom, not as a laudable ambition or a beautiful dream, but as an imperative necessity'. The 'Appeal to all Christian People' acknowledged that

> all those who believe in our Lord Jesus Christ, and have been baptized into the name of the Holy Trinity, as sharing in the universal Church of Christ which is His Body. We believe that the Holy Spirit has called us in a very solemn and special manner to associate ourselves in penitence and prayer with all those who deplore the divisions of Christian people, and are inspired by the vision and hope of a visible unity of the whole Church'.

It then restated the 'Lambeth Quadrilateral'[1] in a slightly modified form, but added a significant rider to show how the historic episcopate in particular might be adapted to the future needs of uniting churches in bringing into being a ministry universally recognised. They asked:

> May we not reasonably claim that the Episcopate is the one means of providing such a Ministry? It is not that we call in question for a moment the spiritual reality of the ministries of those Communions which do not possess the Episcopate. On the contrary, we thankfully acknowledge that these ministries have been manifestly blessed and owned by the Holy Spirit as effective means of grace. . . . If the authorities of other Communions should so desire, we are persuaded that, if terms of union have been otherwise satisfactorily adjusted, Bishops and clergy of our Communion would willingly accept from these authorities a form of commission or recognition which would commend our ministry to their congregations, as having its place in the one family life.

This suggested an attempt to overcome the difficulties of Apostolicae Curae, if they should persist. The effect of this document was to confirm Anglican bona fides in the sphere of ecumenical relations, and was a further indication of her intention to keep eventual union involving Rome in the centre of her picture.

[1] See p. 253 above.

15
THE CONVERSATIONS AT
MALINES

There have been many accounts of the conversations which took place during the years 1922–1926 between a group of Anglicans and some Roman Catholics at the ancient Belgian town of Malines, under the chairmanship of Cardinal Mercier.[1] None has so far been definitive and neither does the present survey, with its wide time span, do more than bring together the more important points of the episode. But even before a full history of the conversations is written, some new light can be thrown on the exchanges by examination of some of the original documents held at Malines.[2]

The histories which recall the Malines dialogues tend to suggest that the origins of the conversations lay on the one hand with the initiative taken by the elderly Lord Halifax and his friend the Abbé Portal who, after their rebuff in 1896, were anxious to make one more attempt to improve Anglican/Roman Catholic relationships during their lifetime; and secondly, it has been indicated that it was Cardinal Mercier's favourable reception of the Lambeth Appeal to all Christian People and his telegram to the Archbishop of Canterbury[3] which caused him

[1] Désiré Joseph Mercier, 1851–1926, Cardinal Archbishop of Malines and Primate of Belgium.

[2] The authors are deeply indebted to His Eminence Cardinal Suenens for permission to read these manuscripts and to the Ecumenical Officer of the diocese, Canon J. Dessain (nephew of Cardinal Mercier's Secretary), for his help and hospitality at Malines.

[3] 21st May 1921. 'May God hearken to the prayers we continually offer for the union of all Christian believers and crown with success your efforts to attain their goal.'

initially to be involved in the proceedings: that Halifax saw
this opportunity and took it. So much is true, but the documents
at Malines reveal the facts to be more complicated than that.
Cardinal Mercier, who had a gallant record of courage and
initiative during the enemy occupation of his country from
1914 to 1918, had shewn these qualities in the religious and
ecumenical field during times of peace. Not only did he offer an
appointment in Belgium to Fr. George Tyrrell, s.j. when that
priest was in difficulties in England, but in the year 1919 he
visited the United States, and went to Detroit in October where
the General Convention of the Episcopal Church of the U.S.A.
was meeting. The House of Deputies invited him to be its
guest at any time during its session and on 20th October he
appeared and was received with considerable warmth; the
accounts of the visit in the Episcopalian periodical *The Living
Church* were indeed expansive.[1]

> It was a dramatic moment when . . . Cardinal Mercier was
> formally received by the House of Deputies. . . . Cardinal
> Mercier advanced amidst tremendous applause up the long
> aisle to the speakers' platform. The galleries had been
> crowded from early morning by expectant throngs. . . .The
> Cardinal, in his sumptuous robes of office, including the
> Cardinal's hat, was the most picturesque figure, it may easily
> be said, that had ever been introduced into a House of
> General Convention. The applause that greeted him was
> tremendous and the audience remained standing until the
> Cardinal himself waved them into their seats.

After a speech of welcome the Cardinal's advance to the
rostrum was the signal for new outbreaks of applause. At the
end of his speech he said:

> I ask to be allowed to add one word more and that is that we
> are brethren in Christian faith [Thundering Applause]. What
> we must know and teach is, that if we are brethren it is
> because we are all sons of the Father who is in Heaven.[2]

The winter of 1920 found him in Rome, and on 21st Decem-

---

[1] October 1919, Vol. 62, pp. 20–1.
[2] Minutes of the *Journal of General Convention*, 1919, pp. 375–8.

ber he addressed a letter to Pope Benedict XV on the subject of Unity[1] and made some suggestions:

> Je m'offre à faire une tentative. Après avoir demandé autour de moi des prières pour une intention secrète de votre Sainteté, j'essayerais d'inviter à Malines successivement un ou deux théologiens de chacune de ces principales églises dissidentes, anglicane et Orthodoxe surtout. Je les retiendrais pendant quelques jours et les mettrais en rapport avec un théologien catholique d'une doctrine sûre et d'un coeur aimant. Dans l'intimité d'un tête à tête avec la grâce de Dieu, la pénétration des âmes peut être beaucoup plus profonde. Mon unique préoccupation serait de préparer les âmes loyales aux solutions que le Saint Siège se réserverait de donner à l'heure et dans la forme de son choix.

It therefore becomes clear that *before* receipt of the Lambeth Appeal or communications from Lord Halifax or Portal (or at any rate those which have come to light so far and have been quoted), Cardinal Mercier was working to promote ecumenical dialogue. Three other pieces[2] of evidence in the Malines Archives corroborate this fact. A letter from Portal,[3] which one might now expect to find, is close at hand, giving information on the Lambeth Appeal and asking if the time had not come to get in touch with the Anglican Church and hold a conference at Brussels.

The next steps are well known: Cardinal Mercier replied to the Lambeth Appeal and Lord Halifax communicated both with the Archbishops of Canterbury and York and wrung a

---

[1] Headed by a pencilled note 'Demande d'approbation de réunions de Malines.' Malines Archives.

[2] (a) Letter from Cardinal Mercier to Mgr. Cerretti, deputy Secretary of State at the Vatican, 25th January 1921, quoting a letter to the Pope relative to the conversations to be held on Orders at Malines. Malines Archives.

(b) Subjects discussed at the interview with Pius XI on 6th February 1922, one of which was 'conversations with Anglicans approved by Benedict XV', see p. 265.

(c) Letter from Mgr. d'Herbigny of the Secretariat of State, Rome, to Cardinal Mercier, 11th March 1922, speaking of the Cardinal's proposal to Benedict XV the year before, 'de réunir (à Louvain) ou plutôt, je crois, à Malines pour des conférences individuelles un dignitaire anglican ou épiscopalien avec un théologian catholique'. ibid.

[3] From Paris, 24th January 1921. ibid.

letter of commendation from Archbishop Davidson to Cardinal Mercier, on the strength of the Cardinal's response and his own belief that the Appeal's wording could be interpreted to include the possibility of dialogue. The Archbishop was cautious in his reference to the impending visit of Halifax to the Cardinal:

> he does not go in any sense as ambassador or formal re-presentative of the Church of England. .... Anything which he says therefore would be an expression of his personal opinion rather than an authoritative statement of the position or endeavours of the Church of England in its corporate capacity. I cannot but think however that you would find a conversation with him consonant with the thought expressed in your Eminence's letter to me . . . and of the visions set forth in the Lambeth Conference Appeal.[1]

This extract aptly sums up the main problems which lay be-hind the dialogue at Malines. Lord Halifax and his compan-ions who went there did not represent current Anglican[2] opinion nor contemporary attitudes towards affairs Roman Catholic. No one understood this better than the Archbishop and this accounted both for his reserve and the secrecy with which the conversations were surrounded in the first place. Furthermore as the dialogue progressed a new complication arose because of the revision of the Book of Common Prayer which was viewed in certain circles as taking too extreme a 'catholic' form. So close a contact with Roman Catholics would further alarm these influences and prejudice the safe passage of the new Prayer Book through Parliament. English public opinion, neither clerical nor lay, was, in general, ready for the Malines Conversations, a fact which makes it even more re-markable that the event took place. And it was because it happened, and moreover was allowed to happen, that the dialogue is of such significance: what was discussed is of secondary importance.

So it will be with the attitudes of Rome and Canterbury (and Westminster) rather than with the actual content of the talks,

---

[1] *Randall Davidson, Archbishop of Canterbury*, G. K. A. Bell, OUP, 1935, Vol. II, p. 1255.
[2] Dean Armitage Robinson was aware of this, as his letters to the Cardinal show; Lord Halifax was less realistic.

that this account will concern itself. Lord Halifax, with the Abbé Portal, saw Cardinal Mercier on 19th October 1921, bearing the Archbishop's cautious letter. According to the *Life* of the Archbishop,[1] the Cardinal, whilst receiving his visitors with great warmth, enquired why they did not address themselves to English Roman Catholic authorities and was told that the disposition of the latter was against it. Cardinal Mercier agreed that a conference be held between Roman Catholics and Anglicans to discuss points which separated the two Churches and said he would go to Rome himself, if necessary, and talk the matter over with the Pope. On his journey home Halifax stopped in Paris to speak with a group of French priests and when back in England invited Fr. Walter Frere,[2] Superior of the Community of the Resurrection, and Dr. Armitage Robinson,[3] Dean of Wells, to join him in Belgium later in the year. The first exploratory conversation was held very quietly in Malines on 6th–8th December 1921.[4] The general basis of the discussions was a memorandum prepared by Lord Halifax dealing with the constitution of the Church and the nature of the sacraments and the Lambeth Appeal; there was also some talk on the difference between fundamental and non-fundamental dogmas.

During that winter Benedict XV died, and Cardinal Mercier, on leaving for the Conclave to elect his successor, received a telegram from Achille Ratti, Archbishop of Milan, (the future Pius XI) suggesting that he might care to stay with him en route for Rome. On 6th Febrary 1922 Pius XI was elected by the Conclave and shortly after Cardinal Mercier was received by his old friend. The Cardinal's handwritten aide-mémoire on the audience is among the Malines papers.[5] No. 5 of the matters he had to discuss with the new Pontiff was the question of private conversations with the Anglicans approved by Benedict XV, and a description of the first conversation which had taken place on 8th–10th December 1921. 'J'en expose le

[1] *Randall Davidson . . .*, Bell, Vol. II, p. 1255.
[2] 1863–1938. Bishop of Truro 1923.
[3] 1858–1933. New Testament and Patristic scholar; 1902 Dean of Westminster; Resigned to become Dean of Wells 1911.
[4] The Roman Catholic members in addition to the Cardinal were his vicar general Mgr. Van Roey and Abbé Portal.
[5] Photostat as illustration.

caractère et les résultats, afin de m'assurer que mes supérieurs m'appreuvent.' The reply from the Pope is also given: 'Je ne vois que du bien à ces réunions. . . .' It was not right only to judge men from ideas suggested by boo'.s. 'J'ai une foi illimitée dans la bonne foi de ceux qui ne sont pas des nôtres dans nôtre église catholique.'

In April Cardinal Mercier received a letter from Cardinal Gasparri,[1] Secretary of State at the Vatican, in answer to one from the Belgian Primate in regard to an exchange with Anglicans. He said that this had been laid before the Pope and the Holy Father had plainly approved of what had been done so far. To lead those who were in error to truth and unity was an apostolic work. The Cardinal was also in receipt of a considerable correspondence during that spring with Mgr. Michel d'Herbigny,[2] It was relayed to Belgium[3] that the Revd. George Bell[4] had written direct to him in Rome from Lambeth sending a copy of the Appeal and asking him to make suggestions as to the method of realising unity between Anglicans and Catholics. d'Herbigny had shown this letter to the Cardinal Secretary of State who suggested that Malines would seem to be the best place for conversations: and in his reply to Bell,[5] d'Herbigny wrote that, while without authority, he could say that the Holy See was happy about those who wished to carry out the wishes of the Saviour on unity; it would be useful to send a delegate of the reverend signatories of the Appeal to Rome and one to Cardinal Mercier to start to confer with competence and authority. Cardinal Mercier was also addressed in June[6] by an English Jesuit from Oxford, Fr. Leslie Walker, who said he understood that there had been an approach for holding a conference between Anglicans and Catholics. He had been in correspondence both with Mgr. d'Herbigny in Rome and George Bell at Lambeth at great length. d'Herbigny had suggested that the idea had been favourably received at Rome

[1] From Rome, 11th April 1922. Malines Archives.
[2] A French Jesuit with an interest in the Orthodox churches; on the staff of the Vatican Secretariat of State.
[3] Palm Sunday (9th April 1922) Mgr. d'Herbigny to Cardinal Mercier. Malines Archives.
[4] The archbishop's chaplain and biographer; later to become Bishop of Chichester and a noted ecumenist.
[5] 11th April 1922. ibid.
[6] From Campion Hall, 13th June 1922. ibid.

and Bell had stated that if a request emanating directly or indirectly from Rome were sent to the Archbishop, something might come of it. A communication from the Pope through the Secretariat of State would be best. Fr. Walker was not over-hopeful of the outcome:

The Anglicans understand that the faith-basis must be ours not theirs and it is on the understanding that we are not prepared to go back on past definitions of faith that they would meet us. The question is whether they can be persuaded to accept our faith-basis.

But if the affair broke down it could not be said that they had not tried to meet the separated brethren half way. If a split occurred in the Anglican Church, which was not impossible, there was a chance of a large party coming over to Rome, rather than setting up independently or in union with the Greeks. If the conference should succeed the benefit to Europe and the world would be incalculable. The suggestions that had been made about meetings with private individuals were of doubtful use: Bell had agreed: private individuals did not represent their church nor would they be prepared to enter into negotiations independently of their bishops: official conferences were called for with duly appointed representatives. Few catholics would approve of such a move, 'But I do not see it would do any harm and might do a great deal of good.'

Despite his letter from Gasparri, curiously enough it was not until September 1922 that the Cardinal told Lord Halifax that he had papal authority to continue the talks. Archbishop Davidson said that an authoritative request from the Vatican was indispensable:[1] whether he was apprehensive solely as to the reactions of his own communion or whether he was sensitive to the feelings of the English Roman Catholic hierarchy also is not known. Cardinal Mercier asked the Pope for the authority[2] and on 25th November he received it from Gasparri: 'Il autorise votre Eminence à dire aux Anglicans que le Saint Siège approuve et encourage vos conversations et prie de tout

[1] Archbishop of Canterbury to Lord Halifax, 20th October 1922. *Randall Davidson. . .*, Bell, Vol. II, p. 1257.
[2] From Malines, Cardinal Mercier to Pius XI, 14th November 1922. Malines Archives.

son coeur le Bon Dieu de les bénir.'[1] Mercier replied 'Nous
allons donc renouer nos relations avec les Anglicans.'[2] Mercier
also wrote[3] to Cardinal Bourne, Archbishop of Westminster, to
tell him about the conversations and Halifax called upon the
Cardinal Archbishop on 29th November. Moreover the Belgian
Primate and the English one began to correspond direct, at
Archbishop Davidson's request. As a result the second conversation took place on 14th and 15th March 1923. The
Cardinal thought the Archbishop was showing great reserve by
a refusal to increase the Anglican participation beyond the
original three, and Portal was disturbed by the emphasis which
Randall Davidson was placing upon the increased connection
between the Church of England and the Eastern Orthodox
Church. The Archbishop had himself been worried about the
Pastoral on the Papacy which Cardinal Mercier had sent to his
diocese on the election of Pius XI, which he considered excessive
in its claims. Among his warnings to the Anglican team were
not to budge an inch on 'the necessity of carrying the East with
us in ultimate reunion steps'.[4] The Dean of Wells informed
Cardinal Mercier of this involvement of the Archbishop in
matters of the Orthodox.[5]

> His Grace is very greatly moved by the seriousness of the
> present opportunity though he is slow to express himself in
> any public way in regard to it. The Russian and still more
> the Greek situation occupies him a good deal, and is unhappily
> not without its political aspect—which again makes him
> specially cautious as to anything he says about Reunion.[6]

During the second conversation the points discussed were of a
practical kind: the nature of the Anglican Communion was
described by its members and the problems of this now world-
wide body which would arise in the event of union: what for
instance would be the relationship of the Archbishop of

[1] From Rome, Secretary of State to Cardinal Mercier, 25th November
1922. Malines Archives.
[2] From Malines, Cardinal Mercier to Cardinal Gasparri, 27th November
1922. Malines Archives.
[3] From Malines, 30th November 1922. ibid.
[4] *Randall Davidson . . .*, Bell, Vol. II, pp. 1260–1.
[5] It being Anglican policy to view the question of unity on a broad front
and not to concentrate on one confession.
[6] From Wells, 15th April 1923. Malines Archives.

Canterbury to the Holy See: the position of the Roman Catholic hierarchy in England: what characteristic Anglican rites and customs could be retained. Each side ended by agreeing to submit a document to their own authorities which they all signed. Archbishop Davidson was alarmed at the sight of these pieces of paper carrying Anglican signatures, since there was a suggestion that the Archbishop of Canterbury and other Anglican metropolitans should receive the pallium;[1] and he considered that whatever arrangements were eventually made for jurisdiction there were great doctrinal issues which must first be faced. He therefore wrote at great length[2] to the Dean of Wells and set out his views in a forthright manner: the fundamental question of the Papacy and papal status, which spread over to such dogmas as Transubstantiation and the Immaculate Conception, must be brought to clear issues. He also warned:

> It is I think possible that our Roman Catholic friends, unfamiliar perhaps with the strength of opinion on these subjects which is prevalent in large sections of the English Church and people, may suppose us to be ready for a more accommodating acceptance of Roman Catholic contentions and claims that I for one, can regard as being either possible or in accordance with our deliberate belief as to what is true.

Here was not caution so much as realism: he repeated his sentiments direct to the Cardinal:[3]

> I do not doubt that your Eminence will agree with me in thinking that, after all, the really fundamental question of the position of the Sovereign Pontiff of the Roman Catholic Church must be candidly faced before further progress can be made. The ambiguity of the term 'primacy' is well known to us all. It has an historic meaning which can be accepted without difficulty. If, however, it is understood as implying that the Pope holds jure divino the unique and solemn position of sole Vicar of Christ on earth, from whom as

[1] An ancient symbol of jurisdiction granted by the Pope in response to obedience.

[2] From Lambeth Palace, 19th March 1923. *Documents on Christian Unity* (ed. G. K. A. Bell) second series, OUP, 1930, pp. 45–50.

[3] *Randall Davidson . . .*, Bell, Vol. II, pp. 1267–8.

Vicar of Christ must come directly or indirectly the right to minister validly within the Church, there ought to be no delay in discussing that implication and expounding its essential bearings. For it would not, in my judgment, be fair to Your Eminence or to others that I should encourage further discussion upon subordinate administrative possibilities without expressing my conviction that such a doctrine of papal authority is not one to which the adherence of the Church of England could be obtained. I say this simply for clearness' sake, and not as meaning that I desire these conversations to end. . . . .

I have explained to my three Anglican friends what I feel upon this anxious and difficult matter, and have encouraged them to look forward to a resumption of the conferences. So great is the importance of this matter and its issues, that no effort on the part of any of us should be spared which may contribute towards the ultimate attainment of Unity within the Church of Christ.

The Cardinal had apprised the Pope of the dialogue to be held in March 1923[1] and on the last day of that month an answer came from the Cardinal Secretary of State.[2] In reply to his detractors His Eminence could reply:

'Le Saint Père connait mes conversations avec les anglicans . . . il ne m'a jamais trasmis le moindre mot de désapprobation; ce qui pour moi est équivalent à un encouragement tacite.' Cette réponse fermera la bouche aux trop zelés defenseurs de la foi. Quant à la seconde, les questions soulevées dans le memorandum sont importantes; elles devront être examinées et résolues, une fois admis le principe de la réunion des Églises. Les Anglicans peuvent être tout à fait reassurés que le Saint Siège fera toutes les concessions possibles pour faciliter la réunion tant desirée.

The third conversations took place on 7th–8th November 1923 and in deference to the Archbishop's wish, discussion was devoted wholly to the position of St. Peter, on the basis of memoranda prepared by both sides. The Anglican party, whose

---

[1] From Malines, 1st March 1923. Malines Archives.
[2] From Rome, 30th March 1923. ibid.

membership had been increased by two, Bishop Gore[1] and Dr. B. J. Kidd,[2] were received by the Archbishop and the advisers he had called in before leaving for Belgium. The Roman Catholic side had been joined by two extra theologians, Mgr. Pierre Battifol[3] and Père Hippolyte Hemmer.[4] Summaries[5] were again drawn up by both groups and although the outcome was far from spectacular there was, as Dr. Kidd wrote to Cardinal Mercier,[6] 'a wonderful atmosphere of good will and we reached an agreement limited, of course, but real, such as I hardly dared to expect'

A most important question which faced those concerned in the dialogue was that of publicity: the facts were leaking out and this, if extended, would do more harm than a statement. The Archbishop decided to write a Christmas letter[7] to the Metropolitans of the Anglican Communion telling them of the conversations and of their nature. This aroused a storm of controversy in which both Archbishop and Cardinal received very sharp criticism. There was, however, some approbation: the Patriarch of Constantinople, Gregory, writing on receipt of a copy of the letter to the Metropolitans, said: 'The recent efforts for fraternal communion with the Church of Rome appear to us also to be such a righteous and godly endeavour.'[8] Archbishop Davidson made his formal answer to his attackers in the Upper House of Convocation on 6th February 1924,[9] in which he emphasised that there had been no negotiations whatever, 'they were private conversations about our respective history and doctrines and nothing more'.[10] He also made clear, what had been challenged by the Roman Catholic side, that the Vatican had been as aware of the conversations as himself.

Meanwhile the Cardinal was also under fire. In December the

---

[1] Charles Gore, 1853–1932. Fellow of Trinity College, Oxford, 1875: Associated with foundation of Community of the Resurrection: 1902 Bishop of Worcester; 1911 Oxford.

[2] Warden of Keble College, Oxford.

[3] 1861–1929. Church historian. At École Ste Barbe in Paris.

[4] 1864–1945. Church historian. Professor at Catholic Institute in Paris.

[5] *Documents on Christian Unity* (ed. G. K. A. Bell) second series, pp. 33–44.

[6] From Keble College, Oxford, 12th November 1923. Malines Archives.

[7] *Randall Davidson...*, Bell, Vol. II, pp. 1282–4.

[8] To Archbishop of Canterbury, June 1924. ibid, p. 1288.

[9] Chronicle of Convocation of Canterbury. 5 and 6 Geo. V. SPCK, pp. 14–21.

[10] ibid., p. 19.

Cardinal Secretary of State[1] wrote saying that the papers had got hold of the conversations and described them as official.

Autant que possible il foudrait empêcher que dans les annonces des journaux les conférences prennent un caractère officiel de la part du Saint Siège.

On the Feast of the Epiphany 1924[2] Cardinal Mercier wrote to Cardinal Gasparri; he mentioned, inter alia, that the English Catholics were becoming suspicious: this was repeated to the Pope by the Belgian Cardinal later that month.[3] Mercier had published in a Pastoral[4] to his diocese a description of the extent of the conversations and had received much criticism. He asked the Pope to encourage him. The Cardinal Secretary of State later replied on the Pope's behalf:[5] the conversations were private under the responsibility of Cardinal Mercier 'ma conosciute e benedette dal Papa'.[6] Moreover, in March Pius XI expressed satisfaction and gratitude for the conferences to the Sacred Consistory.[7]

Two interesting letters, in view of future events, reached Malines in February 1924. One[8] was from Fr. Sordet, a Redemptorist known to the Cardinal. He had just received the Pastoral which he had shown to Cardinal Bourne, Archbishop of Westminster, and currently their guest.

Il en est ravi dans toute la force du terme. Son Éminence m'a dit que son premier plan était de passer par Malines en venant à Rome, mais qu'une pensée de delicatesse l'en avait empêché.

The *Osservatore Romano* had given a translation of the Pastoral, but suppressed the phrase which made reference 'to the encouragement and benediction of the supreme authority given to the conversations'. Cardinal Bourne had pointed this out and produced a letter from Cardinal Gasparri of which he held a copy; also Lord Halifax and the Archbishop of Canter-

[1] From Rome, 30th December 1923, Cardinal Gasparri to Cardinal Mercier. Malines Archives.　　　　　　　　　　　　　[2] ibid.
[3] 14th January 1924. ibid.　　　　　　　　　　　[4] 18th January 1924.
[5] 10th February 1924. ibid.
[6] But known to and blessed by the Pope.
[7] 24th March 1924. *Randall Davidson* . . ., Bell, Vol. II, p. 1302.
[8] From Sant' Alfonzo (the Redemptorist headquarters) in the via Merulana, Rome, 7th February 1924. Malines Archives.

bury. Fr. Sordet had sought to put this right with the paper through Mgr. Giuseppe Pizzardo.[1] Cardinal Bourne had been interested in this manoeuvre and had told Fr. Sordet to acquaint Cardinal Mercier of the fact. The Redemptorist continued:

> Dans sa première audience, le Cardinal Bourne ayant, m'a-t-il dit, trop de matières à traiter n'a pu entamer la question des conversations de Malines. Je crois que son intention est d'en parler au Saint Père dans la seconde audience qui ne tardera pas.

Cardinal Mercier was addressed also in the Spring of 1924, by the Rector of a House of Studies for convert clergymen.[2] He wrote that despite having received over 50 students in the preceding years, since the conversations had become known none had come forward. Those Anglican clergymen who were moving towards the Church were now holding back under the impression that if they waited, they would be able to make special terms. The Cardinal was unaware of the situation in England, it was insinuated: High-Church teaching claimed for the Church of England the status of the Catholic Church of the land. In view of the furore which was to follow, no doubt this information was passed to higher authority.

Meanwhile the talks hung fire for over a year. The Archbishop of Canterbury was anxious for delay: the Prayer Book controversy was warming up. But Cardinal Mercier was sanguine enough on behalf of his superiors, as he wrote to Lord Halifax:

> In proportion as the Sovereign Pontiff, and the Cardinal Secretary of State at the Vatican, affirm with increasing distinctness their confidence in our humble efforts, and thus indirectly disavow certain oppositions of the English Roman Catholics, it would seem as if on our side the nearer hopes of reunion seemed likely to be realised, the more sensitive the good Archbishop of Canterbury seems to grow as to his responsibilities to his own people, and to desire to put off,

[1] Born 1877. Cardinal 1937. Prefect of the Congregation for Catholic Instruction. d. 1973.
[2] From the Revd. H. Barton-Brown, St. Charles, Hatfield, Herts., 12th February 1924. Malines Archives.

rather than to hasten, the definite bringing together of both sides.[1]

In May 1925 the six friends, for such they now were, met in Malines for what was to be the fourth and last conversation. The main subject under discussion was the relationship of the episcopate to the Holy See, with memoranda from both sides prepared as before. The Anglicans felt obliged to say that they saw in papal supremacy, as stated, a grave difficulty: they saw themselves, the Orthodox and some Protestants as preserving certain spiritual elements belonging to primitive Christianity which had been more or less lost in the Church of Rome. Gore[2] went so far as to say that certain Roman doctrines went beyond the original deposit of the faith and seemed to conflict with history and with truth. In his paper 'Unity with Diversity', which concerned itself with what were and what were not fundamental doctrines, and whether there could not be tolerance of diversity determined by the distinction between the two, Gore made the following plea:

> Now what I want to ask, with a sense of my audacity in asking it, is—not for any strictly theological change in the teaching of the Roman Church, nor any alteration in the terms of communion required of those who feel constrained to submit themselves individually to the Roman Church. What I am asking of my friends of the Roman Church, with whom I am having the pleasure of quiet conference, is whether the idea is wholly impossible that, with a view to the corporate reconciliation of the Orthodox Communion and the Anglican Communion, the Roman Church could be content to require not more than the acceptance of those articles of faith which fall under the Vincentian Canon. . . .[3]

The most significant item of this conversation was the paper read by the Cardinal, and produced quite unexpectedly by him, entitled 'L'Église Anglicane Unie non Absorbie':[4] its

[1] 6th March 1925. Malines Archives and *Randall Davidson . . .*, Bell, Vol. II, p. 1289.
[2] *Randall Davidson . . .*, Bell, Voi. II, p. 1291.
[3] From *Recollections of Malines*, Walter Frere, c.r. The Centenary Press, 1935, p. 117.
[4] *Documents on Christian Unity* (Ed. G. K. A. Bell), third series, OUP, 1948, pp. 21–31.

author was not immediately disclosed, but was subsequently revealed to be Dom Lambert Beauduin[1] of the Benedictine Community at Amay. It was a plan for a Uniat Church of England in communion with the Holy See.

The Archbishop commenting on the summaries of these last talks[2] suggested to the Cardinal that whereas he dared not in honesty adopt the phrase used by His Eminence that 'we have made progress in agreement', yet he was increasingly persuaded that the gatherings had been faithful of good, although there had been no signs of the possibilities of modifications or re-statements 'of what are commonly regarded as irreducible doctrinal requirements'. Later[3] he referred to 'that great unremoved mountain of difficulty', the question of the Papacy: for him a corruption of the tenets of primitive Christianity, but for Cardinal Mercier, as Frere said,[4] a logical argument. The Archbishop was however willing for the talks to continue and the fifth Conversation was planned for January 1926.

Meanwhile a furore had broken out between the Archbishopric of Westminster and Malines upon which it is not proposed to dwell. A series of letters passed across the channel which can be found in the biography of Cardinal Bourne by Ernest Oldmeadow, the editor of the *Tablet*, who was himself not blameless in exacerbating the affair. The English Cardinal's main complaints were first that it could be insinuated that differences of opinion existed in the Church of Rome: 'Anglicans openly declare that the views of the Holy See held at Malines are not the same as those taught by us in England':[5] secondly he had been kept in the dark and except for one letter at the end of 1923 had been treated as if he did not exist, whereas the Archbishop of Canterbury had been given full details.[6] From

---

[1] 1873–1960. Entered Benedictine Abbey Mont César 1906. Later at Amay and Chevetogne. Founded ecumenical review *Irenikon* 1925. Exiled from his monastery by Roman authority 1931–1951.

[2] Lambeth Palace, 1st August 1925. *Randall Davidson. . .*, Bell, Vol. II, p. 1294.

[3] To Cardinal Mercier from Old Palace, Canterbury, 9th December 1925. ibid., p. 1298.

[4] *Recollections of Malines*, Frere, p. 50.

[5] 29th October 1925. *Francis, Cardinal Bourne*, Ernest Oldmeadow, Burns Oates, 1944, Vol. II, p. 384.

[6] ibid., p. 365. In fact Cardinal Mercier wrote on 30th November 1922 and Cardinal Bourne replied on 4th December 1922. Malines Archives.

Belgium came several letters of explanation including one which referred to Cardinal Bourne's knowledge of the Pastoral of January 1924 on the Dialogue and a conversation which they had had 'de vive voix' at Sant'Alfonzo in Rome at Whitsuntide of the past year. That the question was now again referred from Westminster to Rome is beyond doubt. Old-meadow, editor of the *Tablet*, visited Cardinal Merry del Val[1] in Rome (whom Portal had earlier described to Halifax as waiting to act in this matter)[2] and they spoke of the earlier prohibition of reunion talks issued by the Holy Office Instruction of 1864.

In December of 1925 Cardinal Mercier's health deteriorated sharply and soon it became known that he was dying. Lord Halifax hurried to Malines. On 21st January 1926 the Cardinal wrote to Archbishop Davidson for the last time thanking him for his expressions of sympathy and repeating the words 'Ut unum sint':[3] two days later he died, mourned by many in his own country and beyond. Portal died in June, and in October the remaining members of the two groups met together under the chairmanship of Mgr. Van Roey, the new Archbishop of Malines, but merely for the purposes of drawing up a report. With the death of the great figure who had been the friend and inspiration of all, and the problems from Westminster (Parliament[4] and Cathedral), the heart had gone out of the Conversations. The publication of the reports presented some difficulties which are hardly of sufficient importance to mention here, except for the fact that Mgr. Van Roey showed himself suffering from some loss of nerve when he suggested[5] that Cardinal Mercier had had certain reserves about Dom Lambert Beauduin's paper on Uniat Status for the Anglican Church. The Belgian Benedictine had already made the late Cardinal's views clear by publishing a comment by Cardinal Mercier on his paper in *Irenikon* in 1927.[6]

[1] *Francis, Cardinal Bourne*, Vol. II, p. 364.
[2] *Charles Lindley, Viscount Halifax*, Lockhart, Vol. II, p. 286.
[3] *Randall Davidson. . .*, Bell, Vol. II, p. 1299.
[4] The Prayer Book Measure was rejected by Parliament (House of Commons) 13th December 1927. See p. 301 below.
[5] In *Libre Belgique*. Lord Halifax to the editor of *The Times*, 22nd February 1930, quoted in *Francis, Cardinal Bourne*, Ernest Oldmeadow, Vol. II, p. 407.
[6] *Documents on Christian Unity* (ed. G. K. A. Bell) third series, pp. 32–3.

An evaluation of the Malines Conversations reveals above all a dimension which had been absent too long in relations between separated Christians: a spirit of charity and fellowship. Inspired initially by Cardinal Mercier, it so permeated the whole group that there are constant references to it in the correspondence between its members. On hearing of the Cardinal's illness, the Dean of Wells wrote[1] that the Belgian Archbishop was daily in his prayers. 'I am bold enough to write, for hearts have been drawn very close together at Malines': strong words from an Englishman. This deep charity of Cardinal Mercier towards those opposed to him doctrinally, in spite of views which could be considered quite extreme,[2] forces a comparison with the great Pope John XXIII who had closely similar characteristics. Both failed in the last analysis to understand the Anglican position,[3] which Mercier showed never more clearly than when he asked Lord Halifax if he would not submit to Rome in April 1924. Where Anglicans saw overturning of primitive doctrine, he did not see the issues. But while the Belgian Archbishop's heart triumphed over his head, the Archbishop of Canterbury's head remained firmly in control, to Halifax's chagrin: as Halifax wrote to him on the draft of the letter to the Metropolitans:[4]

> I wish also very much that it had contained a sentence or two which would have appealed to the heart. The heart and imagination are more compelling forces than any which appeal only to the head.

Doctrinally and immediately the Conversations achieved little. But the relationships established at Malines have endured through several generations of Archbishops on both sides. Now the visits and understanding between the holders of the sees of Malines–Brussels and Canterbury are yielding a rich harvest.

[1] 27th December 1925. Malines Archives.

[2] His Pastoral on the election of Pius XI showed an acceptance of a doctrine of the Papacy which was indeed fulsome: his secretary Canon Dessain (the elder) indicated in a letter to Canon Prestige on Maundy Thursday 1935, in answer to a question, that it was true the late Cardinal had set his heart on furthering belief in the mediation of Our Lady and the devotion to her under this title. Malines Archives.

[3] As Frere pointed out in the case of Cardinal Mercier in his *Recollections of Malines*, p. 50. This is not true of his illustrious successor in office, Cardinal Suenens.

[4] 29th December 1923. *Randall Davidson. . .*, Bell, Vol. II, p. 1282.

16

FROM MALINES TO PIUS XII

Before taking the narrative on from Malines we should make mention of a Commission on 'Doctrine in the Church of England'[1] set up in 1922, which did not report until 1938. It showed a growing uneasiness at the variety of doctrines which were in fact held within the Church, a desire to investigate the facts, lest they should be exaggerated, and a laudable desire to see what limits could be set to individual vagaries and what hope there was of establishing some more precise basis of agreement than in fact there was. This indicated a growing realisation that for ecumenical purposes, among other reasons, the doctrinal basis of the Church of England in the 39 Articles was far from satisfactory. There was no Anglican Summa Theologica, for the Articles do not profess to be that. Much of the essential doctrine of the Church of England was to be distilled from her liturgies, and some could be said to be deducible from the Anglican divines who wrote in the seventeenth century. There was a considerable reluctance to attempt any new set of definitions.

It is of the greatest importance that those engaged in treating with the Anglican churches should not misunderstand their doctrinal pronouncements. William Temple[2] had written:

> It is the great wisdom of our Church that it was not founded to support any particular doctrines, as the Protestant bodies were; it stands as a historic church, which broke with Rome because Rome encouraged definite abuses at that time. But further freedom in doctrine is the life-breath of the Church of England.[3]

[1] See Bibliography.   [2] Archbishop of York 1929, Canterbury 1942–44.
[3] Letter to J. L. Stocks, *William Temple Archbishop of Canterbury*, F. A. Iremonger, OUP, 1948, p. 106.

The terms of reference of the Doctrinal Commission were:

> To consider the nature and grounds of Christian doctrine with a view to demonstrating the extent of existing agreement within the Church of England and with a view to investigating how far it is possible to remove or diminish existing differences'.[1]

Whatever its failures or limitations the very appointment of the Commission was a milestone on the road to Christian understanding. The Church of England knew she would have to show the colour of her doctrinal currency sooner or later if she expected to be taken seriously in discussions on matters of faith.

The next two decades, which span the years between the Malines conversations and the outbreak of the Second World War, can be said, for these purposes, to have two main characteristics. The first is the steady involvement of the Anglican churches in the general ecumenical movement, and the second is the continued relentless, implacable opposition of the Church of Rome at official levels to any participation in it, though during this same period, at many lower levels, and in many places, the seeds of change were beginning to germinate.

The steady move of the non-Roman churches to set up meeting-points was illustrated for the Church of England by the 'COPEC' conference of 1924 (Conference on Christian Politics, Economics and Citizenship) which in turn led in 1937 to the formation of the Life and Work Movement, itself one half of the eventual World Council of Churches.

It should be noted that in the first stages of preparation for COPEC there was Roman Catholic participation. Where it was not thought 'safe' to engage in discussions on Faith and Order a venture might be made on social questions where there was no danger of compromising 'the Faith'. This endured for a time, but it was discovered that divergent views on family ethics made co-operation dangerous, and the Roman Catholics withdrew.

In 1925 came a happy moment for the Anglican Church when her orders were officially recognised by the Old Catholics, a factor not without significance in future dealings with Rome. In 1927 there came into being the other wing of the general

[1] Doctrinal Report, p. 19.

ecumenical movement, at the Lausanne conference on Faith and Order. Bishop Brent of the Episcopal Church in the United States had been particularly diligent in promoting this development since its origins in the Edinburgh Conference of 1910. One of the most influential participants in it was A. C. Headlam, Bishop of Gloucester. Two divergent tendencies emerged in the conference, one pressing for union of agreement on formularies, another saying that such a type of concord should not even be attempted. Headlam enunciated a point which proved to be a catalyst in that particular situation, which still must help to elucidate some of the darker corners of the Roman/Anglican dialogue. He proposed a formula which eventually found general acceptance:

> We accept the faith of Christ as it has been taught us in the Scriptures and as it has been handed down to us in the Creed of the Catholic Church set forth at the Council of Chalcedon, and in the Apostles' Creed.

The words had been carefully chosen. He deliberately used the expression 'Faith of Christ', not 'Creed'; it was the faith not the Creed upon which they were united, something deeper, broader and fuller than any Creed could express, although it might well be expressed by the Creed. Secondly he put at the forefront the Holy Scriptures as the source of their knowledge of the faith of Christ.[1] There are still churches and people who have not assimilated the truths lying behind Headlam's formula at Lausanne.

The attitude of Rome to these movements remained one of non-co-operation. Pius XI was now Pope and there seemed to have been no change of position. A letter of the Holy Office in answer to a question was published in July 1927, one month before the Lausanne Conference, repeating a previous injunction of 1919 to the effect that it was not allowable for catholics

> to be present at or give countenance to meetings of non-catholics, or conferences or societies which have the object of making it appear that all who profess the name of Christian are bound together in one religious covenant.[2]

[1] *Arthur Cayley Headlam, Life and Letters of a Bishop*, Ronald Jasper, Faith Press, 1960.   [2] *Enchiridion Symbolorum*, Denzinger 2199.

But worse was to come, for following close on the heels of the Lausanne Faith and Order Conference the encyclical 'Mortalium Animos'[1] (Epiphany 1928) burst upon the world. The encyclical was a blow aimed at the heart of any possible co-operation between catholics and other Christians in the fostering of Christian union. It not only misrepresented the aims of the ecumenical movement, but tried to discredit it by associating it indiscriminately with inter-faith discussions. After deploring the quarrels and divisions of the time it warned catholics against co-operation with those who sought a facile solution to the problem. It is important to note, in view of subsequent happier times, the full statement of the ultramontane conception of dogmatic truth, the take-it-or-leave-it or all-or-nothing attitude to the faith.

> All true followers of Christ, therefore, will believe the dogma of the Immaculate Conception of the Mother of God with the same faith as they believe the mystery of the august Trinity, the infallibility of the Roman Pontiff in the sense defined by the Oecumenical Vatican Council with the same faith as they believe the Incarnation of our Lord.

The general tenor of this encyclical was so extreme and provocative as to give rise to protests, notably that of Archbishop Söderblom. We now know that the encyclical, and some of the circumstances attending it, began to open the eyes of Roman Catholics themselves to the consequences of the policy being pursued. There was a rigidity in it which contrasted with the tone of the encyclicals of Leo XIII, and which made even the Pascendi of Pius X look moderate in comparison. There are Roman Catholic ecumenists of the present day who date their 'conversion' to a new view of ecumenical matters by a reaction from their first reading of 'Mortalium Animos'.

At this same period occurred the double episode of the Anglican (English) attempt to revise its liturgy, with conspicuous lack of success. The Deposited Book, agreed upon by a majority of 517 to 133 in the Church Assembly in 1927 was rejected by the House of Commons by a majority of 238 to 205. A slight revision, to meet certain Protestant objections, was

[1] *Documents on Christian Unity* (ed. G. K. A. Bell), second series, pp. 51–64.

again rejected in 1928 by the House of Commons. The Book
represented twenty years of hesitations, delays and deliberations. Especially in the Eucharist its revisions were in a
'catholic' direction, and would have made relations with
Rome easier. Perhaps because of that very fact, and no doubt
because of suspicions aroused by the Malines conversations, the
project was defeated by the secular arm. Thus the Church of
England was exposed by her own weaknesses, and the possibility of relationships with other bodies retarded. The nature
of her divisions, and her exposure to State intrusion into
purely ecclesiastical affairs, left her a sorry spectacle, open to
the ecclesiastical public gaze. The bishops felt able, however,
to countenance the use of the rejected book without formal
authorisation, and in that unsatisfactory state the English
Church continued for nearly four decades.

The Lambeth Conference of 1930 had a lot of business
before it, not least the matter of church unity. The resolutions
speak for themselves.

31.   The Conference records, with deep thanks to Almighty
God, the signs of a growing movement towards Christian
unity in all parts of the world since the issue of the Appeal to
All Christian People by the Lambeth Conference in 1920. . . .
32.   Believing that our Lord's purpose for His Church will
only be fulfilled when all the separate parts of His Body are
united,. . . . . the Conference expresses its appreciation of the
courage and Christian charity of Cardinal Mercier in
arranging the Malines Conversations, unofficial and not fully
representative of the Churches though they were, and its
regret that by the Encyclical 'Mortalium Animos' members
of the Roman Catholic Church are forbidden to take part in
the World Conference on Faith and Order and other similar
Conferences.

The Report of the Committee on 'the Unity of the Church'
issued a paper on the 'Historic Episcopate'. Another important
feature of this conference, from the point of view of total
Christian union, was the visit of an Orthodox delegation from
the Patriarchate of Constantinople. At the same time the
Oecumenical Patriarch sent to the Archbishop of Canterbury a
letter notifying him of the acceptance by the Patriarch and the

Holy Synod of Constantinople of the thesis that Anglican Orders possess 'the same validity which those of the Roman, Old Catholic and Armenian Churches possess'.[1]

On the last day of the same year (1930) the Pope issued an encyclical ('Casti connubii') on matters to do with Christian matrimony. This was intended to make the Roman Catholic position clear concerning new ideas, new proposed legislation and changing popular practice. It represents once again a rejection of all liberal attitudes towards divorce, birth control and the status of women. As such it can be said to stand as a further source of divergence between the Anglican Churches and the Church of Rome.

The following year, 1931, saw the publication of another encyclical of Piux XI, 'Quadragesimo anno', taking up the social concern of the 'Rerum novarum' of Leo XIII in 1891, in its fortieth anniversary, and developing it in terms of the post-war economic situation. Mutual discussion in this department of moral theology, steering clear of doctrinal fundamentals, was always more possible than in other fields. To some degree this encyclical helped towards mutual understanding, and offset the prejudice created by 'Casti connubii'.

The formation, in 1932, of the Archbishop of Canterbury's Council on Foreign Relations had been suggested many years previously, and had been the subject of much procrastination. Proposed formally by George Bell, then Dean of Canterbury, its first Chairman was Arthur Headlam, Bishop of Gloucester. These two names appear once more in honourable conjunction (Bell succeeded as Chairman and continued in office until after the Second World War). The Council was formed for 'the survey and promotion of the relations of the Church of England with foreign churches' and has continued to do so since. It was ready to hand as the natural channel of communication from the Archbishop to the leaders of other churches and served largely as a pan-Anglican staff for his office as well until those functions were taken over by the appointment of an 'Anglican Executive Officer' for the communion as a whole.

1937 saw the occurrence, deliberately in relation with one another, of the two movements, 'Life and Work' at Oxford and 'Faith and Order' at Edinburgh. Their juxtaposition was

[1] *Documents on Christian Unity* (ed. G. K. A. Bell), first series, pp. 93ff.

calculated, successfully, to lead on to the formation of the World Council of Churches. The proposal was

> that with a view to facilitating the more effective action of the Christian Church in the modern world, the movements known as 'Life and Work' and 'Faith and Order' should be more closely related in a body representative of the Churches and caring for the interests of each movement.[1]

The birth of the World Council was not without its prenatal difficulties. The reasons for Headlam's opposition were first that he was anxious lest the scheme should lead to the creation of a federation of churches, which would do duty in many peoples' minds for the harder project of corporate union which it might even be effective in postponing. And secondly it might lead to a permanent division of the churches into Roman and non-Roman. Opposing Temple's resolution in the Church Assembly (for Anglican participation in such a scheme) Headlam quoted Temple's own assertion that 'If the new organisation were to win the confidence of the churches, it would do something to provide a voice for non-Roman Christendom'.[2] The Assembly brushed aside Headlam's anxieties and followed Temple, who assured them that he and the other promoters had every intention of involving Rome if they possibly could.

So the Church of England was committed to membership of a world-wide association of churches for the purposes of further understanding and common action. In doing so she believed herself to be implementing the Lambeth Appeal and to be taking a step towards ultimate organic union. She was in no way compromising either her doctrines or her ecclesiological integrity, for membership involved neither of these things. This being so, it was hoped that the Church of Rome might herself feel able to be involved. There had been a certain amount of co-operation in the preparatory stages of the Oxford conference, and even one or two unofficial observers. But when it came to an official approach, there was no change of heart. Nevertheless the World Council was determined to keep the Church of Rome informed, and William Temple, then Archbishop of York, Chairman of the Provisional Committee, sent a letter

---

[1] *Documents on Christian Unity* (ed. G. K. A. Bell), third series, p. 292.
[2] *Headlam*, Jasper, p. 282.

containing the following passage to the Cardinal Secretary of State:

> We understand from previous communications which have passed in connexion with World Conferences held under the auspices of those Movements[1] that the Church of Rome would not desire to be formally associated with the Council. But it seems to us required by courtesy that we should inform the Holy See of what is being done. We hope that it may be permissible to exchange information with agencies of the Church of Rome on matters of common interest and that we should have the help from time to time of unofficial consultation with Roman Catholic theologians and scholars. Such sharing in our activities as Roman Catholics may be ready to undertake will be cordially welcomed by us as a manifestation of fellowship in Christ.[2]

To which he got an answer, not direct, but through the Apostolic Delegate to Great Britain:[3] there was no obstacle in the way of consultation with the bishops and the Apostolic Delegate and nothing in the way of an exchange of confidential information with Catholic theologians. Although this failure to achieve full Roman Catholic participation for the start was a disappointment to many, there were those, in the Church of England and elsewhere, who were able to understand her hesitations, since they had their own. Although the Council was to be called the World Council of Churches, there was a minority who would have preferred some other title on the ground that there were some bodies involved who did not even claim to be churches in the sense normally understood in the title. And although the Church of England, for example, did not feel her position as a church to be compromised under such conditions, it was understandable that the Church of Rome should feel that in view of her claims to uniqueness, compromise would be involved in her case. And no-one was expected to deny their doctrines in order to qualify for membership. Later, when the theological consequences of membership were

---

[1] 'Faith and Order' and 'Life and Work'.
[2] 10th February 1939, *Documents on Christian Unity* (ed. G. K. A. Bell), third series, p. 298.
[3] 2nd July 1939. ibid., p. 299.

qualified by a declaration,[1] this position was considerably changed.

The outbreak of the Second World War put a stop to the further progress of setting up the World Council of Churches. In the same year[2] Pius XI died and was succeeded by Cardinal Pacelli as Pius XII. The severities of war swept across the boundaries of nations and churches and had extensive consequences for the future relations of Christians. Church leaders on all sides, and of all allegiances, found themselves making parallel pronouncements for peace, and exhorting Christians of all denominations to join forces at least for the present, to give sanction to the struggle against a common enemy. We find the new Pope saying (though in a different context, that of an encyclical to the Archbishops and Bishops of the U.S.A. on 'True and False Prosperity', November 1939):

> It is only by united and concerted action that we can foster great schemes. For that reason We are impelled by charity to invite here the co-operation of those whom Mother Church mourns as separated from her communion.[3]

In Britain an attempt was made, largely under the inspiration of Bishop Bell, to assemble the heads of the churches for the purpose of invoking divine aid against war and for peace. Bell had already made attempts, following on the Italian invasion of Albania, to get some Christian expression of the principles of international order. With the good will and co-operation of Archbishop David Mathew, auxiliary of Westminster, approaches were made through the Apostolic Delegate to the Pope. But, as Archbishop Lang of Canterbury had predicted, the suggestion was turned down. It was not likely that an Italian pope would feel able at that moment to make declarations so clearly critical of his own country. And it was perhaps naive of an English prelate to suppose that such a proposal would anywhere be well received if originating from Britain, whose past history had such a signal record of territorial acquisition. The Pope did indeed speak up for peace and put out a declaration of five points on Christmas Eve 1939 which was widely accepted. This was implemented in Britain by

[1] Toronto, 1950. [2] 1939.
[3] *Documents on Christian Unity* (ed. G. K. A. Bell), third series, p. 34.

Cardinal Hinsley's formation in 1940 of the Sword of the Spirit movement, which seemed to come straight to meet the enthusiasm which Bell had been trying to create.[1] This event can be taken to be one of the great steps forward towards closer relations with the churches. On 21st December 1940 there appeared in *The Times* a joint letter over the signatures of the Archbishops of Canterbury and York, Cardinal Hinsley and W. M. Armstrong, Moderator of the Free Church Federal Council, setting out the Pope's five peace points of the previous year and the five economic standards of the Oxford 'Life and Work' conference of 1937. These principles were thought of as the ten foundations of a just peace. Their collocation in one charter was a great moment in Roman/Anglican relationships. Cardinal Hinsley felt able to say:

> Our unity must not be in sentiment and in word only, it must be carried into practical measures. Let us have a regular system of consultation and collaboration from now onwards, such as his Lordship the Bishop of Chichester has suggested, to agree on a plan of action which shall win the peace when the din of battle is ended.[2]

Thus there was established this first essential step in restoring mutual understanding, the ability to take common action on matters of social concern. The rest of this episode contained a certain amount of mutual irritation and suspicion as Roman Catholics began to have reservations about common acts of worship, even the public common recital of the Lord's Prayer, which were seen as involving compromise of theological principle. But it had already become clear that although there was an official rigidity in the hierarchy there were considerable signs of thaw in the lower ranks of the clergy and among the laity which were sooner or later bound to affect the whole situation.[3]

---

[1] In e.g. *Christianity and World Order*, G. K. A. Bell, Penguin Books, 1940.
[2] *George Bell, Bishop of Chichester*, R. C. D. Jasper, OUP, 1967, p. 250.
[3] We have evidence of numerous provincial meetings intended to foster this spirit. A most dramatic instance describes a meeting in Norwich held beneath the sound of German bombers in which the protagonists were Canon Frederick Green, Fr. Georges Fressanges (Roman Catholic) and the Revd. Gilbert Laws, president of the Free Church Council.

The Sword of the Spirit movement was only one of many impulses which the war gave to closer co-operation and understanding between the churches. Millions of men crossed national frontiers, found themselves thrown into situations and contacts, both secular and religious, that would never have occurred before. At the end there emerged a generation with a wider vision who were not likely to be easily contented with national outlooks and denominational formulae. The older patterns of things underwent a transformation. Bishop Bell, for example, found himself going to the British zone of occupation in Germany with a committee of British churchmen which included Mgr. Ellis, Roman Catholic Bishop of Nottingham, together visiting Roman Catholics and Evangelicals, and then together sponsoring the German churchmen's case for better treatment before the appropriate authorities in Britain—the same Bishop Ellis who in 1944 had refused even to join in silent prayer at a meeting of the 'Christian Front' in the presence of the Archbishop of York.[1]

Meanwhile Pius XII involved himself in a number of teaching encyclicals. The first of these, 'Mystici Corporis Christi' (1943) contained new teaching on the Church, and its subsequent interpretation became important for ecumenical conversations. By some it was welcomed (or lamented, according to the commentator's point of view) as confirming traditional teaching. And so to a large extent it did. The Church and the Holy Roman Catholic Church were identified. But others found signs of progress in it. For the appearance in an official document of a spiritual conception of the Church as the Mystical Body of Christ was an improvement on previous juridical descriptions. Theologies of the Church as 'a continuation of the Incarnation' can be seen as far back as J. A. Moehler in 1835, but they had had considerable vogue in the years since the First World War and here can be said to have found their imprimatur. This was an easement in traditional definitions and was the beginning of the road towards the Lumen Gentium of the Second Vatican Council. The ecumenical theology of the encyclical, by present-day standards, is

[1] *Cyril Foster Garbett*, Charles Smyth, Hodder & Stoughton, 1959, p. 362.

traditional in general shape, but here too those who want to trace the pedigree of Vatican 2 can begin to do so. For there is an increasing recognition of the importance of Baptism as a bond between Christians, though acts of heresy and schism can effectively separate men from the communion of the Church. Yet Pius XII's advanced Mariology, which was to find later expression in the promulgation of the dogma of the Assumption, can also be seen developing in this encyclical. 'It was she who obtained, through her most effective intercessions, that the Spirit of the Divine Redeemer, should be conferred at the day of Pentecost . . . on the newly-born Church . . . she who reigns together with her Son',[1] etc.

The next encyclical, 'Divino Afflante Spiritu',[2] later in the same year (1943) came part of the way to meet the progress of modern biblical scholarship, by recognising some of its conclusions (such as the existence of literary genres and early streams of tradition in the gospel narratives) and gave some encouragement to loyal biblical scholars. The further encyclical 'Mediator Dei',[3] though calculated from the Vatican point of view to restrain certain dangerous innovators, could at the same time be said to set forth ecumenical understanding by giving official sanction to what was best in the liturgical movement, and particularly in some most welcome teaching about the Eucharist as the external expression of the inner life of the Mystical Body. As this teaching, largely stemming from Roman Catholic sources in the north of Europe, had begun to have influence in other churches, the importance of the encyclical was considerable, and those who were observing straws in the ecumenical wind took hope. A further occurrence in the same year was an Apostolic Constitution on the necessary shape of Holy Orders (Sacramentum Ordinis) which declared in effect that the porrectio instrumentorum (the delivery of the appropriate instruments) was no longer of the essence of ordination. The main point of the document is in the phrase:

> We do declare by our Apostolic authority, and, even though
> it was once rightly determined differently, we ordain: that at

---

[1] Denzinger, *Ench. Symb.* 2291. [2] ibid., 2294.
[3] ibid., 2297.

least in future the delivery of the instruments shall not be necessary for the validity of the Holy Orders of the Diaconate, the Presbyterate and the Episcopate.[1]

This was of importance as illustrating a willingness to research into the fundamentals of the Theology of Orders such as Anglicans had unsuccessfully urged before Apostolicae Curae; and as showing the ability of Rome to go back on established practice in the interests of a remembered principle—both of which circumstances augured well for the future.

Another retreat from previously held positions which was also a concession to modern critical scholarship was the famous letter to the French Primate (Cardinal Suhard) on the nature of the Pentateuch (January 1948). This letter, which was sent with the knowledge and commendation of the Pope, was widely commented on, and represented another step towards understanding with other Christians. The same degree of progress can not, however, be recorded in the case of the inaugural meeting, later in the year, of the World Council of Churches at Amsterdam. Although there had been some hopes that the Church of Rome might at least send observers to the Assembly without prejudice, this was explicitly forbidden, first in an instruction of the Holy Office (Cum compertum, of June 1948) and a pastoral letter of the bishops of Holland (July 1948): and then the point was rubbed well in in the following year in retrospect by a further instruction from the Holy Office (Ecclesia Catholica) of December 1949. It is interesting to note that from the point of view of Vatican administration this matter was handled by the Holy Office—it was for them first and foremost a theological matter: there was no ecumenical or pastoral machinery to cope with such an issue. But it should be remembered that this very same outlook prevailed for the most part in the large Protestant confessional bodies: for them too, as then constituted, the relationship with Rome was primarily a doctrinal matter and, although they were not yet called upon to make executive decisions, their treatises and studies revealed their assumption that doctrinal differences were insuperable obstacles and that progress in ecumenical relationships (as far as Rome was concerned) was

[1] *Documents on Christian Unity* (ed. G. K. A. Bell) fourth series, p. 14.

primarily a matter of the reconciliation of divergent formulae. And the other notable thing about the Roman Catholic official absence from Amsterdam was the extreme attitude of the hierarchy of Holland—in such strong contrast to the liberal attitudes prevailing in that same province at the present time.

Nevertheless prayer was to be made in all the churches of Holland while the Assembly was on, though the form of it was to be the votive mass Ad tollendum schisma (for the removal of schism). The Holy Office instruction of 1949 went so far as to require that bishops

> should be on their guard against those who under false pretexts stress the points on which we agree rather than those on which we disagree. Such an approach may give rise to a dangerous indifferentism. . . .[1]

The year of the inauguration of the World Council was also the year of another Lambeth Conference. This had before it the problems created by the 'Lambeth Quadrilateral' on reunion, as exemplified by the first practical implementation of it in a reunion scheme, that of South India. This new province of the universal church had 'jumped the gun' by declining to wait for the Anglican dioceses to be officially authorised to join: and by involving them in acknowledging ad interim the orders of ministers in other churches not episcopally ordained. The Conference, however, decided, without difficulty, to accept this fait accompli, to recognise the 'departure' of the dioceses concerned from the Anglican communion and to accept, because of an agreed ordinal, the temporary expedient of a pluriform ministry under the newly consecrated bishops. This gave a clear picture of the sort of thing which might happen through Anglican involvement in union schemes. The Anglican Communion would in effect disappear in stages, to be merged in a world-wide fellowship of dioceses in which the faith and ministry as received from the earliest ages would be effectively preserved.

> Here we desire to set before our people a view of what, if it be the will of God, may come to pass. As Anglicans we believe

[1] *Documents on Christian Unity* (ed. G. K. A. Bell), fourth series, p. 23.

that God has entrusted to us in our Communion not only the Catholic faith, but a special service to render to the whole Church. Reunion of any part of our Communion with other denominations in its own area must make the resulting Church no longer simply Anglican, but something more comprehensive. There would be, in every country where there now exist the Anglican Church and others separated from it, a united Church, Catholic and Evangelical, but no longer in the limiting sense of the world Anglican. The Anglican Communion would be merged in a much larger Communion of National or Regional Churches, in full communion with one another, united in all the terms of what is known as the Lambeth Quadrilateral.[1]

The intention was certainly to preserve under a new dispensation the full 'catholic' status of the Anglican Church, and it was assumed that this arrangement would in no way prejudice future relationships with the Church of Rome. A particular insight into the Anglican Communion consciously preparing itself for wider ecumenical contacts can be studied in a document of the Episcopal Church of the U.S.A. issued in 1949 (the statement having been agreed by Lambeth 1948 as 'being in harmony with the Lambeth Quadrilateral') called 'Statement of Faith and Order'. It described itself as being

> 'not a complete formulation of the faith and order of the Church. It is an exposition of the background and chief implications of the Chicago–Lambeth Quadrilateral. It has been formulated, not as a final pronouncement to which literal subscription should be asked, but as a means of assuring a substantial agreement upon the basis of which formal schemes for Church Union with any other Church may later be drawn up.[2]

This represented an openness which the Anglicans saw as a way forward, though there were other churches who accused the Anglican Communion of being vague and uncertain and therefore difficult to grapple with. Time, however, was to show that

[1] Encyclical Letter of Lambeth Conference, 1948.
[2] *Documents on Christian Unity* (ed. G. K. A. Bell), fourth series, p. 136.

such openness was in fact the only possible way in which the union of the Church could ever be accomplished.

The year 1950 brought forth the dogmatic definition of the Assumption of the Blessed Virgin Mary[1] and the encyclical 'Humani Generis'.[2] Of the former it can be said to have been the climax of a long-standing process, based on a widespread insistence from popular devotion. It was no new invention: the definition had been hoped and prayed for by enthusiasts, but also dreaded by well-disposed ecumenists within and without the Roman Church, for decades. Yet the significance of the eventual promulgation of the dogma lay as much in its form as in its content. For it was admitted that the doctrine was founded neither directly in the Scriptures nor in primitive traditions of the undivided church, and the attempts to demonstrate such connections were acutely disputed even by Roman Catholic scholars. Moreover, there was not complete consultation of the bishops, so that the new dogma was based primarily on the ipse dixit of the Pope himself, and appeared to be the extreme embodiment of what many had feared of the definitions of Vatican 1. The discussions and comment at the time made it clear that there was intended to be further escalation of Marian feasts and dogmas to come. The outlook for ecumenical understanding was black indeed. This impression was further intensified by the encyclical 'Humani Generis'.[3] For this document also carried to the extreme point the fears of many (including almost all members of all other Christian bodies) concerning the Roman Church's attitude to truth itself. It continued the succession of the Syllabus of Pius IX and condemned many recent ideas which seemed to be gaining ground among Roman Catholic scholars, as well as among the other churches and thinkers of the non-Christian world. Chief of the errors named was the philosophy of Existentialism, fast gaining ground in the countries of Europe, and in the U.S.A. Catholics who came under its influence tended to deny the importance of tradition and to value experience higher than revelation as a source of doctrine. The most serious of the

[1] Encyclical 'Munificentissimus Deus', 1st November 1950.
[2] 12th August 1950.
[3] *Enchiridion Symbolorum*, Denzinger, 2305.

condemnations was that of the idea that whereas the fundamental truth remained the same its formulation could and
should be changed from age to age: other condemnations were
of the slightest surrender on the question of the veracity and
total inspiration of the Scriptures (not even excepting the
first eleven chapters of Genesis): and of any attempt to deny
that the Mystical Body of Christ and the Roman Catholic
Church were equal and co-terminous. Thus in 1950 there were
officially condemned what were to be some of the foundation
ideas of the Second Vatican Council. The encyclical could be
described as the last gasp of unchecked 'integrism', the charter
of ultramontanism. It is only fair to say that it was received in
many Roman Catholic quarters with dismay and embarrassment.
But it was nevertheless a pronouncement of the highest 'magisterium' of the Church, and many ceased to hope that the future
could bring anything but endless heart-break and disillusion.
This feeling was further reinforced in the following year, 1951,
on the occasion of the commemoration of the fifteenth centenary
of the Council of Chalcedon, which was widely observed.
While many were hoping that this might have been a peaceful
occasion for the united celebration of a truly catholic and
universal doctrine of the Christian faith, promulgated in the
days of the undivided Church, Rome saw fit in the encyclical
'Sempiternus Rex' to refer to the ancient Orthodox churches,
of the patriarchates of Jerusalem, Antioch, Alexandria,
Byzantium, etc. in the words

> How unfortunate that many in Eastern lands for long
> centuries are pitifully cut off from the unity of the Mystical
> Body of Christ, of which the hypostatic union is such a
> shining example. Is it not holy and salutary and according to
> the will of God that all at long last return to the one fold of
> Christ?[1]

Reference to the Orthodox Churches as 'the Greek schism'
was not of course new to those who were familiar with the details
of Roman ecclesiology; but the likening of communion with the
see of Rome to the internal cohesion of the persons of the

---

[1] *Documents on Christian Unity* (ed. G. K. A. Bell), fourth series, p. 27.

Trinity was a new and unwelcome extravagance to many. A dark night of ecumenical estrangement seemed indeed to have set in, and more hopes again were extinguished. But as so often in the history of the Church the majority were mistaken and a new age was about to dawn. Those who had been keeping watch for the signs of a new day were about to be rewarded. And it is to a study of the last hours of their long vigil that we will now turn our attention.

17

PREPARATION FOR VATICAN 2

In the course of the ten years from 1958 to 1968 an immense change took place in church relationships which none can gainsay, which in its general trend is irreversible. The history of this remarkable decade is still too close for those who have lived through it to be able to diagnose its nature with certainty. At the heart of the interpretation of it is the conviction that this was a stirring of the Spirit, moving as He always does over the face of the churches, being allowed at last to break down some of man's inhibitions. Prolonged and intense prayer for union had borne its fruit and worn away some prejudices. If this was the remoter cause, the proximate can certainly be found in the circumstances of the twentieth-century world, both good and bad. The inspirations of the new Renaissance of knowledge, if that is what we are living in, have broken into the Church and in a measure transformed it. That which all the churches feared and resisted in the nineteenth century has turned out to be a blessing to them in the twentieth. And it is to be hoped that in this particular the history of the twentieth century will have shown a trend in a direction opposite to that of the sixteenth. The new knowledge is not this time separating the churches (it need never have done so), but this time is drawing them closer.

The main impact of the new knowledge has been seen in the study and interpretation of the Scriptures, with all its consequences for doctrine. The importance of the impact has been that it has hit all branches of the Church at the same time and has turned them all to face in the same general direction, so that what were collision courses are at least now parallel, and in many cases are already converging. We have already referred to the École Biblique and the Biblical Commission. They can be said to have polarised the study for the Roman Catholic Church, the former encouraging the new discoveries, the latter guarding the tradition. But it was the encyclical 'Divino afflante spiritu', 1942, which can be said to have been a real turning point, since it seemed, for the first time in papal documents at least, to be administering at last a caution to the cautious about too much caution. The new-turned soil of biblical investigation turned up many buried treasures. It re-emphasised the importance of Scripture as the eventual sanction for the truth of doctrine. Its richness as a source of devotion opened the eyes of many to the poverty of the Liturgy and its need for reform. When the urgent need for new forms of apostolate became apparent in great cities and industrial areas, it was in the Scriptures that many of the best Roman apologists found the 'kerugmatic' theology which filled the need for their contemporary world. And when in the decade preceding the Second Vatican Council the whole of the Roman Catholic Church, theologians, liturgists, canonists and pastors, began to feel the need of new definitions of the Church itself, they discovered with relief a common meeting-place in the new-found rewards of maturing biblical scholarship. And they all found themselves meeting on common ground with the Bible-based scholarship of the Anglican and protestant churches, to their mutual delight. For the non-Roman world was already in search of a new basis for truth, for liturgy, for pastoral action and church structures in an age which had been severely shaken by the decline and fall of biblical fundamentalism. Thus in their common search, from opposite directions, the two traditional adversaries in Christendom found themselves on common ground.

It is impossible in this work to trace the course of the whole liturgical, pastoral, theological and philosophical renewal to which the new biblical scholarship gave rise. But we must at least rehearse the names and places and basic ideas which have ensured themselves a place in the future history books of the Church in the course of it. The École Biblique of Jerusalem suggests Lagrange. The rethinking of the liturgy suggests the great northern Benedictine abbeys and the names of Odo

Casel, Guéranger and Lambert Beauduin. The reclamation of the spiritual life in terms of a biblical centred piety we associate with the Belgian abbeys, with Dom Columba Marmion and Marédsous. Any such list should certainly include the name of Louis Bouyer, Oratorian, an ex-Lutheran and prolific writer on all the foregoing subjects. Biblical studies led to the reflection that many of the standard text-books of the fathers were too selective, too inclined to be used as proof-texts as in the worst uses of the Scriptures themselves. So the same urge brought about a new flourishing of objective studies in patristics, which we might associate with the names of de Lubac and Daniélou, s.j. In basic theology and the rethinking of foundations, in close association with all other aspects of the revival, Jungmann and K. Rahner are the names which had most penetrated into England before the Vatican Council; in the case of the theology of the Church in all its forms that of Yves Congar, Dominican of Le Saulchoir; and in studies leading straight to the heart of the ecumenical problem of Maurice Villain, and Père Dumont of the Istina House in Paris. Anglicans emerging from the shadow of the war were first made conscious that 'there was something going on in France' by the writings of the Abbé Godin and Père Michonneau, by the productions of the Centre Pastorale Liturgique and in particular the psalms of Père Gelineau. To Fr. Gabriel Hebert of Kelham should go the chief credit on the Anglican side of importing into England, and splendidly reinterpreting, some of the great liturgical insights of the continental Roman Church. His writings formed the background and charter of the Parish and People Movement in the Church of England, founded by Henry de Candole[1] and Kenneth Packard.[2] This movement came about partly by spontaneous combustion and was partly also a reflection of and response to the inspiring pastoral and liturgical revival on the continent.

Part of the same upsurging movement, but slightly later in its development, was the theological work of those who set out to confront the new hostile forces of atheism and nihilism which threatened France in particular at its heart. Here again the

[1] Bishop Suffragan of Knaresborough 1949.
[2] Vicar of Sandford St. Martin 1961; Honorary Canon of Christ Church, Oxford, 1965.

glory of the catholic revival lay in its new ability to accept the new knowledge, without fears or condemnations, to sift it, to compare it with authentic sources and then to put out against it a new Christian apologetic. Much of the groundwork for this activity had been done by earlier pioneers in the field of basic theology. In 1941 the Holy Office put on the index a book of Fr. Chenu, like Yves Congar a Dominican of Le Saulchoir, setting out a programme for theological studies which seemed in many ways to by-pass the usual Thomistic pattern.[1] As far back as 1836 Jungmann had published a work which showed that basic theology was going to be exposed to modern scientific disciplines.[2] Another volume which had a wide influence, and which was certainly being read in Anglican circles in the years after the war, was *Le Pélerinage aux Sources* by Lanza del Vasto.[3] The author well remembers the impact of this book and of the first essays of Teilhard de Chardin which were circulated in England long before his works were translated after his death. Another writer whose works on this general subject crossed the English Channel was Gustave Thils, whose *Théologie des Réalités Terrestres*[4] found much acceptance among Anglican readers. It was evident at the time that here was a powerful movement towards theological restatement in a contemporary context which must sooner or later be effective in undermining the exclusive claims of Thomism to be the only philosophical basis of Roman Catholicism. Biology, anthropology, psychology and physiology were going to be allowed to have their say alongside traditional interpretations of revelation and were going to command an authority of their own.

One of the novel ways in which the Church of Rome was to be seen effectively confronting the contemporary world was in the phenomena of the Mission de France and the priest-workers. This latter experiment found its origin in war-time France under Cardinal Suhard, in Paris, from as early as 1941. It ran into certain difficulties at the edges, where the loyalties of some priests were at risk as against their sympathies with extreme Marxist politics. Pius XII took advantage of that situation to inhibit the independence of many of the workers; but it is well

[1] *Une École de Théologie: le Saulchoir.*
[2] *The Good News yesterday and today.*
[3] Paris, 1943.   [4] Vol. I, Paris, 1946; Vol. II, 1949.

to remember that the movement was suppressed by John XXIII,[1] and that it was Paul VI who eventually restored them to the position which they now enjoy. The whole movement of pastoral apostolate which these two experiments represent attracted much attention in England, was the subject of many papers and studies and was the cause of many visits across the Channel by Anglicans to the seminaries of Pontigny and Limoges. The fact that the Roman Catholic brethren of France and the other northern European countries were producing works of this nature opened the eyes of many Anglicans to a situation which was entirely new to them, which loosened many inhibitions and prejudices and opened up attractive ecumenical prospects. This new experience drew the attention of many to the existence of a natural fellow-feeling between the Church of England and the Roman Church in France due not so much to the 'Gallicanism' of former centuries as to the fact that by the mid-twentieth century they were both in the same position vis-à-vis their respective national populations. They had both largely 'lost out' to the eroding forces of secularism and were struggling with the same burden of dead-weight nominal membership. This made a contrast with the case of the Roman community in England, a tight-knit minority taking good care of its integrity and even accustomed to have to fight for its rights.

One of the clearest signs of change in the Church on the continent, as observed from across the English Channel, was the new attitude of Roman Catholics to other Christians. This was firmly based upon the developing theology of the Church, as expounded by Maurice Villian and Yves Congar, already mentioned. The English Church had already been exploiting to the full the possibilities of new contacts and new friendships based on these common experiences and ideas. The Council on Foreign Relations had fostered such contacts from the beginning, but there had been a certain degree of caution about its activities in this respect, for three main reasons: first that the Church of England as a whole would have been reluctant to commit itself to a change in its attitudes without some assurance that they were reciprocal; second that too much publicity for any such activity would be likely to trigger off the

---

[1] See *Documentation Catholique*, No. 1 313, 1959.

phobias of the party in the Church who still didn't want dealings with Rome at any price; and thirdly that the Roman Catholic hierarchy in England would have shown itself distinctly resentful of any relations with Rome which were not channelled through itself. There was therefore no alternative at that stage to the development of relations and contacts by surreptitious means. And this opportunity Bishop George Bell exploited actively through several decades. He encouraged a network of unofficial 'agents', to keep him continually and systematically informed about the developments of Roman Catholic (and of course of all other Christian) life in other parts. And so it was that he was always in possession of a general background picture of what was going on, which no doubt formed the basis of the advice which he gave primarily to the Archbishop of Canterbury and such other people as would benefit by receiving it. This would perhaps be one of the reasons for the undoubted fact that when the possibilities for direct official contacts opened up in the time of Pope John XXIII, the Church of England was the first of the churches to respond to them.

But Bishop Bell and his emissaries were only part of a great company of unofficial travellers, well-wishers and enthusiasts who in the course of the first half of the twentieth century made the eventual achievements possible. He would be a rash character who would undertake to record the list, still less to award a primacy either of time or honour to those who laboured, and no such effort can be undertaken here. Even to select a few names and episodes for mention is to court disaster, but that at least must be attempted. A fuller, but by no means complete, account of these contacts is to be found in the Volume *Anglican Initiatives in Christian Unity*[1] from which some of the episodes in this chapter are drawn.

Gradually individual contacts began to crystallise into group discussions. One of the earliest of these originated in 1936 with the Dominican Order under the aegis of Fr. Henry St. John, himself a migrant from the Church of England. These 'Laxton' conversations took place over a number of years, mainly with members of the Society of the Sacred Mission, Kelham, as the Anglican representatives. These had official approval of

[1] Lectures delivered in Lambeth Palace Library, 1966, SPCK.

their orders on both sides;[1] and the Roman Catholics had the approval of their bishop. In the following year Dr. Leonard Hodgson[2] met Fr. M. Bévenot, s.j. at the Edinburgh Faith and Order Conference. Fr. Bévenot was also put in touch with the Anglican Benedictine Gregory Dix of Nashdom, as a result of the Abbot of Nashdom meeting Bernard Leeming, s.j. in Rome. From these contacts stemmed another series of meetings, this time involving, among others, Abbot Christopher Butler, o.s.b. on the Roman side and for the Anglicans Fr. Hebert of Kelham again, Frs. Geoffrey Curtis, H. E. Symonds, d.d. and Lionel Thornton, d.d. of Mirfield, and Dr. E. L. Mascall. They met at Mirfield in the years leading up to the Second World War. Active pursuit of better understanding was naturally impeded by the outbreak of war, though the war itself was providing international stimulus sufficient to ensure resumption of talks once the hostilities had ceased. Movements and tendencies in all the countries of northern Europe soon showed that the fermentation had increased during the war to a degree that must soon boil over. Even a godly impatience was observable among those who were concerned with the unity of Christendom. It was a matter of seeking for the kind of contacts which would provoke, not suspicion or reaction as some had done in the past, but real basic understanding.

A key figure in such promotions was Fr. Charles Boyer, s.j., professor at the Gregorian University in Rome. Having himself been present at the inauguration of the World Council of Churches in Amsterdam in 1948[3] he believed that the Church of Rome should not ignore the new movement which it represented. Accordingly he allowed himself to be a channel and an agent for such messages and contacts as could use him. In 1949 alone we find that he was contacted by Bishop Stephen Neill,[4] Herbert Waddams[5] and Bishop Bell of Chichester. In the same year Leonard Prestige[6] visited Rome with the full approval

---

[1] Gabriel Hebert and Stephen Bedale, and Bro. George Every. Dominicans were Thomas Gilby, Victor White and Gerald Vann.

[2] Regius Professor of Divinity at Oxford.

[3] As a member of the Press.

[4] Formerly of Tinnevelly, S. India.

[5] Secretary of the Council on Foreign Relations. Later Canon of Canterbury.

[6] d.d., later Canon of St. Paul's.

of the Archbishop of Canterbury and with the encouragement of Mgr. David Mathew, Auxiliary of Westminister, whose concern in these matters was then perhaps unique among the Roman Catholic hierarchy in England. Prestige's visit was particularly important in that it represented the beginning of basic 'soundings' about the possibility of conversations. Prestige kept a diary[1] of his visits, which might well be published. Armed with David Mathew's introduction and encouraged all the time by the good offices of Fr. A. Tindal-Atkinson, O.P. (another 'migrant' from the Church of England), Prestige did the rounds of seminaries and offices in Rome. He saw Cardinal Tisserant and eventually Mgr. Montini, to whom he presented a copy of his 'personal memorandum' setting out what he thought should be the main principles of any future contacts. These were broadly that

> there should not at present be any question of reunion schemes or public demonstrations; that we must not discuss conclusions but examine the reasons why different conclusions are reached—that is where the real crux lies—for different routes lead to different places, and that we should do all that was possible in the way of 'cooperativeness' on practical issues without compromising our loyalties to our respective churches

and to discourage authoritatively all expressions of ill will. Prestige records that Montini was clearly anxious for contacts on these lines to begin and to continue. Considerable discussion ensued as to whether such contacts should be made in England alone, or on the continent. The conclusion seems to have been that whereas they could not (nor should they) be entirely independent of the English scene, most of the contacts would have to be made outside England. Prestige seems to have taken for granted that on a vacancy in the see of Westminster Archbishop Mathew would succeed, and that better relationships would then obtain in England. But neither of these hopes was fulfilled, and the beginnings of the ensuing 'dialogue' were on the continent of Europe, with teams led by Prestige and Boyer. When Prestige died prematurely in 1955 the conversations

[1] Thanks are due to his daughter and son-in-law, the Revd. Robert and Mrs. Collier, for their loan of this interesting document.

were continued on the Anglican side by Dr. A. R. Vidler[1] and
Dr. J. N. D. Kelly.[2] The Roman Catholic team was still
largely French, though Frs. B. Leeming, s.j. and M. Bévenot,
s.j. were included in it. Participants in these discussions have
left the impression that the English Roman Catholic hierarchy
were slightly uncomfortable about them, which is corroborated
by the fact that in 1962 Archbishop Heenan arranged for them
to meet at Worth with an almost entirely English team.[3] But
these contacts were gently preparing the ground for later
advances. Prestige had perhaps not sufficiently stressed that the
Anglican Communion was larger than the Church of England,
though he did suggest (apparently in vain) that, in order to
avoid any 'repetition of Malines' there should be evangelical
representation in every Anglican team. In recording the progress of these important preliminary talks we should note that
the press seemed to do its best to misrepresent Prestige's initial
visit by suggesting, with no authority at all, that it was for the
purpose of starting reunion negotiations, thus ensuring that the
whole affair was surrounded by a maximum of suspicion and
ill will. But an official denial was eventually published and the
bona fides of the visit was accepted by all reasonable people.

A particularly fruitful source of contacts was the religious
orders, where there existed a ready natural sympathy, and no
record of these times would be complete unless it contained a
tribute to them. Besides those whose names have already been
mentioned we should perhaps refer to that of Dom Benedict
Ley of Nashdom, whose ecumenical activities in France so far
back as 1936 are an interesting document of such contacts.[4] He
had stood by the grave of Couturier,[5] and had made an important visit to Niederaltaich (home of the Una Sancta
movement) in 1954.[6]

Behind and beneath all these contacts, discussions and
movements lay the prayers of many souls in many places.
Two items stand out from the pages of this story and demand
attention. The first is the Week of Prayer for Christian Unity

[1] D.D., LITT.D., Dean of King's College, Cambridge, 1956–1967.
[2] D.D. Principal of St. Edmund Hall, Oxford, 1951–1973.
[3] Anglicans were H. Balmforth, Benedict Green, c.r. and Martin Rear-
don.
[4] *Laudate*, Quarterly Review of Nashdom for September 1936.
[5] *Nashdom Abbey Record*, December 1954.   [6] Ibid., December 1955.

and the second the life and work of one man, the Abbé Paul
Couturier. The Week of Prayer tried to give shape to the
aspirations of many that the Churches should come forward and
pray together in public about what many of their members
longed for in private. Its origins can be traced back at least to the
'Church Unity Octave' conceived by two Anglicans, the Revd.
Spencer Jones, and the founder of an American Franciscan
Society (the Revd. Lewis Thomas Wattson). The Octave was
first observed at the latter's friary at Graymoor in 1908. But in
its earliest days it drew its enthusiasm on the Anglican side
almost exclusively from among those who seemed able to remain
in the Anglican Communion while accepting all the 'papal
claims' of the Church of Rome. Wattson and the Graymoor
friars eventually went over to the Roman Church, and the
movement became thereby even less likely to secure the interest
of the general company of Anglicans. In the course of the
Octave's observance in Lyons it attracted the attention of a
humble schoolmaster named Paul Couturier, who immediately
realised that if the observance was ever to be universally
effective it must be given a broader—in effect a more 'catholic'
basis, which he proceeded to do. He acknowledged that his
'Universal Week of Prayer' owed its inspiration to the Octave,
but he wrote to Spencer Jones that

> You know how much I desire the increasing success of the
> Church Unity Octave, which is your work. . . . But I have
> the profound conviction of the absolute necessity of the
> Universal Prayer.[1]

The form which the Unity Octave had assumed not unnaturally gave rise even in official circles in England to alarm,
for it seemed that the impression was being given in France
that the basis of the Octave was widely acceptable to Anglicans.
The Council on Foreign Relations was eventually presented
with a memorandum by its secretary Philip Usher which
suggested that

> if the Octave in this country were reorganised on the lines of
> the French movement under Père Couturier the present

---

[1] *Paul Couturier and Unity in Christ*, Fr. Geoffrey Curtis, c.r., SCM Press,
1964, pp. 63–4.

anxiety of the Council on Foreign Relations as to the impression created abroad would be largely removed.[1]

And so it proved to be.

The Abbé had made many visits to England and had gone to some trouble to make himself familiar with the teachings and practices of the English Church. Becoming soon aware that the Anglican 'papalists' were a very small minority even of the following of the Tractarians he had gone in search of a broader understanding of the Anglican position. He met Archbishop Temple and was impressed and encouraged by the encounter. Most of Couturier's contacts in England were fostered and arranged by the religious communities, through Dom Benedict Ley and Dom Gregory Dix at Nashdom, through Fr. Curtis at Mirfield, Fr. Kelly at Kelham, and Fr. O'Brien at Cowley. Fr. Curtis believes that it was through the last-named that Couturier eventually came to meet the Archbishop of Canterbury (Lang), and so to make an effective friendship which lasted over a number of years. The Universal Week started expanding in the years before the 1939–1945 war, and continued to do so afterwards. It has been outstandingly effective not only in bringing the concept of Church unity before the Church of England in general, but also in facing those members of the protestant churches who needed it up to the challenge of including the Roman two-thirds of Christendom in their vision of unity. When Couturier died in 1956 his work lived after him, and the Week of Prayer, then under the guidance of Fr. Pierre Michalon, continued to be the mainstay of the movement towards better understanding. From 1958 onwards the preparation for the Week was undertaken in conjunction with the World Council, and from then on could be said to be truly ecumenical.

The foregoing is a brief survey of the general trends in church life which prepared the way for change in the first half of the twentieth century. A large-scale revival of biblical studies, new departures in pastoral and liturgical reform, a new orientation of theological thinking away from scholasticism towards an empirical approach to the new knowledge, and an intense aspiration, based deep in prayer, for a reform of the Church

[1] *Ninth Annual Report*, 1938.

which would include a new attitude to other Christians. Yet although this added up to considerable progress, it would have been rash even in 1950 to have predicted with certainty any dramatic change. 1950, after all, was the year of the Assumption doctrine, a dissuader indeed for reformers and ecumenical enthusiasts. The Vatican departmental heads were still in strong control of the Roman Church in all her provinces, and could still reach out to apprehend and to admonish the daring innovators. And it had become a widely accepted principle that contacts and relationships, to be effective, must be at a high official level, must carry confidence and must have wide popular support to have hope of success. Nevertheless, from the hindsight which we now enjoy, it is possible to trace a number of developments in the decade of the '50s which might have indicated that the explosion might not be long in coming. On the Roman side there can be traced a progressive willingness to come closer, and the level at which contacts seemed to be able to be made gradually rose higher. In 1950 Roman Catholic scholars were able to operate freely in the new inter-church Old Testament Society. That permission carried over soon afterwards to New Testament Studies. In 1952 there took place the first of the International Patristic Conferences organised by Professor Cross in Oxford, with full Roman participation. In the same year two Dutch priests Fr. Frans Thijssen and Fr. (later Cardinal) Willebrands set up the Conférence Catholique pour les questions écumeniques, and in doing so were allowed direct contact with the World Council of Churches. Partly as a result of this new creation catholics were able to have a share in the preparation for the Second Assembly of the World Council of Churches at Evanston in 1954, and Fr. Yves Congar was even able to prepare a paper for it. The new attitude which was gradually beginning to show itself at a high level had become possible since the findings of the Toronto Conference on the nature of participation had removed some of the more serious scruples of the more rigid Roman ecclesiologists. As Pius XII grew older there was one figure in the Vatican whose attitudes attracted attention in the outside world, Mgr. G.-B. Montini, to whom reference has already been made above.[1] When Pius seemed unwilling to let the Office of Secretary of

[1] See p. 303.

State out of his own hands two men, opposites in temperament and ecclesiastical outlook, had been obliged to shoulder the main burden of administration. Mgr. Tardini was the other. Montini was soon moved to be Archbishop of Milan, and Tardini reigned alone. In 1955 Montini received a visit from Bishop George Bell, and each took an immediate liking to the other. Bell observed of Montini that

> I was never more impressed, even by my friends among catholic bishops in the north of Europe, than by that man's desire to learn.[1]

On another occasion Bell reported Montini as having said that

> 'although the Holy Father had often urged collaboration between catholics and the separated brethren, he had never indicated how this should be done. . .' He was like a curate being discreetly critical of his Vicar.[2]

In the January Unity Octave of the same year as Bishop Bell's visit (1955) Montini had written, of the problem of the unity of Christendom, that it

> appears more evident in our day . . . in consideration of the effort of the Ecumenical Movement to federate into some unitive form the many separate groups of differing Christian confessions; because of the overcoming of historical motives which originally determined the hurtful separations; in view of the increased desire among Catholics to seek out their distant brethren. . . .[3]

In the following year (1956) Archbishop Montini received at Milan a delegation (arranged by Bishop Bell) of four Anglican priests and a layman[4] who stayed with him some ten days. The object of the exercise was not discussions of controversial topics but the exchange of basic information. The group showed books and photographs and answered endless questions. The

---

[1] Privately to the author.   [2] *George Bell*, R. G. D. Jasper, p. 337.
[3] Pastoral letter to diocese of Milan. *Documents on Christian Unity* (ed. G. K. A. Bell), fourth series, pp. 31–2.
[4] J. C. Dickinson, C. C. W. James, C. L. Gage-Brown and the author. C. J. A. Hickling was the layman. The delegation should have been headed by J. R. H. Moorman (later Bishop of Ripon), who was prevented from attending.

Archbishop was clearly trying to build up for himself a picture of other Christians on a basis of what they said about themselves. Fr. Boyer, s.j. was present on the Roman side, as was Mgr. Sergei Pignedoli, later Secretary of Propaganda Fide and Cardinal. Though the meetings were clandestine in the extreme they were 'leaked' to a few people in England at least, where those who heard about them were glad to learn of a new type of ecumenical encounter 'ultra montes'.

Another encouraging event was the holding of a second 'World Congress for the Lay Apostolate' in Rome in October 1957 which, though conducted under the total surveillance of the Vatican, was able to enunciate what looked like some new principles of catholic ecumenism:

1. Genuine concern for the scandal of separated Christians.
2. Prayer—especially intensive supplication during the January week of prayer.
3. Becoming and keeping well informed on the numerous aspects of the problem of unity.
4. Being in a position to inform others of the Catholic standpoint so as to obviate the major obstacle presented by misunderstanding and prejudice, etc. etc.[1]

Although such events as these quickened the expectations of those who had faith, there was a good deal of scepticism in official quarters that anything of importance might happen at all in the immediate future in Anglican/Roman Catholic relations. A very general view was, regarding the Church of Rome, that 'plus ça change, plus c'est la même chose'. It would not be difficult to make quotations from those who are now in the van of such relationships, who then were sceptics, on both sides of the fence. But there were some who were ready to exploit such opportunities of improving the situation as presented themselves. It is fair to say that officially the Anglican Communion stood ready to meet the slightest suggestion that relationships should be resumed. The Lambeth Conference of 1948 had made its contribution by reasserting its concern with total reunion, and by repeating its determination not to let the Anglican Communion and its distinctive principles

[1] Quoted in *The Churches and Christian Unity*, R. J. W. Bevan, OUP, 1963, p. 71.

disappear into a pan-protestant federation—which was another way of saying that it always had an eye on the possibility of eventual contacts with Rome.

> It would be . . . a betrayal [the Conference said] of our trust before God, if the Anglican Communion were to allow itself to be dispersed before its particular work was done.[1]

And most people understood what was meant.

The instruction Ecclesia Catholica of 1949[2] and the encyclical 'Humani Generis' of 1950[3] had both been mainly dissuasives, but the Lambeth Conference of 1958 decided to make the very most of what little encouragement there was in both of them. The published Report illustrated exactly both the realism and the hopefulness of the Anglican position:

> The observance of the Universal Week of Prayer for Christian Unity (18 to 25 January) becomes wider every year in England, on the Continent of Europe, and in some other parts of the world, with much official Roman Catholic approval. The form of this prayer which is most to be welcomed, and is in fact widespread, is that initiated by the late Abbé Couturier, that the unity of Christians may be achieved as our Lord wills and by the means that he wills. The simultaneous observances of this Week by Roman Catholics and by many members of other Churches are a valuable contribution to the efforts towards unity.

> It is recognised that there will be occasions when Anglicans must adopt a critical attitude towards Roman Catholic utterances or policies when issues such as those concerning the meaning and application of the principle of religious freedom, or the valid claims of Anglicanism, are at stake. Nevertheless we feel certain that Anglicans for their part, while striving at all times for the promotion of truth, frankness, and just dealing between Christians, will wish to do all in their power to secure understanding with Roman Catholics, as part of their efforts to promote peace and unity among all Christian people.[4]

[1] *Report of Lambeth Conference*, 1948, encyclical letter, Part 1, p. 23.
[2] See p. 310 above.   [3] See p. 292 above.
[4] *Report of Lambeth Conference*, 1958, Part 2, p. 49.

It should be remembered that the Chairman of the Conferences of 1948 and 1958 was Dr. Geoffrey Fisher, Archbishop of Canterbury from 1945–1961. He was a zealous promoter of closer relationships with the Methodist Church in England in particular, and with other non-Roman churches in other countries. Not being himself among the first rank of zealots for resuming relationships with Rome, it is all the more to his credit that he faithfully kept the goal of total union including Rome within his target of ambition. It was with the full knowledge and approval of Archbishop Fisher that Bishop Bell went in 1958, before the Lambeth Conference, to pay a visit to Pope Pius XII, then in his last year. He described the interview as 'necessarily brief, but substantial and sympathetic'.[1] In his visit to the Secretariat of State on this occasion it is clear that Bell was able to clear up certain misconceptions in the mind of curial officials concerning the ecumenical intentions of both the Lambeth Conference and the World Council of Churches.[2] The importance of this visit should be rated high. It was perhaps the first really high-level contact which we are able to record so close in to the Vatican, for Bell's influence in the subsequent session of the Lambeth Conference was incalculable. One of the chief sponsors of Bell's visit was Mgr. Cardinale, then an official in the Secretariat of State, whose name should be noted in this regard, for he was the means of introducing many Anglicans into contact with Vatican officials. He has stated that one of his first experiences of wide ecumenical contacts was in the company of the Anglican Archdeacon in Egypt,[3] who with his bishop Llewellyn Gwynne staged an annual gathering of many Christian churches in the Anglican Cathedral in Cairo. Cardinale later became Apostolic Delegate in Great Britain and Nuncio in Belgium. Many influences, of various kinds, had thus been concentrated on the ecclesiastical destinies of the year 1958. In the autumn of that year occurred an event which was destined to usher in for the Church of Rome, and thereby for the rest of Christendom, a new era of life. On the death of Pius XII the conclave elected in his place Cardinal Angelo Roncalli, who took the title of Pope John XXIII.

His election entirely changed the ecclesiastical scene. The

[1] See *George Bell*, R. C. D. Jasper, p. 380.   [2] ibid.
[3] G. F. Allen, later Bishop of Derby.

enigma of his influence has been discussed in many works. He was not a revolutionary, and in most senses of the word not even a liberal. Archbishop (later Cardinal) Heenan wrote of him as:

> the old-fashioned 'garden of the soul' type of catholic. He read his Faber and no doubt regularly recited the Litany of the Sacred Heart. He was not an original thinker. . . . His great achievement was to teach the world of the twentieth century how small is hatred and how great is love. . . . I doubt if he had read many books of contemporary theologians.[1]

He astounded the author by his lack of reliable information about the Church of England: yet he was able to point out with obvious affection the view of the spire of the Anglican Church of All Saints as seen from his window in the Vatican. He was able to pick up, as it were on his spiritual antennae, the Holy Spirit's promptings which led to the Council: but then, in strange contrast, he appointed to its direction quite a number of men who were out of sympathy with his own high hopes for it, and who not infrequently came near to wrecking it. He hoped for a new and simplified expression of the Church's dogma, yet was able almost on the eve of the Council to sign the encyclical 'Veterum Sapientia',[2] insisting that theology must be taught in Latin in all the seminaries of the world. He opened the Council to the presence of observers from the 'separated brethren', yet went himself to dedicate the Council at the shrine of Our Lady of Loreto, of all shrines and devotions the least likely to gain the respect, let alone the devotion, of non-Roman Christians. It is perhaps a pity that the press and the other media of communication have built up the figure of Pope John to a stature which it is not able to bear, all the more because they have made the double error of contrasting it with that of Pope Paul VI to the latter's disadvantage. This has given the unfortunate popular impression that whereas all was sweetness and progress, as far as relationships were concerned, in Pope John's day, the whole climate cooled off in Pope Paul's time. Comparisons are impossible between two such different men. The impression from outside the Church of Rome must certainly be that whereas Pope John's ingenuousness stumbled upon the vision

[1] *Westminster Cathedral Journal*, July 1964.　　　[2] February 1962.

of a new Council and gave it life and breath, it was Pope Paul who guided and weaned it with a sagacity which Pope John would never have commanded. The two men should be held in equally high esteem, but for different reasons.

Pope John had had a most useful apprenticeship, from the point of view of getting to know other Christians, in the papal diplomatic service in Bulgaria, Greece, Turkey and France. Even so it is surprising that he hadn't achieved a deeper understanding of the Orthodox churches of Eastern Christendom. He seemed even in his days as Pope to suppose that if only the Church of Rome would turn eastwards towards them in brotherly affection, they would soon come safely back into the one fold which they had left. No greater illusion can be cherished. We have already referred to the schooling he had had in youth with Catholic Action in the days of the Bishop of Bergamo, Radini-Tedeschi, to whom he was first apprenticed.[1] This must have stirred his splendid pastoral sensitivities into believing that a change was necessary in Vatican political sympathies. His time in restless, largely de-Christianised, France after the Second World War must have introduced him to the agonies of young theologians who were trying to bring theology to grips with the insights of the modern world and yet were in constant repression from the Vatican. From this situation he almost certainly conceived the need for 'aggiornamento', the restatement in the language and symbols of twentieth-century man of the ancient immutable faith. And this could only be accomplished in a Council. So a Council there had to be.

Within the first year of his pontificate Pope John staggered the world by announcing a three-fold project, of a Diocesan Synod for the diocese of Rome, an 'Ecumenical Council of the Universal Church' and the revision of the Code of Canon Law. This intention was first privately announced to a gathering of Cardinals.[2] In the first public notice of it there appeared a phrase which caught the bewildered attention of many people throughout the world, that the Council would contain, among other proposals:

[1] See p. 270 above.
[2] On the feast of the Conversion of St. Paul, 25th January 1959, in St. Paul's Outside the Walls.

an invitation to the separated communities to search for that Unity towards which so many souls aspire.[1]

This was of course no more than a pastoral and sympathetic expression of Pope John's loving but quite traditionalist conception of the Church's unity, which was that of unconditional return to the one and only Church of Christ. The Pope made the point more explicitly when in the following year (Whitsun 1960) he issued a Motu Proprio entitled 'Superno Dei Nutu', in which he said:

A new hope arises that those who rejoice in the name of Christians, but are nevertheless separated from this apostolic see, hearing the voice of the divine Shepherd, may be able to make their way into the one Church of Christ.

There was a similar form of expression in the previous encyclical 'Ad Petri Cathedram'[2] in which he had expressed the hope that the whole triple 'event' would amount to:

a vision which those who are separated . . . may regard as a gentle invitation to seek and to follow that unity which Jesus Christ implored from his heavenly Father with such fervent prayers.

'Old hands' in relations with the Church of Rome were not unduly impressed with these expressions, as merely expressing the old rigidities in a politer form; but the world press lost itself for once in enthusiasm for the possibilities thus opened up, so much so that on the day following the issue of 'Ad Petri Cathedram' the Pope felt obliged to say:

the announcement of the Ecumenical Council has given rise everywhere to most fervent enthusiasm and interest, although there are not wanting suppositions and conjectures which do not correspond with the reality.[3]

Yet although all such expressions played into the hands of pessimists in both camps, there was undoubtedly a charismatic quality about Pope John's conception of the Council which quickly broke through the barriers of prejudice and faithlessness

---

[1] *Osservatore Romano*, 26th January 1959.   29th June, 1959.
[3] Speech to Preparatory Commission, 30th June 1959.

and set it firmly in the centre of ecclesiastical interest all over the world. The agreeable personality of this one man, as reported by the world press, had the immediate consequence that a large majority of Christians everywhere realised that this was their concern. The Roman Catholic Church was in their orbit. The secretary of the World Council of Churches expressed this mood when he said of the forthcoming Council 'Nostra res agitur' (This concerns us).[1]

The preparations for the Council were unpromising in the extreme. Pope John's selection of members of the respective commissions seemed to fall, with one notable exception, on men of conservative opinions. The rumour spread that 'the old guard' (i.e. reactionary elements in the Vatican, and expecially in the Holy Office) were trying to delay the start of the Council, yet behind all the news the inspiring personality of the Pope twinkled and sparkled. Stories began to circulate. It was said, for example, that when Cardinal Tardini reported that they couldn't possibly start the Council in 1963, Pope John said 'Very well, then, we'll have to start in 1962'. But one feature of the preparations had enough promise in it to counterbalance the gloom induced by all the rest, which was the formation in 1960 of the new Secretariat for the Promotion of Unity among Christians, and the appointment as its President of Fr. (later Cardinal) Augustin Bea, the Jesuit head of the Biblical Institute, and of Mgr. Jan Willebrands as Secretary. This gave institutional form at once to the intentions for unity, made a focus for the correspondence and contacts which immediately sprang up between the Church of Rome and the 'separated brethren'. The reactions of the non-Roman world were expectant but cautious. Yet to the Church of England goes the credit of making the first real commitment. Pope John had pledged the Church of Rome to a Council without full canonical consultation of the college of cardinals. Archbishop Fisher of Canterbury made a response to the Pope's gesture by arranging to call upon him in person, also without full consultation of his advisers. This was the first visit of an Archbishop of Canterbury to a Pope since that of Archbishop Arundel.[2] Dr. Fisher called on the Pope[3] on the way back from

[1] See General Secretary's Report, MRCC (Paris), p. 79.
[2] In 1397.
[3] 3rd December 1960.

a visit to the Patriarchs of Jerusalem and Constantinople, no doubt to assure any suspicious Anglicans that he had not lost his sense of priorities. The meeting was historic and has been described elsewhere. Both prelates were impressed with each other's directness and sincerity. Dr. Fisher records that he was able to protest against the suggestion that the restoration of unity represented a return to the Church, or that protestants 'had added anything to the Lord's Prayer'. But he felt able quickly to trust himself to so transparently good and holy a man. The Secretariat of State had done its best to discourage the visit of the Archbishop and had tried to give it the minimum of publicity. There was a brief notice in the *Osservatore Romano* that 'Dr. Geoffrey Francis Fisher [sic] had an audience with His Holiness'. Cardinal Tardini had laid down four conditions for the Archbishop's visit and sent them to H.M. Minister to the Holy See, Sir Peter Scarlett. They were that there should be no photographs of the Archbishop with the Pope, that the Archbishop was not to see Cardinal Bea, that there was to be no press release after the visit, and that the Minister was not to invite any Vatican official to meet the Archbishop at his house.[1] It is important to record this extraordinary state of affairs for two reasons: first as illustrating by contrast how far things had developed by the time Archbishop Ramsey visited Paul VI in 1966, and also as showing how very strong even in 1959 was the determination in the highest Vatican circles to keep other Christians at a distance. Many, probably most, Roman Catholics who read of this state of affairs later were scandalised; yet it was Pope John who appointed Tardini both Cardinal and Secretary of State.

The Pope defeated the machinations of his Secretary of State and ordered that Cardinal Bea, who of course was keen to do so, should meet the Archbishop. As a result of this encounter the Archbishop immediately decided, with the agreement of Cardinal Bea and his Secretariat, to send a representative or 'liaison' to live in Rome to study the preparations for the Council, and to be available to offer any information that might be asked for about Anglican reactions to the problems which arose. Thus in one dramatic stroke three of the damaging

---

[1] See *Fisher of Lambeth*, William Purcell, Hodder & Stoughton, 1969 p. 281.

obstacles to relationships between the Anglican Church and the Church of the Apostolic See of Rome were swept away. The long centuries of total official separation had come to an end and a channel of communication was set up. The principle was automatically established that an exchange of accurate official information at the highest level must be a preliminary to any new relationships; and also it was tacitly assumed by both sides that the situation demanded much more than the exchange of theological ideas. In the new Secretariat for Unity, as at Lambeth, it was made clear that mutual understanding demanded also a comparative study of institutions and ways of life, of pastoral methods and devotional habits. It was the first official recognition of the existence of the 'non-theological factors'.

This tangible response to Pope John's overtures had this additional result, as was realised by the Secretariat for Union. Whereas the enemies of ecumenism in the Vatican confidently prophesied that 'these protestants don't want dealings with Rome anyway—they only want to insult her from a distance', this was promptly demonstrated to be an error by the prompt Anglican reaction. And other churches later sent their representatives too. The author[1] had the honour of being chosen for the appointment, which caused an immense stir in the British press, and was a 'nine days' wonder'.

The reception of the liaison officer in Rome, as might have been expected, was various. It ranged from the thinly-disguised mistrust of some of the curial departments to the total and generous acceptance by the Secretariat for Union. The initial audience with Pope John was cordial in the extreme. Here indeed was a man who had no inhibitions, 'in whom was no guile'—which phrase he immediately applied to Archbishop Fisher, whose visit had evidently pleased him immensely. It is only fair to say that the Pope's lack of objective information about the Church of England was immediately evident in this and in subsequent audiences. He spoke always with ingenuous courtesy. Yet he seemed to be disproportionately concerned, e.g., with the revival of the Walsingham pilgrimage in the Church of England as evidence of a 'return to catholicism'. The framing of a comment on such a remark, at no notice and in a

[1] Then canon residentiary of Ely, etc., later Archdeacon of Canterbury.

foreign language, was not an easy assignment. The task was to convey to such a good and holy man the idea that such was not the Anglican Church's only, or even chief, claim to 'catholicism', without doing injustice to the pilgrimage itself, without appearing to argue, and without directly implying that someone had been giving him an unbalanced picture of the state of affairs in the Church of England. This kind of disappointment was more than compensated by the assurance that the Vatican, and he himself, wanted to know what the Anglican Church said of itself and that it was the 'liaison's' duty to provide the necessary information. Another great encouragement was the clear indication that the Pope had a completely pastoral, non-juridical approach to the problem of better relations.

This most satisfactory relationship having been established, the task became one of studying the preparations for the Council. The proportions of this became quickly evident. Pope John, either through mistaken judgment of individual men, or because of failure to appreciate the nature of the questions involved, appointed to the membership of the preparatory commissions lists of men who were largely of known conservative sympathies, unqualified to handle the widespread demands for reform. Bishops all over the world were showing open disappointment at the composition of the commissions (too many conservatives, too many curial officials and administrators, too few progressives, too few active pastoral bishops); and even more at the preliminary questionnaires sent round to them. The resultant Schemata[1] were circulated to the bishops of the world, and found little favour among those dispersed in the field, who while fighting to defend the faith against the attacks of the contemporary world, were longing for discussion about modern weapons for doing so. A great tide of resentment was obviously building up against the immobilism and reaction of the Vatican curial departments.

We have traced the long years of the separation of the Church of England from the see of Rome. But at last, in 1961, the total separation could be said to be over, and all the essential factors of a new era had appeared. Official communication was

[1] Proposed texts for discussion.

established between the two churches, and the Church of Rome seemed ready at last to consider a programme of reform in discussion with other churches. Whether or not changes satisfactory to the other parties involved in the reunion of Christendom would be achieved in the first attempt, or as a result of it, did not for the moment seem to matter. The contact was made, and it did not seem likely to those closely involved in it that it could ever be broken again. How successful the Second Vatican Council was going to be in narrowing the gap not even the most sanguine could have foreseen.

18

THE SECOND VATICAN
COUNCIL

By setting up the machinery for the Second Vatican Council, and particularly accepting a go-between from the Archbishop of Canterbury as part of its preparations, the Church of Rome had put an end to the long separation. In twenty short years the Council had taken on the dimensions of a world revolution, and the one-man mission has developed into a many-sided dialogue. The day when the new relationships will give place to formal acts of union is still distant, and may not even be in sight, but that they are on the way towards union none can deny. This chapter will make no attempt to trace the detailed progress of the Council, but will only outline the main points in which the issues between the two churches were reduced in number and importance; and Chapter 19 will attempt a sketch of how the findings of the Council have led on to the present stage in these much improved relationships.

The calling of the Council itself was a trumpet-blast which shattered a Vatican wall, for there were many inside who had predicted and hoped that there would never be a Council again. Vatican 1 and the Infallibility decree had created, they hoped, a new channel of revelation which henceforth would make councils superfluous. Even after its announcement there were those who spoke of it as a device for giving conciliar approval to one or two new doctrines which the Pope had in mind. One English Roman Catholic bishop, who must be allowed to remain anonymous, wrote in his diocesan leaflet:

It is an open secret that the bishops are assembling with

great hopes of new definitions to supplement the dogmas of the Catholic Faith already revealed. It is my personal hope that the Holy Father will see fit to crown our love of our glorious and Blessed Mother, Queen of Heaven and Ever Virgin, with the definition of the dogmas of Maria Mediatrix and Maria fons gratiae, which have ever been in the prayers and devotions of the faithful.

The world was reminded that this was no democratic discussion group but 'a solemn act of the highest authority and jurisdiction of the successors of the Apostles, with the successor of St. Peter at the head of them'.[1] Moreover, although there were to be observers, there was no question of the participation even of priests or lay-people, let alone of persons outside the Roman communion:

> Whereas the faithful should take the keenest interest in the proceedings of the Council and will have every opportunity, if they wish to take it, of making suggestions to their bishops before the Council, active participation is only possible for the ecclesia docens. The laity should therefore look up to them in reverent silence, praying that the Holy Spirit will illuminate and encourage them in the highest interests of the Church.[2]

This language was found by some to be discouraging, and there were critics, especially among the press, who repeated that 'plus ça change, plus c'est la même chose'. Yet for those who were prepared to hope, there were considerable signs of new attitudes to old problems. The invitation to the non-Roman churches to send observers who should also have the right and duty to make comments and suggestions through the Secretariat for Union, was a case in point. In addition to the 'liaison' already appointed, the archbishops designated a team of observers for various parts of the Anglican Communion, headed by the Bishop of Ripon (Dr. J. R. H. Moorman). Not all of these were present through the whole Council, but a system of reliefs and substitutes was arranged to ensure that the whole proceedings were observed, commented on, and reported throughout all the sessions.

Pope John's hopes for the Council seemed to the observers

[1] Secretary General of the Council. Press conference, 18th April 1961.
[2] ibid.

to be couched in language with which they were not familiar:

> When we have carried out this strenuous task, eliminated everything which could at the human level hinder our rapid progress, then we shall point to the Church in all her splendour, sine macula et sine ruga ['without spot or wrinkle'] and say to all those who are separated from us: 'Look, brothers, this is the Church of Christ. We have striven to be true to her, to ask the Lord for grace that she may remain forever what He willed. Come, here the way lies open for meeting and for homecoming. . .'.[1]

—and this was not the way in which they thought of the re-integration of the unity of Christians. But the transparent goodness of the Pope and the evident enthusiasm of many of the constituent members of the Secretariat, and of the theological experts (or periti) carried them along and justified some expectation.

Although the Schemata or prepared statements for discussion disappointed the observers from other churches and many of the Roman Catholic bishops, the general syllabus of the Council proved to be full of hope. It was observed that it couldn't have been more satisfactory, from an Anglican point of view, if it had been drawn up at Lambeth. The subjects set out for discussion were, broadly speaking:

1. The nature of the Church
2. The relation of Scripture to Tradition
3. The ministry (particularly the position of the bishops, left undefined in relation to the new dogmas of the first Vatican Council: and consequently of the priesthood)
4. The Laity
5. Relations with other Christians
6. Reform of the Liturgy
7. Religious liberty
8. The role of the Blessed Virgin Mary
9. The Church in the Modern World
10. Non-Christian religions
11. The world of non-believers

There were some protestant observers, and even some

[1] Audience to the General Council of Catholic Action in Italy, 14th February 1960.

Anglicans, who regretted certain omissions from the list, though in the view of the majority it was not reasonable to expect the syllabus for one Council to cover the complete range of all possibilities: and observers had to be reminded that this was in any case primarily a domestic council of the Church of Rome, and not an interconfessional assembly.

In the course of the Council there were unpredicted developments which set forward the general understanding with the non-Roman churches. Even before it had started Pope John had effectively and with good humour stamped upon the efforts of some of the Curial departments to stifle the liberal elements among the bishops and to minimise the importance of the observers. When the Council actually began, and the bishops had the texts in their hands, much further progress was made. It is interesting to observe, especially for those who draw a doubtful line between profound matters and questions of procedure and downgrade the latter in importance, that many of the principal successes of the Council were won by those who saw the spiritual importance of procedural points as they came up. The first which comes to mind was the rebellion of the bishops (led by Cardinals Liénart of Lille and Frings of Cologne) against the suggestion that the Curia would nominate the respective committees. This the bishops took into their own hands, thus wresting a considerable weapon out of the hands of the Curia into their own. In this way they began the process of restoring the rights and duties of the office of bishop after the harm which had been done to them by the first council of the Vatican. A second, vital, procedural turning point occurred at the deadlock in the debate on the two sources of Revelation, when Pope John overruled the regulations, withdrew the original schema and made the two 'schools of thought' sit together on a new committee and produce an entirely new agreed document. This brought a new element into Vatican debating procedure much more like that to which other churches are accustomed. Thirdly it was a procedural point which defeated the ambitions of the Marian protagonists. For, difficult though it may be for non-Roman Christians to believe, they objected strongly to the inclusion of the material concerning Our Lady in the chapter on the Church, giving the impression that she was to be thought of as 'closer to the divine', deserving a chapter of her own. From this mistake, which would have done harm to relationships, the Council was saved by Cardinal Koenig of Vienna who drily observed that the promoters of such suggestions were in effect proposing 'to excommunicate Our Lady'. As a result of this speech an amendment was carried which anchored Our Lady firmly and respectfully in Chapter 8 of the Constitution 'Lumen Gentium'.

The first of the subjects to be discussed, in time, though not in importance, was the LITURGY. This proved to be a fruitful choice as showing the strength of the desire for reform. It is to be remembered that before the Council the Roman Liturgy as practised constituted a major source of misunderstanding between the churches. The mass, recited in Latin by a priest with his back to the people, seemed to invite no participation by the people, who for the most part attended to their private devotions. Communion was discouraged, except at very rare intervals, and even then was administered in one kind only.

The contents and results of the decree on the reform of the *Liturgy* have therefore also changed relationships out of all recognition. For the revised Roman Liturgy, so far from being a cause of dissension, now resembles the Anglican Liturgy very closely. It has also demonstrated the value, under certain circumstances, of an authoritarian government. For instead of the pains and agonies of experiments, objections, counter-objections, and a multitude of parallel revisions existing at the same time, the new Roman Liturgy came into existence simultaneously all over the world. Roman Catholic lay people on the other hand, some of whom find the changes too drastic and too sudden, envy the Anglican laity their ability to have at least some say in the process of change. One of the most important new circumstances is that there is very close correspondence and cross-fertilisation in all discussions on the subject. There have been invited Anglican participants in the Consilium Liturgicum.

The Council decree was concerned only with principles, which corresponded broadly with those of Cranmer's Preface to the Book of Common Prayer. They were:

(a) the translation of services into the vernacular;
(b) the revision of texts with reference to scriptural and patristic models;

    (c) the end of the dominance of the Roman rite;
    (d) the 'declericalisation' of the rites and encouragement of
        the active participation of the laity;
    (e) a playing down of the monastic influence and more
        obvious links with the contemporary world.

Some of the remarks made by bishops in the debates on the reform of the Breviary led one of the observers to comment that 'if this goes on much longer they'll find that they've invented the Book of Common Prayer!' But the new liturgy in many places has outstripped the Liturgy of Cranmer, in spite of the latter's 400 years' start, in its modernity. And there are Anglicans who feel that the English of Cranmer, though a treasure of the literature of its day, is almost as remote from contemporary modes of expression, and therefore as unintelligible, as liturgical Latin. The publication therefore in 1980 of the new Anglican Alternative Service Book has brought the two liturgies still closer together. The liturgy, from being a cause of misunderstanding has thus been transformed into an opportunity for mutual stimulus.

The Constitution on the *Church*, which was basic to most other reforms, also showed itself to be under the influence of new currents of thought, dogmatic and biblical.

There were signs that the boundaries of the Mystical Body of Christ and the Roman Catholic Church are no longer being considered as exactly identical. The eschatological dimension of the Church is deliberately put before a juridical and canonical conception of it. There is an excellent chapter on the pilgrim church (Chapter 2), entirely scriptural and patristic, to which non-Roman Catholics could comfortably subscribe. The Vatican I conception of the Papacy is hedged round by the idea of the collegiality of the bishops, which, to say the least, gives ground for hope that further debate on the nature of the Church's ministerial structure must follow. Then, most important of all, the Constitution gives some ground for supposing that those who are validly baptised are put into a certain relationship to the catholic church herself thereby, the relationship itself being undefined. Sufficient is said to make the subsequent chapter on Ecumenism 'respectable', in that it gives baptised Christians not in communion with the Roman see a status from which to enter into further negotiation. The constitution ends with a memorable chapter on Mary. Considering the fact that the figure of Our Lord's Mother is one of the chief technical barriers between Christians, the results of Vatican 2 in this regard must be counted as particularly fortunate. For, whereas there were many who came to the Council in the firm belief that they would return with two more Marian dogmas to their credit,[1] not only were those hopes disappointed but a real attempt was made to recover the primitive pattern of Mary's role. The chapter is a sober essay in stating the Roman Catholic beliefs about her, relating them carefully to the Scriptures and to patristic norms, and warning against unwarranted exaggerations:

> This Synod earnestly exhorts theologians and preachers of the divine word that in treating of the unique dignity of the Mother of God, they carefully and equally avoid the falsity of exaggeration on the one hand, and the excess of narrow-mindedness on the other. Pursuing the study of sacred Scripture, the holy Fathers, the doctors, and liturgies of the Church, and under the guidance of the Church's teaching authority, let them rightly explain the offices and privileges of the Blessed Virgin which are always related to Christ, the Source of all truth, sanctity, and piety.
>
> Let them painstakingly guard against any word or deed which could lead separated brethren or anyone else into error regarding the true doctrine of the Church. Let the faithful remember moreover that true devotion consists neither in fruitless and passing emotion, nor in a certain vain credulity.[2]

Second in importance to the constitution on the Church from the point of view of understanding between the churches was undoubtedly that on SCRIPTURE and TRADITION.

Remembering the definitions of the Council of Trent (endorsed by Vatican 1) the Council's transactions under this head were very encouraging also. The decree began by being called, in its first draft 'the two sources of Revelation'. In the course of its handling by the Council (which was rough) it was

---

[1] See pp. 320–321 above.
[2] Dogmatic Const. Lumen Gentium, iv. 67.

first withdrawn, then thoroughly recast and given a new title 'On Divine Revelation'. And considering that this represented a tacit admission that previous formulas had over-emphasised the separate identities of the written word and its oral transmission and interpretation, this also represents a movement in a direction towards all protestant beliefs on the subject. Both in the debates and in observers' meetings there was a feeling of identity. Although they were conscious of working together from then on with a common aim, they had approached it from different directions. Roman Catholics had been scandalised with the fragmentation, diversities and confusing varieties of protestant interpretation of dogma and scripture. Protestants were equally scandalised by the Roman insistence that Scripture was to be interpreted by the Church only, and that unaided it could even be a dangerous guide; and by catholic readiness to accept dogmatic formulae which clearly had no Scriptural pedigree at all. In the course of the debates it became clear that the truth, as so often, lay somewhere between two opposite extremes. Protestants, long previous to the Council, had come to see that there were in the Scriptures themselves clearly traceable strands of 'tradition' already interpreting the original oral deposit. And catholics had admitted to themselves that many customs and traditions, and even dogmas, need reshaping in conformity with the Scriptures themselves and with the earliest traditions. The debates gave great satisfaction also, from the Anglican point of view, by coming down heavily in favour of the Biblical Institute and the École Biblique in not only allowing but encouraging the use of modern scientific critical methods in biblical scholarship and in relaxing considerably the hold of the dogmatic department of the Vatican on the free range of biblical scholars. All this boded well for the future, for all dialogue, to be effective, must be able to appeal easily and without restraint to the earliest biblical and patristic sources.

The ground for the decree on ECUMENISM had been prepared in many ways. First by the increasing number of visits and mutual consultations between the churches in the half century preceding the Council and also in the development of the Council itself, particularly in the Constitution on the Church.

The strength of the new practical directions was that they were based on a firm theology set in the Constitution on the Church, which clearly acknowledged the common validity of Baptism rightly administered and recognised that the Holy Spirit was working through other rightly constituted bodies, even though they were out of communion with the see of Rome. In the middle of the Council occcurred the death of Pope John, in 1963, and the succession of Cardinal Montini of Milan as Pope Paul VI. Of all the possible choices (and there might have been many who could have done considerable harm to the Council—to the extent of abrupt closure, which would have been canonical) Montini was the most favoured candidate from the Anglican point of view (it being assumed that for this turn at least it would still be an Italian). The new Pope was familiar with Anglican ways and aspirations, had visited England, and was known to be more liberal in his attitudes than Pope John. His first allocution to the Council after his enthronement contained the memorable passage in which he spoke of:

> the inexpressible consolation and reasonable hope that their presence [the observers'] stirs up within us, as well as because of the deep sadness we feel at their prolonged separation.
>
> If we are in any way to blame for that separation, we humbly beg God's forgiveness and ask pardon too of our brethren who feel themselves to have been injured by us. For our part, we willingly forgive the injuries which the Catholic Church has suffered, and forget the grief endured during the long series of dissensions and separations.

Looking back over the sad centuries of quarrels recorded in this book, it will easily be appreciated how emotive these words were, when uttered for the first time by a Pope in Council. They laid a foundation on which could be built totally new relationships and which might make possible the progressive demolition of the old. The decree on Ecumenism was in tune with this new spirit. It recognised a special relationship with the fellowship of the baptised,[1] a certain correspondence of doctrine,[2] a common inheritance in the Scriptures,[3] and a bond in the celebration of the Eucharist.[4] It went so far as to say, speaking of the 'separated communities of the West':

[1] Section 22.   [2] Section 20.   [3] Section 21.   [4] Section 22.

Among those in which some Catholic traditions and institutions continue to exist, the Anglican communion occupies a special place.[1]

The decree on Ecumenism was followed up by a 'Directory' in two parts, giving practical guidance for its implementation. Since the Council both churches have eagerly exploited its possibilities, both in England and in every area where the Anglican communion is represented.

Under the heading of the *Ministry* the Council was under heavy pressure from many sides to make clearer the status and functions of the various grades of the hierarchy. It was important for the future of the Church of Rome that the episcopate should be clearly understood to have in it the fullness of the priesthood; to which is added certain sacramental functions and juridical authority in the church which the bishop holds in his own right. This was clearly done, and so the function of bishops and their local jurisdiction was established. This right came upon them in their consecration, and though it was to be exercised in tune with the whole 'college' of bishops and in communion with the Bishop of Rome, it derived not from him or them, but straight from Christ, the origin of all ministry in the Church. This again cleared away a possible source of disagreement with other churches, and prevented any further discussion on unity being meaningless.

The status and function of the priesthood had been loudly clamouring for treatment in the Church of Rome throughout the world. There were those who feared that whereas the bishop was just being reduced to the status of a provincial agent of the Papacy, so the priest was becoming a local pawn of the bishop, a machine for the performance of the sacraments, and in particular the offering of the Sacrifice of the Mass, with little functional independence of his own. It is for this reason, among others, that there was no suggestion that the question of Anglican orders should be re-examined in the course of the Council. The press used the point to discredit the serious intentions of the Council: but a council was no place for undertaking such an exercise, and in any case it would have been pointless to do so until much closer agreement had been reached about the

[1] Section 13.

background theology of the ministry. This was to be more closely examined later in the course of the official 'dialogue' after the Council.

In the general work on the priesthood the main direction was given to the Council by Cardinal Suenens of Malines–Brussels, the author of so many other good things in the course of the sessions. Very broadly speaking the new direction which the Council took regarding the function of the priesthood was to restore the pastoral side of the office to its place beside the sacerdotal. The ministry was one of reconciliation in the community, the Body of Christ, accomplished through Word and Sacraments: it was a ministry shared essentially with the lay people, the whole People of God. As such it had a new and exciting function in the less comfortable, less amenable, world in which the majority of the priests were now working. For this ministry, of course, a new, more open, more humane, less cloistered, training, was demanded. This too, had its expression in the decree on Priestly Formation. It opened up a new and more familiar conception of the scriptural and patristic origins of the ministry such as would make any subsequent dialogue about the details and 'validity' of orders much more intelligible.

The position of the Laity in the church had already been greatly improved by the famous Chapter 2 of the *Lumen Gentium*, in which the definition of the whole church as a royal priesthood on the scriptural model was restored to its proper place. The debate on the Decree on the Laity emphasised the need to create machinery for the laity to be able to express their opinions and to take some share in the life and work of the church. A great deal of progress has been made in the attempt to enfranchise the laity to some degree in parishes and dioceses in some parts of the world. But dogmatically the position remains as it was. The hierarchy is still absolute in its role of ecclesia docens,[1] and the place of the laity is to listen and do what they are told. Yet the Church of Rome, though far as yet from any conception of synodical government, has been searching for ways of expressing lay participation. And this has proved an effective point of discussion with the Anglican churches.

1 'The teaching church'.

The decree on *Religious Liberty* also was an important step forward in the possibility of better understanding. For from the Anglican side there had been an impression of intolerance and of the suppression of liberties which if not removed would have been an insuperable obstacle. There were cases where Anglican congregations, and even dioceses, were being denied civil rights by the requirements of Concordats entered into between the Vatican and totalitarian regimes, particularly in South America. The Council virtually turned its face against this situation, decreed that even error had certain rights of expression and laid a foundation for the revision of legal obligations in which the Church was involved. It is a pleasure to record that this decree has brought considerable changes in practice to the extent of removing it from the list of the 'obstacles' to better relationships.

The Pastoral Constitution on the Church in the *Modern World*, known as Gaudium et spes, set a seal on a feature of modern Roman development that was already known and welcomed. Leo XIII's 'Rerum Novarum'[1] and Pius XI's 'Quadragesimo Anno'[2] had steered the Church of Rome towards a realistic confrontation with the problems of the world as they inevitably presented themselves to the Church, as had also John XXIII's 'Mater et Magistra' and 'Pacem in terris'. The main importance of this development, as with the Constitution itself, was that it made possible co-operation between the Church of Rome and the social agencies of other churches. And it has been perhaps in this common contribution to the needs of the world that the co-operation has been closest.

The Council represented a powerful victory of the forces of renewal in the Church of Rome over the conservative immobilism of its centralised government. A good measure of authority has been recognised in and restored to the office of bishop and a stop had been put to what had looked like the endless escalation of papal absolutism. A new framework, pastoral rather than legal and dogmatic, had been set up for the interpretation of

[1] See pp. 217–18.
[2] See p. 283.

divine revelation.[1] The balance had largely been restored between Scripture and tradition. A new situation had been created in the relationships between the Roman Catholic Church and other Christians.

The Anglican observers, therefore, came away from the Council, not to indulge in fanciful dreams about the future, but soberly thankful that so much had been achieved in so short a time against so much opposition. They wrote their impressions and published them to the Anglican world.[2] The head of the Anglican delegation, J. R. H. Moorman, Bishop of Ripon, published his intimate personal impressions of the progress of the Council.[3] It was Bishop Moorman who after the Joint Service on 4th December 1965, at the dismissal of the observers, said:

> The Council is drawing to its end; but the work for Christian Unity is but beginning. We outside the communion of the Roman Church have for long been occupied in prayer, in dialogue and in effort for the union of our respective Churches. Now, with the entry of the Roman Catholic Church into this field, we realise that the Ecumenical Movement has taken on a new dimension. At last we can say that the whole Christian world is engaged in the search for that unity for which Our Blessed Lord prayed.[4]

The theological changes to which the 2nd Vatican Council gave birth derived from a basic modification in the conception of God's revelation to man. Nowhere is this change more easy to perceive than in the theology of the Church. Roman Catholic apologists will be quick to insist that there was not a change in the theology of the Church, or of any other dogma for that matter. And perhaps we ought to be more moderate and say that the change was in the proportion and arrangement of various sections of the doctrine. Before the Council the Church was seen to be a juridicial inflexible entity, rigid in its

---

[1] The decree on Ecumenism says that:

> 'in catholic teaching there exists an order or "hierarchy" of truths, since they vary in their relationship to the foundation of the Christian faith'. (Art. 11)

[2] *The Second Vatican Council* ed. Bernard Pawley O.U.P. 1967.
[3] *Vatican Observed*, J. R. H. Moorman, Darton, Longman & Todd, 1967.
[4] ibid., pp. 211-12.

membership, exlcusive in its relations with the world, sure of its monopolistic claims as the avenue for salvation and dispenser of grace. After the Council the church was seen as the pilgrim people, a congregation of sinners moving along to salvation. It had to shed its triumphalism and clerical monopolism and was seen to consist of lay men and women to whose good the clergy were in service, the Pope himself as servant of servants. The Decree on the Church in the Modern World opened up a different picture of the Church from that of Pius XII's encyclical Mystici Corporis of 1943. Add to these developments the idea of the church as having a diakonia, or duty of service, to the world itself having as its end produce the eschatological salvation of all mankind. This had made possible the idea of the secular mission of the Church and so has redeemed her image in the Third World and sent her into it not primarily to make converts but to act out the healing ministry of Christ.

The changes in the Liturgy effected in the Council decree can be said to be consequent on changes in the doctrine of the Church, or rather mutations in the understanding of the doctrine of the Church. For the new shape of the Liturgy, its performance and its vernacular language are the expression of a church on the march, not of one that is static. It speaks of the service of man as well as of the glory of God. It expresses the worship of a people who are primarily lay people involved in the world rather than of a people subservient to the ministrations of the clergy. For the purposes of our study perhaps one of the most important 'changes' is the restoration of the preaching of the word to a central place in the Liturgy. And considering that this has been taking place contemporaneously with a restoration in the protestant world of the centrality of the Eucharist, it can be seen how these developments represent a real rapprochement between the sundered parts of Christendom.

We have to bear in mind that from the Anglican side relationships with Rome are now conducted on the basis of the world-wide Anglican Communion and that in the dialogue from the Roman side negotiations are in progress with all the other non-Roman churches, so that it is no longer appropriate to think of changes as between the Church of Rome and the Church of England only. This has the additional advantage that gains in one area can be credited to all others who are engaged in the same search. The most significant of these is that the long contention between Rome and Luther in the matter of faith and works and the primacy of grace seems to have been solved 'on the side', and an agreement reached with a minimum of difficulty. The results of this are to be enjoyed by all other non-Roman communities.

The same, however, does not seem to be the case with the question of authority and 'sola scriptura'. That is to say that final agreement does not seem to have been reached, in spite of the Venice agreement and the immense recovery of the status of the Scriptures in the formularies and practice of the Vatican Council itself.

Another notable 'change' of the Council which also involves a modification of doctrine is in the realm of Ecumenism. Present Roman Catholic behaviour in this matter is no passing fashion, but is firmly rooted in the teaching of the Church. The Church is a sign among the nations and its unity is a characteristic 'mark' of it. Its present divisions therefore are a 'ruga et macula' and are to be removed (Art. 1 of the Constitution Lumen Gentium). The Church of Rome is thus doctrinally committed to seek unity, and is clearly working hard to achieve it. No longer does Rome say that it is *the* Church, but that the fullness of catholicity, including unity, 'subsists' in it. The Council even went so far as to say that the Church had erred in certain matters of behaviour towards the 'separated brethren'; and Paul VI even expressed penitence for it.

The theory of the Ministry in its relation to the Church can also be said to have undergone a significant change, as will be seen below, in the matters of the 'collegiality' accorded to the bishops, the rights accorded to the priesthood and the possible 'emancipation' of the lay people. The position of the papacy however remains a question still to be resolved. The Decree on Religious Liberty and the new attitude to the Jews involve such considerable modification of doctrinal attitudes as to justify the belief that other 'modifications' could be expected in the future. But the crown of the dogmatic developments is to be seen in the acknowledgment of a certain essential 'pluralism' in the formulation of doctrines. The Decree on Ecumenism spoke of a 'hierarchy of truths', and Paul VI was heard to divide them into four categories: cardinal doctrines of the faith; those which must be agreed upon for full communion; those which must be accepted for limited ecclesial communion; and 'those which can be said to derive from devotion'. Thus the church had travelled a long way from Humani Generis. The exercise of reconciling these new formulations with the present shape of the magisterium, with its hitherto unmodified doctrine of infallibility, is not going to be easy. The Venice agreement was to be a first attempt.[1]

We must now attempt a catalogue (it can be nothing more) of the advances in understanding which have been made since Vatican 2, against the background of these new dogmatic attitudes.

[1] Made at A.R.C.I.C. meeting 1976 p. 344.

19

SINCE VATICAN 2

By way of demonstrating the Anglican confidence in the future of the progress thus achieved, the Archbishop of Canterbury and his advisers decided to set up an Anglican centre in Rome to act as a channel for the extension of relationships already achieved. This was done with the goodwill of the Secretariat for Union.

The 'dialogue' envisaged by the Decree on Ecumenism and encouraged by Pope Paul VI has exceeded the wildest hopes entertained for it. The theological conversations which have taken place were officially inaugurated by the Archbishop of Canterbury's visit to Rome and to the Pope in March 1966. At this historic meeting in the Sistine Chapel the Pope said to the Archbishop:

> You are rebuilding a bridge, which for centuries has lain fallen, between the Church of Rome and the Church of Canterbury: a bridge of respect, of esteem and of charity. You cross over this yet unstable viaduct, still under construction, with spontaneous initiative and safe confidence. . . . We see the truly spiritual and religious value of our common quest for a common profession of fidelity to Christ, and of a prayer, old and new, which may harmonize minds and voices in celebrating the greatness of God, and His plan of salvation in Christ for all mankind. In the field of doctrine and ecclesiastical law, we are still respectively distinct and distant; and for now it must be so, for the reverence due to truth and to freedom; until such time as we may merit the supreme grace of true and perfect unity in faith and communion.

And the Archbishop to the Pope:

> On the road to unity there are formidable difficulties of doctrine. All the more therefore it is my hope, and the hope of Your Holiness too, that there may be increasing dialogue between theologians, Roman Catholic and Anglican, and of other traditions, so as to explore together the divine revelation. On the road to unity there are also difficult practical matters about which the consciences and feelings of Christian people can be hurt. All the more therefore must such matters be discussed together in patience and charity. If the final goal of unity is yet some way ahead Christians can rejoice already in the fact of their common Baptism into the name of the Triune God, Father, Son and Holy Spirit, and they can already pray together, bear witness to God together and together serve humanity in Christ's name.

As a result of this initiative the 'Commissio Antepreparatoria' set about its work, and after three lengthy residential meetings[1] was able to suggest that there was strong justification for entering into more serious dialogue, with the specific aim of the ultimate union of the churches. Its report was presented to the Lambeth Conference of 1968. The general trend of it can be judged from the following extracts:

> Divergences since the sixteenth century have arisen not so much from the substance of this inheritance as from our separate ways of receiving it. They derive from our experience of its value and power, from our interpretation of its meaning and authority, from our formulation of its content, from our theological elaboration of what it implies, and from our understanding of the manner in which the Church should keep and teach the Faith. Further study is needed to distinguish between those differences which are merely apparent and those which are real and require serious examination.[2]
>
> In considering these questions within the context of the present situation of our two Communions, we propose particularly, as matter for dialogue, the following possible convergences of lines of thought: first, between the traditional

[1] Gazzada, Italy, January 1967; Huntercombe, England, August 1967. Malta, December 1967–January 1968.
[2] Malta Report, Section 4.

Anglican distinction of internal and external communion and the distinction drawn by the Vatican Council between full and partial communion: secondly, between the Anglican distinction of fundamentals from non-fundamentals and the distinction implied by the Vatican Council's reference to a 'hierarchy of Truths' (Decree on Ecumenism, 11), to the difference between 'revealed truths' and 'the manner in which they are formulated' (Pastoral Constitution on the Church in the Modern World, 62), and to diversities in theological traditions being often 'complementary rather than conflicting' (Decree on Ecumenism, 17).[1]

Parallel with this progress in theological understanding has run a continuous programme of events which has served to illustrate and to strengthen the search for deeper unity in life and service. The visit of the Archbishop to the Pope was the official beginning of these activities too. Since then, in many countries and continents, the active pursuit of better relationships has gone steadily ahead. The year 1966 was an annus mirabilis in this particular narrative. For in that year we can record not only the visit of the Archbishop to the Pope, but several other quite significant events as well. The Bishop of Winchester[2] visited Malines to attend the dedication of a memorial tablet in the cathedral to Cardinal Mercier and his work in connection with the Malines conversations, in the presence of his successor Cardinal Suenens. The Belgian cardinal has since attended the dedication in York Minster of a memorial to Lord Halifax. In the same year the Abbot of the Anglican Benedictines was invited to Rome to the General Congress of the whole Order. 1966 also saw the beginnings of a dialogue between Roman Catholic theologians and representatives of the evangelical movement in the Church of England—a development without which the whole encounter would have been unrealistic. In this same year a first attempt was made at the solution of a practical problem which had proved a considerable discouragement to better relations; that of mixed marriages. For in March of that year the Holy Office issued the instruction Matrimonii Sacramentum, which on the surface did not seem

---

[1] ibid., Section 6.
[2] S. F. Allison, Chairman of the Anglican Council on Foreign Relations.

to improve upon the regulations already in existence, though in subsequent years, and in many parts of the world, the possibilities of this document have been taken full advantage of and a better attitude is beginning to show itself in the handling of this vexatious problem. Anglicans had been specially grieved by the severity of Roman legislation up to that point: though they had not given sufficient thought to the problems underlying it for Roman Catholic canonists and pastors. In the past Anglicans have not appreciated how far they have themselves contributed to these difficulties by the apparent willingness of many indifferent nominal churchmen to surrender, without apparent protest or concern, some of their rights in matrimonial contracts. And they have not given full consideration to the fact that Roman Catholic canonists have to legislate in principle for the whole world—which makes it exceedingly difficult for them to accept the validity of all non-catholic Christian marriages, expecially in churches and communities which do not invariably uphold the standard of life-long unions. In England, moreover, they have found it difficult to legislate in the face of the observable fact that so many nominal Anglicans fail to provide their children with any recognisable form of Christian instruction at all. But the situation has steadily eased since the Instructio of 1966. The Instructio has been followed by a papal Motu Proprio, and that has in turn been filled out by a statement of the English hierarchy, each of which steps has gone some way to ease the tension. In many countries the local episcopal conferences have adopted generous attitudes in the matter, and the English Roman Catholic hierarchy has made some concessions: but it cannot be denied that unyielding attitudes still tend to act as a brake on the rate of ecumenical advance.

In spite of such practical difficulties as these the local implementation of the spirit of the ecumenical decree has gone on at an encouraging pace. In the first years after the Vatican Council had opened the floodgates, there swiftly developed situations in which enthusiasm ran away with prudence. But the steady regulation of ways and means of expressing these new impulses has meant that good order has been preserved. The Ecumenical Decree found its expression in a Directory in two parts; and the Directory came to earth as a 'Presentation' in the hands of the local Roman Catholic hierarchy. A great deal of interchange has taken place since then between clergy themselves, both officially and in private, but, what is perhaps more important, the lay people have started neighbourhood groups for the exchange of ideas, and not infrequently for corporate acts of worship and witness. For reasons of our history the progress of ecumenism is slower in this country than almost anywhere else in the world: and although the meetings of the local Roman Catholic and Anglican ecumenical commissions in England have by no means been inactive, much more has been accomplished in the United States and elsewhere, e.g. especially in Latin America.

There have not been wanting critics who have accused both the Church of Rome and the Anglican churches of failing to show fruits of renewal proportionate to their talk about reunion. Yet the Church of Rome has shown remarkable signs of change since the Vatican Council—some directly as a consequence of it, some originating in other causes. A few examples illustrate the theme. First among such changes were those which were initiated by the Pope himself, and they are so many and so extensive as to entitle Paul VI to be thought of as the greatest reformer of the Roman Catholic Church since Hildebrand.[1] The most important single change was the creation of the Synod of Bishops, designed to put the pastoral government of the Church back into the hands of the international episcopate, and to set the exercise of papal government in a new context. This has now had several full sessions, and has set up a permanent cadre to which the Pope and the bishops may refer questions which arise in between meetings. The Pope has also made considerable attempts to internationalise the Curia, by breaking what was more or less a monopoly of Italian control of its major offices. And his appointments to these offices were on the whole in general accord with the spirit of the Council. He appointed to the college of cardinals many non-Italians, so that it was now possible for the Church to elect a non-Italian Pope. This was made even more possible by changes in the method of election of Popes. He set up, and entrusted some important decisions to, a

[1] Pope Gregory VII 1073–1085.

Pontifical Theological Commission,[1] which fulfils a higher function than the Congregation for the teaching of the Faith (formerly the Holy Office). In setting it up he defined its terms in language which was pleasant to non-Roman Catholic ears, for he said in effect that the formulation of the terms of faith was a pastoral as well as an academic responsibility; that the Church must accustom herself to 'a certain pluralism in the theological expression of the one faith', and that the formulation of such expression must always have in mind the effect which its publication might have on those who are not of the Roman obedience that no unnecessary offence should be caused. He personally encouraged the setting up, in concert with certain non-Roman Catholic leaders,[2] of an Institute of Academic Theological Research, on the road between Jerusalem and Bethlehem. This institute has been charged with a programme of research based on the agreed priority of the common examination of 'Salvation history'. He identified himself and the Roman Catholic Church as a whole with the world's great social and economic needs by pilgrimages to the Holy Land, to India, to the United Nations headquarters in New York, and to the Far East. The encyclical 'Populorum Progressio'[3] followed the tradition, in these fields, of Leo XIII and John XXIII. Towards the Anglican Churches in particular he made imaginative and well-informed gestures, of which we might mention two. On the occasion of the canonisation of twenty-two Uganda martyrs in 1963 the Pope, hearing that about the same number of Anglicans were involved in the same martyrdom, invited the Anglican Archbishop of Uganda[4] to participate in the rite in St. Peter's in Rome, and expressed disappointment that the canon law did not yet allow the two churches to make common cause of such an event. On the occasion of the canonisation of the forty martyrs of England and Wales in 1970, he transformed what might have been a cause of contention into an expression of ecumenical charity. It was in the course of this ceremony that Pope Paul said that on the day when the Church

[1] July 1968.
[2] Especially Professor Oscar Culmann of Basle, in whom Paul VI had shown great confidence.
[3] 1967.
[4] Leslie Brown, later Bishop of St. Edmundsbury and Ipswich.

of Rome would embrace firmly her ever-beloved Anglican sister in the one authentic communion of the family of Christ:

> no offence will be afflicted on the honour and sovereignty of a great country such as England. There will be no seeking to lessen the prestige and usage proper to the Anglican Church.

This aspiration has been deliberately followed up, with the Pope's knowledge and encouragement, in more than one instance. In the course of a sermon in the (Anglican) University Church at Cambridge in the week of prayer for Christian unity in 1970 Cardinal Jan Willebrands (now successor to the much revered Cardinal Bea as president of the Secretariat for the Union of Christians) said:

> . . . . . diversity of theological approach and explanation is legitimate, and can be acknowleged within the unity of faith and within the church. . . . May I invite you to reflect on the notion of the typos church . . . and of a plurality of typoi within the communion of the one and only Church of Christ.[1]

And in an article entitled 'United not absorbed' Bishop Christopher Butler, Auxiliary of Westminster, wrote:

> if we are being honest. . . we expect some sort of co-existence, in full ecclesial communion with one another of the Catholic Western Rite . . . and an 'English Rite' with its own bishops, liturgy and theological tradition. . . . It would be obvious that organic union presupposes that dogmatic issues have been successfully dealt with. . . .[2]

This kind of attempt to begin the formulation of a plan for the restoration of union is the general result of papal initiatives, for which the Anglican churches should be grateful.

In spite of this programme of reform and renewal the 'means of communication' have on the whole soft-pedalled it and have high-lighted instead those few events in the history of Pope Paul's pontificate which have not shown him in the same progressive light (as seen from an Anglican perspective). The first of these was the encyclical on birth control and family

[1] *Tablet*, 24th January 1970, p. 73.   [2] *Tablet*, 7th March 1970.

planning ('Humanae Vitae'). This was a world-wide disappointment, not only to Anglicans, but to Roman Catholics at large; but the case against it was argued by most commentators without adequate statement of the other side. Perhaps it is easier for an Anglican to appreciate that a Pope must find the greatest difficulty in reversing the clear teaching of his four predecessors on this matter (John XXIII not excepted), and that Roman Catholics, in so far as they were asking to do so, were putting a greater strain on the man and on the office than it was possible for him to bear. In many Anglican eyes Roman Catholics were trying to lay on the shoulders of one Pope the blame for what was in fact a flaw in the conception of authority and in the moral theology of the Church. The other case was the reluctance of Paul VI even to permit the discussion of clerical celibacy at the meetings of the Synods. The difficulties of this too were appreciated by some Anglican commentators who, though disapproving both the original rule and the prohibition of its discussion, could see the immense problems which a general, and even more a local, relaxation of the rule, would cause for the Church of Rome. Yet in spite of these two exceptions, the flow of reforms initiated by the Pope himself has been almost uninterrupted, and the present state of papal government, when compared with that of only fifteen years ago, represents improvements, as seen from an Anglican point of view, which then would have been impossible to foresee.

To the changes which have flowed out from the centre can be added the spontaneous developments which have been occurring in the provinces throughout the world. The adventurers of the Roman Catholic Church in Holland have amazed the world by their innovations. In the third of a series of Pastoral Councils (bishops, clergy and laity) in 1969 they passed the following resolutions, among others:

1. 'that the statements on birth control in the encyclical "Humanae Vitae" were not convincing on the arguments put forward';
2. 'that obligatory celibacy as a condition for exercising the ministry must be abolished';
3. 'that married people should have the opportunity to be admitted to the priestly office'; etc. etc.

We might also mention the phenomenon of the Focolarini, a revival movement founded by Chiara Lubich in Trento, N. Italy, and now diffused throughout the world. This spontaneous expression of renewed personal religion comes very close to the spirit of the evangelical emphasis in the Anglican Churches, and could well provide a bridge across which many might come to a new understanding.

The social concern of Archbishop Helder Camara of Recife, Brazil; the pioneer sociological work of the Jesuits in Chile; the bewildering changes which are observable in the life and habits of the Religious Orders; and Cardinal Suenens' struggle to get attention for his vision of co-responsibility in the Church are among the items which have attracted notice, but they represent a desire for renewal which is widespread. It is one of the many features of the present ecclesiastical situation which should encourage all those who are working for the restoration of the unity of Christendom. It prompts the reflection that the Anglican churches would have done well if they had come so far in so short a time. They have not been entirely untouched by the winds of reform. Of those which might be said to improve the situation of the Church of England vis-à-vis the Church of Rome there have been in recent years:

(a) an honest attempt to approach a solution of the problem of 'authority' by a series of commissions on the nature of the 'establishment', which have resulted so far in generous consultation of the laity in episcopal and other appointments;
(b) the 'Enabling Act' and 'Synodical Government' as reforms in the matter of self-government;
(c) the re-introduction of a reformed Canon Law;
(d) liturgical revision, in close consultation with other churches;
(e) the beginnings of reconsideration of the 39 Articles as a document of assent to the faith.

Another result of the visit of Archbishop Ramsey to Pope Paul VI in 1966 was the decision to set up a continuation Commission. So there came into being the Anglican–Roman Catholic International Commission, commonly called ARCIC, with nine delegates from each Church under the chairmanship of the Right Reverend H. R. McAdoo, Bishop of Ossory, Ferns and Leighlin (now Archbishop of Dublin), and the Right Reverend A. C. Clark, Auxiliary Bishop of Northampton (now Bishop of East Anglia). It decided that the three subjects to which it should first devote its attention would be Eucharist, Ministry and Authority. (The recommendation that the subject of Mixed Marriages should be dealt with by a separate joint commission was accepted.)

The first Agreed Statement, on *Eucharistic Doctrine*, was completed at Windsor in September 1971. It was followed by that on *Ministry and Ordination* at Canterbury two years later. The third Statement, on *Authority in the Church*, after meetings held at Venice was completed in 1976.

The discussion on the Eucharist set a good precedent for its successors by recognising implicitly that its problems were by no means primarily theological. The whole history of the controversy had been distorted by political, cultural and social considerations. The discussion rightly therefore arrived at a minimum of doctrinal definition, of which there had been too much in the past. It concentrated on basic differences, and when possible summoned up new, or resurrected old, terminology. To define the relationship of the Eucharist to the sacrifice of Christ it returned to the ancient word 'commemoration' or 'memorial' (anamnesis). In tackling the hoary problem of the nature of Christ's presence in the Eucharist it used the simple phrase 'the bread and wine which, in this mystery, become his body and blood' (para. 6) in the hope that this would leave room for wide interpretation of the nature of the mystery. It is hoped that it will be able to do so. In this and in the other two statements it was not to be expected that the Commission would be able to produce a comprehensive treatise, but only to see whether there was substantial agreement, sufficient to justify continuing the dialogue. This they claimed emphatically to have done. There was no attempt made to discuss the problems of intercommunion, these being left deliberately to a subsequent commission to discuss practical consequences.

After examining the suggestions and criticisms received under this head, the pamphlet *Elucidations* comes to the following conclusion:

That there can be a divergence in matters of practice and in theological judgements relating to them without destroying a common eucharistic faith, illustrates what we mean by *substantial* agreement. Differences of theology and practice may well coexist with a real consensus on the essentials of eucharistic faith—as in fact they do within each of our communions.

The statement on Ministry and Ordination followed the same general pattern as regarding principles involved. There was a considerable attempt to explain the meaning and limitations of the idea of priesthood and its relation to other forms of ministry; and to clarify the sacramental implications of ordination.

No sustained attempt was made to deal with the question of the Ordination of Women or the reconsideration of the question of Anglican Orders. The further questions raised by the implementation of the Covenant in the Church of England have of course occurred since the issue of the Statement and will presumably be dealt with by the subsequent general Commission on practical consequences which is eagerly awaited at the time of this second edition. This Statement again claims to have reached a 'substantial agreement', though it clearly leaves a number of unexplained conundrums. The chief of these, according to subsequent comment was undoubtedly the mysterious assertion that the ministry of the priesthood 'is not an extension of the common Christian priesthood but belongs to another realm of the gifts of the Spirit'.

Elucidations summarises the position thus:

Mutual recognition presupposes acceptance of the apostolicity of each other's ministry. The Commission believes that its Agreements have demonstrated a consensus in faith on eucharist and ministry which has brought closer the possibility of such acceptance. It hopes that its own conviction will be shared by the members of both our communions; but mutual recognition can only be achieved by the decision of our authorities. It has been our mandate to offer to them the basis upon which they may make this decision.

There were, of course, more considerable problems to be faced in the third of the three exercises, that on Authority in the Church. Here again the object was not to conduct a headlong confrontation with the controversial decisions of the first Vatican Council, universal jurisdiction of the papacy, infall-ibility, etc., but to search out the origins of the problem of transmitting the authority of Christ to all Christians throughout the ages and across the world. What started as an almost impossible impasse soon took on the more promising shape of a joint search for a common problem, traceable back to first origins and capable of being expressed in terms of common loyalty to the Saviour's commands. Catholic teaching had tended more and more to pile all authority first on the hierarchy and then onto the shoulders of the Bishop of the see of Rome. Protestant attempts to solve the same problems had led to the exaltation of the words of Scripture, leaving untouched the question of who was to resolve the ambiguities and contradic-tions of the texts. Starting from these two intractable positions it was remarkable that the Commission came to find common ground at all, and a matter of thanksgiving that they felt able to issue a statement claiming to have won much common ground and to see great possibilities in the synodical and conciliar authority of the Church. This statement was widely accused of having been issued too soon and to have left unsolved the two major problems, of infallibility on one side and of apparent chaotic indiscipline on the other.

There is no doubt that in some of the language used of the primacy the joint commission overstepped what all the Churches feel able to accept, at least up to the moment. But in the end, although the theologians were aware of these difficulties, the great gain was that they were to reach agreement in saying that even these two problems were capable of solution in the end and would eventually be able to be removed from the list of obstacles. Each side could learn from the other.

By the time these Statements had been read and considered by the respective churches there was a new Archbishop of Canterbury, Donald Coggan, who decided to pay a visit to the Pope with a view to considering what was to be the future of the dialogue. This took place in April 1977. Para 2 of their Common

Declaration stated that:

> As the Roman Catholic Church and the constituent
> Churches of the Anglican Communion have sought to grow
> in mutual understanding and Christian love, they have come
> to recognize, to value and to give thanks for a common faith
> in God our Father, in our Lord Jesus Christ, and in the Holy
> Spirit; our common baptism into Christ; our sharing of the
> Holy Scriptures, of the Apostles' and Nicene Creeds, the
> Chalcedonian definition, and the teaching of the Fathers; our
> common Christian inheritance for many centuries with its
> living traditions of liturgy, theology, spirituality and mission.

Para. 26 of the Venice Statement concluded:

> The Malta Report of 1968 envisaged the coming together of
> the Roman Catholic Church and the Churches of the
> Anglican Communion in terms of 'unity by stages'. We have
> reached agreements on the doctrines of the Eucharist,
> Ministry, and apart from the qualifications of para. 24,
> Authority. Doctrinal agreements reached by theological
> commissions cannot, however, by themselves achieve the goal
> of Christian unity. Accordingly, we submit our Statements to
> our respective authorities to consider whether or not they are
> judged to express on these central subjects a unity at the level
> of faith which not only justifies but requires action to bring
> about a closer sharing between our two communions in life,
> worship, and mission.

As a result of these events a new omnibus Commission is now
in being which has the objective of addressing itself to the next
stage of the debate. A series of 'Elucidations' carefully considering objections, difficulties and amendments, has already been
published.

Meanwhile the situation evolves on all sides. Cardinal Hume,
in his address to the Benedictine monks gathered in
Westminster Abbey immediately after his consecration said:

> The sister Churches can now look back on a past that is dead
> and buried. We can look forward to a new life, to new hope
> and in God's time to the goal of Christian unity. Already in

the last decade we have seen much achieved to reunite the two sister Churches.

One of the chief obstacles from the Anglican side, to progress (not normally thought of as such) is the hesitation on the Roman side to give any enfranchisement to the lay people; so that when the findings of these commissions are submitted to Rome for adjudication the world can only hear the verdict of the hierarchy. 'Roma locuta est' means only that 'Hierarchia Romana locuta est'. Thus contrary to what is commonly supposed, there is uncertainty about the Roman Catholic position. It is to be hoped that in the not-too-distant future the voice of the 'people of God' will be able to be heard. If and when it is heard progress on the ecumenical front will be faster. We must look for straws in the wind, and these are to be seen perhaps in the National Pastoral Councils, such as are increasingly being introduced in many parts of the world. In the 1980 Council in Liverpool we note the following sentence in the Common Declaration:

> We profess our growing conviction of the need for more profound unity with our fellow Christians and we will continue to search for more effective ways of achieving that unity.

Of the future intentions and aspirations from the Anglican side there can be no doubt. The Lambeth Conference in 1978 resolved that the Conference:

1. welcomes the work of the Anglican–Roman Catholic International Commission which was set up jointly by the Lambeth Conference of 1968 and by the Vatican Secretariat for Promoting Christian Unity;
2. recognizes in the three Agreed Statements of this Commission a solid achievement, one in which we can recognize the faith of our Church, and hopes that they will provide a basis for sacramental sharing between our two Communions if and when the finished Statements are approved by the respective authorities of our Communions;
3. invites ARCIC to provide further explication of the

Agreed Statements in consideration of responses received by them;

4. commends to the appropriate authorities in each Communion further consideration of the implications of the Agreed Statements in the light of the report of the Joint Preparatory Commission (the Malta Report received by the Lambeth Conference 1968—see p. 134 of its report), with a view to bringing about a closer sharing between our two Communions in life worship, and mission. (Resolution 33).

In these last years a new star has risen in the Christian firmament, in the person of Pope John Paul II (Wojtyla). Coming as he does from the restrictions of his native Poland he cannot be expected to have his ecumenical attitudes as neatly arranged as were those of his predecessor but one. Unhappily some agencies of the media have tended to assume, we think wrongly, that his attitudes will be cautious and unco-operative. We believe this to be mistaken, and can only quote his own words. In the discourse to the cardinals on the morning after his election he said:

It does not seem possible that there should still remain the drama of division among Christians—a cause of confusion, perhaps even of scandal. We intend, therefore, to proceed along the way already begun, by favouring those steps which serve to remove obstacles. Hopefully, then, thanks to a common effort, we might arrive finally at full communion.

It can also be a matter of thanksgiving that in an important speech to the whole curia on the 28th June 1980 the Pope said:

In less than two years, and in a spirit of Christian friendship, I have had exchanges with two Archbishops of Canterbury: Dr. Coggan, who kindly attended the solemn inauguration of my pontificate, and Dr. Runcie, who met me in Africa. At these meetings I saw reflected the intentions of so many Anglicans for the restoration of unity.

This intention instils strength in so many dialogues and so much collaboration in progress in the English-speaking world. This is an experience that must lead us to follow in prayer the work carried out by the joint Commission between the Catholic Church and the Anglican Communion, the results of which, very important ones, will be presented at the end of the next year.

Some events of his pontificate have given the impression of a sterner grip on the discipline of the Church. 'L'affaire Küng' has received world-wide publicity and has slightly lowered the ecumenical temperature. The episode offers a good opportunity for understanding. Roman Catholic doctrine and discipline being what it is, it is not surprising that the chief pastor should eventually have to put the brake on teaching which explicitly denies a major doctrine, under review indeed for possible modification, but still 'on the books'. The Dutch theologian Schillebeeckx was indicted about the same time and ex-onerated. It behoves Anglicans on the other hand to try to understand Roman Catholic dismay at Anglican failure to take any action at all against authorised teachers who impugn cardinal doctrines of the faith.

Those interested in evaluating the position of John Paul II would profit from studying his reactions to the 'Latin American problem'. Paul VI had gone well across the central line to show sympathy with the liberation hopes of oppressed peoples at the conference at Medellin. John Paul II, on the other hand, was more cautious when he visited the episcopal conference at Puebla in 1978, but even there he felt able to refer sympatheti-cally to the fact that human rights were being betrayed in some of the South American regimes. But he seemed to be even more concerned with the threat from advancing communism to the liberties of the church.

And against the Pope's apparent rigidities with regard to the marriage of priests and the ordination of women to the priesthood, Anglicans should remember that the spasmodic and piecemeal introduction of the ordination of women and the uncertainties of the introduction of the Covenants in England and Wales have caused hesitations on the Roman side.

Those who have the long-term vision of unity in view are learning to bring a maximum understanding and tolerance to bear on each development as it occurs.

We have now brought this narrative up-to-date.[1] It represents a long upward struggle against the waywardness of man, and a spectacular token of God's grace, a cause for much thankfulness. The process is not at an end but is relentlessly on the move. The churches have advanced, by God's grace from hostility and misunderstanding to friendliness and toleration. The situation as we find it at the time of writing is that theologians have gone far, perhaps as far as they can go, in removing obstacles and in setting up acceptable agreements. We are now entering on a new phase which must consist in considering the practical consequences and opportunities of the present situation. Assuming that it would never be possible to achieve detailed agreement on all points of doctrine, discipline and morals, have we now reached a point at which the churches could enter into some kind of relationship? After these words had been written the Archbishop of Canterbury delivered a lecture in Westminster Abbey in which he used these words:

> I begin with the idea of the Anglican Church united not absorbed. . . . I want to suggest some questions Anglicans should now be asking Roman Catholics in order to elucidate what unity not absorption would mean.
>
> Some hard questions must be asked about Vatican centralization. As early as the close of the second century Pope Victor was threatening the excommunication of the whole of the Asian episcopate because they kept Easter on a different date from the West. Fortunately Irenaeus put him right. But the tendency to uniformity still seems to be a Roman attitude of mind. . . . To put it more directly, would Anglicans be expected to accept the 'Latin' attitudes and rulings of the various Vatican Congregations? The question is acute when we consider moral issues relating to particular interpretations of Natural Law and the anglo-saxon tradition of the informed Christian conscience.
>
> Ultimately, the theological question can be put like this: what is involved (and what is *not* involved) in acceptance of the universal ministry of the Bishop of Rome; is this ministry not solely concerned with the basic unity of the faith in the world-wide communion of the Churches and their God-given

[1] March 1981.

diversity; would this mean, at the most, a form of universal presidency, in charity when essential matters of faith are at stake; what relation, then, would the Vatican have to the various Synods of the Anglican Communion. There are, therefore, some questions about the Anglican acceptance of a universal primacy which cannot be answered until Anglicans and Roman Catholics have come to some consensus on what acceptance actually involves. . . . We are now at the stage of dialogue where the hard questions need to be put—and Rome will have some tough questions to put to Anglicans as well. In this exchange both traditions will be purified and renewed. Both will have something to give to the other. . . . It is therefore my profound hope that when the present successor of Pope Gregory comes to this country next year St. Augustine's present successor and he will be able to take a step together towards that unity—towards the mutual exchange which will show both traditions more clearly what visible structures that unity in diversity requires.

In these words, the expression of firm faith and powerful intention, we can see the emergence of a new era in these relationships. The theologians having brought us so far along the road of agreement, the remaining few sources of difference can be more clearly seen.

Through 400 years, therefore, the Church has watched the bitter night of past separation change gradually into the light of twentieth-century day. It has seen extensive changes, and changes for the better, begin to command the acceptance of twentieth-century churchmen, until hostility has yielded to confrontation and confrontation to friendship. 'Now', to use Cardinal Suenens' words 'instead of looking at one another the churches are looking together in the same direction'. They have come so close together that there is no reason now why they should not go steadily on to build up an effective organic relationship. And the Pope and the Archbishop of Canterbury have publicly declared their intention that the churches should respond in this way to the movement of the Spirit.

BIBLIOGRAPHY

BOOKS

Abbott, Walter M. *The Documents of Vatican II*. Geoffrey Chapman, 1967.

Albion, G. *Charles I and the Court of Rome*. Burns & Oates, 1935.

Allies, Mary H. *Life of Pius VII*. Burns & Oates, 1897.

Altholz, J. *The Liberal Catholic Movement in England*. Burns & Oates, 1962.

Amand de Mendieta, E. *Rome and Canterbury*. Herbert Jenkins, 1962.

Amhurst, W. J. *The History of Catholic Emancipation and the Progress of the Catholic Church in the British Isles, 1771–1820*. Kegan Paul, 1886.

Anglican Participants. *An Official Report of the Conversations at Malines*. OUP, 1927.

Ashwell, A. R. *Life of Samuel Wilberforce* (vol. I only; vols. II and III by Wilberforce, R. G.). John Murray, 1880.

Aspinall, A. (ed.). *Letters of George IV*. CUP. 1938.

Atkinson, James. *Rome and Reformation*. Hodder & Stoughton, 1966.

Aubert, R. *Le Saint-Siège et l'union des Églises*. Brussels, 1947.

———. *La Théologie Catholique au milieu de XXᵉ Siècle*. Paris; Casterman, 1954.

Ayres, Philip. *The Reuniting of Christianity*. John Winter for William Gilbert, 1673 (reprinted 1708 with Appendix by Bishop Atterbury).

Barberi, Dominick. *The Lamentation of England or the Prayer of the Prophet Jeremiah applied to the same*. Leicester; A. Cockshaw, 1831.

Barrington, Shute. *Sermons, Charges and Tracts*. 1811.

Battiscombe, Georgina. *John Keble: a Study in Limitations*. Constable, 1963.

Baum, Gregory. *That They May Be One: a Study of Papal Doctrines (Leo XIII–Pius XII)*. Bloomsbury, 1958.

Bayne, C. G. *Anglo-Roman Relations, 1558–65* (Oxford Historical and Literary Studies, vol. II). OUP, 1913.

355

Bea, Augustin. *The Unity of Christians*. Geoffrey Chapman, 1963.

Beck, G. A. *The English Catholics, 1850–1950*. Burns & Oates, 1950.

Bell, G. K. A. *Randall Davidson, Archbishop of Canterbury* (2 vols.). OUP, 1935.

——. *Christianity and World Order*. Penguin Press, 1940.

——. *Christian Unity: the Anglican Position*. Hodder & Stoughton, 1948.

——. (ed.). *Documents on Christian Unity* (1st series, 1920–4, OUP, 1924; 2nd series, 1924–9, OUP, 1930; 3rd series, 1930–48, OUP, 1948; 4th series, 1948–57, OUP, 1958).

Benson, A. C. *The Life of Edward White Benson—Sometime Archbishop of Canterbury* (2 vols.). Macmillan, 1899, 1900.

Berington, Joseph. *Memoirs of Gregorio Panzani*. Birmingham; Swinnen & Walkes, 1793.

——. *The State and Behaviour of English Catholics from the Revolution to 1780*. F. Faulder, 1780.

Berkeley, Joan. *Lulworth and the Welds*. Gillingham, Dorset; The Blackmore Press, 1971.

Bevan, R. J. W. *The Churches and Christian Unity*. OUP, 1963.

Bill, E. G. W. (ed.). *Anglican Initiatives in Christian Unity*. SPCK, 1967.

Birkbeck, R. K. *Life and Letters of W. J. Birkbeck*. Longmans, Green, 1932.

Birkbeck, W. J. *Russia and the English Church*. Rivington, 1895.

——. *Essays and Articles* (ed. Athelstan Riley). SPCK, 1917.

——. (ed.). *Russia and the English Church. A correspondence between Mr. William Palmer, Fellow of Magdalen College, Oxford, and M. Khomiakoff in the years 1844–1854*. SPCK, 1895.

Bivort de la Saudée, Jacques de. *Documents sur le Problème de l'union Anglo-Romaine, 1921–1927: Anglicans et Catholiques*. Paris, 1949.

——. *Anglicans et Catholiques: le Problème de l'union Anglo-Romaine, 1833–1933*. Paris, 1949.

Black, J. B. *The Reign of Elizabeth, 1558–1603*. OUP, 1936.

Blakiston, Noel (ed.). *The Roman Question. Extracts from the Despatches of Odo Russell from Rome, 1858–70*. Chapman & Hall, 1962.

Bloxam, J. R. *A Register of the Members of St. Mary Magdalen's College, Oxford* (vols. I–VII). Oxford, 1853.

Bolton, A. *A Catholic Memorial to Lord Halifax and Card. Mercier*. Williams & Norgate, 1935.

Bossy, J. *The English Catholic Community, 1570–1850*. DLT, 1975.

Bowle, John. *Henry VIII*. Allen & Unwin, 1965.

Boyer, Charles. *Unus Pastor: Rome 1948* (English trans. from French), *One Shepherd: the Problem of Christian Reunion*. New York, 1952.

Brady, W. Mozière. *Memoirs of Cardinal Erskine, Papal Envoy to Court of Geo. III.* (Anglo-Roman Papers, III). Alexander Gardner, 1890.

——. *Annals of the Catholic Hierarchy in England and Scotland, 1585–1876*. J. M. Stark, 1883.

Brandreth, H. R. T. *Ecumenical Ideals of the Oxford Movement*. SPCK, 1947.
——. *Dr. Lee of Lambeth*. SPCK, 1951.
——. *Episcopi Vagantes and the Anglican Church*. SPCK, 1947.
Bricknell, W. S. *The Judgment of the Bishops upon Tractarian Theology*. Oxford, 1845.
Broderick, J. F. *The Holy See and the Irish Movement for the Repeal of the Union with England, 1829–47*. Rome; Gregorian University, 1951.
Broderick, James. *Robert Bellarmine* (2 vols.). Burns & Oates, 1928.
Brownlow, W. R. *The Reunion of England and Rome*. 1896.
Burnet, Gilbert. *History of His Own Time* (2 vols.). Joseph Downing, 1734.
Burton, Edwin H. *Life and Times of Bishop Challoner*. Longmans, Green, 1909.
Butler, Charles. *Philological and Biographical Works* (5 vols.). 1817.
——. *The Book of the Roman Catholic Church, in a series of letters addressed to R. Southey*. John Murray, 1825.
——. *Historical Memoirs of the English Catholics* (4 vols.). John Murray, 1822.
Butler, Dom Cuthbert. *Life and Times of Bishop Ullathorne*. Burns & Oates, 1926.
——. *The Vatican Council, 1869–1870*. Collins and Harvill Press, 1930 (reprinted 1962).

Capovilla, Loris (ed.). *Mission to France. Angelo Giuseppe Roncalli Pope John XXIII*. Geoffrey Chapman, 1966.
Caraman, Philip. *The Years of Siege. Catholic Life from James I to Cromwell*. Longmans, Green, 1966.
——. *The Other Face. Catholic Life under Elizabeth*. Longmans, Green, 1960.
Cardinale, Archbishop E. *Signs of the Times and Ecumenical Aspirations*. SPCK, 1967.
Chadwick, Owen. *The Reformation*. Penguin, 1964.
——. *The Mind of the Oxford Movement*. Adam & Charles Black, 1960.
——. *The Victorian Church*. Adam & Charles Black, Part I, 1966; Part II, 1970.
——. *From Bossuet to Newman. The Idea of Doctrinal Development*. CUP, 1957.
Christie, W. D. *Life of A. A. Cooper, 1st Earl of Shaftesbury*. Macmillan, 1871.
Church, Mary (ed.). *Occasional Papers of R. W. Church* (2 vols.). Macmillan, 1897.
——. (ed.). *Life and Letters of Dean Church*. Macmillan, 1894.
Church, R. W. *The Oxford Movement, 1833–45*. Macmillan, 1891.
Cobb, Gerard. *The Kiss of Peace or England and Rome at one on the Doctrine of the Holy Eucharist*. J. T. Hayes, 1867.
——. *Sequel to The Kiss of Peace*. J. T. Hayes, 1868.

Congar, Yves M. J. *Chrétiens Désunis*, Paris, 1937 (English trans. *Divided Christendom: a Catholic Study of the Problem of Reunion*). Geoffrey Bles, 1939.

Coulson, John (with Allchin, A. M. and Trevor, Meriol). *Newman: a Portrait Restored*. Sheed & Ward, 1965.

——. and Allchin, A. M. (ed.). *The Rediscovery of Newman; an Oxford Symposium*. Sheed & Ward and SPCK, 1967.

Courayer, P. F. le. *Dissertation on the Validity of the Ordinations of the English Church, with an Historical Introduction*. OUP, 1844.

Creighton, Louise. *Life and Letters of Mandell Creighton* (2 vols.). Longmans, Green, 1905.

Creighton, Mandell. *A History of the Papacy from the Great Schism to the Sack of Rome* (6 vols.). Longmans, Green, 1897.

Cross, F. L. *The Oxford Movement and the 17th Century*. SPCK, 1933.

——. *The Tractarians and Roman Catholicism*, SPCK, 1933.

Curtis, Geoffrey. *Paul Couturier and Unity in Christ*. SCM Press, 1964.

Davenport, Christopher (Franciscus a Santa Clara). *Deus, Natura, Gratia*. Lyon, 1634.

——. *Paraphrastica Expositio Articulorum Confessionis Anglicanae* (ed. Lee, F. G.). Hayes, 1865.

Davidson, Thomas Randall, and Benham, William. *Life of Archbishop Tait* (2 vols.). Macmillan & Co., 1891.

Davies, Godfrey. *The Early Stuarts, 1603–1660*. OUP, 1959.

Dessain, C. S. *Life, Letters and Diaries of John Henry Newman*, vols. XI–XXII (vols. XIV and XV with Blehl, V. F.), Nelson, 1961–72. Vols. XXIII and XXIV (with Gornall, Thomas), Oxford; Clarendon Press, 1973.

De Vere, Aubrey. *Recollections*. New York, 1897.

Dix, Gregory. *The Question of Anglican Orders*. Dacre Press, 1944.

Dockery, John Berchmanns. *Christopher Davenport*. Burns & Oates, 1960.

Doctrine in the Church of England (The Report of the Commission on Christian Doctrine appointed by the Archbishops of Canterbury and York in 1922). SPCK, 1957.

Dodd, Charles (pseudonym Hugh Tootel). *Church History of England from the beginning of the 16th century to the Revolution of 1688* (5 vols, with Notes by Tierney, M. A.). Charles Dolman, 1839–43.

Döllinger, Ignaz von. *Lectures on the Reunion of the Churches* (trans. and with a Preface by Oxenham, H. W.). Rivington, 1872.

Doyle, Dr. James, Bishop of Kildare and Leighlin. *Letters on the State of Education in Ireland and other works, together with a reply to a charge by Dr Magee, Archbishop of Dublin*. Dublin, 1824.

Ehrlich, Rudolf J. *Rome: Opponent or Partner?* Lutterworth Press, 1965.

Ellis, J. T. *Cardinal Consalvi and Anglo-Papal Relations, 1814–1824*. Washington; Catholic University of America Press, 1942.

Enchiridion Biblicum. Documenta Ecclesiastica Sacram Scripturam Spectantia, 3rd edition. Rome, 1956.

Enchiridion Fontium Historiae Ecclesiasticae Antiquae, 5th edition. Herder, 1941.

Enchiridion Symbolorum. 31st edition. Herder, 1957.

Falconi, Carlo. *The Popes in the 20th Century.* Weidenfeld & Nicolson, 1967.

Fey, Harold E. (ed.). *The Ecumenical Advance, 1948–68.* SPCK, 1970.

Figgis, J. N. and Laurence, R. V. (eds.). *Selections from the Correspondence of the first Lord Acton.* Longmans, Green, 1917.

Fitzpatrick, W. J. *Life, Times and Correspondence of the Rt. Revd. Dr Doyle, Bishop of Kildare and Leighlin* (2 vols.). Dublin; James Duffy, 1861.

Forbes, A. P., Bishop of Brechin. *An Explanation of the 39 Articles.* Oxford; Parker, 1867.

Forbes, William. *Considerationes Modestae et Pacificae Controversiarum* (Library of Anglo-Catholic Theology), 4th edition, Oxford, 1850–6.

Forster, Charles. *The Life of John Jebb.* James Duncan, 1836.

Fowler, John. *Life of R. W. Sibthorpe.* W. Skeffington & Son, 1880.

Frere, Walter, C. R. *Recollections of Malines.* The Centenary Press, 1935.

——. *The English Church in the Reigns of Elizabeth and James I, 1558–1625.* Macmillan, 1904.

Froude, Hurrell. *Remains.* Rivington, 1838.

Gardiner, S. R. (ed.). *Constitutional Documents of the Puritan Revolution, 1625–1660.* OUP, 1889 (reprinted 1947).

Gasquet, Aidan. *Great Britain and the Holy See, 1792–1806.* Rome, 1919.

——. *Leaves from My Diary, 1894–96.* Burns & Oates, 1911.

——. (ed.). *Lord Acton and his Circle.* Burns & Oates, 1906.

Gee, Henry, and Hardy, W. J. (eds.). *Documents Illustrative of Church History.* Macmillan, 1896.

Gibbard, Mark, *Unity is Not Enough.* Mowbrays, 1965.

Gooch, G. P. *Correspondence of Lord John Russell, 1840–78.* 1925.

Grant, Frederick C. *Rome and Reunion.* New York; OUP, 1965.

Gwynn, Denis. *Lord Shrewsbury, Pugin and the Catholic Revival.* Hollis & Carter, 1946.

——. *The Struggle for Catholic Emancipation.* Longmans, Green, 1928.

——. *A Hundred Years of Catholic Emancipation.* Longmans, Green, 1929.

——. *Cardinal Wiseman.* Dublin; Browne & Nolan, 1929.

——. *Father Domenic Barberi.* Burns & Oates, 1947.

Haile, Martin, and Bonney, Edwin. *Life and Letters of John Lingard, 1771–1851.* Herbert & Daniel, 1912.

Hales, E. E. Y. *Pio Nono*. Eyre & Spottiswoode, 1960.
——. *Revolution and the Papacy, 1796–1846*. Eyre & Spottiswoode, 1965.
——. *Pope John and his Revolution.* Eyre & Spottiswoode, 1965.
Halifax, Charles Lindley, Viscount. *Leo XIII and Anglican Orders*. Longmans, Green, 1912.
——. *A Call to Reunion*. Mowbrays, 1922.
——. *The Conversations at Malines, 1921–25*. Philip Allan, 1930.
Hebert, A. G. *Liturgy and Society*. Faber & Faber, 1935.
Heenan, J. C. *Cardinal Hinsley*. Burns & Oates, 1944.
—— (ed.). *Christian Unity—A Catholic View*. Sheed & Ward, 1962.
Hemmer, H. *Fernand Portal, 1855–1926: Apostle of Unity* (trans. from French *Monsieur Portal, Prêtre de la Mission*, and ed. Macmillan, A. T.). Macmillan, 1961.
Hemphill, Basil. *The Early Vicars-Apostolic of England, 1685–1750*. Burns & Oates, 1954.
Heylyn, Peter. *Cyprianus Anglicus, or The history of the life and death of William, Archbishop of Canterbury*. A. Seile, 1668.
Hodgson, Leonard. *Convictions (Questions answered on Lausanne Faith and Order Conference, 1927)*. SCM Press, 1934.
Hooker, R. *Of the Laws of Ecclesiastical Polity*. Oxford; Clarendon Press, 1885.
Horton, Douglas. *Vatican Diary* (3 vols.). Philadelphia; United Church Press, 1963–5.
How, F. D. *Archbishop Maclagan*. Wells, Gardner, Darton & Co., 1911.
Hughes, J. J. *Absolutely Null and Utterly Void*. Sheed & Ward, 1968.
——. *Stewards of the Lord*. Sheed & Ward, 1970.

Iremonger, F. A. *William Temple, Archbishop of Canterbury, his Life and Letters*. OUP, 1948.

Jasper, Ronald. *Arthur Cayley Headlam, Life and Letters of a Bishop*. Faith Press, 1960.
——. *George Bell, Bishop of Chichester*. OUP, 1967.
Jewel, John. *Works* (3 vols.). Cambridge; The Parker Society, 1845–8.
Jones, O. W. *Isaac Williams and his Circle*. SPCK, 1971.
Jones, Spencer. *England and the Holy See. An Essay towards Reunion*. Longmans, Green, 1902.

Küng, Hans. *The Council and Reunion*. Sheed & Ward, 1961.
——. *The Living Church*. Sheed & Ward, 1963.
——. *Infallible?* Collins, 1971.
——. *The Church Maintained in Truth*. SCM Press, 1980.

Lacey, T. A. *The Unity of the Church as Treated by the English Theologians*. SPCK, 1898.
——. *A Roman Diary and Other Documents relating to the Papal Inquiry into English Ordinations*. Longmans, Green, 1910.
——. *The Universal Church: A Study in the Lambeth Call to Union*. Mowbrays, 1921.

Laud, William. *Diary* (Wharton's trans., with Notes by Dr Bliss). *Works*, vol. III. Library of Anglo-Catholic Theology, 136; OUP, 1853.

—— (ed. Simpkinson, C. H.). *A Relation of the Conference between William Laud and Mr Fisher the Jesuit*. Macmillan, 1901.

Lee, F. G. *The Validity of Holy Orders of the Church of England Maintained*. J. T. Hayes, 1869.

Leeming, Bernard. *The Vatican Council and Christian Unity*. Darton, Longman & Todd, 1966.

——. *The Churches and the Church*. Darton, Longman & Todd, 1960.

Leslie, Shane. *Henry Edward Manning: His Life and Labours*. Burns & Oates, 1921.

——. *Cardinal Gasquet*. Burns & Oates, 1953.

Liddon, H. *Life of E. B. Pusey* (4 vols.). Longmans, Green, 1893–7.

Lindbeck, G. A. *The Future of Roman Catholic Theology*. SPCK, 1970.

Lingard, John. *History of England* (up to vol. X, 6th edition, Dublin and London; James Duffy, Paternoster Row, 1878; vol. XI, Hilaire Belloc, Sands & Co.; 1915).

Lloyd, R. *The English Church in the 20th Century* (2 vols.). Longmans, Green, vol. I, 1946; vol. II, 1950.

Lockhart, J. G. *Cosmo Gordon Lang*. Hodder & Stoughton, 1949.

——. *Charles Lindley, Viscount Halifax* (2 vols.). Geoffrey Bles, 1935–6.

Lupton, J. H. *Archbishop Wake and the Prospect of Union between the Gallican and Anglican Churches*. George Bell & Sons, 1896.

McClelland, V. A. *Cardinal Manning, his Public Life and Influence, 1865–92*. OUP, 1962.

McCormack, Arthur. *Cardinal Vaughan*. Burns & Oates, 1966.

McDonagh, Enda. *Roman Catholics and Unity* (Star Books on Reunion). Mowbrays, 1962.

McDowell, R. B. *Social Life in Ireland, 1800–45*. Dublin, 1957.

——. *Public Opinion and Government Opinion in Ireland, 1801–46*. Faber & Faber, 1952.

—— and Curtis, Edmund (ed.). *Irish Historical Documents, 1171–1922*. Methuen, 1943.

McIlwain, C. H. *Political Works of James I*. 1918.

MacKay, Donald J. *Bishop Forbes, a Memoir*. Kegan Paul, 1888.

Mackie, J. D. *The Earlier Tudors, 1485–1558*. OUP, 1952.

Mathew, David. *Catholicism in England, 1535–1935*. Longmans, Green, 1936.

——. *James I*. Eyre & Spottiswoode. 1967.

——. *Acton, the Formative Years*. Eyre & Spottiswoode, 1946.

——. *Lord Acton and his Times*. Eyre & Spottiswoode, 1968.

——. *The Age of Charles I*. Eyre & Spottiswoode, 1951.

Meinhold, Peter. *Christenheit in Bewegung*. Hamburg; Hoffman und Campe, 1964.

Messenger, E. C. *Rome and Reunion: a Collection of Papal Pronouncements.* Burns & Oates, 1934.

Meyer, A. O. *England and the Catholic Church under Queen Elizabeth.* Routledge & Kegan Paul, 1914.

——. *Clemens VIII und Jakob I von Schottland.* Quellen und Forschungen aus italienischen Archiven & Biblioteken VII. Rome, 1904.

Middleton, R. D. *Magdalen Studies.* SPCK, 1936.

——. *Newman and Bloxam: an Oxford Friendship.* OUP, 1947.

——. *Newman at Oxford,* OUP, 1950.

Montague, Richard. *De Originibus Ecclesiasticis Commentationum.* 1640.

Moorman, John R. H. *A History of the Church in England.* Adam & Charles Black, 1953.

——. *Vatican Observed.* Darton, Longman & Todd, 1966.

Morley, John, Viscount. *Life of Gladstone* (3 vols). Macmillan, 1903.

Mosheim, J. L. *Ecclesiastical History* (5 vols, trans. Maclaine, A.). 2nd edition, 1758.

Moss, C. B. *The Old Catholic Movement: its Origins and History.* SPCK, 1948.

Mozley, Anne (ed.). *Letters and Correspondence of J. H. Newman during his Life in the English Church* (2 vols). Longmans, Green, 1891.

Mozley, Thomas. *Letters from Rome, 1869–70* (2 vols). Longmans, Green, 1891.

Muller, J. A. *Stephen Gardiner and the Tudor Reaction.* SPCK, 1926.

Neill, S. C., and Rouse, Ruth (ed.). *A History of the Ecumenical Movement, 1517–1948.* SPCK, 1954.

Newman, J. H. *Apologia Pro Vita Sua* (Everyman edition). J. M. Dent & Sons, 1864.

——. *Tract 90 on Certain Passages in the 39 Articles,* with a Historical Preface by E. B. Pusey. Oxford; Parker, 1865.

Newsome, David H. *The Parting of Friends: A Study of the Wilberforces and Henry Manning.* John Murray, 1966.

Nichols, P. *The Pope's Divisions.* Faber, 1981.

Noel, G. *The Anatomy of the Catholic Church.* H & S, 1980.

Oldmeadow, Ernest. *Francis, Cardinal Bourne.* Burns & Oates, 1944.

Ollard, S. L. *Short History of the Oxford Movement.* Mowbrays, 1915.

——. *Reunion.* Robert Scott, 1919.

Oman, Carola. *Mary of Modena.* Hodder & Stoughton, 1962.

Ornsby, Robert. *Memoirs of James Robert Hope-Scott,* 1884.

Outler, Albert C. (ed.). *John Wesley.* New York; OUP, 1964.

Overton, J. H. *The Non-Jurors.* Smith, Elder & Co., 1902.

Oxenham, H. N. (ed.). *Proposal for Catholic Communion by a Minister of the Church of England, 1704* (reprinted by George Bohham, Dublin, 1781). New edition with Introduction under title *An Eirenicon of the 18th Century.* Rivington, 1879.

Pares, Richard. *King George III and the Politicians*. OUP, 1953.

Pastor, Ludwig. *The History of the Popes from the Close of the Middle Ages* (40 vols.). Kegan Paul, 1938–53.

Paton, David M. *Anglicans and Unity* (Star Books on Reunion). Mowbrays, 1962.

Paul, Herbert (ed.). *Letters of Lord Acton to Mary Gladstone*. Macmillan & Co., 1913.

Pawley, Bernard C. *Looking at the Vatican Council*. SCM Press, 1962.

—— (ed.). *The Second Vatican Council*. OUP, 1967.

Pearson, Hesketh. *The Smith of Smiths*. Penguin Books, 1948.

Perchenet, A. *The Revival of the Religious Life and Christian Unity*. Mowbrays, 1969.

Perry, W. *A. P. Forbes, Bishop of Brechin, the Scottish Pusey*. SPCK, 1939.

Pol, W. H. van de (trans. from the Dutch). *The Christian Dilemma: Catholic Church—Reformation*. 1952.

——. *Anglicanism in Ecumenical Perspective*. USA; Duquesne University Press, 1964.

Pollard, A. F. *Thomas Cranmer and the English Reformation, 1489–1556*. Putnam, 1904 (new edition, 1926).

Pollen, J. H. *The English Catholics in the Reign of Elizabeth*. 1920.

Prothero, G. W. (ed.). *Select Statutes and other Constitutional Documents Illustrative of the Reigns of Elizabeth and James I*. OUP, 1913.

Prothero, Rowland E. *Life and Letters of Dean Stanley*. Nelson, 1909.

Pullan, Leighton. *Religion since the Reformation*. Oxford: Clarendon Press, 1923.

Purcell, E. S. *Life of Cardinal Manning* (2 vols.). Macmillan & Co., 1895.

——. *Life and Letters of Ambrose Phillipps de Lisle* (2 vols.). Macmillan & Co., 1900.

Purcell, William. *Fisher of Lambeth*. Hodder & Stoughton, 1969.

Ramsey, Michael. *The Gospel and the Catholic Church*. Longmans, Green, 1936.

Ranke, Leopold von. *History of England; principally in the 17th Century* (6 vols). Oxford: Clarendon Press, 1875.

——. *History of the Popes, their Church and State, and especially of their Conflict with Protestantism in the 16th and 17th Centuries* (3 vols., trans. Foster, E.). Bohn, 1847–8.

Rankin, Charles (ed.). *The Pope Speaks. Pius XII*. Faber & Faber, 1940.

Raymond, John (ed.). *Queen Victoria's Early Letters*. B. T. Batsford, 1907; reprinted 1963.

Roe, W. G. *Lammenais and England*. OUP, 1966.

Rouse, Ruth, and Neill, Stephen Charles (ed.). *The History of the Ecumenical Movement, 1517–1948*. SPCK, 1967.

Rynne, Xavier. *Letters from Vatican City* (4 vols.). Faber & Faber, 1962–5.

St. John, Henry. *Essays in Christian Unity, 1928–1954*. Blackfriars Publications, 1955.

Scarisbrick, J. J. *Henry VIII*. Eyre & Spottiswoode, 1968.

Scarisbrike, E. *Life of Lady Warner*. 1691.

Simpson, W. J. Sparrow. *Roman Catholic Opposition to Papal Infallibility*. John Murray, 1909.

Smith, B. A. *Dean Church, the Anglican Response to Newman*. OUP, 1958.

Smith, Thomas. *A Pacifick Discourse of the Causes and Remedies of the Differences about Religion*. 1688.

Smyth, Charles. *Cranmer and the Reformation under Edward VI*. CUP, 1926.

——. *Cyril Foster Garbett, Archbishop of York*. Hodder & Stoughton, 1959.

Snead-Cox, J. G. *Life of Cardinal Vaughan*. Burns & Oates, 1910.

Southern, A. C. *Elizabethan Recusant Prose, 1559–82*. Sands & Co., 1950.

Stafford, H. G. *James VI of Scotland and the Throne of England*. New York and London; D. Appleton-Century Co., 1940.

Subscription and Assent to the Thirty-nine Articles: a Report of the Archbishops' Commission on Christian Doctrine. SPCK, 1968.

Suenens, Cardinal Léon-Joseph. *Co-responsibility in the Church*. Bruges; De Brower, 1968.

Sykes, Norman. *Church and State in England in the 18th Century*. CUP, 1934.

——. *Old Priest and New Presbyter*. CUP, 1956.

——. *William Wake, Archbishop of Canterbury, 1657–1737* (2 vols.). CUP, 1957.

——. *From Sheldon to Secker*. Ford Lectures, CUP, 1959.

Symonds, H. E. *The Council of Trent and Anglican Formularies*. OUP, 1933.

——. *The Church Universal and the See of Rome*. SPCK, 1939.

Tavard, Georges. *Petite Histoire du Movement Oecuménique*. Paris, 1960.

——. *Two Centuries of Ecumenism* (trans. Hughes, R. W.). Burns & Oates, 1961.

——. *The Quest for Catholicity*. Burns & Oates, 1963.

Thils, Gustave. *Histoire doctrinale du Movement Oecuménique*. Louvain, 1955; nouvelle édition, 1963.

Thurian, Max. *Marie, Mère du Seigneur Figure de l'Église*. Les Presses de Taizé, 1962.

Trevor, Meriol. *The Pillar and the Cloud*. Macmillan, 1962.

——. *Light in Winter*. Macmillan, 1962.

——. *Pope John*. Macmillan, 1967.

Ullathorne, W. B. *From Cabin Boy to Archbishop*. Burns & Oates, 1941.

Vane, Charles William, Marquess of Londonderry (ed.). *Correspondence, Despatches and other papers of Viscount Castlereagh, 2nd Marquess of Londonderry* (12 vols.). John Murray, 1848–53.

Vidler, A. R. *A Century of Social Catholicism*. SPCK, 1964.

Villain, Maurice. *Introduction a l'Oecuménisme*. 3rd edition, Tournai. 1961. (English trans., *Unity: a History and some Reflexions*. Harvill Press, 1963.)

——. *La Vocation de l'Église*. Paris, 1953.

——. *L'Abbé Couturier, Apôtre de l'Unité Chrétienne: souvenirs et documents*. 3rd edition, Tournai and Paris, 1959.

Waddams, Herbert. *The Church and Man's Struggle for Unity*. Blandford Press, 1968.

—— (ed.). *The English Church and the Continent*. Faith Press, 1959.

Walpole, Spencer. *Life of Lord John Russell* (2 vols.). Longmans, Green, 1889.

Walsh, W. *The Secret History of the Oxford Movement*. Church Association, 1899.

——. *The History of the Romeward Movement in the Church of England, 1833–60*. James Nisbet, 1900.

Ward, Bernard. *The Dawn of Catholic Revival in England, 1780–1803* (2 vols.). Longmans, Green, 1909.

——. *The Eve of Catholic Emancipation* (3 vols.). Longmans, Green, 1911–12.

——. *The Sequel to Catholic Emancipation* (2 vols.). Longmans, Green, 1915.

Ward, Maisie. *The Wilfrid Wards and the Transition*. Sheed & Ward, 1934.

Ward, W. G. *The Ideal of a Christian Church*. Toovey, 1844.

Ward, Wilfrid. *Aubrey de Vere: a Memoir*. Longmans, Green, 1904.

——. *W. G. Ward and the Oxford Movement*. Macmillan, 1889.

——. *W. G. Ward and the Catholic Revival*. Macmillan, 1893.

——. *Life and Times of Cardinal Wiseman* (2 vols.). Longmans, Green, 1897.

——. *Life of John Henry Cardinal Newman* (2 vols.). Longmans, Green, 1912.

Watkin, E. I. *Roman Catholicism in England from the Reformation to 1950*. OUP, 1957.

Watson, J. Steven. *The Reign of George III*. OUP, 1960.

Wesley, John. *Works* (14 vols.). Michigan; Zondervan Publishing House, 1958–9.

Wickham Legg, J. *English Church Life, 1660–1833*. Longmans, Green, 1914.

Wilberforce, R. G. *Life of Samuel Wilberforce* (vols. II and III). John Murray, 1881–2.

Williams, Basil. *The Whig Supremacy, 1714–1760*. OUP, 1939.

Willson, D. Harris. *James VI and I*. Jonathan Cape, 1956.

Wiseman, Nicholas. *Letter respectfully addressed to the Revd J. H. Newman upon some passages in his letter to the Revd Dr Jelf*. Dolman, 1841.

Wiseman, Nicholas. *A Letter on Catholic Unity addressed to the Rt Hon the Earl of Shrewsbury*. Dolman, 1841.

——. *Three Lectures on the Catholic Hierarchy, Dec. 5, 1850*. Richardson & Son, 1850.

——. *Essays on Various Subjects* (2 vols.). Dolman, 1853.

——. *Recollections of Four Last Popes*. New York; P. O'Shea, 1875.

Wordsworth, John, *The Episcopate of Charles Wordsworth, 1853–1892*. Longmans, Green, 1899.

ARTICLES

Allison, A. F. 'Richard Smith, Richelieu and the French Marriage: the political context of Smith's appointment as bishop for England in 1624', *Recusant History*, vol. 7, no. 4, Jan. 1964.

Brandreth, H. R. T. 'Grégoire Panzani et l'ideal de la réunion sous le regne de Charles 1er d'Angleterre', *Irénikon*, tome XXI, 1948.

——. 'Le Courayer', *Reunion*, vol. V, no. 31, June 1944.

Butler, Charles. 'An Address to the Protestants of England, 1813', from *Works of Charles Butler*, vol. IV. London, 1817.

Church Quarterly Review. 'Pierre François le Courayer', vol. XVI, art. IV, Apr.–July 1883.

Clancy, Thomas. 'English Catholics and the Dispensing Power, 1570–1640', *Recusant History*, vol. 6, no. 3, Oct. 1961.

Cleary, J. M. 'Dr Morys Clynog's Invasion Projects of 1575–6', *Recusant History*, vol. 8, no. 6, Oct. 1966.

Cobb, Gerard. *Separation not Schism: a plea for the position of Anglican Reunionists*. G. K. Palmer, 1869.

——. *A Few Words on Reunion and the Coming Council at Rome*. G. K. Palmer, 1869.

Crehan, J. H. 'Black Market in Episcopal Orders (Story of O.C.R.)', *The Month*, Dec, 1970, pp. 352–8.

English Historical Review. 'James VI and Rome', vol. VI (1905), pp. 126–7.

Fisher, Archbishop Geoffrey. *Feeling Our Way: three sermons preached in Jerusalem, Istanbul and Rome*. Church Information Office, 1960.

Gaselee, Stephen. 'British Diplomatic Relations with the Holy See', *Dublin Review*, Jan. 1939, pp. 1–9.

Gladstone, W. E. *The Vatican Decrees in their Bearing on Civil Allegiance*. John Murray, 1874.

——. *Vaticanism*. John Murray, 1875.

Lee, F. G. (ed.). *Essays on Reunion of Christendom by Members of the Roman Catholic, Oriental and Anglican Communions*. 1st, 2nd and 3rd series (3rd Intro. By E. B. Pusey, 1867).

McLean, G. R. D. 'Archbishop Wake and Reunion with the Gallican Church', *Church Quarterly Review*, vol. CXXXI, no. 262, Jan.–Mar. 1941.

McNeile, Hugh. *Fidelity and Unity: a letter to the Revd. E. B. Pusey.* London; Hatchard & Co., 1866.

Mackie, J. D. 'Secret Diplomacy of James VI in Italy prior to his Accession to the English Throne', *Scottish Historical Review*, vol. XXI, 1923–4.

Manning, H. E. *The Unity of the Church.* John Murray, 1842.

——. *The Working of the Holy Spirit in the Church of England: a letter to E. B. Pusey.* Longmans, Green, 1864.

——. *The Reunion of Christendom: a pastoral letter to the clergy.* London, 1866.

——. *England and Christendom.* Longmans, Green, 1867.

——. *The Ecumenical Council and the Infallibility of the Roman Pontiff: a pastoral letter to the clergy.* Longmans, Green, 1869.

Mercier, Cardinal D. J. *L'Unité Chretienne, texte et discours.* Maay s/Meuse, 1927.

Meyer, A. O. 'Charles I and Rome', *American Historical Review*, vol. XIX (1913), pp. 13–26.

Newman, J. H. *Lecture on Anglican Difficulties.* Basil Montagu Pickering, 1876.

——. *A Letter to the Bishop of Oxford on the Occasion of Tract 90.* Oxford, 1841.

——. *A Letter to the Revd. E. B. Pusey on his Recent Eirenicon.* Longmans, Green and Reader & Dyer, 1866.

Oxenham, H. N. *Dr Pusey's Eirenicon Considered in Relation to Catholic Unity: a letter to the Revd. Fr. Lockhart.* Longmans, Green, 1866.

Phillipps, Ambrose de Lisle (later called Phillipps de Lisle). *A Letter to the Earl of Shrewsbury on the Re-establishment of the Hierarchy of the English Catholick Church and the Present Posture of Catholick Affairs in G.B.* London, 1850.

——. *On the Future Unity of Christendom.* London, 1857.

Pollen, J. H. 'Fomenting of the Irish rebellion of 1579 by Gregory XIII', *The Month*, July 1902.

Pusey, E. B. *The Articles Treated on in Tract 90 Reconsidered and their Interpretation Vindicated in a Letter to the Revd. R. W. Jelf.* Oxford; J. H. Parker, 1840.

——. *A Letter to the Rt. Revd. Richard Lord Bishop of Oxford on the Tendency to Romanism, imputed to Doctrines Held of Old, as Now, in the English Church, with a Preface on the Doctrine of Justification.* Oxford; J. H. Parker, 1840.

——. *A Letter to the Archbishop of Canterbury. A Present Crisis in the Church.* Oxford; J. H. Parker, 1842.

——. *The Church of England, a Portion of Christ's One Holy Catholic Church, and a Means of Restoring Visible Unity. An Eirenicon. In a letter to the author of the 'Christian Year'.* John Henry & James Parker and Rivingtons, 1865.

——. *First Letter to the Very Revd. J. H. Newman (2nd Eirenicon).* Oxford; James Parker, 1869.

Pusey, E. B. *Is Healthful Reunion Impossible? (3rd Eirenicon). A Second Letter to the Very Revd. J. H. Newman*, Oxford, 1870.

Ramsey, Michael. *Rome and Canterbury. A public lecture in Dublin, 23.6.67.* SPCK, 1967.

Rowlands, Marie. 'Staffordshire Clergy, 1688–1803', *Recusant History*, vol. 9, no. 5, Apr. 1968.

——. 'Education and Piety of Catholics in Staffordshire in the 18th Century', *Recusant History*, vol. 10, no. 2, Apr. 1969.

Seton, Walter W. 'Relations of Henry, Duke of York, with the British Government', *Transactions of the Royal Historical Society*, 4th series, vol. II (1919), pp. 94–112.

Sitwell, Gerard. 'Leander Jones' Mission to England, 1634–5', *Recusant History*, vol. 5, no. 5, Jan. 1960.

Stone, J. M. 'Corporate Reunion in the Reign of Charles I', *Scottish Historical Review*, Apr. 1889.

Ullathorne, W. B. *The Anglican Theory of Union. Second letter to the clergy of the diocese of Birmingham.* 1866.

Ward, A. W. 'James VI and the Papacy', *Scottish Historical Review*, vol. II (1905), pp. 249 *et seq.*

Wiseman, Nicholas. *Pastoral out of the Flaminian Gate. 7 Oct. 1850.* T. Hooker, 1850.

Wordsworth, Christopher. *Visible Unity. The price to be paid for it.* London, 1865.

BIBLIOGRAPHIES

Brandreth, H. R. T. *Unity and Reunion. A Bibliography.* Adam & Charles Black, 1945.

'Confraternity of Unity', Bulletin II. Baltimore, 1928 (Bibliography of Anglican–Roman Books and Articles).

Society for Catholic Reunion. Books recommended for study. Compiled by J. T. Plowden-Wardlaw, with additions by Harris, S. M. (Anglican–Papalist position).

NEWSPAPERS AND PERIODICALS

Christian Review.
Church of England Newspaper.
Church Quarterly Review (ceased 1971).
Church Times.
Civiltà Cattolica (Rome).
Contemporary Review.
Documentation Catholique, La (fortnightly; Paris).
Dublin Review.
Dublin University Magazine.
Guardian, The (1846–1951).

Informations Catholiques Internationales (fortnightly; Paris).
Irénikon (bi-monthly; published by Benedictines of Chevetogsne).
Living Church, The (USA).
Month, The.
Nineteenth Century, The.
One in Christ (quarterly; London).
Pilot, The (a few numbers in 1876).
Recusant History.
Rambler, The (1848–62).
Reunion (organ of the Confraternity of Unity).
Reunion Magazine (quarterly; published by Lee, F. G., Banstead;
    1877–9, 1909–11).
Revue Anglo-Romaine (weekly; Paris; 1895–6).
Tablet, The.
Times, The.
Union Newspaper (1857–62).
Union Review (1863–75).
Unitas (bi-monthly; Rome).
Weekly Register (1849–50; continued as *Catholic Magazine and
    Register*).
Westminster Gazette.

ARCHIVES

Birmingham Archdiocese Archives.
Archdiocese of Malines Archives.
Propaganda Fide.
Public Records Office.
Rinieri, P. Ilario. *Diplomazia Pontificia nel secolo XIX* (Printed
    Vatican Archives) Rome; Civiltà Cattolica, 1904.
Vatican Archives, especially the private archives of Pius IX.
Westminster Cathedral Archives.

REPORTS AND MINUTES

Chronicle of Convocation: Convocation of Canterbury. SPCK.
*Journal of General Convention of the Protestant Episcopal Church of the
    U.S.A.*
Lambeth Conferences—*Reports*. (1867–1948; SPCK, 1948. 1958;
    SPCK, 1958. 1968; SPCK, 1968.)
Parliamentary Debates (Parliamentary History of England,
    Hansard, until 1803; Parliamentary Debates, *Hansard*, 1803–)

MANUSCRIPT MATERIAL

THESES
Greenfield, R. H. 'The Attitude of the Tractarians to the Roman

Catholic Church, 1833–50' (an unpublished doctoral thesis in the Bodleian).

Jurich, Fr. s.j. 'The Ecumenical Relations of Victor De Buck, s.j. with Anglo-Catholic Leaders on the Eve of Vatican I, 1854–68' (unpublished thesis, Université Catholique de Louvain, Facultie de Theologie, 1970).

LETTERS

J. R. Bloxam and Ambrose Lisle Phillipps (afterwards Phillipps de Lisle) (Library, Magdalen College, Oxford).

Mrs. (Ann) Capper, her father the Revd. Isaac Saunders, and her sisters, 1825–35 (Mrs. A. J. M. Saint, 65, Ramsey Road, Headington, Oxford).

A. P. Forbes, Bishop of Brechin and Ambrose de Lisle Phillipps (Pusey House, Oxford).

A. P. Forbes, Bishop of Brechin and Dr. F. G. Lee (Brechin Diocesan Archives).

William Gladstone and Ambrose Phillipps de Lisle, 1874–7 (British Museum).

William Gladstone and Margaret de Lisle (Mill Hill Convent and British Museum).

J. H. Newman and Ambrose Lisle Phillipps (Birmingham Oratory).

Ambrose de Lisle to Mgr. Talbot (English College, Rome).

Ambrose de Lisle with Cardinal Wiseman, Canon Morris (secretary) and Archbishop Manning (Oblates of St. Charles, St. Mary of the Angels, London W2.)

R. W. Sibthorpe and J. R. Bloxam (Library, Magdalen College, Pusey House, Oxford).

R. Simpson and Victor De Buck, s.j. (Archives of Jesuit Province of Northern Belgium, Brussels).

Cardinal Wiseman and Ambrose Lisle Phillipps (Westminster Cathedral Archives).

Fr. V. De Buck, s.j., E. B. Pusey and A. P. Forbes, Bp. of Brechin (Pusey House).

DIARIES

Diary of Laura de Lisle (The Squire de Lisle).

Diary of the Revd. Canon Prestige for the period of his visit to Rome in 1948 (Mrs. R. H. Collier, Shabbington Vicarage, Aylesbury).

INDEX

371